m.kabela

Contemporary Philosophy and Its Origins

TEXT AND READINGS

SHELDON P. PETERFREUND
Professor of Philosophy, Syracuse University

and

THEODORE C. DENISE
Professor of Philosophy, Syracuse University

D. VAN NOSTRAND COMPANY, INC.
PRINCETON, NEW JERSEY
TORONTO   LONDON

Van Nostrand Regional Offices: *New York, Chicago, San Francisco*

D. Van Nostrand Company, Ltd., *London*

D. Van Nostrand Company (Canada), Ltd., *Toronto*

Copyright © 1967, by D. VAN NOSTRAND COMPANY, INC.

Published simultaneously in Canada by
D. Van Nostrand Company (Canada), Ltd.

No reproduction in any form of this book, in whole or in part (except for brief quotation in critical articles or reviews), may be made without written authorization from the publisher.

PRINTED IN THE UNITED STATES OF AMERICA

Preface

A DISTINCTIVE PEDAGOGICAL PRINCIPLE has influenced us in the preparation of this book: Both *apprenticeship to leading philosophical thinkers* and *historical perspective* are necessary if the student is to understand the philosophic positions of a given period.

The historical perspective which we have in mind is not that of *extrinsic* history. However interesting the lives and personalities of philosophers, however important the mechanisms of intellectual dissemination, however decisive historical events for philosophical reflections, it remains true that such historical facts in and of themselves fail to illuminate philosophy *qua* philosophy. Understanding philosophy as a chronological set of events bears no logical relation to understanding philosophy itself. The historical lore of a philosophy may whet the appetite for the study of philosophy proper; indeed, if space and time had permitted, we might have included more of it. Yet to know that the philosopher Abelard was enamored of Heloise is not revelatory of his attempted solution to the nominalist-realist problem; to know that Plato's *Timaeus* was translated into Latin by Cicero is not at all to know that Augustine's concept of eternity is like Plato's, however much it may stimulate us to search for such similarities; and even to know that Hitler's rise was accompanied by philosophical expressions pleasing to Nazi Germany, and that all other philosophical expressions were publicly denounced, is not to know either the philosophical weaknesses or the strengths of the "official" view.

Meanwhile there is an *intrinsic* history which can take a line just as irrelevant. While extrinsic history can lose the thought in the name of the thinking person, intrinsic history can lose the thinker in the name of the thought. Unfortunately numerous are the books that confidently set forth the genealogy of the "isms." We learn, for example, that the extreme rationalism of the eighteenth century gave rise to the romanticism of the nineteenth century, which, like a child, renounced its parent. When a book of this sort discusses individual thinkers, it does so with an unwitting condescension for which the thinker is reduced to a mere instrument articulating the ism which permeates his culture. Such books ignore the conditions under which intellectual contributions are produced, and accordingly ignore the conditions for the development of new movements in thought—which, if successful, become isms. Plato did not set out to express Platonism, Locke did not set out to express Empiricism, and Peirce did not set out to express Pragmatism. Each man was impressed by a set of intellectual problems and combined old modes of thought with newly invented modes in order to attack these problems. For example, a conspicuous number of the modern isms for philosophers, scientists, and humanists alike can be traced back to Immanuel Kant's detailed effort to answer the technical philosophical question, "How are synthetic *a priori* judgments possible?"

There is a second criticism that attaches to the injudicious use of the intrinsic history of philosophy. It is this. When we look for identifiable continuity in a complex intellectual domain, we tend to accept lower standards of similarity between the articulations of selected thinkers. For example, the similarity between Peirce and James, which is strict for only their theories of meaning, has been extended beyond defensible bounds by those with a propensity for schools of thought. Such writers declare for the overall similarity of these two American philosophers on the grounds that each provides an articulation of pragmatism, a cluster of ideas which, though variously expressible, is nevertheless a distinctive entry in the realm of ideas. Yet each of the isms in this realm—which includes Pragmatism, Idealism, Realism, Thomism, Rationalism, Empiricism, Existentialism, and a host of others—is being conceived as transcending any philosopher's or set of philosophers' actual detailed inquiries. Thus, a recommendation for more than a passing interest in a Peirce or a James as individuals is but a demand that we take their specific philosophical investigations as the basis for serious comments about them, rather than concern ourselves with fitting them into some convenient classificatory system. There are exactly as many notable philosophies as there are notable philosophers.

True, no philosopher lives in an intellectual vacuum: the raw materials and gross processes of thought have been made available to him. A philosopher like Friedrich Nietzsche, for example, whose philosophy is oriented by an idea of evolution the features of which were available to someone gaining instruction in philosophy in his time and place, did not develop his distinctive view *ex nihilo*. Yet his idea of evolution is not precisely that of nineteenth-century evolutionists like Darwin and Lamarck nor even that of the early Greek evolutionists. Nor is it merely an assemblage of features adapted from his predecessors. Furthermore, even while Nietzsche was developing his idea of evolution, his contemporaries Henri Bergson and Herbert Spencer were developing evolutionary ideas different from his and from each other's. Thus, while the intellectual climate may provide the necessary condition for a thinker to develop a fruitful concept, it does not constitute a sufficient condition for that concept.

Admittedly the tale we hope to tell makes exacting demands of the teller. We wish as much as anyone else that it could be told in terms of a cosmic dialectic of isms. Can we analyze the precise nature of the relationship between a man's philosophy and the intellectual present and past? Perhaps it is enough here to deny the simple adequacy of either an extrinsic history of the world and the thinker or the intrinsic history of ideas. Events viewed extrinsically do not provide philosophical illumination, while a set of ideas viewed intrinsically does not expose the specific issues which a given philosopher is concerned to answer. Our point is purely a pedagogical one. We are not advocates of either the extrinsic or intrinsic forms of historical reductionism. Yet the history of philosophy can serve pedagogy, and that for the following typical reasons:

- The history of philosophy directs attention to problems which are currently at issue and indicates the frameworks of ideas within which solutions are being sought.
- The history of philosophy indicates incomplete patterns of thought which attract people to attempt their completion.
- The history of philosophy provides us with themes against which certain contemporary efforts may be viewed as variations, with analogues for certain contemporary presuppositions.
- The history of philosophy impresses us with the magnitude of the philosopher's task.

A generous invocation of history is accordingly an outward feature of our book—perhaps a distinctive feature. Meanwhile something else quite as important lies at the core—the words of the best advocates and expositors that we could find for the five positions explored. Once more, good pedagogy suggests that readings in philosophy must do more than expound. They must illuminate the central ideas and they must provoke a dialogue with the reader. A sound course of reading is more than a collection of snippets attached to great names. Accordingly, the substantial extracts we have selected are notably readable, notably clear—and notably provocative.

Although by design each of the chapters in this book is introductory and conceptually self-contained, we recommend that at least on the instructor's first use of the book the chapters be taken in the order of their occurrence. Our experience in the classroom with these materials indicates that this is a sensible arrangement both for the level of their pedagogical difficulty and for their relation to the current philosophical scene. While we cannot know with any precision how difficult the various chapters will seem to the student, we can surmise that, for example, Chapter I, Realism, in and of itself, is more easily understood than Chapter V, Philosophical Analysis. It is our hope, of course, that when the chapters are studied in order, the accumulation of vocabulary and concepts will keep the level of difficulty uniform throughout. The instructor may wish to lecture in a broader vein on the schools represented. Our text and readings should facilitate his doing so by lessening his concern over some of the central features to which the student *must* be exposed.

Syracuse, New York   S.P.P.
January 1967   T.C.D.

Contents

PREFACE • The History of Philosophy and Pedagogy   iii

CHAPTER I • REALISM   1
    Democritus and Epicurus   2
    Hobbes, Galileo, and Descartes   4
    Locke   7
    Berkeley   8
    Reid   9
    Kant and Continental Idealism   11
    Brentano and Meinong   12
    Moore and Russell   13
    Realism in America   15

    Readings in Contemporary Realism
      LOVEJOY: Cartesian Dualism and Natural Dualism (*The Revolt Against Dualism*)   19
      LOVEJOY: The Nature of Knowing as a Natural Event (*The Revolt Against Dualism*)   32
      MONTAGUE: The Knower and the Known: A Dialogue (*The Ways of Knowing*)   45

    Guide to Further Readings in Contemporary Realism   58
      Realism and Knowledge
      Realism and Value
      Realism and Metaphysics
      Allied Movements: Phenomenology and Naturalism

Notes   62

CHAPTER II • IDEALISM 63

    Heraclitus and Parmenides 64
    Plato 65
    Aristotle 69
    Augustine and Medieval Philosophy 71
    Berkeley 74
    Spinoza and Kant 76
    Hegel 79
    Bradley and Royce 83

    Readings in Contemporary Idealism
      BLANSHARD: Coherence as the Nature of Truth (*The Nature of Thought*) 85
      BLANSHARD: Concrete Necessity and Internal Relations (*The Nature of Thought*) 91
      JOACHIM: The Idealist Position (*Logical Studies*) 103

    Guide to Further Readings in Contemporary Idealism 115
    Idealism and History
    Idealism and Knowledge
    Idealism and Metaphysics
    Idealism and Language

    Notes 118

CHAPTER III • PRAGMATISM 120

    Sophists 121
    Plato and Aristotle 123
    Epicurus 124
    Augustine and Duns Scotus 127
    Bacon, Copernicus, and Galileo 128
    Pascal 131
    Kant, Comte, and Mill 132
    Nietzsche 136
    Peirce 137
    James 138

    Readings in Contemporary Pragmatism
      DEWEY: Nature, Means, and Knowledge (*Experience and Nature*) 143
      DEWEY: The Question of Method (*Experience and Nature*) 159
      LEWIS: A Pragmatic Conception of the A Priori 168

Guide to Further Readings in Contemporary Pragmatism   177
    Pragmatism and Social Philosophy
    Pragmatism and Value Theory
    Pragmatism and Philosophy of Science
    Allied Movements: Pragmatics and Naturalism

Notes   180

CHAPTER IV • EXISTENTIALISM   182
    Socrates, Plato, and Aristotle   183
    Augustine and Pascal   185
    Hegel   188
    Kierkegaard   189
    Nietzsche and Bergson   192
    Husserl and Heidegger   195

Readings in Contemporary Existentialism
    SARTRE: Nausea (*Nausea*)   198
    TILLICH: Types of Anxiety (*The Courage to Be*)   206
    TILLICH: Courage and Transcendence (*The Courage to Be*)   217

Guide to Further Readings in Existentialism   228
    Existentialism and Religion
    Existentialism and Society
    Existentialism and Literature
    Existentialism and Thomism

Notes   231

CHAPTER V • ANALYSIS   232
    Eubulides   234
    Plato   236
    Aristotle   239
    Roscellinus, William of Champeaux, and Abelard   241
    Locke   242
    Berkeley and Hume   245
    Kant   249
    Russell   250
    Moore and Wittgenstein   252

Readings in Contemporary Analysis
   SCHLICK: Meaning and Verification   255
   AUSTIN: Other Minds   282

Guide to Further Readings in Contemporary Philosophical Analysis   312
   Analysis and Ethics
   Analysis and Knowledge
   Analysis and Logic and Mathematics
   Analysis and Theory of Mind
   Analysis and Philosophy of Science

Notes   320

INDEX   321

I · Realism

Do the existence and nature of objects depend, to any extent, on their being experienced or known? In all ages the common-sense answer to this question has been no. To the man who has never entered into philosophical inquiry, the issue is trivial because the answer is so obvious. He is firmly convinced that there are external objects, that their characteristics do not in any way depend on him, and that the existence and nature of the external world are open for discovery by others as well as himself. He is confident, too, that he has *direct* knowledge of the objects about him. He will admit that his senses do deceive him on occasion and that as a consequence he must exercise caution not to be taken in by various illusions. Finally, he is aware that the experiences of his inner life of feeling, imagination, and abstract thought are different from those sense experiences that disclose the external world.

The philosopher Hermann Lotze (1817–1881), characterizing this common-sense level of belief, said:

> The world lies around [us] as illuminated by its own radiance, and . . . outside of us tones and odours cross and meet one another in the immeasurable space that plays in the colours belonging to things. Our senses sometimes close themselves against this continual abundance, and confine us to the course of our inner life; sometimes they open like doors to the arriving stimulus, to reserve it as it is in all its grace or ugliness. No doubt disturbs the assurance of this belief, and even the illusions of the senses, insignificant in comparison with the preponderance of consentient experience, do not shake the assurance that we here everywhere look into an actual

world that does not cease to be as it appears to us, even when our attention is not turned to it. The brightness of the stars seen by the night watch will continue to shine over [us] in slumber; tones and perfumes, unheard and unsmelt, will be fragrant and harmonious, afterwards as before; nothing of the sensible world will perish save the accidental perception of it which consciousness formerly possessed.[1]

But if we pause to reflect, are we satisfied that such a common-sense report is complete? It does not seem to be. We have indicated, for one thing, that some of our sense experiences seem truly to reveal the natural world, while others do not, and for another, that some of our experiences refer to an external world, whereas others refer to an inner life. We have not indicated, however, the ways in which we distinguish between the real and the illusory, between public and private realms. In short, our common-sense perspective introduces the broad problem of appearance and reality but does not provide for its resolution.

DEMOCRITUS AND EPICURUS

Numerous philosophers have accepted in good faith the minimum thesis of "realism"—that *objects exist independently of human experience*—and have been confident that they could solve the problems that such a belief poses. A group of early Greek philosophers known as the *atomists* embraced realism in conjunction with a thoroughgoing materialism. The three best known of these philosophers were Leucippus (440 B.C.) Democritus (460–370 B.C.), and Epicurus (341–270 B.C.). The atomistic theory, conceived by Leucippus and developed by Democritus, asserts that the basic constituents of the universe are atoms and void (empty space) and that these alone exist. The eternal atoms, occupying empty space, are infinite in number and differ only in size and shape. The term "atom," derived from the Greek *a-* (not) and *tomos* (cut), suggests indivisibility and indestructibility. Constantly in motion, atoms fall by mechanical necessity into various temporary arrangements; the qualitative distinctions that are experienced in this world, such as differences in color, taste, odor, and sound, are functions solely of the quantitative differences among the atoms—that is, their differences in size and shape—and of their collective arrangements.

The most striking Democritean reduction of the qualitative to the quantitative occurs in Democritus' theory of psychology. Being a materialist, he had to regard mind as a certain configuration of atoms. Sensations and thoughts are impressed on the mind by the successive impacts of thin veils of atoms that are patterns (effluences) emanating from corporeal bodies as their source. In this view a sensation of red cannot represent an intrinsic characteristic either of the atoms of the corporeal body or of the mind, or again, of atoms in any special arrangements. Sense experiences, as well as thoughts, are products—or better yet, mere by-products (epiphenomena)—of the interaction between the effluences and the mind.

But what is the effect of this mechanistic-materialistic world view, with its corpuscular theory of perception? In gaining the feeling of security which comes from affirming that there is a real world independent of us, we have lost confidence in our ability to know it directly. What is experienced (colors, sounds, etc.) is apparent rather than real, and what is real (atoms) is beyond experience.

The Democritean view of nature was adopted and somewhat modified by Epicurus. Believing that the primary task of a metaphysical theory (theory of reality) is to remove the basis for those pervasive human fears which militate against happiness, Epicurus deliberately selected the Democritean account of things. He saw in it a way of supplanting explanations which provoked fear of the unknown through their appeal to supernatural causes with naturalistic explanations, explanations which appeal solely to concrete reality. Superficially at least, Epicurus could claim to provide therapy for those afflicted with superstition. On reflection, however, it becomes clear that his prescription for removing belief in those unseen entities which distort the ordinary man's ethical thinking proceeds on the assumption of a reality which is not only unseen but also unseeable—the atoms.

Epicurus himself was distressed whenever his naturalistic or materialistic explanations seemed to depart from common sense. He was particularly reluctant to follow the Democritean reduction of quality to quantity —that is, he was unwilling to accept the view that the world is in reality qualitatively featureless. Although he accepted the Democritean claim that individual atoms are devoid of sense qualities, he spoke of these properties as "belonging to" collections of atoms. Like most men, he was reluctant to say that the rich world of the senses was merely an appearance, a phenomenon without causal efficacy, an epiphenomenon. As a result, he created a philosophical puzzle of the first magnitude and one that is not solved by employing such vague phrases as "color belongs to the object," or "the object is characterized by color," or even "color is a property of the object." What is the color of the rose? What is the sound of the bell? Granting that a condition of their emergence is the compounding of atoms, what is the status of the sense qualities themselves?

Can an effect (a sense quality) be identified with its cause (a configuration of atoms)? Only by arguing affirmatively could Epicurus maintain that sense qualities are real. But in such an argument, does not the cause-effect relationship lose its meaning? On the other hand, if Epicurus had accepted the view that cause and effect are not identical, he would have had to accept the epiphenomenalism of Democritus. He simply left these questions unanswered.

HOBBES, GALILEO, AND DESCARTES

Thomas Hobbes (1588–1679) was a realist and materialist whose views were very much in line with those of the early Greek atomists. As the first great modern mechanistic-materialist, he maintained that all processes, physical and mental, were reducible to "matter in motion." He defined matter or body as "that which, having no dependence upon our thought, is coincident or coextended with some part of space," [2] and he averred that the world in its entirety is corporeal.

In his theory of knowledge (epistemology), Hobbes made two major points: first, that all knowledge of external things begins with sensation; second, that knowledge of external things as afforded by sensation is indirect rather than direct. He defined sensation as an agitation of the central nervous system caused by the motions of an external body. However, he frequently described sensations as "phantasms," "seemings," apparitions"—in short, as subjective experiences. Sensations viewed either as internal motions or as the experience of internal motions do not resemble their remote causes, material bodies. Hobbes reasoned that if the familiar sense qualities were inherent in the object, they could not be separated from their original sources; for example, color could not be reflected by a mirror and sound could not echo across a valley.

It is to Hobbes' credit that he recognized the difficulty for any theory of knowledge (epistemology) that his philosophy created by its demand that genuine knowledge proceed from effect to cause. As an epiphenomenal interpretation, his problem becomes extremely acute, because knowledge involves movement not only from effect to cause, but also from effect of one *kind* to cause of another *kind*. He warned that "whatsoever accidents or qualities our senses make us think there be in the *world*, they be *not* there, but are *seeming* and *apparitions* only: the things that really *are* in the world without us, are those motions by which these seemings are caused. And this is the *great deception of sense*." [3] But Hobbes' warning cloaks a deeper problem. Granted that external objects are the cause of our sensations, how can one know that the cause is or is not different in *kind* from the effect? Clearly his senses do not reveal this directly; but if they do so indirectly, then an explanation of this indirect knowledge is urgently needed. Hobbes failed to provide such an account.

The epistemological predicament that arises when one can no longer naively assume that the world is simply and wholly as it appears to be was felt not only by Hobbes but by many of his contemporaries. The scientists of the period sought to avoid this philosophic difficulty by concentrating on the relatively stable, metric features of objects, such as extension and motion, and by ignoring the relatively transient, nonmetric qualities, such as color and sound. The great physicist Galileo (1564–1642), for example, marked off the domain of science by distinguishing the qualities of objects that are primary from those that are secondary and by insisting that science, with its mathematical method, is properly concerned only with the former. He drew the basic distinction in these words:

> I feel myself impelled by the necessity, as soon as I conceive a piece of matter or corporeal substance, of conceiving that in its own nature it is bounded and figured in such and such a figure, that in relation to others it is large or small, that it is in motion or remains at rest, . . . that it is single, few or many; in short, by no imagination can a body be separated from such conditions; but that it must be white or red, bitter or sweet, sounding or mute, of a pleasant or unpleasant odour, I do not perceive my mind forced to acknowledge it necessarily accompanied by such conditions; or if the senses are not the escorts, perhaps the reason or the imagination by itself would never have arrived at them. Hence I think that these tastes, odours, colours, etc., on the side of the object in which they seem to exist, are nothing else but mere names, but hold their residence solely in the sensitive body; so that if the animal were removed, every such quality would be abolished and annihilated.[4]

René Descartes (1596–1650) answered the challenge to philosophy that science presented—to account fully for the observable world. He too distinguished between the primary qualities of an object (shape, size, position and motion)—that is, the qualities intrinsic to the object—and the secondary qualities of the object (color, sound, taste, smell, and feeling)—that is, the qualities attributable to the object only because of the object's effect on man's sense organs. But he went beyond the distinction itself to embrace openly the view of metaphysics that it seemed to imply: he asserted that there are two distinct and irreducible substances instead of one—mind and matter. The essential attribute of mind is thought or consciousness, while the essential attribute of matter is extension or spatiality.

Two problems follow immediately from the Cartesian metaphysical dualism, one involving the mind-body relationship and the other the knower-known relationship. The first problem consists in explaining how there can be a causal relationship between disparate substances. How can mind, which is nonspatial, influence matter or how can matter, which is nonmental, influence mind? The second and related problem consists in explaining how the mind can know a body. How can mind which is nonspatial, know what is spatial? In answer to the first question, Descartes did little more than assert that there is *causal interaction* between the two basic substances. In answer to the second question, which constitutes a puzzle within a puzzle, he was content to show that the mind apprehends the *essential* generic nature of material objects—that is, their extension. This is disclosed by the rational power of mind. Interestingly enough however, although he claims that reason can disclose the existence of one's self, he hesitated to assert that the existence of the external world (material substance) can be similarly known.

Descartes resolved to clear the ground for constructive philosophy through the "method of systematic doubt." Showing first that it is impossible to distinguish, on rational grounds, between dreaming and waking states, and illusory and genuine experiences, he cast doubt on the senses as the bases of absolutely certain knowledge. The senses neither reveal the *essential nature* of the external world nor, indeed, necessitate belief in the *existence* of one. His second great doubt concerned the capacity of reason itself to reach beyond one's inner life to an outer reality. Attracted to mathematics as the model of systematic knowledge—just as Galileo had been—Descartes nevertheless came to realize that mathematical "clearness and distinctness" did not provide a guarantee of external reality.

The climax of Descartes' search for indubitable truth occurred when he realized that one cannot doubt that he is doubting. That is, in the very process of doubting, being a doubter (thinker) is affirmed. His famous Latin sentence, *cogito ergo sum*, "I think; therefore I am," captures this basic intuition. Having established the existence of mental substance, Descartes proceeded to deduce the existence and nature of God. As a consequence of these arguments, which we need not examine for our present purposes, he asserted that God guarantees the reliability of the method of reason (*rationalism*) which proceeds from the clear and distinct ideas of the mind. He avoids making the claim, however, that it is possible to have either intuitive knowledge (as in the case of the self's existence) or demonstrative knowledge (as in the case of God's existence) of the external world's existence. In brief, then, it is possible to have at best probable knowledge that the external world exists; but, provided that it does exist, it is possible to have certain knowledge of its general nature.

The problems of dualism were clearly stated by Descartes, but his answers were merely the forerunner of further intensive inquiry.

LOCKE

John Locke (1632–1704) was concerned particularly with the problem of how the mind gains genuine knowledge of external reality. In dealing with this issue, he gave a clear statement of what has come to be known as the *representative theory* of perceptual knowledge. This theory arises from the conviction that the mind is confined to perceptions of visual, auditory, tactile, olfactory, and gustatory data which are not themselves the actual qualities of the external world. A person is confined to his own ideas and is forever precluded from direct or immediate awareness of the external world. One must settle for knowledge of an indirect sort, which comes about because some of the ideas are copies or representations of external objects.

The "simple ideas," as Locke terms them, which are representations are called "ideas of primary qualities," and any which are not representations are called "ideas of secondary qualities." External objects have the power of producing ideas of qualities inherent in the object, such as solidity, motion, shape, size and number. In addition, they have the power to excite ideas of qualities not intrinsic to the object, such as color and sound. The latter set of ideas is entirely nonrepresentative of external reality.

Thus the elements of perceptual ("sensitive") knowledge are the following: conscious mind, the ideas that it entertains, and the external objects that are their causes. Locke asserted that this kind of knowledge involves the "agreement or disagreement" between ideas and external reality. The inevitable question arises: How can one determine whether or not there is agreement? Since the real world is not perceived directly, one is in no position to know whether ideas agree or disagree with reality. How is this situation any different from that of a Hottentot who has never seen and will never see a skyscraper, but possesses only a picture of it? He can not know whether his picture is an adequate likeness of the actual skyscraper, or indeed, whether there is such a building.

It is fair to say, then, that John Locke's view appears to have the serious and obvious limitation that there seems to be no way in which to establish either the existence or the nature of the external world, a limitation which has its origin in his belief that each person is confined to the realm of his own ideas. In attempting to make the doctrine of realism more plausible, Locke left it exposed to criticism which made it implausible.

BERKELEY

Bishop George Berkeley (1685–1753), an avowed opponent of realism, is nevertheless important for understanding the modern phases of the movement. He had studied critically both Descartes and his followers and Locke, and saw a way out of their major epistemological and metaphysical difficulties. In large measure, the root of their difficulties lay in their insufficiently examined assumption that the natural sciences, so important after the time of Galileo, required the existence of a *material* world. Awestruck by science on the one hand and, quite properly, unwilling to sacrifice the mental life on the other, they were driven unhappily to their dualistic positions. Berkeley resolved to make a more "commonsensical" accommodation to science:

> I do not pretend to be a setter up of new notions. My endeavors tend only to be to write and place in a clear light that truth which was before shared between the vulgar and the philosophers, the former being of opinion that *those things they immediately perceive are the real things*, and the latter, that *the things immediately perceived are ideas which exist only in the mind*. Which two notions put together do, in effect, constitute the substance of what I advance.[5]

It is quite clear, as Berkeley said, that the ordinary man takes the objects of our sense perception to be real, but it is perhaps equally clear that the ordinary man believes that matter is real. In short, it never occurs to him to distinguish between the two; he remains a satisfied naive realist. Berkeley takes his stand only against the materialistic phase of common sense. With his interpretation of the first proposition—"whatever we immediately perceive is real"—it becomes absurd to believe in the reality of matter. He interpreted the proposition to mean that *only* those things we perceive are real. This is captured in his famous phrase *esse est percipi*, "to be is to be perceived." Thus to say, for example, that an apple being eaten exists is to assert no more than that the eater is having certain experiences of color, sound, odor, and so on. In presenting this account of the collection of sensed qualities, a complete description of the apple is given. There is no need to refer to some material substratum in which these sense qualities inhere. In fact, when from force of habit one does speak of a "material substance," he has no idea whatsoever in mind.

Locke and Berkeley were in agreement that ideas are what are immediately perceived. But they disagreed about the *status* of ideas. For Locke, ideas were merely "representative" of reality. Berkeley insisted that the statement "I have an idea of something" means simply "I directly perceive something." This is a *presentative theory* of reality.

It is worthy of note that Berkeley's account of the presentative theory was placed in the context of an idealistic metaphysics. The second of Berkeley's propositions—"the things immediately perceived are ideas which exist only in the mind"—committed him to the thesis that reality is mind-dependent. And to believe that reality is mind-dependent is to believe that reality is mental. His critics, however, have insisted that the admission that something *depends* on mind does not justify the inference that it is mental in character.

Berkeley's answer to the question "Does the world about me depend on *my* perception of it?" is among the most famous and controversial in the history of philosophy. An affirmative answer to this question is termed *solipsism*, the belief that only the individual mind and its states exist. Berkeley avoided the solipsistic predicament by affirming that the infinite mental substance, God, guarantees the continued existence of things, even when finite minds are not perceiving them. This question immediately gives rise to another: How can I have an idea of a nonsensible being when "ideas" are limited to what is experiential? While denying that we have an "idea" of God, Berkeley claimed that we may, however, have a "notion" of Him—that is, we can have a meaningful concept of an active agent as a source of perceptual effects.

REID

The first major critic of Berkeley was the Scottish "common sense" realist Thomas Reid (1710–1796). His attack was directed against Berkeley's idealism and not against the presentative theory of reality. He summarized Berkeley's position in the following manner: "[1] If we have any knowledge of a material world, it must be by the senses; [2] But, by the senses, we have no knowledge, but of our sensations only; [3] and our sensations have no resemblance of any thing that can be in a material world." [6] Reid accepted propositions [1] and [3] but attacked proposition [2]. It is to be noted that he elected in his formulation to use the term "sensation" rather than the familiar Berkeleian "idea." The crucial question for Reid became: Are all objects of sense, sensations (ideas)? Berkeley's answer was yes; Reid's was no.

Reid said that Berkeley employed "idea" so broadly as to include not only "sensation" but also what Reid called "perception." Sensation is a completely psychical event—that is, it is a feeling or operation of the mind which is primitive and noncognitive. For example, the sensations of odor, taste, and sound are directly experienced; only by association are they related to objects like a rose, sugar, a bell. On the other hand, perception involves not only the psychical event of sensation but also an object of sense that is distinct from the act of sensing. Berkeley had failed to acknowledge the instances in which it is possible to distinguish properly between the *act* of experiencing and the *object* of experience; he treated both of them as sensations. Reid focused his attention on the crucial error of Berkeley in the following analysis:

> Suppose I am pricked with a pin, I ask, Is the pain I feel a sensation? Undoubtedly it is. There can be nothing that resembles pain in any inanimate being. But I ask again, Is the pin a sensation? To this question I find myself under a necessity of answering, That the pin is not a sensation, nor can have the least resemblance to any sensation. The pin has length and thickness, and figure and weight. A sensation can have none of these qualities. I am not more certain that the pain I feel is a sensation, than the pin is not a sensation; yet the pin is an object of sense; and I am as certain that I perceive its figure and hardness by my senses as that I feel pain when pricked by it.[7]

Reid was saying that men of common sense tend to neglect sensations in favor of the objects of sense, and that Berkeley tended to neglect the objects of sense in favor of sensations. He carefully acknowledged both aspects in his view of experience. For example, when one slaps a chair, hardness and pain are inseparable features of the experience. Reid contended that a common-sense quality such as hardness appropriately characterizes the property of objects as such, but fails to characterize the experiencing mind. Conversely, the word "pain" is improperly used in describing the object but is properly used in describing the experiencing mind. Therefore the Berkeleian presumption against external qualities is baseless and Reid was free to follow the assumption of common sense that characteristics exist independent of mind. It is for this reason that his view is called "common-sense realism." Thus Reid rejected Berkeley's idealism as an incomplete analysis of experience, and at the same time rejected Locke's representative realism because it posited an unnecessary and undesirable "veil of ideas" between man and the world.

KANT AND CONTINENTAL IDEALISM

A brief reference to the German philosopher Immanuel Kant (1724–1804) is a necessary condition for understanding the next development in realism. Kant is celebrated for his analysis of the structure of experience. He finds experience to consist of both material and formal elements, the former being contributed *to* us and the latter being contributed *by* us. The mind "fashions" the "given" into experienced and intelligible objects by imposing perceptual forms (space and time) and conceptual categories (causality, substance, etc.) on it. Without such activity of the mind, experience and understanding of the observable (phenomenal) world would be impossible. According to Kant, however, a condition of another sort must also be recognized before the analysis of experience can be regarded as complete. That is, there must be an independently existing source or cause of the materials that the mind structures, since something cannot come from nothing. Kant termed this independent reality "things-in-themselves," as opposed to phenomena, the objects of experience. Unfortunately, these things-in-themselves must remain unknowable because they are unexperienceable.

A succession of philosophers following Kant rejected his notion of things-in-themselves on logical grounds. They argued that the notion of a thing-in-itself as the *cause* of phenomena is unintelligible, since cause itself is a conceptual category having its application and basis solely within the phenomenal realm. One way to summarize the logical difficulty that these men recognized is as follows. It is self-contradictory to speak of an unknowable existence, since to know that it exists as a cause is to have knowledge of it. The elimination of Kant's things-in-themselves cleared the way for more stringent forms of idealism in which both the content and form of objective experience were regarded as products of the mind.

But the Kantian philosophy led not only to a militant idealism on the continent, but also to a hesitant realism. The philosopher-psychologist Johann Herbart (1776–1841), while sympathetic to the idealist criticism leveled against things-in-themselves, nevertheless deemed it necessary to acknowledge that there were ultimate reals. He felt that any account of *objective* experience which failed to make reference to reals was fanciful and subjective and amounted to a return to Berkeley.

BRENTANO AND MEINONG

A significant continental movement toward a modern realism was initiated by the philosopher-psychologist Franz Brentano (1838–1917). Following the lead of some scholastic thinkers, Brentano regarded the central feature of psychical phenomena to be their "intentionality." Seeing or hearing, for example, he regarded as a mental act in which something beyond the act itself is necessarily referred to or *intended*. When a patch of green is seen, it is not the green that is mental but rather it is solely *the act of seeing it* that is mental. A perception then, according to Brentano, is by its very nature always a psychical act directed toward a nonmental object. A point of essential agreement between Brentano and Reid lies in their insistence that reality is directly and immediately grasped. But it must be understood that whereas Reid portrayed the mind as a relatively passive agent confronted by external objects, Brentano, influenced by Kant, depicted the mind as aggressively reaching out for its objects.

Alexius Meinong (1853–1920), Brentano's student, broadened his teacher's theory of intentional reference into a "general theory of objects." He sought to establish a science in which all the various types of objects can be classified, regardless of whether they are perceived, conceived, or imagined. Meinong proposed to treat as real not only physical existents but also ideal and what are commonly referred to as fictitious entities. A key to his basic thinking is provided by the following quotation:

> Whether I have an idea of a church-steeple or a mountain-peak, a feeling or a desire, a relation of diversity or causality or any other thing whatsoever, I am in every case having an idea. In spite, therefore, of the unlimited variety of their objects, all these mental processes manifest a common feature which makes them ideas, and this is the act of having an idea. On the other hand, ideas, in so far as they are ideas of distinct objects, cannot be altogether alike; however we may conceive the relation of the idea to its object, diversity of object must in some way go back to diversity of idea. That element, therefore, in which ideas of distinct objects differ, in spite of their agreement in the act, may be properly called the content of the idea. This exists, is therefore real and present, and is of course mental, even when the object presented by its aid does not exist, is not present, and is not mental.[8]

In brief, what ideas have in common is that they are mental acts; they differ in their content or meaning.

Meinong made it quite clear that the total class of real objects includes not only what are normally called *actual* objects—that is, those that *exist* and can be pointed to—but also those nonactual entities about which it is possible merely to think or imagine, such as the ideal objects of mathematics and the obviously fictitious objects of classical mythology. He emphasized the fact that no intelligible account of the actual world could be made without reference to such ideal entities as relations ("north of," "older than") and number. These *subsist* rather than exist. As for the nonactual, fictitious entities designated by expressions like "golden mountains" and "unicorns," Meinong insisted that these too subsist and that they are immediately grasped by mind. His reasoning seems to be that one *knows* what he means even when he asserts that "neither golden mountains nor unicorns exist."

Perhaps the most philosophically significant type of object that Meinong identified is what he termed "objectives," a subclass of ideal objects. An objective is an object of judgment—that is, it is what is referred to when one makes a judgment or assumption. For instance, to say "the sky is blue" is to refer to a state of affairs involving a thing (sky) and a property of the thing (blueness). But the object of the assertion is neither the thing nor its property, but rather the thing and property intrinsically related. Meinong contended that the test of an objective lies in its capacity to be true or false. Meinong's notion of "objectives" helped shape the theory of propositions in modern logic.

The philosopher whose views contrast most strikingly with those of Meinong is Berkeley. In Berkeley's system (disregarding his notion of God, as many subsequent philosophers have) *all* objects of experience (percepts, thoughts, etc.) are dependent on finite minds. In contrast, in Meinong's account *no* objects of experience (percepts, concepts, etc.) are mind-dependent. Just as objectivity was made to give way to subjectivity in Berkeley's system (because of the principle *esse est percipi*), subjectivity gives way to objectivity in Meinong's view (because of the act-object distinction). Can we in all seriousness be satisfied with either of these extreme views? Can we seriously believe either that the world of sticks and stones is merely ideas in our minds or that the world is somehow populated not only with sticks and stones but also with numbers and golden mountains?

MOORE AND RUSSELL

The campaign against Berkeley in particular and idealism in general was pressed in earnest by the British philosophers G. E. Moore (1873–

14 CONTEMPORARY PHILOSOPHY AND ITS ORIGINS

1958) and Bertrand Russell (1872–), as well as by others. A demand to refute the idealists point for point had been astir for some time in both England and America. The kind of discontent, whether justified or not, is indicated in the following autobiographical comment by Russell:

> During 1898, various things caused me to abandon both Kant and Hegel [an antirealist philosopher]. I read Hegel's *Greater Logic*, and thought, as I still do, that all he says about mathematics is muddle-headed nonsense. I came to disbelieve Bradley's [an Hegelian] arguments against relations, and to distrust the logical bases of monism. I disliked the subjectivity of . . . [Kant's] "Transcendental Aesthetic." But these motives would have operated more slowly than they did, but for the influence of G. E. Moore. He also had had a Hegelian Period, but it was briefer than mine. He took the lead in rebellion, and I followed, with a sense of emancipation. Bradley argued that everything common sense believes in is mere appearance; we reverted to the opposite extreme, and thought that *everything* is real that common sense, uninfluenced by philosophy or theology, supposes real. With a sense of escaping from prison, we allowed ourselves to think that grass is green, that the sun and stars would exist if no one was aware of them, and also that there is a pluralistic timeless world of Platonic ideas. The world, which had been thin and logical suddenly became rich and varied and solid.[9]

In 1903 G. E. Moore wrote an article, "The Refutation of Idealism," which served as a call to arms in Great Britain and America for numerous philosophers who were discontented with the prevailing idealism of the century. In this article Moore followed and developed the act-object distinction of the German neorealists Meinong and Brentano, in an effort to refute Berkeley's claim that there is a necessary connection between *esse* and *percipi*. Russell has given a clear statement of the impact of Moore's argument:

> Berkeley's view, that obviously the colour *must* be in the mind, seems to depend for its plausibility upon confusing the thing apprehended with the act of apprehension. Either of these might be called an "idea"—probably either would have been called an idea by Berkeley. The act is undoubtedly in the mind; hence, when we are thinking of the act, we readily assent to the view that ideas must be in the mind. Then, forgetting that this was only true when ideas were taken as acts of apprehension, we transfer the proposition that "ideas are in the mind" to ideas in the other sense, *i.e.* to the things apprehended by our acts of apprehension. Thus, by an unconscious equivo-

cation, we arrive at the conclusion that whatever we can apprehend must be in our minds. This seems to be the true analysis of Berkeley's argument, and the ultimate fallacy upon which it rests.[10]

Since "objective idealism," the form advocated by the important British philosopher Francis Herbert Bradley (1846–1924) and others, did not make conspicuous use of Berkeley's "to be is to be perceived," it seemed unaffected by the foregoing kind of criticism. In fact, the objective idealists themselves opposed the Berkeleian subjectivism whereby reality is made to depend on finite minds. In their account, reality imposes the demand on thought that the world of facts be viewed as interdependent and interrelated. Accordingly, they laid great stress on the all-inclusiveness and self-consistency of the Real and warned against pluralistic world-views and methods of analysis leading to piecemeal and artificial results. Pushing the principles of the objective idealists to the extreme, one would have to conclude that no thing can be fully understood short of understanding its relationship to every other thing. As it occurs in the context of Bradley's philosophy, this doctrine is expressed in the following ways: "A relation must at both ends affect and pass into the being of its terms"; and "every relation essentially penetrates the being of its terms, and is, in this sense, intrinsical." [11] This doctrine of *internal relations* became another target of realist concern.

The realists, led by Russell and Moore, countered with the doctrine of *external relations*, on the grounds that it assumes less about the nature of reality and that in addition, it is psychologically more appealing. (In developing criticisms on these grounds, the realists united with the pragmatists in their revolt against idealism.) They maintained that in such a relation as aRb, the relation R in no way affects or modifies either the term a or the term b. For example, the fact that the book a is "spatially above" the book b in a bookcase in no way affects either of the books, whether they are regarded as merely physical objects or as products of the human mind. (It is to be observed that the realist criticism of Berkeley's *esse est percipi* is a special application of the doctrine of external relations: when a mind a is in a cognitive [perceptual] relation with an object of experience b, the cognition of b by a in no way affects either b's existence or b's nature.)

REALISM IN AMERICA

A widespread neorealistic movement was initiated by Moore and Russell through critical thrusts and through their insistence on a positive reorientation in philosophy. A particularly striking venture, known as American

New Realism, was signaled in 1910 by the appearance of the "Program and First Platform of Six Realists." This uncompromising manifesto was set forth by E. B. Holt (1873–1946), W. T. Marvin (1872–1944), R. B. Perry (1876–1957), W. B. Pitkin (1878–1953), E. G. Spaulding (1873–1940), and W. P. Montague (1873–1957):

> 1. The entities (objects, facts, etc.) under study in logic, mathematics, and the physical sciences are not mental in any usual or proper meaning of the word mental.

This tenet is in the tradition of Meinong's general theory of objects.

> 2. The being and nature of these entities are in no sense conditioned by their being known.

This tenet negates Berkeley's *esse est percipi*.

> 3. The degree of unity, consistency, or connection subsisting among entities is a matter to be empirically ascertained.
> 4. In the present stage of our knowledge there is a presumption in favor of pluralism.
> 5. No self-consistent or satisfactory logic (or system of logic) so far invented countenances the "organic" theory of knowledge or the "internal" view of relations.

Tenets 3, 4, and 5 deny the objective idealist's presumption that nature must necessarily be understood as a unified whole; they affirm that the character of nature is precisely as revealed by experience (empiricism); and they acknowledge the evidence of science that nature is only an aggregate of parts rather than an organic unity.

> 7. There are certain principles of logic which are logically prior to all scientific and metaphysical systems. One of these is that which is usually called the external view of relations.

This tenet expresses an important presupposition of a pluralistic metaphysics.

> 11. Realism holds that things known may continue to exist unaltered when they are not known, or that things may pass in and out of the cognitive relation without prejudice to their reality, or that the existence of a thing is not correlated with or dependent upon the fact that anybody experiences it, perceives it, conceives it, or is any way aware of it.

This tenet amounts to a summary of the general realistic thesis.

12. Cognition belongs to the same world as that of its objects. It has its place in the order of nature.
13. The objective content of consciousness is any entity in so far as it is responded to by another entity in a specified manner exhibited by the reflex nervous system. Thus physical nature, for example, is, under certain circumstances, directly present in consciousness.
14. The specific response which determines an entity to be content of consciousness does not directly modify such entities otherwise than to endow them with this objective status. In other words, consciousness selects from a field of entities which it does not create.

In tenets 12, 13, and 14 the New Realists objected to the prevailing view that consciousness is either an entity itself or an attribute of a substantial mind. They offered in its place a relational theory of consciousness. For them, the objects of the world are as they are, whether or not they enter into a cognitive relationship. That is, things are known directly, and in being so known, are not altered in any way.

The New Realists, in their discussion of the cognitive relationship, provided a philosophical prolegomenon to the psychological theory of behaviorism: the "perceiver" or "knower" refers to a responding nervous system; and the "knowing relationship" refers merely to a form of selective environmental response.

16. The realist holds that things known are not products of the knowing relation nor essentially dependent for their existence or behavior upon that relation. He holds that this doctrine has three claims upon our acceptance: first, it is the natural, instinctive belief of all men, and for this, if for no other reason, puts the burden of proof upon those who would discredit it; secondly, all refutations of it presuppose or even actually employ some of its exclusive implications; and thirdly, it is logically demanded by all the observations and hypotheses of the natural sciences, including psychology.[12]

The New Realists' claim that their view is supported by common sense needs to be examined. They assert quite properly that each of the following propositions is instinctively believed: (a) the nature and existence of things are independent of our knowing them; (b) all of the qualities that we experience in connection with an object are actually qualities of that object; and (c) both objects and their qualities are known directly.

We may question, however, whether other propositions that they espoused gain support from common sense. Consider, for example, these additional New Realist propositions: (*d*) consciousness is not located within the brain but rather in that portion of the external world to which the brain is responding; (*e*) dreams and hallucinations are not subjective experiences, but rather are objective experiences. The New Realist's distinction between the illusory and the genuine cannot be based on the familiar contrast between private and public worlds but must be explained as a distinction within the public realm itself.

We can say of the New Realists generally that they adopted what we have called the "presentative theory of knowledge" and that this led them to adopt "epistemological monism" as well. They reasoned that since we know objects directly, the distinction between objects as such and objects as experienced is artificial. It thus became natural for them to suppose that the cognitive relationship involved no more than one kind of reality. However, they did not agree about what this one reality was. Some viewed it as physical and were called "physicalists," or less appropriately, "materialists"; others considered it to be a neutral stuff which was neither mental nor physical, and were called "neutral monists."

Another group of American realists, the Critical Realists—G. Santayana (1863–1952), A. O. Lovejoy (1873–1962), J. B. Pratt (1875–1944), C. A. Strong (1862–1940), D. Drake (1878–1933), A. K. Rogers (1868–1937), and R. W. Sellars (1880–   ) arose primarily in opposition to the New Realist epistemological monism, with its "uncommonsensical" implications. On the other hand, they also recognized the pitfalls of the naive dualism of Locke and Descartes. Accordingly, they attempted to modify the representative theory of knowledge in such a way that the old objections disappeared. Although their individual theories differed quite radically, they were agreed that the content of experience is not external objects but rather sense data ("character-complexes," "essences") which, in some fashion, mediate between our minds and the independently existing external world.

We have selected readings from two men to serve as the "voices of realism." The first is from the Critical Realist A. O. Lovejoy's *The Revolt Against Dualism,* and the second is from the New Realist W. P. Montague's *The Ways of Knowing.* Although each man stands as a representative of his group, each brings fresh insight to his presentation.

A. O. Lovejoy: CARTESIAN DUALISM AND NATURAL DUALISM

Lovejoy is concerned to point out that there is a set of beliefs which it is natural for men to hold and that these natural beliefs about the world establish the basis for what might be called a dualistic theory of knowledge. For example, a belief that there have been past events is most easily accounted for by presuming that although the awareness of an event such as Lyndon B. Johnson's inauguration can only be a present experience, the event of which one is aware occurred in the past. Note that this presumption involves not only a temporal distinction between the present and the past, but also a qualitative distinction between consciousness and its objects. Lovejoy is confident that such analyses point up the artificiality of rejecting the realistic creed that things exist independent of mind but nevertheless are knowable.

The source of the following exposition is Lovejoy's The Revolt Against Dualism, *1930, pp. 11–24, and it is reprinted here with the kind permission of the publisher, Open Court Publishing Co., La Salle, Illinois.*

Let us take epistemological dualism. . . . Men are normally led to accept it simply because they have formed certain preconceptions as to what an object of knowledge ought to be, and then comparing the characteristics of the thing directly presented in their experience with these preconceptions, have found that the two do not match. In knowing, or attempting to know, man makes certain claims or pretensions, the remarkable nature of which he usually fails to see because he makes them so confidently and habitually. He assumes that, in so far as he ever succeeds in one or another form of the cognitive enterprise, some very curious things must be true about the known fact's or object's relation to himself and his act of knowing. These assumptions are no far-fetched inventions of the philosopher; they are all manifestations of the primary and most universal faith of man, his inexpugnable realism, his two-fold belief that he is on the one hand in the midst of realities which are not himself nor mere obsequious shadows of himself, a world which transcends the narrow confines of his own transient being; and, on the other hand, that he can himself somehow reach beyond those confines and bring these external existences within the compass of his own life, yet without annulment of their transcendence. It is precisely this achievement that men naturally mean by "knowing"; I have but put in general and explicit terms what everyone (except, possibly, a few philosophers) supposes himself to be doing when he is engaged in true perception, retrospection, forecast, or social communication. In the persistent human demand that this singular achievement shall be possible, and the consequent necessity of making intelligible how it can be possible, of describing precisely what happens when it is accomplished, lie the perennial sources of that most human of all the activities of reflective thought which is called epistemology. Man, in short, is by nature an epistemological animal; for his irrepressible knowledge-claim is itself a thesis *about* knowledge, and therefore about himself and his relation to nature and to the life of his fellows; and it is a thesis which cries out for clarification, and for correlation with the conclusions about other natural phenomena to which this natural phenomenon of knowing has brought him. So long as he continues to feel any normal curiosity about himself and his role amid the rest of things, he will necessarily wish to know himself *as* knower, and therefore to understand the seeming mystery and challenging paradox of knowledge—the possibility which it implies of going abroad while keeping at home, the knower's apparent transcendence of the existential limits within which he must yet, at every moment of his knowing, confess himself to be contained.

Specifically, men naturally make at least five assumptions (we need not yet ask whether they are valid assumptions) about the character or status of what may, for short, be called *cognoscenda*— the things-to-be-known-if-possible. (1) Many *cognoscenda*, including most of those to be known, if at all, visually, are assumed to be at places in space external to the body of the percipient. Man may be described biologically as an animal whose habitual and paradoxical employment is the endeavor to reach outside his skin. As a physical organism *homo sapiens*, like other creatures, has a definite spatial boundary of rather irregular outline, formed chiefly of a single material substance. All that, physically or spatially speaking, constitutes the organic functioning of an individual of the species takes place within the narrow room defined by this epidermal surface. What the man as a biological unit is, and what the events that make up his life are, are sought by the biologist wholly within those confines. Yet man is forever attempting, and, as he is wont to believe, with success, to apprehend, to "get at," things which lie beyond this surface. The individual's actual existence, as it appears to *him*, can in only very small part be described as a succession of subcuticular events. The stuff of which it *seems* to be mainly composed consists of entities and happenings on the far side of the boundary, some of them so slightly removed from the epidermal surface that they are said to be in contact with it, others incalculably remote. The human animal, in short, does not for the most part live where its body is—if an organism's life is made up of what it really experiences; it lives where the things are of which it is aware, upon which its attention and feeling are directed. (How far this may be true of other creatures we cannot judge.) One of the most curious developments in the entire history of thought is the invention in our day of what may best be named the Hypodermic Philosophy—the doctrine, resulting from the application to a cognitive animal of the biological concepts found sufficient in the study of animals assumed to be non-cognitive, that the organic phenomenon of knowing may be exhaustively described in terms of molecular displacements taking place under the skin.

(2) Equally insistent in man, and yet more paradoxical—had most men but the capacity for philosophic wonder which would enable them to see it so—is the demand that he shall have a real traffic with things that are not, because they are by-gone or have not yet come into being. What time and nature have extinguished he makes the matter of his present contemplation, and gains thereby his power to foresee what is still unborn. In memory and in forecast and anticipation he expressly conceives himself to be apprehending entities or events (even though they may be only other experiences of his own) which are not co-existent with the acts or states through which they are apprehended—to be reaching what is nevertheless at that moment in some sense beyond his temporal reach.

(3) An even more exigent desire for knowledge normally arises in man—though some philosophers who profess to have rid themselves of it would have us believe that it is equally wanting in others. Besides his craving to reach that which is spatially and temporally external to himself at the moment of cognition, there is, plainly, in the natural man a wish to attain an acquaintance with entities as they *would be if unknown*, existences not relative to the cognitive situation—in short, with things as they literally are in themselves. He has a persistent, if not easily gratified, curiosity about what M. Meyerson calls the *être intime*, the private life, of things. Tell him that at every moment of his existence he is contemplating noth-

ing but the ghostly offspring of that moment's contemplation itself—even though they be projected into other places—and you contradict one of the most tenacious of his convictions—and, as he will point out to you, if he should be something of a dialectician, you also contradict yourself. He may, under pressure from philosophers, surrender this conviction with regard to one and another limited class of the contents of his experience; surrender it wholly, neither he nor the most subjectivistic philosopher has ever really done.

And (4) this tenacity in believing that through what goes on within the individual's experience he can know what is other than that experience and as real as it is, is greatest with respect to his knowledge of the experiences of others of his kind. There are a few philosophers among us who profess not only to be satisfied with automatic sweethearts and mindless friends, but also to be unable to attach meaning to the proposition that these automata have any being beyond that which they have in the philosopher's own private and (as some would add) corporeal existence. (It is, of course, evident that if this philosophy is true—supposing the word "true" still to have meaning—there are not several such philosophers, but only one.) But this queer affectation, a hypertrophy of the logic of scientific empiricism, is manifestly belied at every moment by the behavior and speech of the philosophers who assume it: it denies the meaningfulness of a belief which every creature of our kind seems inevitably to hold and from which all the distinctive quality of man's moral consciousness and all the tang and poignancy of his social experience derive—the belief that he is surrounded by beings like himself but not himself, having inner lives of their own which are never in the same sense *his* own, but of which, nevertheless, he can attain some knowledge, and to whom, reciprocally, he can convey some understanding of that which is going on within himself. This social realism also, which is manifestly a piece of pure epistemology, seems to be one of the specific characters of *homo sapiens*, as properly a part of his zoölogical definition as his upright posture or his lack of a tail. It is implicit in all his most distinctive modes of feeling and behavior—his elaboration of language and art as means of expression, his craving for affection, the curious and immense potency over the individual's conduct which is possessed by his beliefs about the thoughts and feelings of others about himself, and his occasional ability to recognize the interests of other sentient creatures as ends in themselves. Apply the principle of relativity to men's apprehensions of one another, and you destroy the very idea of a society of the characteristically human type.

(5) Finally, the *cognoscenda* which the individual knower ascribes

to places and times in the external world where his body is not, and in which his cognitive act is not occurring, he also conceives to be potentially, if not actually, apprehensible by these other knowers; they must be things capable of verification in experiences other than the one experience in which, at a given moment, they are in some sense before him. Out of his belief in a multiplicity of knowers other than himself, or a multiplicity of knowings which, though now knowable by him, are not *his present* knowing, he has framed the category of publicity, the notion of a world of objects for common knowledge; and he tends to treat this attribute of common verifiability as the criterion of that independence of the percipient event or the cognitive act which he naturally attributes to the *cognoscendum*. In other words, his character as a social animal has profoundly and permanently infected his very notion of knowing, so that the experience of objects which he has when, in dream or madness, he steps aside into a world of his own—be it never so vivid and never so coherent—is not, when seen to be thus private, taken as equivalent to that access to reality which he seeks.

These, then, are the five articles of the natural and spontaneous epistemological creed of mankind—a creed which, as I have said, contains its own apparent mysteries, or diverse aspects of the one mystery of the presence of the absent, the true apprehension, by a being remaining within certain fixed bounds, of things beyond those bounds. Epistemological dualism arises when reflection, initially accepting these articles, inquires about their implications and brings them into connection with certain familiar facts of experience. There is, indeed, as should be evident from what has already been said, a sense in which all realism is intrinsically dualistic; in all its forms, namely, it asserts that the thing known may be other in time and place and nature than the *event or act by means of which* the thing is known. Thus the event of seeing, as we have remarked, if conceived physiologically as a neuro-cerebral change, does not appear to occur either where the visual object is seen or where the real object is assumed to be. A happening inside of a given body somehow achieves the presentation, in the individual stream of experience connected with that particular body, of an entity outside the body. And even if the cognitive event be conceived as a purely psychic and non-spatial act of awareness, that act has at least a date which need not (*e.g.*, in memory) be the date, and a *quale* [quality] which is by hypothesis not the *quale* of the object known. But it is not this fundamental sort of dualism necessarily inherent in any realistic theory of knowledge which we shall here mean by "epistemological dualism"; the term stands for the assertion of quite another (though not unrelated) duality, that of the content or datum at a given moment immediately and indubitably presented, and the reality said to be known thereby. Even the datum, of course, *seems*, in the case of sight and touch, to be situated outside the body, though whether it truly is or not must be a matter for subsequent consideration. I do not actually see the desk inside the head of which I at the same time can see a small bit—namely, the tip of my nose—and to the rest of which I give in thought a spatial position definitely related to that bit. But epistemological dualism (as here understood) declares that not even the visible desk which is thus directly perceived as spatially external to the perceived body is the same existent as the "real" desk, *i.e.*, the *cognoscendum*. And the existential distinctness of datum and *cognoscendum* which is thus held by the dualist to be exemplified in the case of visual perception is also asserted by him, *mutatis mutandis*, in the case of other modes of perception and other forms of cognitive experience; so that, in his view, all knowing is mediated through the presence "before the mind"—as the traditional phrase goes—of entities which must be distinguished from an ulterior reality which is the true objective of knowledge.

Now you obviously cannot discuss whether two particulars—two in the sense that they have been provisionally distinguished in discourse—are identical unless you already know or assume something about both. If you are in a state of blank ignorance about either one, no question concerning the nature of their relations can be raised. It is therefore necessary to know, or postulate, certain propositions about the class *cognoscenda* before we can compare it with the class "data" to ascertain whether the two satisfy our criteria of identity. To assert their non-identity is to ascribe to the one a spatial or a temporal or a spatio-temporal position, or a set of qualities, which is inconsistent with those empirically exhibited by the other. Philosophers, it is true, have often attempted to go about the matter in what seems a different way. They have begun by provisionally assuming that they know nothing whatever except the passing immediate datum, and have been sought to determine, by reflecting upon the nature or implications of this, how much knowledge of existents which are not immediate data they must, or may, suppose themselves to possess. This was, of course, essentially the method of Descartes, though he applied it confusedly and inconsistently. But it is not the natural road to epistemological dualism. That road starts from the position of natural realism—from the assumption that we already have certain information about realities which are not *merely* our immediate, private, and momentary data; and it leads to the discovery, or supposed discovery, that this very assumption forbids us to believe that our acquaintance with these realities is at first hand. The time, place, context, or qualities which we have ascribed to them prove inconsistent with those which belong to the data. Not only is this the natural approach to the dualism of datum and *cognoscendum*, but it is also the only approach which is at all likely to be persuasive to those averse to that theory. The argument starts from the premises of those who would, if possible, avoid its conclusion. We shall, then, in this . . . lecture, not attempt an affectation of universal doubt, but shall tentatively accept—with nearly all of the early and many even of the later insurgents—the broad outlines of the picture of nature familiar to common sense and sanctioned by the older physics. We shall, in particular, not initially question the supposition that there are extended external objects, such as pennies, tables, planets, and distant stars, having at least the primary and possibly also the secondary qualities; having determinable positions in a space like that of visual and tactual perception, whether or not it is identical with it; capable of motion and causal interaction; acting, by means of processes in space, upon our sense-organs; and thereby conditioning the presence in our experience of the data which, whether or not identical with the objects, are our sources of information about them. When these natural assumptions are provisionally adopted, there nevertheless prove to be at least five familiar aspects of experience in which it seems plain that the object of our knowing must be different in the time or place or mode of its existence, or in its character, from the perceptual or other content which is present to us at the moment when we are commonly said to be apprehending that object, and without which we should never apprehend it at all.

(1) Of these, the first is implicit in the second of the above-mentioned articles of man's natural realistic creed. Intertemporal cognition, the knowing at one time of things which exist or events which occur at another time, seems a patent example of a mode of knowledge which we are under the necessity of regarding as potentially genuine and yet as mediate. When I remember, for example, not only is there a present awareness distinct from the past memory-object (that alone would imply only the duality of act and content), but the present awareness manifestly has, and must have, a compresent content. But the past event which we say the memory is *of* cannot be this compresent content. In saying this I am, it is true, including among the natural grounds of epistemological dualism an assumption which some dualistic philosophers—and even some who repudiate the naïvely dualistic theory of memory—regard as unsound. Mr. Broad, for example, has said that there "is no general

metaphysical objection to such a theory" on the ground that when an event is past it ceases to exist. "Once an event has happened it exists eternally"; past events, therefore, "are always 'there' waiting to be remembered; and there is no *a priori* reason why they should not from time to time enter into such a relation with certain present events that they become objects of direct acquaintance." This view, however, implies an inconceivable divorce of the identity of an event from its date. The things which may be said to subsist eternally are essences; and the reason why they can so subsist is that, by definition, they have no dates. They do not "exist" at all, in the sense in which dated and located things do so; and if "events" externally existed after they had "once happened" (and when they were no longer "happening"), they would likewise exist before they happened; eternalness can hardly be an acquired character. The present image and the past event may be separate embodiments of the same essence; they are not identical particulars, because the particularity of each is undefinable apart from its temporal situation and relations. The duality of the memory-image and the bygone existence to which it refers seems to be inherent in what we *mean* by remembrance; if the two were one our intertemporal knowing would defeat its own aim of apprehending the beyond, by annulling its beyondness. The very wistfulness of memory implies such duality; the past, in being known, still inexorably keeps its distance. Plainest of all is it that a man's own experienc*ing* of yesterday, the even of his then *having* an experience, does not seem to him, in being remembered, to become to-day's experiencing. Common sense, however much inclined in its more self-confident moments to believe in direct perception, has never, I suppose, believed in direct memory; it has been well aware that what is present in retrospection is a duplicate which somehow and in some degree discloses to us the character, without constituting the existence, of its original.

(2) It is not alone in the case of memory that there is a temporal sundering, and therefore an existential duality, of the content given and the reality made known to us through that content. This second reason for dualism has not, it is true, like some of the others, always been discoverable by the simplest reflection upon every-day experience. But the fact upon which it rests has long been one of the elementary commonplaces of physical science; and the probability of it had suggested itself to acute minds long before its verification. There had at times occurred to him, wrote Bacon in the *Novum Organum*, "a very strange doubt," a *dubitatio plane monstrosa*, "namely, whether the face of a clear and starlight sky be seen at the instant at which it really exists, and not rather a little later; and

whether there be not, as regards our sight of heavenly bodies, a real time and an apparent time (*tempus visum*), just as there is a real place and an apparent place taken account of by astronomers." For it had appeared to him "incredible that the images or rays of the heavenly bodies could be conveyed at once to the sight through such an immense space and did not rather take some appreciable time in travelling to us." Unfortunately for his reputation Lord Bacon was able to overcome this doubt by invoking against it several bad reasons, which need not be here recalled; but his subtler medieval namesake had not only propounded but embraced and defended the same conjecture three centuries earlier. Roemer's observation in 1675, through which it became established as one of the fundamental theorems of empirical science, is not usually mentioned in the histories of philosophy; but the omission merely shows how badly the history of philosophy is commonly written, for the discovery was as significant for epistemology as it was for physics and astronomy. It appeared definitely to forbid that naïvely realistic way of taking the content of visual perception to which all men at first naturally incline. The doctrine of the finite velocity of light meant that the sense from which most of our information about the world beyond our epidermal surfaces is derived never discloses anything which (in Francis Bacon's phrase) "really exists" in that world, at the instant at which it indubitably exists in perception. It is with a certain phase in the history of a distant star that the astronomer, gazing through his telescope at a given moment, is supposed to become acquainted; but that phase, and perhaps the star itself, have, ages since, ceased to be; and the astronomer's present sense-data—it has therefore seemed inevitable to say—whatever else they may be, are not identical with the realities they are believed to reveal. They might perhaps be supposed to be identical with the peripheral effect produced by the light-ray on its belated arrival at the eye—in other words, with the retinal images; but two present and inverted retinal images *here* are obviously not the same as one extinct star formerly existing elsewhere, and the duality of datum and object would therefore remain. This particular hypothesis, moreover, is excluded by the now familiar fact established by the physiological psychologists, that there is a further lag—slight, but not theoretically negligible—in the transmission of the neural impulse to the cortical center, and therefore—since the percept does not appear until the impulse reaches the brain—a difference in time between the existence of a given pair of retinal images, or any other excitation of peripheral nerve-endings, and the existence of the corresponding percept. Never, in short, if both the physiologists and the physicists are right, can the datum or character-complex presented in the perception of a given moment be regarded as anything but the report of a messenger, more or less tardy and more or less open to suspicion, from the original object which we are said to know by virtue of that perception.

(3) Another class of empirical facts which are familiar, in their simpler forms, to all men have seemed by the plainest implication to show that perceptual content, even though it appears as external to the physical organs of perception, is not identical with the particular objects about which it is supposed to convey information. It is commonly assumed that the object, or objective, of a given perception can, first of all, be identified, at least roughly, by its position in space and time. What I am "perceiving" at a certain moment is the ink-bottle two feet away from my hand, or the star a hundred light-years distant. Even if the position is defined only vaguely, the thing is at least supposed to be (or have been) "out there" somewhere. This identification of the object referred to is, obviously, possible only by means of the same perception; yet, assuming such identification, experience shows that what I perceive is determined by events or conditions intervening in space and time between that object and my so-called perception of it. The qualities sensibly presented vary with changes which appear to occur, not in the place where *the* object is supposed to exist, but in regions between it and the body itself, and, in particular, in the very organs of perception. The examples are trite: a man puts a lens before his eyes, and the size or shape or number or perceived distance of the objects presented is altered; he puts certain drugs into his stomach, and the colors of all the perceived objects external to his body change; he swallows other drugs in sufficient quantity, and sees outside his body objects which no one else can see, and which his own other senses fail to disclose. The discovery of this primary sort of physical relativity, which is really one of the most pregnant of philosophical discoveries, begins in infancy with the earliest experience of the illusions of perspective, or the observation that the objects in the visual field change their spatial relations when looked at with first one eye and then the other. If *homo sapiens* had at the outset been blind, the first seeing man, a paleolithic Einstein, when he reported this astonishing fact—the relativity of position to the motions of eyelids—to his fellow cave-men, would presumably have seemed to them a deviser of intolerable paradoxes, and have been made acquainted with those more effective methods for repressing strange doctrines which cave-men, no doubt, knew how to employ. The evidence of this dependence of the nature of what is perceived upon happenings which, as themselves experienced, do not happen in the right place to per-

mit them to be regarded as changes in the *cognoscendum* itself, has constantly increased with the progress of the sciences of optics, neuro-cerebral physiology, and psychology; the eventual determination of the character of the percept has been removed farther and farther, not only from the external object, but even from the external organ of sense. As Professor Dewey remarked, "it is pure fiction that a 'sensation' or peripheral excitation, or stimulus, travels undisturbed in solitary state in its own coach-and-four to either the brain or consciousness in its purity. A particular excitation is but one of an avalanche of contemporaneously occurring excitations, peripheral and from proprioceptors; each has to compete with others, to make terms with them; what happens is an integration of complex forces." And even in the earliest and easiest phases of this discovery, the variability of the percept with conditions extrinsic to the object to be perceived manifestly affects those attributes by which the very identity of the individual object should be defined: it is not colors only but shapes, not shapes only but perceived positions, that prove to be functions of the processes spatially and temporally intervenient between the object and the perception, and therefore not attributable to the former. Thus what is actually perceived could be regarded only as the terminal effect of a more or less long and complex causal series of events happening at different places and times, only at the perceptually inaccessible other end of which series the *cognoscendum* was supposed to have—or rather, to have had—its being. Aside from any empirical evidences of the sort mentioned, it has apparently seemed to many minds virtually axiomatic that, if the *cognoscendum* in perception is conceived (as it is in ordinary thought and in most physical theory) as a "causal object" acting upon the bodily organs of perception in the determination of the character of the content experienced, that which is acted *upon* must also have a part—must, indeed, have the last and decisive word—in determining the character of that content. How under these circumstances the exterior causal object would be known at all is an obviously difficult question; this argument for epistemological dualism, and especially the rôle assigned in it to the organs of perception, gives rise to that "crux of realistic theories" which Mr. C. A. Strong has very precisely expressed: "to explain how a sensation which varies directly only with one physical object, the nervous system, can yet vary with another physical object sufficiently to give knowledge of it." But with these ulterior difficulties we are not for the moment concerned; whatever *their* solution, they obviously do not annul the difficulty, for any realistic philosophy, of identifying the end-term with the initial term of the physico-physiological causal series.

(4) This physical and physiological conditionedness of the data manifestly implies that the contents of the experience of percipients having different spatial and physical relations to a postulated external object cannot be wholly identical. But this implication is independently confirmed and extended through that communication and comparison of experiences which is supposed to be possible through language. While the many knowers are, by the fifth article of the natural epistemological creed, dealing with what is said to be one and the same object—and if they are not doing so are not achieving what is meant by knowledge—they notoriously are not experiencing the same sensible appearances. There is an assumed identity of the region of space at which the observers are all gazing, and this serves for the requisite antecedent identification of the common *cognoscendum*; but what they severally find occupying this supposedly single locus consists of character-complexes which are not merely diverse but (according to the logic almost universally accepted until recently) contradictory. So long as it is assumed either that there are certain sets of sensible qualities—*e.g.*, two or more colors—which are incompatible, *i.e.*, cannot both occupy the same place or the same surface of a material object at the same time, or that there are in nature "things" which at a given moment have a single and harmonious outfit of geometrical and other properties, the conclusion has seemed inevitable that the many discrepant appearances cannot "really" inhabit the one place or be the one thing at that place. So soon as the dimmest notion that there is such a phenomenon as perspective distortion dawned upon men, they began *eo ipso* to be epistemological dualists. It is of course conceivable, so far as the present consideration goes, that *one* of the discordant appearances might be identical with the object-to-be-known or with some part of it; but even so, since all the other observers are also supposed to be apprehending the object, *their* apprehension, at least, must be mediated through data which are *not* identical with it. Nor does it seem a probable hypothesis that, while *almost* all perception is mediate, a few privileged observers now and then attain direct access to the object.

(5) Finally, the experience of error and illusion, however difficult it may be to render philosophically intelligible, seems to have at least one direct and obvious implication: namely, that the thing which at any moment we err about—otherwise than by mere omission—cannot be a thing which is immediately present to us at that moment, since about the latter there can be no error. It, at least, *is* what it is experienced as. In so far as *cognoscendum* and content are

identified, error is excluded; in so far as the possibility of error is admitted, *cognoscendum* and content are set apart from one another. It may perhaps seem that this reasoning applies only to the cases in which there *is* error, and that in true judgments (or in veridical perception) the content may still be the same as the *cognoscendum*. And if the term "true judgments" includes the mere awareness of an immediate datum, then in such judgments there is in fact no duality. But these constitute, at best, only a tiny part of the subject-matter of our claims to potential knowledge, the range of our possible judgments at any given time; and it is, indeed, an obviously inconvenient use of language to call them judgments at all. For the most part we are occupied, when judging, with matters conceived to be so related to us that we are not, from the very nature of that relation, necessarily immune against error; doubt as to the validity of our judgments about them is assumed to be not meaningless. But where error is *conceivable*, the relation between content and *cognoscendum* must be the same as in the case of actual error. The generic nature of judgments-potentially-erroneous must be conceived in such a way as to permit the genus to have both judgments actually true and judgments actually false as its species—and to make it intelligible that the latter are aiming at the same mark as the former without hitting it. But a judgment is about something in particular; it has to do with a specific portion of reality. Since in actually erroneous judgments it is impossible that that portion can be the immediate datum, error must consist in attributing some character now present in perception or imagery, or represented by a verbal symbol, to *another* locus in reality, where it in fact is not present; and the species of actually true judgments will correspondingly be defined as the attribution of some such character to another locus in reality where it in fact *is* present. In all this, once more, I have only been putting explicitly the way of thinking about truth and error which seems to be common to all mankind, barring a few philosophers of more or less recent times. That bit of baldly dualistic epistemology known as the correspondence-theory of truth is one of the most deeply ingrained and persistent of human habit; there is much reason to doubt whether any of the philosophers who repudiate it actually dispense with it; yet *it* is not merely an instinctive faith, but has behind it certain simple and definite logical considerations which it appears absurd to deny. This also, among the five points of natural epistemological dualism, may plausibly be supposed to have been a part of the unformulated working epistemology of our race from an early stage in the progress of intelligence; for there can hardly have been many featherless bipeds so naïve as not to have learned that man is liable to error, and so dull as to be unable to see, at least dimly, that in direct contemplation there is no room for error. . . .

A. O. *Lovejoy:* THE NATURE OF KNOWING AS A NATURAL EVENT

Lovejoy insists that in order to be adequate, any epistemological theory must adopt the view that we gain knowledge indirectly rather than directly, that knowledge is "mediate" rather than "immediate." Idealism, in many of its forms, has sought to avoid this feature by assimilating all knowledge to the model of perception, a model in which the mistake of equating ideas and their objects is difficult to detect. It becomes clear that the doctrine of mediate knowledge is unavoidable when we analyze our claims to past and future knowledge. Lovejoy admits, however, that to understand the need for a dualistic account of knowledge does not show how it is possible. He then turns his efforts to answering those chronic questions which led to the "revolt against dualism": How can it be established that there is a resemblance between ideas and objects, and granted such resemblance, in what sense can we be said to know objects through the mediation of such ideas? The general thesis which Lovejoy develops to answer these questions is that the content of ideas has a significance which goes beyond their occurrence as psychological experiences.

The pages below are reprinted from Lovejoy's The Revolt Against Dualism, *1930, pp. 303–318, by kind permission of the publisher, Open Court Publishing Co., La Salle, Illinois.*

If you are to believe in a real physical world, then . . . you must necessarily be a dualist in both senses of the term: you must hold (*a*) that there are given in experience particular existents which are not parts of the world, and you must hold (*b*) that whatever knowledge of real objects you have is indirect or representative, that the datum whereby you know any such object is not identical with the object known. Resuming our inquiry at this point . . . we proceed to consider two further questions, relating exclusively to the second of these propositions. The first question is whether that proposition is valid not exclusively from the standpoint of the realist, but from any standpoint—in other words, whether epistemological dualism must be accepted by anyone, be he realist or idealist or phenomenalist or pragmatist, who believes that the phenomenon called knowing ever does actually occur. The second question is whether, in final analysis, epistemological dualism itself is tenable—whether the notion of the apprehension of an existent (whatever be its metaphysical nature) by means of the immediate presence in experience of *something other than itself* is psychologically intelligible, or even conceivable without self-contradiction. Our two questions, then, more briefly stated, are: (1) Is the mediate character of knowledge implied by idealism (or kindred doctrines) as well as by physical realism? (2) Is mediate knowledge possible—and if so, how?

The comment will, of course, naturally suggest itself here that the second question ought to come first, and that, indeed, it should have been dealt with at the very beginning of our whole inquiry. But this order of procedure would, I think, be a mistaken one, in spite of its air of logicality. It is, for reasons which I have already suggested, better to begin with hypothetical questions, to make explicit the necessary but frequently overlooked implications, with respect to a given problem, of the various types of opinion which have been held by philosophers, or by common sense, instead of attacking directly the seemingly fundamental and decisive issues. And the advantages of this procedure are well illustrated in the case of the questions now before us. One of the principal and most plausible grounds for accepting idealism, as a metaphysical doctrine, has at all times consisted in the assumption that epistemological dualism is a gratuitously complicated, or even an intrinsically absurd, account of what occurs when anything is known, and that idealism is a way, and the only way, of escaping from this supposed absurdity. But if it is the fact—as I think we shall find it to be—that the idealist as well as the realist is irretrievably committed to the theory of indirect or representative knowledge, then both of them are likely to come with more open minds to the question whether that theory is really so gratuitous or so absurd as had been supposed. They are, indeed, under such circumstances, likely to come to it with a rational presumption in its favor. For—unless one is prepared to admit in advance that there is an absurdity inherent in the very idea of knowledge—it would appear antecedently improbable that a conclusion which is equally inevitable from the standpoint of either of the two possible general types of metaphysical doctrine is itself impossible. When this improbability is realized, a less hasty and prejudiced examination into the supposed difficulties of that conclusion should result.

(1) We turn, then, to our first question. The answer to it is to be found in some very simple considerations already intimated. The idealist does, of course, avoid an admission of epistemological dualism with respect to the knowledge of the physical world, inasmuch as he denies that there is—in the sense in which we have been using the term—any physical world to be known. He is content (in this matter) with his private world of perceptual content. His sense-data have an indubitable, if transitory, existence; each of them is precisely what it is immediately experienced as being; and he seeks for nothing possessing similar generic characters beyond or behind them. The being of sensible things is simply their being sensed; and their true characters are therefore their sensed characters. And it is because he has, in dealing with the special problem of perception, thus contrived very easily and summarily to rid himself of the difficulty of understanding how things can be known indirectly, that the idealist has often supposed that he has avoided that difficulty altogether. But this is an illusion, and a very naïve and transparent one, arising chiefly from an excessive preoccupation of epistemologists in the past with the problem of perception.

For the type of cognitive—or putatively cognitive—experience with which a systematic epistemological inquiry ought to begin is not perception but retrospection, or, more specifically, remembrance. This is the primary mode of knowing, which must be presupposed, tacitly or explicitly, in any reflection upon the implications of what is sensibly given; and it is the kind of knowledge about the reality of which there is least disagreement. It is the one which involves the smallest transcendence of absolute scepticism, and from which it is improbable that the most resolutely subjectivistic of philosophers really dissents. Its thin end is of an exceeding thinness; it amounts to no more than the assumption that one was not born at this moment, that one has had experiences of which one now knows, though they are not the experiences which one is now having. If Descartes had been as critical and methodical in rebuilding his world as he was in shattering it, he would have seen that the existential proposition which, in his reconstruction, should have immediately followed the *cogito ergo sum* was *memini ergo fui* [I remember, therefore I was]. He could not, indeed, have formally deduced this from the *cogito*;

Realism: A. O. Lovejoy   35

he could not, strictly speaking, have justified it by reasoning; but he could, by simply keeping his attention fixed upon his own consciousness, have, so to say, seen *cogito* transforming itself into *memini* before his eyes. Small as this step might have seemed, it would have altered the direction of Descartes' subsequent course of reasoning; and if he had taken it, the history of modern philosophy might well have been widely different from what it has been, and less involved in confusion.

For any belief in the possibility of true remembrance is not only a step out of subjectivism; it is also a step into epistemological dualism. Why this is true was briefly indicated in the first of these lectures; but it is perhaps advisable to recapitulate and complete the argument here. In memory and other retrospection there is a conscious and intrinsic reference to a reality other than the content given. The perceptual datum, as Berkeleian idealists and neo-realists both like to remind us, is not presented in unreflective experience as standing for an existent not itself; *merely* to perceive is not to be explicitly aware of a contrast between datum and *cognoscendum*. But merely to remember *is* to be aware of a contrast between the image presented and the event recalled. No man doubts that, when he recollects today the acts he performed yesterday, those acts are not occurring today and yet that something which somehow exhibits their character is an item in his experience today; or that when, for example, he brings to mind the look of a dog he owned when a boy, there is something of a canine sort immediately present to and therefore compresent with his consciousness, but that it is quite certainly not that dog in the flesh. Retrospection is thus a case in which the duality of the datum and the thing known is immediately manifest, so that to deny the duality is to deny that the kind of knowing which retrospection purports to be is possible at all; whereas in the case of perceptual knowledge the duality becomes evident only through an analysis in which certain postulates about the external world are necessary. The direct evidence for epistemological dualism from the nature of the memory-experience is, then, as plain for an idealist as for a realist, if the idealist admits that he had a past and is not wholly unacquainted with it. Everyone who ever says "I remember," and uses the word in its natural and familiar sense, is bearing witness to the possibility of mediate or representative knowledge.

It is, of course, true that some philosophers and psychologists profess to reject this account of what occurs when a man remembers. Two opposite objections to it have been raised. (*a*) With the first I have already dealt: it consists in the assertion that the thing remembered has *not* ceased to exist, and may therefore now be directly contemplated. This, if literally meant, is a paradox, begotten of a theoretical prejudice, which I find it impossible to take seriously; and if it is not literally meant, it is irrelevant. From the standpoint of physical realism its absurdity is doubly evident; for what is remembered is not only, by the assumption inherent in memory itself, something past, but it is often also, by the assumption of the realist, something not present in the physical world. The dog remembered was once flesh and blood; it is now dust; but it is a dog not dust that is the object of the remembrance. But from any standpoint, again, the absurdity is patent. To remember is *eo ipso* to assign to the object a date in a temporal sequence which is not the date of the act of retrospection nor of the givenness of the image. Even if what is called the same individual thing still exists, it is to a bygone phase of its existence that memory refers; to apprehend a present state of anything is not to remember. And, of course, if memory consisted in the actual presence in consciousness of the object to be known, it would necessarily be infallible. (*b*) The other way of attempting to escape from the dualistic implication of the fact of memory is by denying the existence of memory-images. When a man says "I remember," there no doubt is, it is granted, something of a peculiar sort given in his experience, or, at all events, taking place in his body; but this, whatever it be (about which theories may differ), is neither an actual past event nor a simulacrum referred to a prior date. It is merely some distinctive present form of sensory content or physiological behavior. About this only two brief remarks need, I think, be made. In the first place, it is simply a dogmatic denial of the occurrence of a type of experience which most persons are quite as certain of having had as they are certain of anything. It is true, indeed, that memory-content is often of a highly abstract and symbolic or verbal sort; what is now introspectibly present may be rather the name than the likeness of a vanished object or a by-gone happening. Yet it is also true that the content is often of a more or less vividly imaginal character; the testimony to this is far too definite and abundant to be summarily set aside. Empirical science is presumably science which is based upon human experience; and a psychological theory which tells us that there are no such things as images experienced when people are remembering rejects *a priori* a voluminous mass of empirical evidence which does not happen to accord with the theorist's preconceptions. And, in the second place, be the memory-content as non-imaginal and abstractly symbolic as it may, it is still symbolic *of* something, and that something is apprehended as past; this is the distinctive *quale* of the retrospective experience. Even if we should attempt to give a purely behavioristic account of what is *present* in memory, should describe it as a particular kind of muscular "set," or as a movement of molecules in the larynx or some other anatomical region, unless this were in some fashion conceived as corresponding with or referring to some antedated event, at least to some earlier behavior, it would not be to anything of the nature of memory that our description would be pertinent.

These attempts to conceive of retrospection in general, and of memory in particular, in a non-dualistic way are, then, unsuccessful; when not equivalent to denying that we ever remember at all, they are equivalent to admitting that memory is a mode of representative knowledge. In short, there is either no such phenomenon as retrospection, or else in it, at least, the relation of the immediate content to the fact or object known is of that loose, indirect, mediate sort which the epistemological dualist supposes to be characteristic of knowing in general. . . .

Of the other form of intertemporal cognition, actual or supposed—that is, foreknowledge or expectation—the dualistic implications are, if possible, even more manifest; and thus those pragmatic philosophers who curiously tend to conceive of the future as the sole region upon which our interest and our intellection are directed must, not less certainly than the idealist, admit that the *cognoscendum* is not apprehended through actual possession. For such pragmatists knowledge is pre-presentative if not representative. Future events not only are not now being experienced, but they have never entered into experience nor into existence, *as* events; and upon them no sane mortal can suppose his cognitive grasp to be direct and assured. Yet unless we can truly be said in some sense to be capable of referring to and foreknowing some future events, all our other knowing is, not, indeed, spurious, but—as the pragmatist rightly enough insists—barren, and irrelevant to the occasions which chiefly make knowledge needful to the expectant, purposive, and plan-devising creatures that we are.

Both retrospection and forecast, then, are crucial and undeniable examples of the fact that knowing—if there *is* any such phenomenon—may, and at least in certain cases must, consist in the apprehension of a particular existent through the presence in a given experience of some existent other than itself. To deny this is to deny not only that we can have any knowledge of an external world, but also that we can have, or even conceive the possibility of having, any knowledge of any experience beyond the immediate and certain content of a single specious present of a single knower. Here, at least, the object is present vicariously or not at all. If there were in this mode of knowing no recognized contrast between what is given and what is meant, it would not do for us what, in the perpetual flux of consciousness, and in our urgent need to escape from the limitations of that flux, we want knowing to do; and, on the other hand, it would permit no doubts about the truth or adequacy of our apprehension of the object upon which our cognitive act is directed, and demand no venture of faith when we go about our business tentatively taking that which now appears to us as evidence of that which truly has been and is to be.

We pass now to our second question. It concerns the truth of the thesis—frequently maintained by philosophers who are themselves, as we have just seen, epistemological dualists—that any theory of indirect or representative knowledge is redundant and, in the last analysis, self-contradictory. This general type of criticism takes two forms, according as the point of difficulty in the dualistic view is conceived to be (*a*) the assertion that the object is not *directly* known or (*b*) that it nevertheless *is* known. (*a*) Those who fix upon the first point declare that to say that a thing is not known directly—is not itself "before the mind" at the time of the cognitive event—is equivalent to saying that it is *not* at that time known and that verification of a judgment concerning it at any time is impossible. Any correspondence-theory of knowledge, it has been endlessly reiterated, is tantamount to a denial of the possibility of knowledge. If the realities about which we judge, in our perceptual or other judgments, are forever beyond our grasp, it is mere irony to speak of our "apprehending" them. The two supposedly correspondent existences, idea and object, can never be brought together for actual comparison; and the truth of the judgment can therefore never be established. (*b*) And, on the other hand, it is argued, the dualist in distinguishing between the datum which he apprehends directly and the "real object" which he professes to apprehend indirectly, implies that he *has* the latter as well as the former present to his consciousness—and present with precisely the status of "objectivity" or "realness" whereby it is supposed to be differentiated from the mere datum. But if so, it is not only superfluous but inconsistent to maintain that it is through a substitute which is not in the same sense "real" that the object is known. In short, an object is at any moment "before the mind" or it is not. If it is not, it obviously is not at that moment being known. If it is, then it is *that* object, and not some other entity, that is before the mind. Epistemological dualism is thus a self-refuting thesis; it cannot be stated without being in that statement implicitly denied. The dualist may, it is true, introduce a verbal distinction between data which are "merely present" for awareness and those which are "present-as-absent"; but the distinction is unintelligible. There are not two ways of being present for awareness, but only one.

These arguments, and especially the latter, were among the more serious and plausible of the considerations which originally gave rise to the revolt against dualism. They are arguments against the possibility of mediate knowledge as such, and are therefore pressed by both the realistic and idealistic critics of dualism. That they cannot legitimately be used by the former has already been shown on two quite different grounds—first, because realism proves unable, in any of its forms, to assign to the datum the characters and spatio-temporal situations and modes of action which it ascribes to the real physical object; and second, because the monistic realist's position is liable to the same type of objection which he here brings against the dualist. His doctrine implies what he reproaches the dualist for plainly asserting. For it implies that he and other men can be aware of things which are not, as existents, immediately present for awareness. If he does not admit this, he denies the knowable reality of things independent of awareness. He, too, is by the inherent logic of his doctrine committed, though against his own intention, to affirming that content may be within the circle of actual experience as if extraneous to it. The present objection to dualism is thus at bottom an objection to all realism, including that residuum of realism which inevitably remains even in the doctrine of the idealist. But to show that the vicarious presence of objects, at least in intertemporal cognition, is implied by everybody who believes such cognition to be possible, is not to eliminate the apparent paradox of vicarious presence. It is, therefore, as we have recognized from the outset, incumbent upon the dualistic philosopher to attempt to make clear finally, not only (to use an apposite distinction of Bradley's) *that* the doctrine of the mediate character of knowledge *is* true, but also *how* it *may* be true—to "explain how consciousness can be of an absent object."

To do this, however, the dualistic philosopher need only invite men to observe yet more carefully what they are doing when they are, or conceive themselves to be, knowing the past or the future. In the case of retrospection or anticipation, as in other cases, knowing manifestly does not consist in blankly glaring at isolated and unrelated bits of content. The content is permeated with relational categories; its parts are given as having diverse situations in one or another schema of relations, of which the temporal distinctions of relative date—before-and-after, past-present-and-future—are one type. We can know yesterday today, and know it *as* yesterday, without either actually going back to it or bringing it again into present existence, simply because what is before the mind today is a pattern of dated events. The pattern is given, and has its psychological existence, today, but it *includes the relative date of its own existence as one of its terms* or components; and in this pattern its own date or locus of existence is recognized as identical with that of our awareness, and as not identical with that of the particular event, within the pattern, upon which our cognitive attention is specifically directed. To experience at a given moment a pattern of temporal succession is not the same as passing through a succession of experiences. In a historical chart the relations both of simultaneity and of succession of certain happenings are alike simultaneously spread out in a spatial arrangement which you may take in at a glance. Nevertheless, if you are acquainted with the plan upon which the chart was drawn up, you perfectly clearly distinguish between the spatial pattern which you see and the temporal relations which it symbolizes; and you do not, because the names or descriptions of the historical events in question are before your eyes all at once, have any difficulty in understanding that what the historian intended to convey was not that these events occurred all at once. It is, then, this power which we obviously have—one without which there could be no historians, inasmuch as historical propositions could have no meaning—of thinking relations of succession without thereby experiencing them, that makes retrospection possible, and defines the sense in which remembered events are present-as-absent. It is their symbols only, the images or the words which represent them, that are literally and indubitably present. But the remembered events, though not in this sense present, are presented. For the given characters of the symbols are referred to a situation in the conceptual schema which is external to that which the symbols are recognized as having therein. The symbols, in short, have a date of givenness and a date of reference, which are clearly distinguished. The practical function of knowledge, upon which it is the current fashion to lay so great emphasis, is secondary to this function of intertemporal transcendent reference, and derivative from it. Knowledge is, no doubt, among other things, an instrument of control and a means of adaptation to the predetermined conditions and limitations of purposive action. But its distinctive efficacy for this end lies in its power to bring past and future within the scope of present consciousness; and its uncertainty and fallibility lie in the fact that it does not bring the *actual* past and future within the confines of time or place that bound the existence of present consciousness and of its data.

Realism: A. O. Lovejoy 41

The solution, then, of the supposed difficulty in the conception of knowing as mediate is evident. To claim knowledge of what is not temporally coexistent with the knowing, is *not* to have the intended object of knowledge *in propria persona* "before the mind"; and the epistemological dualist in expressing his thesis does not fall into the contradiction of asserting that he has that object before his mind and at the same time asserting that he knows it only through the presentation in his experience of something which is not that object. What his thesis means, or should mean, is that at the moment when any man believes himself to be, *e.g.*, remembering, there is before him both a particular concrete datum—usually an image— and the conception of a mode of relatedness in which mutually external existences, including this datum, may stand to one another; and that the character of the datum either is ascribed to a locus (in that relational order) conceived as other than that in which it is actually given (other, namely, than the here-and-now locus), or is at least regarded as capable of presence in that other locus. This ascription of the character to some locus of the not-present and not-given is not equivalent to, and is in knowledge—when, at least, it is at all reflective—not confused with, its veritable presence in such a locus; for it is as an externality in *existence* that the mutual externality of the loci is conceived. The notion of existence, which is so often treated as mysterious and incomprehensible, appears to be so only because it is fundamental in our thinking and irreducible; intelligence cannot take a single step without employing it. Those who think they have dispensed with it are transparently deceiving themselves. We are empirically acquainted with its meaning by ourselves being—and by the being, at any moment, of our present data. But we can, and must, and persistently do, extend it to objects and events to which we impute positions not our own in that order of temporal relations which we conceive as including and transcending our own position and that of our data. And when we do this we mean something more than the fact of our so extending it—more, that is, than the fact that those objects are now presented to us as so situated in that now presented frame. We mean, precisely, that that to which we extend it had, or will have, existence in its own position as truly as we and our data (including our concept of the temporal order of relations) now have existence; but in that order, the only part of which we are now *experiencing* the existence, and of which we can assert the present existence, is the part within which we and our data are situated. Thus it is that we can, at a given moment, contrast the reality of a not-present event with the givenness of the datum (whether percept or image) by which we apprehend it, and even with the givenness of the conceptual schema by means of which we are enabled to frame the distinction between the present and the not-present, the datum and the *cognoscendum*.

The "how" of mediate knowing being thus made intelligible primarily by a scrutiny of intertemporal knowledge, of which the mediate character is certain, the purely epistemological paradox supposed to inhere in any dualistic theory of perception disappears. There is nothing more paradoxical in the conception of a knowledge of physical objects by means of sensa not identical with those objects than there is in the conception of a knowledge of past events by means of memory-images not identical with those events. . . .

We have been considering the knowing of particular existences from, so to say, the inside; we have been observing what it appears as to the knower. Accepting the results thus reached, we may now define the distinctive character and the role of knowledge in the economy of nature. Essentially, knowing is a phenomenon by which the simple location of things is circumvented without being annulled. Upon any metaphysical theory deserving of serious consideration reality is an aggregate of *partes extra partes* [parts outside of parts]. Every particular is in its own time, or its own place, or its own point-instant in space-time; or (for the idealist) it is an act of consciousness, or a subject of consciousness, or a presentation in the experience of some supposedly "windowless monad," each of these being numerically distinct from other entities of the same type. Existents, in short, whether they are physical or mental or both, are many, they are bounded, and the bounds of their being mean mutual exclusion. This is not equivalent to asserting that they are without relations, or that they do not causally interact, or even that they may not be mutually implicatory. But it is mere confusion of thought to suppose that any of these interconnections between particulars amount to a transcendence of the separateness and identity of the particulars. If things are said to be related, it is so much the more evident that they do not (with respect to any determinate mode of relation) escape from their reciprocal exclusiveness; for it is only where there are distinct terms that there can be said to be real relations. But though things exist in their own places and not elsewhere, they may get-reported elsewhere; and the being-known of a thing is its getting-reported where it does not exist—and its getting-reported there *as* existing at the locus or region in which it does exist. Any theory of knowledge which does not recognize both these distinctive peculiarities of the cognitive phenomenon, fails to provide either for actual knowledge or for possible error.

According to the contention of these lectures (with respect to the

Realism: A. O. Lovejoy 43

epistemological issue) this two-fold requirement for a thing's getting-reported is fulfilled, and can be fulfilled, only in one way—in the way, namely, of partial or symbolic reproduction in the awareness of a cognitive organism which is at the same time capable of thinking of some general scheme or order in which existences have separate and mutually exclusive situations, and of referring attributes of the data (*i.e.*, sensa or images) of which it is directly aware to external situations in that order. These situations may be "external" in one or both of at least two respects. (*a*) They *must* be external to the situation of the event by which the representation is proximately generated, or by which the awareness of it is conditioned. Thus, if it is admitted that there is a spatial order containing real bodies, including those of cognizing organisms, the event in question occurs somewhere within the region defined by the organism's body, and probably within its brain. If any character of any object or event whatever, other than a single brain-event, at any time gets reported—even the vague character of being something-or-other outside the brain and causally related to the datum—this first sort of externality is obviously implied. But it is also implied by any non-solipsistic form of idealism. The existent known is at least external to the cognitive mental event assumed to take place in "an" individual mind—namely, it is either "in" some other mind, or has a different temporal locus in the series of events constituting the history of the same mind. (*b*) Some data, *e.g.*, visual sensa, are directly presented as spatially external to the locus of the event which is (at least by the realist) assumed to generate them or to condition the awareness of them; they are, that is, perceived as having spatial positions outside the perceived body. It is partly this fact which has led to the belief of the naïve realist that "external" objects can get reported directly. But there are empirical reasons—set forth in the earlier lectures of this course—why the sorts of existences which the realist believes himself to know through perception cannot be identical in their spatial or temporal situations with such visual data; and there therefore may—and by the realist must—be recognized a second sort of externality, namely, spatial or temporal externality to the loci in which the sense-data appear. Thus—with the very debatable exception of pure self-awareness—the existents which get-reported must (irrespective of the difference between realists and idealists) always be admitted to be in fact external to the situations of the knower, of the cognitive event, and of the data without which, nevertheless, those existents would remain unknown.

Since it is admitted—again upon any theory—that the data by which external existences get-reported are conditioned by particular cognitive events (either physical or mental), and since there are familiar empirical reasons for supposing that the peculiarity of any such event (or of the organism or mind in which it occurs), as well as other circumstances external to the locus of the original existent in question, affect the character of the datum, there arises from the standpoint of the knower a characteristic difficulty inherent in the nature of the cognitive phenomenon—that of discriminating, if possible, those features of the datum which can be taken as reporting characters possessed by the external existent at the locus of reference, and those which are to be taken as additions or modifications due to the cognitive event, or to other extraneous circumstances, and therefore as existing only at the locus of givenness. There is no summary and purely logical way of complete escape from this embarrassment; for the two opposite assumptions which might seem to eliminate it are both manifestly impossible. If we could show, or even legitimately postulate, that the percipient or other cognitive event is always purely "instrumental"—that what is presented in awareness can never differ, by addition or alteration or dislocation, from the *cognoscendum*—we should escape the difficulty. But when thus generalized, the instrumental theory is equivalent to the assertion of human infallibility; and if not generalized, it leaves the situation unaffected. At the other extreme is what I have termed the theory of a perspectivity of the characters of data. This too, if generalized, would, in a sense, eliminate the difficulty; but also, if generalized, it would be equivalent to the denial of the possibility of any knowledge whatever. No existent at one place could ever get itself in any degree truly reported at another place to another existent. Since we can admit neither man's complete inerrancy nor his continuous and complete ignorance of aught but his momentary, private, self-generated content, the line must be drawn somewhere between these extremes—and is by every man, when actually functioning as a cognitive animal, always tacitly or explicitly drawn somewhere between them. Upon the question where it is to be drawn, certain considerations have already been suggested; but with this question we are not at this point concerned. For so long as it is admitted that *some* knowing of external existences occurs, that there are realities not now, not here, and not ourselves, which get reported to us here and now, the existence of differences of opinion as to the precise extent of what is thus known cannot affect the validity of the conclusion which we have reached as to the *generic* nature and natural function of knowing. And it is highly important in philosophical procedure to keep this general question distinct from and unconfused by ulterior questions of detail. . . .

W. P. *Montague:* THE KNOWER AND THE KNOWN: A DIALOGUE

THE SECTION *of the Dialogue reproduced here (from Montague's* The Ways of Knowing, *1925, pp. 382–398, by kind permission of the publisher, The Macmillan Company) is largely an exchange between Hylanous and Lovelace. Hylanous speaks for Montague and is listed officially as a "realist." It is his view that "Philosophy's primary interest is in the ways of things rather than in the ways of knowing them." Lovelace is called a "dualist" and represents Lovejoy and other Critical Realists who subscribe to epistemological dualism. The minor figures in this section of the Dialogue are Partridge, an "objectivist," who reflects a philosophical attitude of many American and British New Realists, and Bryce, a "subjectivist," who represents such idealists as Royce and Creighton.*

HYLANOUS: Now that both Bryce, as representing subjectivism, and Partridge, as representing objectivism, have assented to my compromise, I am hopeful of winning over the dualistic member of our group. For it seems to me that a solution of the epistemological problem which satisfies representatives of the two extremist attitudes ought to appeal to Lovelace even more. For his dualism, like my realism, is an attempt to mediate between the opposite positions of objectivism and subjectivism in epistemology.

LOVELACE: Well, Hylanous, your realism, as you call it, and my dualism might superficially appear to resemble one another as compromise doctrines. But in reality they are quite different. For while your compromise would include the points essential to both objectivism and subjectivism, my compromise has a less ambitious, and— if you will pardon my saying so—a more sensible aim. You try to combine the merits of the two opposed theories, and, in my opinion, succeed only in combining their errors. My dualism, on the other hand, is frankly incompatible with each of the extremes in epistemology. Without any pretence at a higher synthesis, I aim to steer a straight common-sense course midway between the Scylla of objectivism and the Charybdis of subjectivism.

HYLANOUS: Why, Lovelace, I thought you agreed with Partridge in holding that there is a real world independent of our experience, and that at the same time you thought that Bryce was right in his theory that any object of which we can be *directly* conscious is an inseparable state of the knower, that is, a mere idea or sensation.

LOVELACE: Of course, in that sense and to that extent, my view, like yours, recognizes an element of truth in each of the epistemological extremes. But there the resemblance between us ends. For I believe that the situation in which an individual cognizes the world outside him is clearly and irremediably dualistic, involving on the one side a set of internal states or ideas which constitute the individual's consciousness, and on the other hand, a set of absolutely external things which make up the world of reality. The second set is the cause of the first set, but is in no sense identical with it. Extra-organic things are not ideas, and ideas are not extra-organic things. And in view of this duality, I reject as futile the epistemological monism of the objectivist for whom the content of experience is an aspect of the material world; and I reject as equally futile the epistemological monism of the idealist for whom physical objects are aspects of experience. While as for your attempt to combine both of these monisms, it seems to me, as I said, to involve a double set of errors. You took the objectivism of Partridge, and after admitting to him that every content of experience had an objective nature and status that was independent of consciousness, you proceeded to modify his doctrine by denying his claim that the objects of illusion and dreams were existent objects. Yet even on this, your only point of criticism, you conceded that the non-existent objects of experience, such as the straight stick that appears bent in the water, and the parallel rails that appear to converge, were existential in the sense that they were physically explicable effects of the actually existent, and might to that extent be regarded as distorted aspects of extra-organic bodies. In short, you conceded to Partridge the essentials of his objectivistic monism, merely substituting potential existence (or, if definitely illusory, a distorted and relative existence) for the actual existence which he wished to attribute to every particular object in a perceptual field. Again, in dealing with the idealism of Bryce you gave in to his epistemological monism of the subjectivistic variety, merely substituting possible experience for the actual experience to which he wished to reduce all reality.

HYLANOUS: Yes, Lovelace, that was it exactly. I thought to eliminate the paradoxes of epistemological monism by substituting the concept of *possible* for the concept of *actual*. To the Partridge-monists I said: "*The immediately experienced is numerically identical with what might be (but need not be) an independent existence.*" To the Bryce-monists I said: "*The independently existent is numerically identical with what might be (but need not be) immediately experienced.*" Why do you object to this way of dealing with the situation?

LOVELACE: Well, for one thing, the whole business is too far-fetched and complicated to suit me. There is a chair on the floor in front of me. I press my eyeball in and out and the chair that I directly experience jumps up and down; but in the meantime the real external chair that you and I believe in, and that we can sit upon, remains quite unmoved by the gyrations of my perceptual image. The one chair varies independently of the other, so why not recognize their obvious duality? The chair in my experience is one thing, the chair in the physical world is another. Why should you go to work and by an elaborate *tour de force* attempt to show with the Objectivist that the chair in my consciousness is an aspect or even a potentiality of the physical chair, and then with the Subjectivists attempt with equal elaboration to prove that the physical chair is a potentiality of the chair inside my mind? I tell you the thing is artificial and fantastic.

HYLANOUS: Do you use this epistemological dualism in teaching your classes? I admit that it sounds very simple and clear.

LOVELACE: Yes, Hylanous, I do use it in my classes, and it works very well. And what is more, just by way of experiment, I have tried several times to interpret the knowledge situation and to define truth and error in terms of each of the opposed forms of epistemological monism. Those efforts of mine were not successful. After learning the elements of the physiology of sense-perception, as generally taught in a beginners' course in psychology, the students found it difficult to see any sense in which states of consciousness could be identical with material objects. For that reason I returned to my dualism, and I have never since had any trouble. In teaching, I usually represent the bodies and events in the external world by the large letters of the alphabet A, B, C, . . . , and the corresponding mental states which are their effects and from which their existence is inferred by the small letters a, b, c, ...

HYLANOUS: I understand; and when our ideas are good copies of the things outside we have truth, and when they are bad copies we have error; is that it?

LOVELACE: Well, yes. Only, you must remember that the essential point about this so-called copying is not that the specific ideas and sensations shall resemble the bodies and properties, but only that the *relations* between the terms in the one system shall resemble the *relations* between the terms in the other system. Or, to put it in another way, there must be a correspondence rather than a similarity between the two sets of entities. For example, it is not necessary that the ether waves which cause a colour sensation should themselves have any quality resembling the colour quality of the sensation which they cause; it is sufficient if there is a one-to-one correspondence between specific colour qualities and specific ether vibrations.

HYLANOUS: Then, if I understand you, your epistemological dualism is concerned to defend only a numerical duality or non-identity of the contents of a person's experience on the one side and the external causes of those contents on the other; while as to the *ontological nature* of the internal experiences and the external things that cause them, your epistemology is neutral. Is that the case?

LOVELACE: Yes, Hylanous, that is the case. The internal states or contents of which alone we have direct awareness may be the states of a psychic agent, a soul or a transcendental ego; or on the other hand, the self may be only the brain, and the states of consciousness may be modifications of neural substance or forms of neural energy; or, finally, the self and its experience may be partly material and partly immaterial. With respect to these rival theories as to the nature of the self and its states, our dualistic epistemology is, as you have said, wholly neutral. While as for the external realities themselves, they may be (1) exact duplicates of the effects which they produce in consciousness (naïve realism); or (2) similar to our experience only as regards the primary or spatial properties (scientific or critical realism); or (3) of a nature quite unknown to us; (4) psychic in their own right, either (*a*) as aspects of a cosmic self, or (*b*) as complete souls like the Leibnizian monads, or finally (*c*) as aggregates of "mind-stuff" or "mind-dust," which is panpsychism, the view which most of the present group of epistemological dualists are inclined to accept, though our epistemological dualism as such is compatible with any of the ontological theories which I have mentioned.

HYLANOUS: Yes, I understand. It is only the so-called numerical duality or difference in position which you insist upon, from the standpoint of epistemology. What we can be aware of directly are the states inside our brains, and from these internal data we can infer with more or less probability the nature of the causes outside.

LOVELACE: Precisely.

HYLANOUS: You have said that you always found it easy to convince students of the soundness of your epistemology and to make clear to them the nature and the causes of true knowledge and of error by using the large letters A, B, C, ... to symbolize the external realities of the physical world, and the small letters *a*, *b*, *c*, to symbolize the internal effects or ideas, of which alone we can have direct apprehension. But tell me honestly, did you never have any objections or criticisms of this copy theory of knowledge?

LOVELACE: Well, I must admit that once or twice objections were made to this procedure.

HYLANOUS: What were the objections, Lovelace?

LOVELACE: Well, one of them was the old objection that is usually advanced against Locke's form of our theory. It runs as follows: If we can never apprehend anything but our ideas, which are copies of objects, how can we ever tell whether these copies resemble their originals, that is to say, how do we know anything about things as they really are? This apparent difficulty I have always disposed of by appealing frankly to probability. If, for example, the assumption of a system of atoms and electro-magnetic vibrations enables me to predict successfully the sequences of sensations that will ensue when wood is set on fire or when any two chemicals as they appear in experience are mixed together, there is a probability (which becomes stronger with the multiplication of instances) that the reason why the assumption tallies with our experience is because it is true. In other words, if instead of atoms and ether the world were made of something quite different, it would be extremely unlikely that the effects of that something could be explained and predicted by the atom and ether assumptions. It is here very much as with our inference of other minds. If from my auditory and visual sensations of you, I infer the existence of you as a human being like myself, with an interest in the epistemological problem, I am able to rationalize and predict those future experiences of mine which I describe as seeing your behaviour and hearing your remarks. And so, although it is possible that you have no objective existence at all, and that the cause of my visual and auditory experience is wholly different from what I assume, yet this latter possibility is extremely improbable, as you yourself will be the first to admit.

HYLANOUS: Yes, I feel the force of that, Lovelace. And I suppose that we must admit that the experience of any complex of qualities is conditioned not only by external causes but also by our own natures; and that consequently it must always be a matter of inference and probability as to just which of the experienced qualities are the existent properties of things in their own right, apart from their relation to the organism. And we should probably agree that there is sufficient ground for regarding the primary or spatio-temporal qualities as existentially objective irrespective of any relation to the knowing self, but that the status of the secondary or non-spatial qualities, such as colour, tone, odour, and savour, is more doubtful. That is to say, it is possible that the secondary qualities are only effects produced upon the brain or self by energies which are themselves lacking in those qualities. In short, we should both agree that the extent to which things out of relation to the organism resemble their appearance when related to the organism is a matter for empirical investigation, and that whatever difference there might be between things and their appearances would depend upon the distortion of the forms and periodicities of the energies in the passage from their extra-bodily origin to their terminals in the brain.

LOVELACE: Indeed, Hylanous, all that you say is correct; but you are speaking quite in the manner of an epistemological dualist.

HYLANOUS: I have much more sympathy for your dualism than you give me credit for. But now I wish to go back to something you said a little while ago in connection with your success in teaching epistemological dualism as compared with your experience with both forms of epistemological monism. Did not your students ever point out any further difficulties in the dualistic conception? Did they always find it satisfactory?

LOVELACE: Well, I must confess that some of the more acute students raised one or two other objections which led to a good deal of confusion.

HYLANOUS: What were those objections?

LOVELACE: Two or three of the students asked how it was possible to differentiate between the conceptual space and time in which the external causes of perceived objects are inferred to exist and the space and time which are actually experienced. These students claimed that any conceptual or inferred space and time could be thought of only as a continuation of the space and time we immediately apprehend as containing and relating our perceptual objects. And they went on to illustrate their objection by pointing out that if the space in which the stars are perceived to be located is assumed by the dualist to be merely an intra-cranial copy of a genuinely real extra-cranial space, the latter can be conceived only as spatially beyond or outside the space that we perceive. But inasmuch as the extent of perceived space has no limits except the accidental limits put upon it by clouds, stars, and other opaque objects, it seems impossible to conceive of or believe in any space outside of that of the alleged copy-space of perceptive experience. Hence they concluded that if *perceived* space is inside us, *conceived* or inferred space must be equally so. And as to perceptual and conceptual time, this same claim for identity was made. Thereupon the class divided into two groups; one group insisted that this identification of perceptual space and time with the space and time that we infer meant that the so-called external objects of inference were as subjectively internal and dependent on consciousness as were the objects of perception; while the other group took the opposite position of extreme objectivism, and argued that the realm of so-called internal percepts was as externally objective as anything could be. My class of contended dualists was thus transformed into two warring factions: subjectivists and objectivists! And my own position seemed as foolish as that of a pacifist in the middle of a battlefield, neglected by all and respected by none.

HYLANOUS: I see. The claim was that inferred space and perceptual space must be identical; and therefore that if you are to get to a world beyond your own states in inference, you must in perception. In short, if you don't get outside your head in perception you can't get outside at all.

LOVELACE: Yes; and those who accepted the subjectivist horn of the dilemma urged that the objects that a man infers to exist are as relative to his condition and prejudices and as dependent upon his mental states as are the objects of perceptual experience. It was argued that men differ at least as much in what they believe as in what they see.

HYLANOUS: How did you deal with this disintegration of the dualistic epistemology?

LOVELACE: Well, I admitted that there was a puzzle about the independence and externality of perceptual space and time as such, but I reverted to the rock-fact on which dualism is founded, namely, the demonstrable independence of the sensory experience of objects, and the system of causes outside the organism which we must infer in order to explain the order of our perceptions. In the case of the stereoscope, for example, it cannot be denied that I see a spherical object in front of me; but neither can it be denied that the cause of that apparent sphere is two flat disks acting separately upon my two eyes.

HYLANOUS: But in what place do you locate the stereoscopically apparent sphere?

LOVELACE: In the space in front of me.

HYLANOUS: And in what place are the two flat disks located?

LOVELACE: In the space in front of me.

HYLANOUS: Is it not plain, then, according to your own admission that the space of the illusory sphere and of the existent disks is the same? And, in general, that the space of real objects in which you believe is no more and no less external than the space of immediate perception?

LOVELACE: It would seem so; and yet to admit it would be absurd. For it would do away with the duality of the merely apparent and the real.

HYLANOUS: No, Lovelace. We can do full justice to the duality on which you rightly insist by making it a duality of *context* and of *causal conditions* rather than of *position*.

LOVELACE: I do not understand you.

HYLANOUS: Take once more the illustration of the stereoscopic illusion which was discussed at length with Partridge. In this case the real objects and the apparent object are differentiated by their internal natures—flat disks on the one hand and solid sphere on the other. But why do you call the sphere merely apparent, and the disks real?

LOVELACE: Because the disks stand in relation of causal efficiency to photographic plates, to scales, and in general to the totality of other objects in addition to and independently of their effect upon my consciousness; while the sphere has no effects except upon my conscious states at the moment of perception.

HYLANOUS: Just so; the actual and practical reason for condemning certain contents of experience to a status of illusion is not that they are located in an intra-cranial space (for, as we have seen, real and unreal are located in the same space), but that their *effective relations are* restricted to an individual's private field of experience; while what we call the real objects are not thus restricted, but exert their effects upon the totality of other objects, regardless of their membership in anyone's private experience. This difference of behaviour is the practical criterion for distinguishing between the real and the illusory; why is it not also adequate to serve as the theoretical or final criterion of the difference?

LOVELACE: Do you mean that illusory objects such as the stereoscopic sphere, the convergent appearance of the rails of a train track, and the chair that dances up and down as the result of my pressing my eyeball, are actually located in the same external space as that of the real objects which are the bases for these distorted images?

HYLANOUS: For a thing to be apparent it must operate through the brain of an individual. For a thing to be only apparent, it must operate only through the brain of an individual. Real objects operate causally on the totality of things. The duality between the immediately perceived and the independently existent is a duality of behaviouristic context and not of spatial location.

Realism: W. P. Montague   53

LOVELACE: What is the advantage of substituting your duality of relational context for my duality of spatial location?

HYLANOUS: There are two points of advantage. In the first place, my view makes the theoretical criterion for distinguishing the objectively real from the merely subjective or illusory, identical with the practical criterion that we actually use. In the second place, my view of the situation makes it possible to explain how in the case of true perception the object perceived can be identical with the real object.

LOVELACE: I do not understand this second point of advantage.

HYLANOUS: Why, according to your view all immediately apprehended objects are internal states of the knower, and as such can never be identical with the objects external to his organism whose existence he infers. You can never know external reality; the nearest you can come to it is to apprehend mental states which stand in one-to-one correspondence with external objects. Moreover, as we have already seen, even conception and inference cannot properly avail to give you a consciousness of anything outside yourself. For the conceptual order of extra-organic objects in which you believe is no more than a rearrangement of perceptual qualities; and the space and time of the inferred objects, if it means anything at all, must mean the same space and time as that of your perceptual objects. In short, if you are correct in your assumption that the realm of perception is intra-cranial, you are forced to admit that the realm of conception and inference is equally intra-cranial, and your dualism degenerates into a monistic subjectivism. Now the view which I am proposing substitutes for the impossible duality of locus a duality of relational context. It defines a content as subjective in so far as it stands in immediate causal relations to your other perceptions and to your cerebral processes. It defines a content as objective and externally real in so far as it stands in immediate causal relations to the totality of other objects. This definite duality of subjective and objective contexts does not preclude any content from having membership in both orders simultaneously. The private field of an individual experience and the public field of extra-organic objects can intersect and overlap. Whenever a thing is known truly it is known *as it is*. The known object and the real object are identical. Consider two curves which are continually intersecting. Each curve is a system of points determined by a law or formula of its own. The points of intersection enjoy membership in both systems without prejudice to their identity. Their duality of context is no bar to their oneness of essence and existence. So it is with the subjective order of events in consciousness and the objective order of events in the physical world. The one order of events is determined by intra-organic processes of the individual knower, the other by the extra-organic processes of the physical world. Yet despite this duality of causal conditions there is constant intersection and overlapping of the two orders, so that one and the same event can be a member of both orders, which is the situation involved in true apprehension.

LOVELACE: Will you give a concrete illustration of the way in which this duality of context would permit of intersection or identity of the perceived and the real?

HYLANOUS: Certainly. Take the case of the chair which you perceive in front of you. Apart from the question of its secondary qualities, you infer and believe, for all sorts of reasons, that there is really, out there, independent of your consciousness, an object that in shape, size, mass, and position is indistinguishable from the object that you perceive. The chair in the room and the chair in your consciousness are one and the same thing. Now, press your eyeball and the chair which you experience dances about, while the chair on which you can sit and which you can photograph remains at rest. In short, you are no longer apprehending a reality. The dancing chair is purely subjective. Now this shows that the chair that you perceive depends for its behaviour primarily and directly upon causes within your organism, while the behaviour of the real chair depends upon causes quite different. So that the one can vary independently of the other. Your view interprets this situation to mean that the perceived chair is inside your brain. My view would hold, on the contrary, that it is only the determiners of the perceived chair that are inside your brain, and that the perceived chair may be in exactly the same extra-bodily space as the chair which we infer to exist.

LOVELACE: You say that the chair in consciousness is controlled by intra-organic conditions, and that so long as these conditions are such as to make the chair *appear* in the space where the real chair actually is, the two chairs are identical and our perception is true?

HYLANOUS: Yes.

LOVELACE: And that as soon as the intra-cerebral processes (which are themselves in part, though only in part, the effect of the external chair's activity upon the sense-organs) become such as to produce the appearance of a chair different in nature or position from the external chair, that then our perception becomes false?

HYLANOUS: Yes.

LOVELACE: Well, to make your view clearer, tell me just how many combinations of the subjective and objective orders there are and to what situations they correspond.

HYLANOUS: There are obviously four logically possible combinations of the two orders with respect to any element or object.

(1) An object can have membership in both the subjective or intra-organic and in the objective or extra-organic orders. It is then both apprehended and externally existent. For example, the stationary chair perceived as such. This is the situation of *actualized truth*.
(2) An object can have membership in the subjective or intra-organic order and no membership, or no corresponding membership, in the objective or extra-organic order. It is then apprehended, but not externally existent. For example, the chair in a dream or the chair that dances when the eyeball is pressed. That is the situation of *actualized error*.
(3) An object can have membership in the objective or extra-organic order, but not in the subjective or intra-organic order. It exists externally, but is not apprehended. For example, the things on the other side of the moon. This is the situation of *potential truth*.
(4) An object can have membership neither in the objective or extra-organic order nor in the subjective or intra-organic order. It neither exists nor is apprehended. For example, any of the unreal objects which have not been believed in or thought of, such as a moon made of purple cheese. This is the situation of *potential error*.

LOVELACE: Well, Hylanous, I think that I might accept this compromise of yours, according to which the duality of the apprehended and the real is interpreted in terms of separate causal conditions rather than separate places, were it not for the fact that consideration of the mechanism by which perceptions are produced shows quite clearly that the qualitative natures of the things which we perceive and also the spatial and temporal relations between them are just what we should expect to appear if the world were mirrored in our brains, or represented in the system of brain-states, which are the effects of extra-organic causes. You admit that the happenings in the brain determine the objects of perception. But you hold that the latter are genuinely extra-organic in their location. How could intra-organic processes determine extra-organic objects? What could be the means by which perceived objects were reprojected into that outer space and past time from which their causes initiated their action? How much simpler it would be to make the perceived objects identical with the intra-organic effects of the real objects.

HYLANOUS: I will admit that the cerebral states of an individual constitute a kind of simulacrum of reflection of the world outside his organism.

LOVELACE: Will you admit that that simulacrum might be perceived by an external observer, if the brains of the observer and the subject could be grafted together?

HYLANOUS: Yes; but in such a situation the observer would perceive only the brain-states of the subject and not the extra-organic world which the subject himself perceived by means of those brain-states. It would be like seeing the words without seeing the meanings.

LOVELACE: If the subject's brain-states in a case of true perception have a one-to-one correspondence with the contents of his perception, why do you fear to identify them?

HYLANOUS: I fear to identify the brain-states of the subject with the objects which are perceived by them for the same reason that I fear to identify the words in a book with the things outside the book which they mean and reveal. The words are in one-to-one correspondence with their meanings, they might even be pictures resembling their meanings, but they are not identical with the things which they mean. The things meant may be existent or merely subsistent, real or unreal, but the words designating them are always existent and particular. Even the idealists admit a difference between the mental state or image and the meaning attached to it. You have now, let us say, the thought of Socrates. Perhaps there is in your brain or in your mind a more or less accurate image of the man. But that image, visual, kinesthetic or what not, is located in some sense within your organism and occurs at the present moment. It gives you the thought of Socrates, but it is not Socrates. Nothing that exists in your head to-day can be identical with what existed outside your head and in the distant past.

LOVELACE: I understand; you do not deny the possibility that the world outside an individual can produce an image of itself inside that individual, but you hold that these cerebral or mental states, like words, have a meaning or implication of what is outside them, in the sense of occurring in other times and spaces than their own, and that it is this implication of the brain-states rather then the brain-states themselves which the individual apprehends.

HYLANOUS: Exactly so. What a man will perceive or conceive depends entirely upon the processes or states of his nervous system, just as what a book describes depends entirely upon what words are printed on its pages; but to argue from this that a man could apprehend only his own states would be as absurd as to argue that a book could describe only its own words and pictures.

LOVELACE: Your analogy between words and brain-states makes clear your meaning, but it leaves totally unexplained the manner in which the effects produced in the brain can imply or reveal their extra-cerebral causes. Words reveal the things for which they stand in virtue of a mind which comprehends their meanings. But in your theory the brain-states are like words which interpret themselves. They are at once the book and the reader.

HYLANOUS: I admit that my analogy as such offers no explanation of the manner in which the cortical states transcend themselves and afford an experience of objects other than themselves. The question of how this is possible is a matter for psychology rather than epistemology. I have on various occasions expressed my belief that the self-transcending implications of the brain-states could be understood as a corollary of the truth that they are forms of potential energy into which the kinetic energies of the sensory nerve currents had been converted, and that as such they could contain, intensively, reference to other times and places than those which they occupy. But I am not concerned here to defend this particular psycho-physical theory as to the nature of brain-states and the manner in which they refer to a world beyond themselves. It is necessary only to accept the fact that in some manner the internal states of an organism are the indispensable conditions for an apprehension or consciousness by that organism of a space and time other than that of the states themselves. And that in so far as the internal states agree with or correspond to the objects existing in the outer world, there is consciousness of reality or truth; while in so far as the brain-states, by reason of the distorting influence of the media, physical and physiological, through which the stimuli must pass before they can affect the brain, are not in correspondence or agreement with their extra-organic causes, then there will be consciousness of what does not exist—in other words, error. In either case, inner states of the brain reveal an outer world, but in the one case that outer world will be real, in the other case it will be unreal.

LOVELACE: I think I understand. Outer things, in so far as they are implied by a system of self-transcending brain-states, are members of a subjective order, and are controlled by intra-organic causes; while in so far as they are in inter-action with the totality of other objects in space, and not merely with any one brain, they are members of the objective or existential order, and are controlled by extra-organic causes. An object such as a chair can have membership in both orders together, in either singly, or in neither. And the duality of what is apprehended and what is real expresses a duality of intra-organic and extra-organic causal conditions, and not a duality of intra-organic and extra-organic location.

HYLANOUS: Yes. Your own epistemological dualism noted correctly the capacity of real objects and perceived objects to vary independently of one another, and it also noted correctly the existence in every percipient organism of a set of internal states by which consciousness was determined. But in interpreting this situation by identifying the objects *of* which we are conscious with the brain-states *through* which we are conscious, it made a chasm between an inner world that we can know but which is not real and an outer world which is real but which we cannot know. The compromise which I offer does full justice to the power of the real and the perceived to vary independently, and it does equally full justice to the duality involved in the intra-cerebral images of an extra-cerebral world; but by refusing to make the brain-states their own objects we permit the real objects and the known objects to be members of intersecting contexts rather than of separate realms. They are independent without being mutually exclusive.

LOVELACE: Well, I am more nearly satisfied than I expected to be by your compromise. But I cannot quite see how you can grant so much of my epistemological dualism and still keep your theory satisfactory to the monistic objectivism of Partridge and the equally monistic subjectivism of Bryce.

HYLANOUS: I have contended throughout our whole discussion that it was possible to reconcile the three classic types of epistemological theory which you three friends respectively represent. And the eirenicon which I have proposed is constructed by cutting out from each of your three theories that element which, unessential in itself, has nevertheless sufficed to keep you in disagreement with one another, and if I may say it without offence, in equal disagreement with the facts of the knowledge situation.

GUIDE TO FURTHER READINGS IN CONTEMPORARY REALISM

REALISM AND KNOWLEDGE

George Santayana (1863–1952), who wrote broadly and eloquently in philosophy, identified himself epistemologically with the critical realists. He rejected presentative realism in favor of representative realism but at the same time denied that the existence of a thing can be inferred from intuited essences or data. Knowledge was for him a matter of faith or belief. "This belief is native to animals and precedes all deliberate use of intuitions as signs or descriptions of things. . . ."[13] See especially his *Scepticism and Animal Faith* (London: Constable, 1923).

R. B. Perry (1876–1957) provided one of the most intriguing neorealist arguments against idealism. Conceding that *"no thinker to whom one may appeal is able to mention a thing that is not an idea*," [14] Perry argued that this admission indicates only a methodological difficulty rather than a metaphysical one. See particularly his articles "The Ego-centric Predicament," *Journal of Philosophy*, 7 (1910): 5–14, and "Realism as a Polemic and Program of Reform," *Journal of Philosophy*, 7 (1910): 337–353.

Additional Readings
  Drake, D., et al., *Essays in Critical Realism*. New York: Macmillan, 1920.
  Findlay, J., *Meinong's Theory of Objects*. London: Oxford University Press, 1933.
  Holt, E. B., et al., *The New Realism*. New York: Macmillan, 1912.
  Moore, G. E., *Philosophical Studies*. London: Kegan Paul, 1922.
  Russell, B., *The Analysis of Mind*. New York: Macmillan, 1921.
  ——— *An Inquiry into Meaning and Truth*. New York: Norton, 1940.
  ——— *Our Knowledge of the External World*. Chicago: Open Court, 1914.
  ——— *The Problems of Philosophy*, New York: Oxford University Press, 1912.

REALISM AND VALUE

G. E. Moore (1873–1958) was an ethical as well as an epistemological realist. In opposition to all subjectivists and relativists, he contended for example, that "good" is a characteristic of things which exists independent of human desires and interests and that it is capable of being known intuitively. His *Principia Ethica* (Cambridge: Cambridge University Press, 1903) was a landmark in modern ethical analysis.

Nicolai Hartmann (1882–1950) developed a theory of values that reflected the influence of the neorealistic movement on the continent. He argued that "values are essences"; although values have no spatiotemporal existence, they nevertheless subsist and are discovered by mind. Without these values, which are known through intuition, events would be totally lacking in significance. See especially his *Ethics* (New York: Macmillan, 1932), I.

Additional Readings
  Ewing, A. C., *The Definition of Good*. New York: Macmillan, 1947.
  Hartmann, N., *Ethics*, 3 vols. New York: Macmillan, 1932.
  Moore, G. E., *Ethics*. London: Home University Library, 1912.
  ———, *Philosophical Studies*. New York: Harcourt, Brace, 1921.

REALISM AND METAPHYSICS

Samuel Alexander (1859–1938) was permanently influenced in his thought by G. E. Moore's "Refutation of Idealism," *Mind*, 12 (1903), and by the presentative theory of perception as elaborated by American New Realists such as E. B. Holt and R. B. Perry. He warned, however, that while epistemology is an important part of metaphysics, it is not its indispensable foundation. Accordingly, Alexander was one realist who concerned himself with such diverse metaphysical problems as the nature of freedom and of the deity. Rejecting the static reality of materialism for the dynamic view of emergent evolution, with its stress on growth and novelty, he advanced the view that things are simply complexes of motion and that reality is properly conceived as infinite and continuous space-time. See especially *Space, Time and Deity* (2 vols.; New York: Macmillan, 1920).

Alfred North Whitehead (1861–1947) proposed the most comprehensive and complicated metaphysical theory on the contemporary scene. In spirit and rough outline, he was in accord with the thought of Alexander. Although Whitehead was an epistemological realist, he criticized other realists for committing the "fallacy of misplaced concreteness." After the manner of Newtonian science, most realists conceive experience as marked by such things as points, instants, and event-particles, and forget that these are merely convenient abstractions and not at all descriptive of reality. The real world presents patterns of dynamic, interrelated events rather than collections of static, independent entities. Whitehead's philosophy is essentially an elaboration of the theme "the actual world is in process." For introductory purposes, see particularly his *Science and the Modern World* (New York: Macmillan, 1925).

Additional Readings

    Alexander, S., *The Basis of Realism*. London: Oxford University Press, 1919.
    Gilson, E., *God and Philosophy*. New Haven: Yale University Press, 1941.
    ———, *Philosophical and Literary Pieces*. London: Macmillan, 1939.
    Russell, B., *Philosophical Essays*. New York: Longmans, Green, 1910.
    Whitehead, A. N., *The Concept of Nature*. Cambridge: Cambridge University Press, 1920.
    ———, *Principles of Natural Knowledge*. Cambridge: Cambridge University Press, 1919.

———, *Process and Reality*. Cambridge: Cambridge University Press, 1929.

ALLIED MOVEMENTS: PHENOMENOLOGY AND NATURALISM

Edmund Husserl (1859–1938) initiated the movement in philosophy known as *phenomenology*. As the name indicates, phenomenology investigates the items of experience. Phenomena, far from being ideas representative of reality as Locke would have us believe, are *intentional objects*—that is, meanings or essences with which the mind is confronted. (Here Husserl showed his intellectual indebtedness to Brentano and Meinong.) Basic to his philosophy is a method by which all questions concerning the existence of experienced items can be temporarily suspended. Only in this way can the essential relations between the contingent features of things be discovered. Somewhat like mathematicians and symbolic logicians, Husserl begins his investigations by ignoring the existential aspects of experience to discover the ideal structures that underlie the factual realm. Secure in his knowledge of these structures he can then hope to give a significant theory of reality. See especially his *Ideas*, translated by W. R. B. Gibson (New York: Macmillan, 1931).

Frederick J. E. Woodbridge (1867–1940) was regarded by the New Realists as one of them; however, he resisted identifying himself with their movement, insisting that his epistemological and metaphysical realism were but a part of his *contemporary* naturalism. Determined to avoid reductive materialism, reductive idealism, and all other reductive philosophies, Woodbridge sought to study nature in all its qualitative variety. His philosophy resembles that of Aristotle more than it resembles any other past philosophy. Like the Greek philosopher he represented all objects of the natural realm with respect to their essential traits—that is, their structure, behavior, and purpose. When man recognizes himself as a part of nature, he frames his aspirations in accordance with the means available to him in nature. See especially his *Nature and Mind* (New York: Columbia University Press, 1937).

Additional Readings

Cohen, M., *Reason and Nature*. New York: Harcourt, Brace, 1931.

Farber, M., *Philosophical Essays in Memory of Edmund Husserl*. Cambridge: Harvard University Press, 1940.

———, *The Foundation of Phenomenology*. Cambridge: Harvard University Press, 1943.

Woodbridge, F. J. E., *An Essay on Nature*. New York: Columbia University Press, 1940.

NOTES FOR CHAPTER I

1 Rudolf Hermann Lotze, *Microcosmos* (4th ed.; New York: Scribner and Welford, 1890), III, 345.
2 William Molesworth (ed.), *The English Works of Thomas Hobbes* (London: Bohn, 1839–40), I, 102.
3 *Ibid.*, IV, 8.
4 Galileo Galilei, *Il Saggiatore*, quoted in E. A. Burtt, *Metaphysical Foundations of Modern Science* (New York: Harcourt, Brace, 1925), p. 75.
5 "Three Dialogues Between Hylas and Philonous," in *The Works of George Berkeley*, A. A. Luce and B. Jessop (eds.) (London: Nelson, 1949), II, 262.
6 Thomas Reid, *Essays on the Powers of the Human Mind* (London: Griffon, 1827), p. 93.
7 *Ibid.*, p. 93.
8 J. Findlay, *Meinong's Theory of Objects* (London: Oxford University Press, 1933), p. 22.
9 Paul Schilpp (ed.), *The Philosophy of Bertrand Russell* (Evanston and Chicago: Northwestern University Press, 1944), pp. 11–12.
10 Bertrand Russell, *The Problems of Philosophy* (New York: Oxford University Press, 1912), p. 42.
11 Francis Herbert Bradley, *Appearance and Reality* (2nd ed.; New York: Macmillan, 1897), pp. 364 and 392.
12 E. B. Holt, *et al.*, "Program and First Platform of Six Realists," *Journal of Philosophy*, 7 (1910): 393–401.
13 George Santayana, *Scepticism and Animal Faith* (London: Constable, 1923), p. 179.
14 Ralph Barton Perry, *Present Philosophical Tendencies* (New York: Longmans, Green, 1912), p. 129.

II · Idealism

WHICH IS the ultimate reality—mind or matter? Perhaps no question in the history of reflective thinking has divided men as much as this. Those who have regarded it as necessary to satisfy the common-sense belief in a world of substantial things have tended to view matter alone as constituting reality, while those who have been preoccupied with the life of ideals and aspirations have tended to view the world as spiritual. But, we may well ask, aren't the strengths of each position more than offset by the weaknesses? The idealist argues that the materialist condemns man to live as a hopeless exile in a bleak world of dead things; the materialist charges that the idealist tempts man to escape into an airy world of idle fancies and dreams. Which is man's proper task—to reconcile himself to a stubborn world of fact or to assume his responsibilities as an integral part of an intelligible and purposive world order?

Idealism not only has a psychological advantage over materialism for those who insist that human existence is purposive and significant, but also carries a comparable benefit for those who are primarily concerned that society be safeguarded from the erosion of moral relativism. Since Plato (427–347 B.C.) materialism has been indicted time and again as socially insidious because it provides an excuse for irresponsible behavior.

> [Materialists] say . . . that the honorable is one thing by nature and another thing by law, and that the principles of justice have no existence at all in nature, but that mankind are always disputing about them and altering them; and that the alterations which are made by art and by law have no bases in nature, but are the authority

for the moment and at the time at which they are made. ...
These, my friends, are the sayings of wise men, poets and prose writers, which find a way into the minds of youth. They are told by them that the highest right is might and in this way the young fall into impieties.[1]

But it is one thing for the sensitive-minded man to favor a philosophy that suits his personal and social preferences and quite another for him to justify it on a rational basis. Concluding that something *is* the case simply because we *hope* it is clearly constitutes a non sequitur. Let us turn, then, to the philosophical arguments that the idealists have advanced for the truth of their view.

HERACLITUS AND PARMENIDES

One of the idealists' theses asserts that we must go beyond the disclosures of sense to discover what is real or intelligible, since the real and the intelligible are characterized as unchanging and orderly and are thus essentially one and the same. This view is a recurrent theme of Greek thought: *there can be knowledge only of what is permanent and stable.* Heraclitus (535–475 B.C.), who championed the doctrine that the objects of our experience are in perpetual flux, honored the thesis. While insisting that the world disclosed to sense is one of incessant change, he nevertheless attempted to show that change follows lawful patterns and that these patterns are the proper objects of knowledge. Only when the senses are employed in conjunction with intelligent understanding can knowledge be achieved. This is suggested in his metaphorical saying, "Eyes and ears are bad witnesses for men unless they have souls that understand the language."

Parmenides (515–440 B.C.), Heraclitus' younger contemporary, carried to its logical extreme the theme that what is real or intelligible is unchanging. He argued that the Heraclitean admission about the transitory nature of sense experience was tantamount to a *complete* denial of its intelligibility. For this reason, he declared, the changing world of perception must properly be regarded as illusory and unreal. Even Heraclitus had granted that our knowledge of a sensible object can never be more than approximate, since the perceived object is always in process of changing from what it is to what it will be. Such a notion of becoming requires us not only to think about what an object is (being) but also to think about what an object is not (nonbeing). Parmenides insisted that this requirement cannot be met, since nonbeing or nothing is unthinkable; "You cannot know what is not," and "When you think, you think of

Idealism 65

something." It is thus the Parmenidean view that transitory objects of sense are only apparent objects of knowledge and that our generalizations about them are mere opinion. The only way of truth, then, is through reason, which discloses an unchanging realm of being.

Let us look more closely at the kind of analysis that Parmenides employed in developing his position. Consider his statements "What *is not* is not" and "What *is* is." While each of these appears to be a simple tautology, Parmenides insisted that the first is without meaning. We cannot actually conceive what *is not* (nothing, nonbeing), because in attempting to do so, even when our purpose is to say that it is not, we must be conceiving of *something*. Manifestly, this involves us in a contradiction and therefore it is unintelligible; it cannot be regarded as making an assertion about reality. On the other hand, when we assert, "What *is* is," we can draw more specific implications: what *is* is indestructible, uncreated, unchanging, indivisible, and eternal. The Parmenidean arguments which establish that these are indeed the characteristics of Being exhibit a similar pattern of thought. Let us take as a representative case: "What *is* is indestructible." Suppose that what *is* is destructible. It would mean that what *is* is capable of becoming what *is not*. But this would involve the possibility that "what *is* is not"; however, one cannot hold the latter conception, since it is, by its very nature, self-contradictory. One must then reject the original supposition in favor of its contradictory, "What *is*, is indestructible." Bolstered by such seemingly irrefutable argument, subsequent Greek thinkers—whatever their philosophical predilections—had to face the uncompromising dictum of Parmenides:

> Come now I will tell thee—and do thou hear my word and heed it—what are the only ways of enquiring that lead to knowledge. The one way, assuming that being is and that it is impossible for it not to be, is the trustworthy path, for truth attends it. The other that not-being is and that it necessarily is, I call a wholly incredible course, since thou canst not recognize not-being (for this is impossible), nor couldst thou speak of it, for *thought* and *being* are the same thing.[2]

PLATO

In the wake of Parmenides and Heraclitus some philosophers were led inevitably to the conclusion that there can be no genuine knowledge—that is, no knowledge of that which both relates to experience and is certain, objective, eternal, and unalterable. They rejected Parmenides' view by giving it an extreme representation in which the supposed objects of knowledge were absolutely irrelevant to sense experience; they rejected Heraclitus' view because of a misunderstanding in which the supposed objects of knowledge were equated with sense objects. On the basis of this misinterpretation it follows that no two people can properly be said to *know* the same thing at the same moment. But even more radically, an individual cannot *know* a real object because, at the instant of his perception, it has become something other than it was; and again, not only the *known* changes during perception, but also the *knower*.

Protagoras (481–411 B.C.), despairing of the possibility of knowledge while at the same time remaining acutely aware of the ongoing problems of life, advised men to resign themselves to mere opinion. He maintained that the capacity of reason is limited to organizing our subjective impressions and feelings for practical purposes, and that those philosophers who persist in the belief that reason can disclose truth deceive themselves. The prescription for living advanced by Protagoras consists simply in recognizing as myth the claim that reason can discover absolute standards for knowledge and conduct. Insofar as man feels the need for standards, he will arbitrarily create his own.

Socrates (469–399 B.C.) became the self-appointed opponent of the Sophistic doctrine that "Man is the measure of all things." ("Sophistic" refers to the practices of the Sophists, a group of teachers who employed the art of verbal persuasion to win philosophical arguments.) In particular, he abhorred both the portrayal of man as only a complex animal gratifying his immediate desires and the consequent conception of society as merely a collection of such brutish individuals operating under the force of convention and the relative natural strength of its members. Pointing out in concrete terms the hideous ramifications of such a view, he demonstrated the logical absurdity of the Sophistic position. He argued that in the very act of propounding their radical relativism, the Sophists were presuming that men have the common basis of understanding required for communication. Numerous Socratic dialogues suggest that where there is neither constancy in the meaning of terms nor agreement about their proper use, there can be no intelligible discourse. The analysis of meaning so courageously initiated by Socrates was developed systemically by his great disciple, Plato.

According to the Socratic-Platonic analysis, communication is possible only in a context in which our terms can be clearly defined, and such definitions of terms involve common recognition of meanings. Common recognition of meanings, in turn, implies that each of us is apprehending one and the same thing. Since as Heraclitus and Protagoras rightly

Idealism 67

pointed out, no two people perceive the same thing, it follows that the kind of apprehension basic to definition must be conceptual rather than perceptual. Thus, since a given definition is itself invariant whereas the objects of the sensible world to which it may apply are in flux, what we apprehend through definition is something nonsensible rather than sensible, universal rather than particular and, in general, transcending the spatiotemporal realm of sense. We can illustrate this account of meaning by a passage concerning the Idea of "equality" in Plato's *Phaedo*:

> And shall we proceed a step further, and affirm that there is such a thing as equality, not of one piece of wood or stone with another, but that, over and above this, there is absolute equality? Shall we say so?
>
> Say so, yes, replied Simmias, and swear to it, with all the confidence in life.
>
> And do we know the nature of this absolute essence?
>
> To be sure, he said.
>
> And whence did we obtain our knowledge? Did we not see qualities of material things, such as pieces of wood and stones, and gather from them the idea of an equality which is different from them? For you will acknowledge that there is a difference. Or look at the matter in another way: —Do not the same pieces of wood or stone appear at one time equal, and at another time unequal?
>
> That is certain.
>
> But are real equals ever unequal? or is the idea of equality the same as of inequality?
>
> Impossible, Socrates.
>
> Then these (so-called) equals are not the same with the idea of equality?
>
> I should say, clearly not, Socrates.
>
> And yet from these equals, although differing from the idea of equality, you conceived and attained that idea?
>
> Very true, he said.
>
> Which might be like, or might be unlike them?
>
> Yes.
>
> But that makes no difference: whenever from seeing one thing you conceived another, whether like or unlike, there must surely have been an act of recollection?
>
> Very true.

But what would you say of equal portions of wood and stone, or other material equals? and what is the impression produced by them? Are they equals in the same sense in which absolute equality is equal? or do they fall short of this perfect equality in a measure?

Yes, he said, in a very great measure too.

And must we not allow, that when I or any one, looking at any object, observes that the thing which he sees aims at being some other thing, but falls short of, and cannot be, that other thing, but is inferior, he who makes this observation must have had a previous knowledge of that to which the other, although similar, was inferior?

Certainly.

And has not this been our own case in the matter of equals and of absolute equality?

Precisely.

Then we must have known equality previously to the time when we first saw the material equals, and reflected that all these apparent equals strive to attain absolute equality, but fall short of it?

Very true.[3]

The Platonic theory of knowledge forcefully underscores the thesis that the facts of the observable world can be understood only as Ideas—that is, objects or essential natures apprehended by mind, as distinguished from particular mental experiences. These Ideas (universals, forms, principles, laws) are neither reducible to nor derivable from sensible entities. The former are more *real* than or *logically prior* to the latter in that we can only know the latter if we presuppose the former. That is, while any intelligible account of particular things depends on knowledge of universals, the converse does not hold. I can only adequately understand what a cat is—that it is both an animal and yet distinct from all other animals in essential rather than accidental ways—if I have the Idea of catness. Moreover, even at the initial level of understanding, in which I merely identify the obvious characteristics of objects, I am dependent on knowledge of universals. For example, I can designate a particular cat as a black thing only if I have the Idea of blackness.

In addition to their being *logically prior* to sensible things, Platonic Ideas are more *real* in still another way—namely, as more *perfect* than their particular embodiments. The very fact that we refer to certain animals as cats, even though no two are exactly alike, indicates that our Idea of catness functions as a standard of perfection or an ideal that is only approximated in the sensible world. Although experience may be said to provide occasions for apprehending certain Ideas rather than others, Plato insists not only that the apprehension of Ideas is absolutely independent of sense experience but also that the circumstance of their apprehension need not depend on sense experience. This latter point is especially important in connection with our moral judgments about the individual and society: a man can *know* what constitutes justice even when he lives in an unjust society. In the Platonic view, the man who contemplates the ideals of truth, beauty, and justice—the rational man—more nearly fulfills his love of reality than the ordinary man, who incessantly seeks reality in material things.

But we have not exhausted the Platonic analysis of reality and morality. Just as particular objects and events are intelligible only because they "partake of" the Ideas or universals, so the Ideas or universals constitute an intelligible whole only because they derive from the ultimate source of intelligibility, the Idea of the Good. Thus Plato's prescription for men is as follows:

> In the world of knowledge the Idea of the Good appears last of all, it is seen only with an effort; and, when seen, is also inferred to be the universal author of all things beautiful and right, parent of light and of the lord of light in this visible world, and the immediate source of reason and truth in the intellectual; and this is the power upon which he who would act rationally either in public or private life must have his eye fixed.[4]

ARISTOTLE

The attack by Aristotle (384–322 B.C.) on Plato's theory of Ideas has had a lasting impact on idealism. He insisted that Plato's concern for the immutable and eternal things led him to depreciate the changing world of concrete particulars and to retreat from the natural world of sense experience. He criticized Plato for separating the essential or universal features of the objects of our experience from their particular embodiments. Rooting himself firmly in a naturalistic position, Aristotle maintained that universals, like predicates of sentences, cannot stand alone. At the common-sense level, he held that sense experience is necessary for knowledge of reality, because it both discloses the existence of particular things and provides particular instances from which the essential nature of things may be extracted.

In his most strident moments, Aristotle criticized Plato for adhering to the view that there are two realms rather than one: the world of sensible objects and the world of Ideas. Epistemologically, Plato's position was unsound because it ignored the fact that knowledge has its origin in experience. Ontologically and metaphysically, the dualism is untenable because it becomes impossible to explain that relationship which must be presumed to hold between two realms that are absolutely different in kind. Psychologically and morally, it is impotent because it is "otherworldly"—that is, the norms and ideals that reason discloses are themselves transcendent and unapproachable in our daily lives, rather than immanent and approachable.

Yet the difference between Plato's account of knowledge and Aristotle's must not be exaggerated. Both represent the objects of genuine thought as unchanging universals that the mind apprehends or discovers rather than creates or invents. Moreover, they agree that particulars can be understood only in relation to universals. As suggested, the difference between these philosophers consists primarily in their respective doctrines of existence. From Aristotle's viewpoint, Plato mistakenly believes that there are two kinds of existents: that which is intelligible by its very nature (form) and that which is made intelligible by form (matter). Such a division into two classes of existents entirely misrepresented the basic ontological truth, that particulars alone exist. The Platonic fallacy involved mistaking the legitimate separation of form and matter *in thought* for a separation of form and matter *in actuality*.

Aristotle regarded particular things dynamically rather than statically. That is, they are spatiotemporal objects whose essential development is internally directed but whose accidental changes are externally influenced. Every natural object has within it a directive principle or purpose which shapes the course of its action and development, and it is only in accordance with this principle or "final cause" that the natural object becomes intelligible. These principles constitute the sole objects of genuine knowledge. To "know" the tadpole, for example, is to know that this complex union of form and matter is in process of becoming a frog. Furthermore, Aristotle depicted the universe as a pyramid of interconnected purposes in which the formed matter at one level functions as matter still to be formed at another level. The mature and regenerative frog that is the actualized tadpole stands as matter to be utilized in the growth process of higher animal forms. The purpose achieved at one level becomes the means whereby the purpose at the next higher level may be fulfilled. Aristotle was not suggesting, however, that everything is *consciously* striving to achieve its ideal end, although he recognized that man is conscious of such striving. Again, there is little support in his metaphysics for the religious contention that this purposive universe is the product of a divine plan. The

Idealism 71

teleology (purposive principle) of which he spoke is an immanent one—that is, by virtue of the fact that a thing exists, it is good for something.

Roughly speaking, Aristotle reasoned that since the growth, development, or any other kind of natural change in the universe represents a movement from imperfection toward perfection, a utilization of means toward ends, it follows that the flux of events depends on final causes or goals. Furthermore, since each final cause can only be accounted for in terms of other final causes—frogness presupposes amphibiousness, amphibiousness presupposes animality, and so on—the existence and motion of natural objects indicate the logical reality of a fixed hierarchy of purposes. Finally, since the notion of an *infinite* collection of purposes is unintelligible, there must be an ultimate purpose, an unmoved mover (God) toward which all things in the universe tend:

> . . . but evidently there *is* a first principle, and the cause of things are neither an infinite series nor infinitely various in kind. For neither can one thing proceed from another, as from matter, *ad infinitum* (e.g., flesh from earth, earth from air, air from fire, and so on without stopping), nor can the sources of movement from an endless series (man, for instance, being acted on by air, air the sun, the sun by strife, and so on without limit). Similarly, the final causes cannot go on *ad infinitum*,—walking being for the sake of health, this for the sake of happiness, happiness for the sake of something else, and so one thing always for the sake of another. . . . If there is no first, there is no cause at all.[5]

AUGUSTINE AND MEDIEVAL PHILOSOPHY

While the general tone of Aristotle's philosophy is naturalistic, his minimal support of the Platonic thesis that universals or ideas are logically prior to the concrete objects makes him important in the history of idealism. Furthermore, because Aristotle's theology was more thoroughly stressed in the medieval period than his physics—that is, because his remarks about the nature of the unmoved mover or God were emphasized more than his statement about concrete objects—his thought contributed to the idealistic tradition. A basis for his influence can be seen in the following passage:

> Since there is something which moves without being moved, a being purely actual, this being can in no way be otherwise than it is. For, though locomotion is the primary kind of change, as circular motion is the primary kind of locomotion, it is induced by a first mover. The first mover, accordingly, is a necessary being. . . . On such a principle, accordingly, the heavens and nature depend. It is a

life such as ours is in its best moments. It is always at its best, though for us this is impossible. The first mover's action is enjoyable, even as we, too, most enjoy being awake, conscious, and thinking, whence come the joys of hope and memory. Thus, knowing by its very nature, concerns what is inherently best; and knowing in the truest sense concerns what is best in the truest sense. So intellect finds its fulfillment in being aware of the intelligible; for it becomes intelligible by contact with intelligibles and in its exercise of knowledge so that mind and the intelligible are the same. For what is capable of receiving intelligible or essential being is mind. But mind is active in so far as it has the intelligible as its possession; hence, the possession of knowledge is the divine aspect of mind and it is the activity of intellectual vision that is most pleasant and best. If the divine, then, is always in that good state in which we are at times, this is wonderful; and if it is in a still better state, this is ground for still more wonder. Now, it is in this better state that the divine has its being and its life. For the activity of mind is also its life and the divine is that activity. The self-sufficient activity of the divine is life at its eternal best. We maintain, therefore, that the divine is the eternal best living being, so that the divine is life unending, continuous, and eternal.[6]

Thus Aristotle may be regarded as an important link between the formalism of Plato and the theism that modern idealistic philosophers inherited from medieval philosopher-theologians.

A rough comparison of Plato, Aristotle, and one of the greatest of the early medieval thinkers, St. Augustine (354–430 A.D.), will be instructive at this point. All three accepted as a manifest truth that intelligibility depends on forms or universals. In Plato's theory, forms constitute an independent realm, but one which he warned is grounded in a still higher form, "the Good." Aristotle corrected the theory by arguing that the forms can only be separated from matter in thought; but in an apparent inconsistency warned against by Plato, he identified God exclusively with pure intellectual activity. Augustine accepted Plato's theory as corrected by Aristotle, but also heeded Plato's warning.

Unlike Aristotle, Augustine did not think God's intellect constitutes the totality of His nature. In addition to being pure intellectual activity, God is the ground for the truths contemplated, just as Plato's "the Good" is the warrant for all lesser forms. Furthermore, the Augustinian depiction of God as eternally contemplating His own essence is more comprehensive than Aristotle's, since it includes God as creative. Divine self-contemplation involves God's forming a finite, sensible world that reflects His essence.

Certain observations about the background from which modern idealism emerges are now possible. Let us imagine Platonic, Aristotelian, and Augustinian responses to the famous idealistic thesis, *the real is the rational and the rational is the real,* paying particular attention to the status of the natural world of the senses in this account. Granting his definition of "real," Plato might well have accepted the thesis. For him this term designated universals or Ideas. These alone make things intelligible, and these alone meet the criteria of knowledge by being eternal, necessary and certain, and absolute. The objects of sense experience and belief fail to satisfy these criteria because they are respectively spatio-temporal objects and temporal events. As a result, they are fleeting rather than eternal, contingent and accidental rather than necessary and certain, relative rather than absolute.

Aristotle would have rejected the idealistic thesis, although he would have supported some of the thinking that underlies it. He might well have argued that while the term "real" designates the concrete particulars of experience we can only apprehend these particulars through their forms (universals). Thus, in Aristotle's system, the study of that which exists—his ontology—and the study of our knowing that which exists—his epistemology—are not identical, but they are intimately connected. Universals do exist, but they exist only in particulars—that is, as embodied forms. This constitutes their ontological status. Universals are what we may be said to know and as objects of thought are separated from their embodiment. This constitutes their epistemological status.

Augustine would have accepted the idealistic dictum, but would have insisted that it be understood within a fuller, theological context. As we have seen, he contended that although rationality is of the essence of God, it does not exhaust His essence, since God is also the ground of rationality. Finite thinkers must recognize that the world depends on God as a creative intelligence and, even more, that each concrete particular depends on Him for both its existence and its nature. Thus Augustine, like Aristotle, termed concrete objects real but, unlike Aristotle, regarded them as necessary reflections of the divine ideas. Employing *real* in this ontological sense, we may say that Augustine expressed the first half of the idealistic criterion—namely, *the real is the rational.* In this way he took a long step toward incorporating Aristotlelian empiricism into the developing framework of idealism. But Augustine also conceived the term "real" in a quasi-Platonic sense. Since universals and Ideas constitute the active mind of God, whose rationality is intrinsic to His being, they are real in the sense of being intelligible. Using "real" in this epistemological sense, we may say that Augustine expressed the whole idealistic dictum, *the real is the rational and the rational is the real.*

BERKELEY

There are two major strains in modern idealism: the first, and less influential, is illustrated by the *subjective idealism* of Berkeley and the second by the *objective idealism* of Hegel.

Speaking generally, Berkeley's philosophy derived from three related convictions: (1) that the existence of particular objects depends on mind; (2) that particular objects are essentially mental in nature; and (3) that all genuine ideas are particular rather than universal. The Augustinian principle that every natural object is a creation and manifestation of the infinite mind of God is a forerunner of the first two Berkeleian principles. But Berkeley's third principle breaks radically with the Greek and medieval traditions. Furthermore, it accounts for the way in which he formulated his first two principles.

Berkeley's denial of universals and affirmation of particulars can be traced to the raging nominalist-realist controversy of the middle and late medieval period. Among the most important nominalists was William of Ockham (1280–1349), who maintained that universals are merely general names for particular things and that they exist in the mind only as terms or names rather than as entities. He insisted that explanations which employ universals, essences, substantial forms, and so on, increase the inexplicable instead of diminishing it. Taking the position that our knowledge derives solely from immediate experience of concrete particulars, he urged the rejection of all those expressions which complicate this simple, direct state of affairs by referring to inexperienceable entities. This methodological principle of simplicity has come to be known as "Ockham's razor."

In Berkeley's hands, nominalism became an even more extreme doctrine. It manifested itself most dramatically in his attack on the traditional belief that there are "abstract ideas":

> He who is not a perfect stranger to the writings and disputes of philosophers must needs acknowledge that no small part of them are spent about abstract ideas. . . . We are told, the mind, being able to consider each quality singly, or abstracted from those other qualities with which it is united, does by that means frame to itself *abstract ideas*. . . . The mind having observed that in the particular

extensions perceived by sense there is something common and alike in all, and some other things peculiar, as this or that figure or magnitude, which distinguish them one from another, it considers apart, or singles out by itself, that which is common; making thereof a most abstract idea of extension; which is neither line, surface, nor solid, nor has any figure or magnitude, but is an idea entirely prescinded from all three. So likewise the mind, by leaving out of the particular colours perceived by sense that which distinguishes them one from another, and retaining that only which is common to all, makes an idea of colour in abstract; which is neither red, nor blue, nor white, nor any other determinate colour.[7]

To anyone who held this doctrine Berkeley laid down the following challenge: Demonstrate that you have the capacity for experiencing anything other than particulars.

For myself, [I dare be confident I have it not]. I find indeed I have a faculty of imagining, or representing to myself, the ideas of those particular things I have perceived, and of variously compounding and dividing them. I can imagine a man with two heads; or the upper parts of a man joined to the body of a horse. I can consider the hand, the eye, the nose, each by itself abstracted or separated from the rest of the body. But then whatever hand or eye I imagine, it must have some particular shape or colour. . . . To be plain, I own myself able to abstract in one sense, as when I consider some particular parts of qualities separated from others, with which, though they are united in some objects, yet it is possible they may really exist without them. But I deny that I can abstract from one another, or conceive separately, those qualities which it is impossible should exist so separated; or that I can frame a general notion, by abstracting from particulars in the manner aforesaid. . . .[8]

Berkeley combined the principle that all genuine ideas are particulars with the definition of "idea" that he believed most nearly conformed to the views of common sense—that all ideas are immediate objects of awareness or experience. As a consequence, he insisted that it is idle—or better, meaningless—to assert that one can have an idea of an inexperienceable object. It is precisely on this ground that he rejected the idea of matter. Berkeley asked what was meant by "matter"—that is, what item of sense experience was referred to when that term was used. It was futile to follow the lead of those important thinkers who stated that matter referred to an unperceivable substratum, since their statements were self-contradictory. Their claim was tantamount to asserting that it is possible to experience what is inexperienceable (substratum or matter). Recognizing this contradiction led to awareness that the term "matter" can represent no more than a "collection of sensible qualities." Berkeley accepted this use of the term but feared that it would prove confusing in ordinary discourse. Consequently he abandoned the term "material" and adopted the term "real." For example, he underscored that which is immediately experienceable (tactile and visual) when he asserted that a chair is real. Thus Berkeley believed he had exploded the age-old myth that the intelligibility of things depends on entities that transcend our experience.

It was manifest then that ideas are—just as the word suggests—completely dependent on mind or consciousness, since matter was shown to be inconceivable. As a result, the question concerning the status of so-called public objects became crucial. Berkeley was acutely aware that philosophers might accuse him of being a solipsist—that is, one who believes that things exist only for the perceiver and only while he is perceiving them. But he was confident that careful reasoning would show this conclusion to be invalid. That existent things depend on mind does not imply that they depend on any finite mind. In addition to this logical point, there is the psychological fact that, unlike figments of the imagination, the "furniture of the world" falls outside volitional control. These considerations support the conclusion that sensible objects depend for their persistent existence and regularity, their reality, on the supreme mind, God (see page 9).

In Berkeley's system of idealism, then, only the mind and its ideas—particular ideas—are real. His reduction completed, he claimed that he had not sacrificed any of the principles required for a genuine understanding of the universe. For example, neither the facts of ordinary experience by which men directed their actions (that fire burns and can cause death) nor the facts of science (that gases expand when heated) were any less valid in his system than in any other. In both cases, these regularities are the "consistent, uniform workings" of God's will.

SPINOZA AND KANT

To understand objective idealism, the more important strain in modern idealism, let us examine briefly several features in the philosophies of Spinoza (1632–1677) and Kant (1724–1804). The influence of these men on Hegel, the outstanding exponent of objective idealism, arose both from what he regarded as their philosophical successes and from what he considered their philosophical deficiencies.

Spinoza's philosophy depicts the universe as an organic unity comparable to a single, living being. Just as the eye and ear have separate functions but are nevertheless dependent on the whole of which they are parts, an individual man, so all observable objects are separated from one another but depend on and are contained in the unique whole, which Spinoza sometimes termed God or Substance. "By God [Substance], I understand that which is in itself and is conceived through itself; in other words, that, the conception of which does not need the conception of another thing from which it must be formed."[9] Thus, whenever he said, "All things depend upon God," he did not mean that God underlies, pervades, or creates all individual things; rather, he meant that God is the logical ground, the *immanent cause* of their being. God's relationship to the world of existent things is one of logical entailment, such as obtains between a genus and its species.

Although Spinoza suggested that God can be known through intuition, he denied that He can be known cognitively (definitionally). To say that God can be defined would be to deny His unity, since a definition can occur only in the circumstances in which a genus provides not only the things to which the differentiae (defining characteristics) apply but also the things to which a differentia does not apply. To define something, then, is not only to affirm that it is something, but also to deny that it is something else. For Spinoza, the role of definition is in distinguishing the part from the whole. After denying that we can cognize God's essence, he admits that we can characterize God by His manifestations in the world of experience: the basic characterization is that God has the parallel attributes of extension and thought. By conceiving God as at once an extended and a thinking substance, and by successively applying appropriate differentiae to each genus concept (extension and thought, respectively), we can distinguish, in parallel fashion parts of the whole until we reach the level of ordinary physical objects and mental events.

The philosophy of Spinoza invites several comments that may aid in understanding the Absolute Idealism of Hegel. In the first place, Spinoza's Substance is somewhat comparable to Hegel's Absolute. Hegel and Spinoza agree that when one asserts that Substance is infinite, he is not asserting that it is undetermined. Both would have insisted that the infinite is *causa sui*—that is, self-determining. Hegel, however, rejected as inconsistent with the foregoing the additional doctrine about Substance that Spinoza apparently supported: since Substance is infinite, no essential properties may be ascribed to it. In Hegel's view, to speak of a featureless reality is to say nothing at all. Moreover, each man's philosophy follows to a great extent from his conception of definition. It is in fact the difference

78 CONTEMPORARY PHILOSOPHY AND ITS ORIGINS

with regard to the concept of definition that makes all the difference. While, as we have seen, Spinoza pointed out that defining anything involves the correlative processes of affirming and denying, Hegel subordinated the former process to the latter. He, and his many followers, insisted that the degree to which something is known depends on the degree to which what it is not is known.

The position of Immanuel Kant with regard to idealism is ironic. Although he was an explicit opponent of the current subjective idealism,[10] he stood as an unwitting *sine qua non* of subsequent objective idealism. Any idealistic tendencies in Kant do not result from his conscious effort to promote idealistic theses but rather from his effort to meet effectively the skeptical challenge posed by David Hume (1711–1776).

The following four propositions provided the basis for Humean skepticism. (1) All knowledge of the real world is based on experience. (2) By its very nature, experience confines us to the realm of phenomena. (3) Experience reveals no necessary connections between things, so that it serves as a basis for no more than probability judgments. (4) The belief that there are necessary connections in the real world derives from a habit-induced feeling. Of these four, Kant accepted (1) and (2), but rejected (3) and (4). In rejecting the conclusion of (3), he insisted that Hume's analysis of experience committed a serious error of omission and, as a consequence of this, dismissed Hume's psychological account of causality, as expressed in (4), as philosophically irrelevant. Kant, however, saw that an adequate refutation of Humean skepticism would require him to show how it is possible to have certain knowledge about the sensible world—that is, how it is possible to make judgments about the world that are universal and necessary. In solving this problem Kant showed that phenomena fall into necessary relations because of the organizing activity of the mind in its experiencing and understanding.

The force of the Kantian arguments may be illustrated by the following example, which is calculated to show that phenomena depend logically on space but not the converse:

> Space is a necessary *a priori* representation [independent of all experience of phenomena], which underlies all outer intuitions. We can never represent to ourselves the absence of space, though we can quite well think it as empty of objects. It must therefore be regarded as the condition of the possibility of appearances, and not as a determination dependent upon them. It is an *a priori* representation, which necessarily underlies outer appearances.[11]

Idealism 79

From such considerations as this, meticulously and systematically developed at the levels of both our sensation and our understanding, Kant concluded that the *a priori* forms of the sensibilia, space and time, constitute the preconditions for experience and that the categories of the understanding, such as causality and substance, constitute the preconditions for intelligible experience.

Interestingly enough, Kant's extensive critical analysis of experience depended on an unexperienceable entity, the thing-in-itself or *Ding an sich*. Turning to the ancient distinction of form and matter, one may say that, for Kant, mind was a source of form but not a source of matter. Speaking more strictly, we can say that mind provides the structural framework for having and understanding experience, without supplying its content. Kant was satisfied to say that what produces the data of experience transcends experience; and since the source is beyond experience, one cannot properly apply to it the *a priori* forms of the *sensibilia* and the categories of the understanding. That is to say, the noumenal realm is, on principle, both unexperienceable and unanalyzable.

It was Kant's thesis, then, that the mind has a creative role in determining *how* experience is organized but not in determining *what* is organized. Subsequently, idealists accepted the positive but not the negative portion of this formula. They argued that following Kant would force them into the enterprise of trying to answer unanswerable questions: How can we know that which is unexperienceable? How can we know that to which the forms and categories of the mind are inapplicable, when knowing something involves their application? [12]

HEGEL

Kant's successor, Hegel (1770–1831), brought the idealistic movement developing from Kantian philosophy to maturity. Hegel's major thesis was that all attempts to establish the existence of things independent of mind would result in absurdity. He warned all realists that even though they carefully avoided such statements as "We know the unknowable exists"—an obvious self-contradiction—in favor of such assertions as "The unknowable may exist without our knowing it," their case would remain hopeless. The second formulation turns out to be self-contradictory as well. Hegel insists that, since whatever exists is and must be an object of conscious thought, even to say that "The unknowable may exist without our knowing it" presumes an act of conscious thought about the unknowable. But this is self-contradictory in that the intent of the statement is to deny precisely what is being presumed. Using idealistic terms, the existence of anything necessarily depends on mind; speaking in terms critical of the realist, nothing can exist independent of mind. For Hegel, the world of experience, both actual and possible, *is* the world.

One way of portraying Hegel's break with Kant is to contrast their answer to the question, "How is knowledge possible?" Kant's answer requires that the object of knowledge or the phenomenal object be regarded as doubly dependent: on the perceiving mind for its form and on the thing-in-itself for its content. As we have seen, Hegel rejected Kant's thing-in-itself. Furthermore, he was sensitive to the peril of a Berkeleian-like subjectivism resulting from the Kantian formula amended to make the object of knowledge wholly dependent on a knowing mind. Taking a notion from Spinoza, he suggested instead that the distinction between the knower and the known is relative—that is, that the knowing mind and the thing known constitute but two ways of viewing the same reality. The possibility of knowledge, according to Hegel, arises precisely because of the essential identity of the mind and its object.

Let us take a closer look at Hegel's basic claim that thought and being are identical. Concede that the mind can think *only* by way of concepts or universals. This means that the *thought* of an object can consist of no more than a convergence of universals, that in thinking of a horse, for example, thought is wholly constituted by such universals as being hoofed, brown, and four-legged. To object in the name of common sense that thought of a *specific* horse contains more than is describable through universals is to attribute to common sense the absurdity of conceiving the inconceivable. But again, the same range of considerations that applies to *thought* of objects applies to *objects* of thought. To maintain in the name of common-sense realism that the object of thought is different from the thought of the object is merely another way of subscribing to the fallacy of conceiving the inconceivable. Thus it is not too far-fetched to say that in the history of thought Hegel is Parmenides reborn: ". . . that not-being is and that it necessarily is, I call a wholly incredible course, since thou canst not recognize not-being (for this is impossible), nor could thou speak of it, for *thought* and *being* are the same thing." [13]

The force of Hegel's idealism manifests itself in his pattern of philosophical analysis. To illustrate, let us apply his method both to Democritus' objective materialism and to Berkeley's subjective idealism (i.e., Berkeley's philosophy with the notion of God deliberately excluded).

Democritus' world view represents minute particles of matter or atoms as the real objects in this world and regards them as independent of mind,

Idealism 81

indestructible, eternal, hard, and so on. Hegel maintained that this view possesses truth when it is seen within the context of the philosophical perspective. The materialist insists, quite correctly, that the atoms (ultimate reality) are objective rather than subjective and are, in this sense, logically independent of the knower. But placing materialism in proper perspective also discloses that in the very process of speaking about the atoms as objective, such concepts or universals as indestructibility, eternality, and hardness are necessarily and exclusively employed. Thus although the materialistic account honors the objectivity of things, it fails to recognize the fact that things can be characterized as objective only *within* the context of thought.

Now let us apply the Hegelian analysis to subjective idealism. The weakness of the materialist, his failure to account for the ability to know objects, becomes the strength of a Berkeleian idealist, who insists on the kinship between mind and objects. Specifically for Berkeley, the objects of knowledge are sets of particular ideas (images) dependent on the individual mind. According to Hegel, although this account recognizes the fact that things can only occur within the context of thought, it fails to honor the objectivity of things. By presenting the objects of knowledge as purely psychical events, Berkeley could account for the logical independence of objects only with great difficulty.

Our illustration, however, is intended less to show the errors of Democritus and Berkeley than it is to display their essential insights into the cognitive relationship. Looking at them generally, we may say that these radically opposed views contributed jointly to a more comprehensive and consistent theory and specifically to one that began to approximate the basic Hegelian principle of the identity of thought and being. Hegel would have accepted the Democritean emphasis on the object as objective, while at the same time acknowledging the Berkeleian emphasis on the object as knowable. However, in the Hegelian unity, the Democritean objective object is recognized to be an object *for thought* and the Berkeleian knowable object is recognized to be a thought *about the object*. The wisdom of Democritus—the logical independence of the object—is included in such a synthesis, while the error of the object's unknowability is excluded. Again, Berkeley's insight into the knowability of objects is included, while his error concerning the object's mind-dependence is excluded.

The foregoing sketch of how the conflict between objective materialism and subjective idealism may be resolved made use of Hegel's distinctive philosophic technique or method, termed the Hegelian dialectic. To philosophize systematically, however, Hegel advises that we begin our dialectical process with that principle or category of reason which is presupposed by all others. Like many philosophers before him, he found this ultimate category to be that of *being,* the concept that alone applies to every conceivable object. Consider any two objects. The one may be red while the other is blue, the one may be square while the other is round, and so on, but whatever their differences in specific qualities, it remains that they have *being* in common. Hegel then proclaimed that he had found the very key to reality and our understanding of it. The mind, reflecting on the category of being, is led dialectically to deduce all other categories—that is, those universals or concepts—unity, plurality, cause, effect, substance, quality, existence, nonexistence, and so on—which stand as the necessary conditions of all experience. The thought of *being* necessarily involves the concept of *nothing,* for in asserting that an object has being, all its specific determinations are disregarded. But in shifting attention to the latter concept, nothing, the former, being, is inexorably considered. If the concept of nothing means the total absence of specific determinations, then the circumstance in which being may be said to apply is inevitably returned to.

But the mapping of thoughts at this abstract level is not yet completed. For the ceaseless movement back and forth between being and nothing involves still another concept, *becoming,* which balances the tension between the two. *Becoming* explicates the very processes in which we have engaged—that is, the thought of being becoming the thought of nothing and the thought of nothing becoming the thought of being. Just as we stated earlier that Hegel was a modern Parmenides, so we may note that he was a modern Heraclitus, since his dialectic is an application of the Heraclitean doctrine that stability constitutes a balance of tensions.

The first triad (being-nothing-becoming) is typical of the Hegelian dialectic. The basic pattern of thought involves an alternation between a thesis or positive assertion and its antithesis or negative assertion, which movement leads to a synthesis unifying the opposing concepts. The synthesis then becomes the thesis and the process is repeated, until its culmination in a final synthesis which—unlike all preceding synthesis—does not contain a contradiction within itself. This culmination of the dialectical process, the final category of the mind, Hegel termed the *Absolute Idea.*

But in proceeding dialectically from the category of being to the Absolute Idea, Hegel remained within the confines of the abstract or logical realm. It is as if he showed that a deductive order prevails within Plato's transcendent realm of Ideas or among Kant's *a priori* categories of the understanding. At this juncture, Hegel faced that root problem which he maintained his predecessors failed to resolve: What is the relationship of the categories to experience? It was Hegel's contention that the Absolute Idea is itself a thesis in a final triad in which whole-bodied nature stands as its antithesis and Spirit as its synthesis. Hegel's account of this triadic movement is less than clear, and it is less than clear to his critics that this movement is comparable to the dialectic processes previously exhibited.[14] Leaving aside the precise status of the dialectical method, however, Hegel, like Augustine, insisted that ideas (thesis) are incomplete unless they are embodied—i.e., unless they are externalized or find objective concreteness (antithesis). For Hegel, this dichotomy between ideas and objects of experience achieves its synthesis through the cosmic mind or the Absolute.

BRADLEY AND ROYCE

Hegelian idealism had a profound effect on the philosophy of the late nineteenth and early twentieth century. The locus of the objective idealist movement shifted from the Continent to Great Britain, where a favorable climate had been set in literature by such figures as Coleridge, Carlyle, and Ruskin and in philosophy by J. S. Mill, whose empiricism remained in the Berkeleian tradition. The three most important British neo-Hegelians were T. H. Green (1836–1882), B. Bosanquet (1848–1923) and F. H. Bradley (1846–1924).

Although Bradley is quite properly called a Hegelian for classificatory purposes, his philosophy is strikingly different from Hegel's in its detail. For example, whereas Hegel is concerned to deduce a system of the categories of the mind, Bradley rejected such an effort as logically impossible. In a most difficult and subtle analysis, he found that the familiar categories—substance, causation, and so on—fail to honor the fact that thought is relational in nature and that, since thought *is* relational, it is incapable of fully grasping reality for two reasons. First, to know reality we would have to know both things and the relations that obtain between them, but it is the nature of discursive thought to apprehend only relations and not the things related. Thus, on principle, our reason can provide only a limited knowledge of reality. Second, to know reality we would have to know the total relatedness of all things, which is manifestly beyond the limit of human capabilities. Bradley supported his general thesis, that conceptual or discursive knowledge is systematically limited, by showing that each alleged category of mind leads to self-contradiction.[15]

Contemporaneously with Bradley, the great American philosopher

Josiah Royce (1855–1916) was developing another form of objective idealism. Working from an acute analysis of the "knowing" situation, he charged that others had failed to recognize the proper relationship between the idea and the object. Subjective idealists following Berkeley and objective idealists following Hegel tended to assimilate the object to the idea, while their natural opponents, the realists, irreparably separated objects from ideas. Seeking to avoid both extremes, Royce warned his fellow idealists that a suitable place must be found for objects as well as ideas, and condemned realists for failing to bridge the gap between ideas and objects in experience. His own answer to this problem was that every idea has both *internal* and *external* meaning, the internal meaning constituted by the intention or goal of the idea to become embodied, and the external meaning constituted by the idea as embodied.

But if the world of fact is, as Royce suggested, the fulfillment of conscious purpose, the question arises, *Whose* purpose? Holding that one cannot, with conviction, believe the world to be his private experience nor, again, the collective experience of a group of finite selves, Royce, in Berkeleian fashion, concluded that there must be a universal consciousness, the Absolute. Individual selves are continuous rather than discontinuous with this Infinite Self, and the world of fact, to which finite selves must submit, is the embodiment and the full realization of the conscious purposes of the Infinite Self.

Since the early twentieth century, idealism expressed in the grand manner of Hegel and Bradley has virtually disappeared in American and Britain. This is not to say, however, that there have been no recent idealistic philosophers of importance. J. E. Creighton (1861–1924), J. M. E. McTaggart (1866–1925), H. H. Joachim (1868–1938), and B. Blanshard (1892–   ) may be taken as representative. But in general the idealistic tradition has become diffuse and its influence more indirect than direct. The following observations indicate roughly the role that idealism plays on the contemporary intellectual scene. (1) The pattern of idealistic thought permeates much of religion, literature, and social science. (2) Some of the basic idealistic tenets are incorporated into the doctrines of dominant schools of thought. (3) The tradition of idealism serves as a rich source of insight for critical analysis of current philosophical doctrines.

Brand Blanshard's *The Nature of Thought* (2 vols.; New York: Macmillan, 1940) and Harold Henry Joachim's *Logical Studies* (Oxford: Clarendon Press, 1948) provide well-reasoned and forceful presentations of the central doctrines of idealism. We now turn to readings selected from these works.

Brand Blanshard: COHERENCE AS THE NATURE OF TRUTH

BLANSHARD *proposes to investigate the questions concerning the relation of thought to reality. It seems clear to him that thinking is constituted by the attempt to link that which we do not understand with that which we do understand in such a way as to form a systematic and intelligible whole. He goes on to point out that the test to which all thinking must submit is a logical one, namely, coherence. He admits that the question as to why we think is unanswerable and, what is more important, admits that there can be no conclusive demonstration that reality actually conforms to the way in which we think about it. However, Blanshard insists that the idealist contention that "thought is related to reality as the partial to the perfect fulfillment of a purpose" is the only plausible one to make. Roughly speaking, his argument is that since thinking by its very nature must be coherent, it can only be presumed to relate to a reality which is itself coherent.*

The passages below come from Blanshard's The Nature of Thought, *1940, pp. 260–266, 266–267, and 267–269. They are reprinted by kind permission of The Macmillan Company.*

Coherence is in the end our sole criterion of truth. We have . . . to face the question whether it also gives us the nature of truth. We should be clear at the beginning that these are different questions, and that one may reject coherence as the definition of truth while accepting it as the test. It is conceivable that one thing should be an accurate index of another and still be extremely different from it. There have been philosophers who held that pleasure was an accurate gauge of the amount of good in experience, but that to confuse good with pleasure was a gross blunder. There have been a great many philosophers who held that for every change in consciousness there was a change in the nervous system and that the two corresponded so closely that if we knew the laws connecting them we could infallibly predict one from the other; yet it takes all the hardihood of a behaviourist to say that the two are the same. Similarly it has been held that though coherence supplies an infallible measure of truth, it would be a very grave mistake to identify it with truth.

The view that truth *is* coherence rests on a theory of the relation of thought to reality, and since this is the central problem of the theory of knowledge, to begin one's discussion by assuming the answer to it or by trying to make one out of whole cloth would be somewhat ridiculous. . . . First we shall state in *résumé* the relation of thought to reality . . . and sketch the theory of truth implicit in it.

To think is to seek understanding. And to seek understanding is an activity of mind that is marked off from all other activities by a highly distinctive aim. This aim . . . is to achieve systematic vision, so to apprehend what is now unknown to us as to relate it, and relate it necessarily, to what we know already. We think to solve problems; and our method of solving problems is to build a bridge of intelligible relation from the continent of our knowledge to the island we wish to include in it. Sometimes this bridge is causal, as when we try to explain a disease; sometimes teleological, as when we try to fathom the move of an opponent over the chess board; sometimes geometrical, as in Euclid. But it is always systematic; thought in its very nature is the attempt to bring something unknown or imperfectly known into a subsystem of knowledge, and thus also into that larger system that forms the world of accepted beliefs. That is what explanation is. *Why* is it that thought desires this ordered vision? Why should such a vision give satisfaction when it comes? To these questions there is no answer, and if there were, it would be an answer only because it had succeeded in supplying the characteristic satisfaction to this unique desire.

But may it not be that what satisfies thought fails to conform to the real world? Where is the guarantee that when I have brought my ideas into the form my ideal requires, they should be *true*? . . . If thought and things are conceived as related only externally, then knowledge is luck; there is no necessity whatever that what satisfies intelligence should coincide with what really is. It may do so, or it may not; on the principle that there are many misses to one bull's-eye, it more probably does not. But if we get rid of the misleading analogies through which this relation has been conceived, of copy and original, stimulus and organism, lantern and screen, and go to thought itself with the question what reference to an object means, we get a different and more hopeful answer. To think of a thing is to get that thing itself in some degree within the mind. To think of a colour or an emotion is to have that within us which if it *were developed and completed*, would identify itself with the object. In short, if we accept its own report, thought is related to reality as the partial to the perfect fulfilment of a purpose. The more adequate its grasp the more nearly does it approximate, the more fully does it realize in itself, the nature and relations of its objects.

Thought thus appears to have two ends, one immanent, one transcendent. On the one hand it seeks fulfilment in a special kind of satisfaction, the satisfaction of systematic vision. On the other hand it seeks fulfilment in its object. . . . Unless they are accepted as one . . . [there is] . . . no alternative to scepticism. If the pursuit of thought's own ideal were merely an elaborate self-indulgence that brought us no nearer to reality, or if the apprehension of reality did not lie in the line of thought's interest, or still more if both of these held at once, the hope of knowledge would be vain. Of course it may really be vain. If anyone cares to doubt whether the framework of human logic has any bearing on the nature of things, he may be silenced perhaps, but he cannot be conclusively answered. One may point out to him that the doubt itself is framed in accordance with that logic, but he can reply that thus we are taking advantage of his logico-centric predicament; further, that any argument we can offer accords equally well with his hypothesis and with ours, with the view that we are merely flies caught in a logical net and the view that knowledge reveals reality. And what accords equally well with both hypotheses does not support either to the exclusion of the other. But while such doubt is beyond reach by argument, neither is there anything in its favour. It is a mere suspicion which is, and by its nature must remain, without any positive ground; and as such it can hardly be discussed. Such suspicions aside, we can throw into the scale for our theory the impressive fact of the advance of knowledge. It has been the steadfast assumption of science whenever it came to an unsolved problem that there was a key to it to be found, that if things happened thus rather than otherwise they did so for a cause or reason, and that if this were not forthcoming it was never because it was lacking, but always because of a passing blindness in ourselves. Reflection has assumed that pursuit of its own immanent end is not only satisfying but revealing, that so far as the immanent end is achieved we are making progress toward the transcendent end as well. Indeed, that these ends coincide is the assumption of every act of thinking whatever. To think is to raise a question; to raise a question is to seek an explanation; to seek an explanation is to assume that one may be had; so to assume is to take for granted that nature in that region is intelligible. Certainly the story of advancing knowledge unwinds as if self-realization in thought meant also a coming nearer to reality.

That these processes are really one is the metaphysical base on which our belief in coherence is founded. If one admits that the pursuit of a coherent system has actually carried us to what everyone would agree to call knowledge, why not take this ideal as a guide that will conduct us farther? What better key can one ask to the structure of the real? Our own conviction is that we should take this immanent end of thought in all seriousness as the clue to the nature of things. We admit that it may prove deceptive, that somewhere thought may end its pilgrimage in frustration and futility before some blank wall of the unintelligible. There are even those who evince their superior insight by taking this as a foregone conclusion and regarding the faith that the real is rational as the wishful thinking of the "tender-minded." Their attitude appears to us a compound made up of one part timidity, in the form of a refusal to hope lest they be disillusioned; one part muddled persuasion that to be sceptical is to be sophisticated; one part honest dullness in failing to estimate rightly the weight of the combined postulate and success of knowledge; one part genuine insight into the possibility of surds in nature. But whatever its motives, it is a view that goes less well with the evidence than the opposite and brighter view. That view is that reality is a system, completely ordered and fully intelligible, with which thought in its advance is more and more identifying itself. We may look at the growth of knowledge, individual or social, either as an attempt by our own minds to return to union with things as they are in their ordered wholeness, or the affirmation through our minds of the ordered whole itself. And if we take this view, our notion of truth is marked out for us. Truth is the approximation of thought to reality. It is thought on its way home. Its measure is the distance thought has travelled, under guidance of its inner compass, toward that intelligible system which unites its ultimate object with its ultimate end. Hence at any given time the degree of truth in our experience as a whole is the degree of system it has achieved. The degree of truth of a particular proposition is to be judged in the first instance by its coherence with experience as a whole, ultimately by its coherence with that further whole, all-comprehensive and fully articulated, in which thought can come to rest.

But it is time we defined more explicitly what coherence means. To be sure, no fully satisfactory definition can be given; and as Dr. Ewing says, "it is wrong to tie down the advocates of the coherence theory to a precise definition. What they are doing is to describe an ideal that has never yet been completely clarified but is none the less immanent in all our thinking" [*Idealism*, p. 231]. Certainly this ideal goes far beyond mere consistency. Fully coherent knowledge would be knowledge in which every judgment entailed, and was entailed by, the rest of the system. Probably we never find in fact a system where there is so much of interdependence. What it means may be clearer if we take a number of familiar systems and arrange them in a series tending to such coherence as a limit. At the bottom would be a junk-heap, where we could know every item but one and still be without any clue as to what that remaining item was. Above this would come a stone-pile, for here you could at least infer that what you would find next would be a stone. A machine would be higher again, since from the remaining parts one could deduce not only the general character of a missing part, but also its special form and function. This is a high degree of coherence, but it is very far short of the highest. You could remove the engine from a motor-car while leaving the other parts intact, and replace it with any one of thousands of other engines, but the thought of such an interchange among human heads or hearts shows at once that the interdependence in a machine is far below that of the body. Do we find then in organic bodies the highest conceivable coherence? Clearly not. Though a human hand, as Aristotle said, would hardly be a hand when detached from the body, still it would be something definite enough; and we can conceive systems in which even this something would be gone. Abstract a number from the number series and it would be a mere unrecognizable *x*; similarly, the very thought of a straight line involves the thought of the Euclidean space in which it falls. It is perhaps in such systems as Euclidean geometry that we get the most perfect examples of coherence that have been constructed. If any proposition were lacking, it could be supplied from the rest; if any were altered, the repercussions would be felt through the length and breadth of the system. Yet even such a system as this falls short of ideal system. Its postulates are unproved; they are independent of each other, in the sense that none of them could be derived from any other or even from all the others together; its clear necessity is brought by an abstractness so extreme as to have left out nearly everything that belongs to the character of actual things. A completely satisfactory system would have none of these defects. No proposition would be arbitrary, every proposition would be entailed by the others jointly and even singly, no proposition would stand outside the system. The integration would be so complete that no part could be seen for what it was without seeing its relation to the whole, and the whole itself could be understood only through the contribution of every part. . . .

Now if we accept coherence as the test of truth, does that commit us to any conclusions about the *nature* of truth or reality? I think it does, though more clearly about reality than about truth. It is past belief that the fidelity of our thought to reality should be rightly measured by coherence if reality itself were not coherent. To say that the nature of things may be *in*coherent, but we shall approach the truth about it precisely so far as our thoughts become coherent, sounds very much like nonsense. And providing we retained coherence as the test, it would still be nonsense even if truth were conceived as correspondence. On this supposition we should have truth when, our thought having achieved coherence, the correspondence was complete between that thought and its object. But complete correspondence between a coherent thought and an incoherent object seems meaningless. It is hard to see, then, how anyone could consistently take coherence as the test of truth unless he took it also as a character of reality.

Does acceptance of coherence as a test commit us not only to a view about the structure of reality but also to a view about the nature of truth? This is a more difficult question. . . .

Suppose that, accepting coherence as the test, one rejects it as the nature of truth in favour of some alternative; and let us assume, for example, that this alternative is correspondence. This, we have said, is incoherent; why? Because if one holds that truth is correspondence, one cannot intelligibly hold either that it is tested by coherence or that there is any dependable test at all. Consider the first point. Suppose that we construe experience into the most coherent picture possible, remembering that among the elements included will be such secondary qualities as colours, odours, and sounds. Would the mere fact that such elements as these are coherently arranged prove that anything precisely corresponding to them exists "out there"? I cannot see that it would, even if we knew that the two arrangements had closely corresponding patterns. If on one side you have a series of elements a, b, c . . . , and on the other a series of elements $[a', b', c']$ . . . , arranged in patterns that correspond, you have no proof as yet that the natures of these elements correspond. It is therefore impossible to argue from a high degree of coherence within experience to its correspondence in the same degree with anything outside. And this difficulty is typical. If you place the nature of truth in one sort of character and its test in something quite different, you are pretty certain, sooner or later, to find the two falling apart. In the end, the only test of truth that is not misleading is the special nature or character that is itself constitutive of truth.

Feeling that this is so, the adherents of correspondence sometimes insist that correspondence shall be its own test. But then the second difficulty arises. If truth does consist in correspondence, no test can be sufficient. For in order to know that experience corresponds to fact, we must be able to get at that fact, unadulterated with idea, and compare the two sides with each other. . . . Such fact is not accessible. When we try to lay hold of it, what we find in our hands is a judgment which is obviously not itself the indubitable fact we are seeking, and which must be checked by some fact beyond it. To this process there is no end. And even if we did get at the fact directly, rather than through the veil of our ideas, that would be no less fatal to correspondence. This direct seizure of fact presumably gives us truth, but since that truth no longer consists in correspondence of idea with fact, the main theory has been abandoned. In short, if we can know fact only through the medium of our own ideas, the original forever eludes us; if we can get at the facts directly, we have knowledge whose truth is not correspondence. The theory is forced to choose between scepticism and self-contradiction.

Thus the attempt to combine coherence as the test of truth with correspondence as the nature of truth will not pass muster by its own test. The result is incoherence. We believe that an application of the test to other theories of truth would lead to a like result. The argument is: assume coherence as the test, and you will be driven by the incoherence of your alternatives to the conclusion that it is also the nature of truth. . . .

Brand Blanshard: CONCRETE NECESSITY AND INTERNAL RELATIONS

>BELIEVING *he has shown that thought can be related to a world which is an intelligible whole, Blanshard addresses himself to the task of detailing the nature of the relations which obtain between the parts of that whole. The doctrine of "internal relations" is the key conception. In his presentation, the idealist adage—things are what they are in virtue of their relations—involves drawing the following inference. Since the relations in which a thing is involved determine*

what properties it has, a change in the thing's relations constitutes a change in the nature of the thing itself. After clarifying and defending this conception through examples and arguments, Blanshard reinforces the doctrine by showing that it is utilized by all of us in our daily lives and by scientists in their painstaking attempts to understand the natural world. He maintains that the concept of causality, for example, whether at the ordinary or scientific level, depends on the presumption that logical necessity connects past, present, and future events.

The passages below, from The Nature of Thought (*pp. 475–477, 478–479, 487–490, 492–496, 499–500, 503–504, 506–509, 511, 515, 517*), *are reprinted by kind permission of* The Macmillan Company.

Is there any positive reason for believing that the nature of things is intelligible? We have seen that the world could be accounted intelligible only if it were a system, all-inclusive and perfectly integrated, and that such integration would be achieved only if the parts were internally related. By an internal relation between two parts we mean a relation such that neither could be different without entailing a difference in the other. We have agreed that first appearances impose an all but overwhelming veto upon belief in such interdependence; and if it were not for the pressure of the implicit ideal of thought, making itself insistently felt in the scientific search for connection behind apparent irrelevance, and surging up continually in the long line of speculative thinkers who have held to the unity of things, the belief would probably have been discarded long ago as fanaticism or perversity. This verdict *may* be the right one. We have said repeatedly that *proof* of the rationality of things was not logically possible, since it would assume validity for a supposedly independent world of the very canons whose applicability was at issue.

But if the question is not whether logic is applicable to some unexperienced *Welt-an-sich*, but whether our known world of persons and things might with a keener wit be understood or intelligibly construed, we have suggested that an affirmative answer can be established as at least probable. That such an answer would also be desirable need hardly be pointed out. An answer in the negative would mean that the enterprise of thought was doomed from the outset, since the conditions of understanding could not be fulfilled; of some arrangements in the system the question why would have no answer. Even uncertainty about the answer, if genuine, would leave us perpetually in the dark, not only as to whether we could find answers to our questions, but whether there were any answers to be found. We have seen that scientific and speculative practice has assumed a reply in the affirmative; not that scientific men, for example, can be put down as speculative rationalists, but that at each successive step, when they have asked the question Why? have assumed an intelligible answer to be waiting, whether they found it or not, and that rationalism is only a generalization of this assumption. Unhappily the desirability of anything hardly proves that it exists. If evidence is to be offered that the world thought is seeking to construe is a whole of internally related parts, it must be drawn from other and more difficult sources. Some of these sources we now propose to explore.

(1) Consider, first, an argument of Hegel's, which derives perhaps from Plato. It is an argument designed to show that the internal relation of each to each is a condition implicit in the very being of anything at all. For if a thing is to be at all, says Hegel, it must be this *rather than that*, and the "rather than that" belongs as truly to its essence as the "this." "Something is in this relation to Other from its own nature and because otherness is posited in it as its own movement: its Being-in-Self comprehends negation, through which alone it now has its affirmative existence . . . it is just as this cancellation of its Other that it is Something." This is Hegel's forbidding way of making a comparatively simple point. To use an illustration of his, a meadow is clearly *not* a wood or a pond; on that all would agree. But few reflect on what, nevertheless, is a fact, that "not to be a wood is a part, and an essential part, of the nature of the meadow." Putting it generally, everything is related to everything else by the relation of difference at least. If it were not so related, it would clearly not be the thing it is, since then it would not differ from that which is admittedly other than itself. But a relation that could not be theoretically changed without changing the thing itself is precisely what we mean by an internal relation. Whence it follows that everything is related internally to everything else.

Common sense will no doubt be unmoved by this argument. But if so, this is not, so far as one can see, because the argument is unsound, but because common sense is unaccustomed to moving among considerations so abstract. If it could do so, what would it say? It might contend that difference is not a relation. The natural reply to this would be a definition of relation such that, while including difference, it obviously answered to men's common thought of relation; but from this reply we are cut off, since "relation" is indefinable. But of course the indefinability of a term does not mean that there is anything either arbitrary or indefinite in our thought of it. And I think that on careful inspection we shall see that difference does fall within the common meaning of relation. Likeness and difference go together in our thought as having the same sort of being; but likeness is plainly a relation, and it would be odd if difference were not. And if it really is not, what else can it be? To call it a substance, or a quality, or an event, or a way of behaving, or indeed anything *except* a relation seems forced and unnatural. We must conclude that it is either a relation or some form of being that is unique; and this it clearly is not. . . .

(2) Consideration shows that what holds in this respect of the relation of difference holds of other relations also. The nature of any term, unless the term is itself a relation, consists of attributes or properties (in the non-technical sense); by the nature of an apple we mean its roundness, its redness, its juiciness, and so on. Thus a change in any of the properties would be a change in the apple's nature. Now is a relation a property? No. Nevertheless it seems clear that whenever a term does have a relation of any kind to anything else, it also has a property in virtue of that relation—what Dr. Moore calls a "relational property"—and that this property belongs to its nature as truly as does any other. "If A is father of B, then what you assert of A when you say that he is so is a *relational property*— namely the property of being father of B; and it is quite clear that this property is not itself a *relation*, in the same fundamental sense in which the relation of fatherhood is so. . . ." [G. E. Moore, *Philosophical Studies*]. A relation, then, though not a property, gives rise to a property. And these properties are part of the nature of that which has them; the properties of being "above the beasts of the field," "a little lower than the angels," and "the father of B" belong to A as part of his nature. Now could the relations be different without the properties also being different? Obviously not. Could they be different without a difference in the nature of their terms? Obviously not, again; for the properties *are* part of the nature of the terms. Thus it holds of all relations that if they were different, their terms would also be different. But this means that all relations are internal. . . .

(3) The argument just offered, however, has been applied only to the unique, and we shall at once be reminded that even if it holds

of the unique, it may not hold of universals. And the case for internal relations must, if complete, apply to both. For the doctrine means that terms *as such or generally*, and not merely concrete existing things, are what they are in virtue of their relations. Now is there any reason to think that an abstract character or attribute is so connected with others, and ultimately with all others, that none of its relations to these could be different without involving a difference in itself? This is harder to believe. There are probably many persons who would admit that in order to say fully what this unique thing is, one must exhaust its relations to other things, but would draw back from the same suggestion as applied to a universal. Thus red-headedness may appear in a great variety of persons who have different temperaments, antecedents, and states of health. It therefore bears relations to all these characters, as it does indeed to countless others. Can one seriously say that red-headedness would not be red-headedness *unless* it were thus related? If this were true, we should have to hold that no one could know what red-headedness was without knowing all its relations to the mental and bodily traits of the people who had it. And is not that preposterous? For surely we do *not* know all these relations while we *do* know perfectly well what red-headedness is. That is, we actually possess knowledge which, on the theory, would be impossible. Hence the theory must be wrong.

But, for all its plausibility, this argument does not prove what it seeks to prove. What it proves is that we can have *some* knowledge of red-headedness without knowing all the relations of red-headedness. What it ought to prove is that we can know red-headedness *fully and as it really is* without such knowledge. And between these two there is an enormous difference. We admit that if the theory of internal relations asked us to deny the first, it would be asking something absurd. For it is obvious that we do attach some meaning to red-headedness even though we do not know all its relations. But what defender of internal relations has ever denied this? To deny it would be to take the self-destructive position that every bit of knowledge that we possess is equally and utterly illusion, since nothing ever comes before us whose relations we know exhaustively. And why anyone who holds, as do believers in internal relations, that all knowledge is a matter of degree, should be supposed to accept also this nihilism in knowledge is very far from apparent. Indeed it is the essence of the doctrine of degrees to hold that we *can* have *some* knowledge without an exhaustive grasp of relations. Between us and our critics, then, there is important common ground. It is agreed that when we use the term "red-headedness" we do use it with a meaning, we do have some knowledge of the attribute it names, even though we do not know all the relations of that attribute.

But is this equivalent to saying that the red-headedness now explicitly presented in thought is all there is to that attribute as it exists in the nature of things? That is what is implied in the criticism just offered us; for unless this criticism means that we can know the real nature of an attribute without knowing its relations, it is saying nothing from which we should differ. But to assume that what is now presented in idea does give the whole nature of what is referred to is not only to beg the question; it is to adopt a position that we have already examined and found false. An idea always points beyond itself; it always means more than it is; it always refers to more than it includes within the circle of its explicit content. Indeed that is what makes it an idea. This difference we have carefully studied under the head of immanent and transcendent meaning. That there is such a difference is undeniable; it is the difference exemplified (though of course not perfectly, since transcendent meaning can never be captured wholly) by the interval between what presents itself to the schoolboy when he thinks of Napoleon's loss of Waterloo and what presents itself to the historian; both refer to the same things, but by general admission the historian's explicit grasp is nearer to the fact than the school-boy's. *What makes the second grasp better than the first?* We have seen that is the fuller grasp of context, that is, of the antecedents, methods and bearings of the engagement. The school-boy must lay hold of these things if he is to see the defeat as it really was, and as he apprehends the context more fully his thought at once remoulds itself internally and approximates to the fact without. Similarly of the more trivial thought we have taken in illustration. For purposes of everyday intercourse on the level of common sense, the ordinary notion of it suffices. Does our notion at this level therefore exhaust the nature of the object? There is no more reason for thinking so than that our ideas of anything else on this level are truly adequate to their objects. Little, perhaps, as would be the point of reflecting on it ordinarily, it still remains the fact that red-headedness is an integral part of an organism, and indeed is so bound up, for example, with the structure of hair-fibres, and this in turn with all manner of constitutional factors determining racial and individual differences that our common notion of it supplies scarcely more than a signpost to its real or ultimate nature, i.e. to what it is as embedded in its own context. As we grasp these further relations, our explicit thought of the attribute is modified while our reference remains the same; we see that we are advancing toward the character as it really is. . . .

Idealism: Brand Blanshard

(4) Further evidence for internal relations is to be found in the nature of causality. There are two propositions about causality which, if made out, would establish that everything in the universe is related internally to everything else. These propositions are, (i) that all things are *causally* related, directly or indirectly; (ii) that being causally related involves being *logically* related. We believe that there are sound reasons for accepting both propositions; and since the conclusion they carry with them is so important for our position, we must examine them, particularly the second, in some detail.

(i) First, is everything related causally to everything else? If anyone denies this, it is pretty certain to be on one or other of two grounds, either (a) that some events are not caused at all, or (b) that if all events are caused, at least they are not each of them related causally to all of the others. (a) Until lately, the first of these grounds would have been considered almost absurd. The universality of the law of causation was generally accepted without question. But recent work in quantum physics has raised grave doubts about it. . . . An adequate discussion of these views would demand more space and far more knowledge of physics than the present writer has at his disposal. Two remarks will have to suffice. [1] Some physicists of the first competence in this realm have not been persuaded that the new results point validly to any suspension of causality, for example Einstein and Planck, Lodge and Rutherford. Thus whichever side the layman takes, he will at least have high authority with him. [2] Some competent writers who have examined the Heisenberg principle [the principle which asserts that it is impossible to determine simultaneously both the position and the velocity of a particle accurately] are clear that it confuses indeterminacy in our knowledge with indeterminism in fact. . . .

(b) But there is another ground of objection to the view that everything is causally related to everything else, a ground that does not lie in any doubt whether causation is universal, but in the belief that, granting its universality, there are spheres of causal influence that are closed to each other. Thus, what is happening now in the sun can be neither cause nor effect of anything now happening on earth; for no causal agency, not even gravitation, can travel faster than light, and it takes light an appreciable time, about eight minutes, to make the journey from sun to earth. But there is nothing in such facts to disturb us. We should not contend that everything is connected *directly* with everything else, i.e. that one could pass from any event to any other by following a single line of causation forward or backward. Obviously one could not. What does seem extremely probable, however, is that everything is connected directly *or* indirectly with everything else. Events now happening in the sun are traceable to causes occurring only a few minutes ago which in turn did affect the course of events on earth. Thus events in the two regions, even when neither is the cause of the other, are connected through *common* causes. Nor, if this mode of connection is recognized, does there seem to be any region or any event that is cut off from any other. There is of course nothing startling in this to the contemporary scientist. It is almost certain, writes Sir James Jeans, that "every body pulls every other towards it, no matter how distant it may be. Newton's apple not only exerted its pull on the earth, but every star in the sky, and the motion of every star was affected by its fall. We cannot move a finger without disturbing all the stars."

Our first proposition about causality was that every existent is causally related to every other. If the causal relation is really universal, which we saw no compelling reason to deny, and "causal relation" is interpreted to include indirect causal relation, this proposition has an excellent claim to be believed.

(ii) What about the other proposition? That proposition was that causality involves an element of necessity in the logical sense. This is far less likely to be accepted without protest than the first. Time was when it was accepted as evident by thinkers of the first rank, but this confidence was destroyed by Hume, and the prevailing tendency at present is to follow writers like Mach, Pearson and Russell in holding that there is nothing in causal law but regular antecedence and consequence. According to this view, all we are justified in meaning when we say that *a* causes *b* is that neither is ever found without the other. But it has become reasonably clear that this notion will not serve. There can be no doubt that we *mean* more than this by causality, and it can be established pretty certainly that there *is* more in it. We have not the space either for a complete discussion of the regularity theory or for an analysis of causality into its factors; but our purpose will be served if we show that among these factors logical necessity is one.

(a) That necessity does thus enter into causality is easier to see in some cases than in others, so we shall take at once the case in which its presence seems to us clearest. Consider any instance of reasoning, for example our old case of the abbé and the squire. "Ladies," says the abbé, "do you know that my first penitent was a murderer?" "Ladies," says the squire, entering shortly afterward, "do you know that I was the abbé's first penitent?" A conclusion was of course produced in the ladies' minds, and our question is as to the nature of the causation that produced it. It would be agreed between holders of the regularity theory and ourselves that the ladies' entertainment of the premises had something causally to do with the emergence in their minds of the conclusion. The question is whether, when we say that the one contributed causally to the other, our only proper meaning is that whenever the first appears the second does, or whether we must say also this, that the special logical relation in which the content of the premises stands to the content of the conclusion had something to do with the appearance of that conclusion. To us it seems plain that it had. According to the regularity theory our only ground for expecting the judgment that arose rather than some other quite different one, e.g. that Florida raises grapefruit, is that thoughts of the first kind have regularly been followed by thoughts of the second; the question *why* what followed did follow is one on which we are, and must remain, in total darkness; the connection between the events is no more intelligible than the connection of lightning and thunder for a savage. We must confess to feeling that there is something perverse in talk of this kind. If the ladies were asked how they came to have the belief with which they ended, they would say that it was because this belief was obviously implied by what they were thinking the moment before; and we are convinced that this answer, which is the natural one, is also substantially the right one. Not that no other causes contributed to the result; we are not suggesting, of course, that causality *reduces* to logical necessity. What we hold is that when one passes in reasoning from ground to consequent the fact that the ground entails the consequent is one of the conditions determining the appearance of this consequent rather than something else in the thinker's mind. . . .

(*b*) But inference is of course only one of many mental processes. Can the influence of necessity which is displayed in it so plainly be traced in others also? We think it can. Not that its presence in those other processes is equally plain; nor would it be fair to expect this, since inference is concerned with necessity in a special manner. But we must remember what we have found earlier, that necessity, whatever our first impressions, is a matter of more and less, and that between a complete demonstration and a mere accidental conjunction it may be present in very many degrees. A process of rigorous inference approximates to the first of these extremes; association by mere contiguity approximates to the second; and between them are numerous processes in which there is more contingency than in inference, but more necessity than in association. Consider some examples. A painter is painting a landscape that is half completed, and he finds himself moved to put a tree in the foreground. Is such a development normally quite unintelligible? Certainly most painters would not say so. Is it then an example of pure necessity? No again; it clearly falls somewhere between. Or let us say that a man is intensely afraid of dogs. With the help of psycho-analysis he discovers that at an early age he was badly injured by the attack of a dog; it may come to him as a quasi-intuitive insight that it was this that caused his fear; and let us suppose that in this belief he is right. Can one say in such a case that it remains absolutely unintelligible to him how the fear arose? We do not think so. . . .

(c) There is thus good reason to think that not only in inference but also in many other mental processes the causal relation involves necessity. But what of causation in physical nature? This is the field in which most cases of causation are considered to fall, yet current philosophies of science are disposed to agree that no relation whatever is discoverable between physical cause and effect but one of regular conjunction. Certain it is that between the blow of a hammer and the sinking of a nail, or between the motion of one billiard ball and that of a second, no one has shown the same transparent relation that appears in a course of inference and may be recognized under veils of varying depth in other processes of the mind. The challenge laid down by Hume to show *why* any particular physical event was followed by any other has not been met. Nor do we propose to add one more to the list of futile attempts to meet it. But we should be clear as to what is implied in the failure to meet it. Does such failure in particular cases show that causality generally is nothing but regular sequence? Very far from it. Indeed I think it can be shown that regular sequence is not enough, that there must be some intrinsic connection between cause and effect, and that this intrinsic connection probably is, or includes, one of logical necessity. We must dwell on this a little, since it is important for our position that it should be seen.

In order to overthrow the regular-sequence theory, nothing more, strictly speaking, need be shown than what has been contended for already. It will hardly be denied that mental processes supply genuine cases of causality, and any case at all in which the relation involves necessity is enough to invalidate an account which asserts that it never does. But we are dealing now with causality in physical nature. It seems to me that even there the theory has been disposed of by certain criticisms that have recently been made of it. . . .

But further, even those who accept the regularity view are compelled, sometimes in the statement of this view itself, to assume that it is false. When they say that events have causes in the sense of regular and special antecedents, they intend this to apply to the future as well as to the past. But they have not experienced the future, and hence they must be using an *argument: Because b* has followed *a* in the past, it will continue to do so. Now unless *a* is connected with *b* by something more than mere conjunction, there is no ground for this argument whatever. What, apart from such connection, could be our reason for saying that uniform sequence in the past would carry with it uniform sequence in the future? We may say of course that when we have argued from such uniformities in the past to their continuance in the future, we have found our expectations verified, but plainly this will not do, for the uniform sequence of verification upon expectation is only another sequence, on a par with the original ones, and is entitled to no special privileges when the question is as to our right to argue from *any* past sequence to others. Again, if we make it a matter of probability, and say that a conjunction frequently recurrent is more likely to be maintained than broken, this either repeats the old assumption whose basis is in question, that the past is a guide to the future, or else is clearly false, since if *a* and *b* are really unconnected, there is no more reason to expect them to continue together than there is to expect an unloaded penny to go on giving heads because it has just done so ten times running. When this old puzzle about induction is raised, the answer usually given is that we "postulate" the uniformity of nature, viz., that the same cause is always followed by the same effect. But what is the status of this postulate? Is it merely an arbitrary assumption? Clearly not; in some sense it arises out of experience. Is it then a conclusion derived from experience? No, for, as has been pointed out times without number, the argument would be circular; unless we assumed "same cause, same effect," we could not argue that the same cause as in the past would be followed by the same effect. But then the question arises, what part *does* this assumption play in the argument? And the answer is that it is the *principle* of the inference, just as the principle of syllogism is the canon involved in any syllogistic reasoning. Now can the principle of an argument or inference be totally without necessity? We can only say that, if so, the "inference" to which it applies is no inference at all, and quite without cogency. We are not maintaining, of course, that the principle of uniformity has the clear and definite necessity of geometric demonstration, nor is that to be expected while the terms that pass muster as causes and effects remain so loose and vague. We do maintain, however, that the passage from past to future sequences is clearly an argument, that the principle of the argument, as of inferences generally, must be more than a chance conjunction of symbols or characters, and hence that the linkage between cause and effect in virtue of which we predict their future sequence is always implicitly taken as intrinsic.

Indeed, whatever the difficulties of finding the true connection between cause and effect, the difficulties of holding that they are not connected at all except by *de facto* conjunction is far greater. We have no room here to develop these in full, but by way of rounding out our brief case against this theory, we may set down the following paradoxes. (1) If causality *means* regularity of sequence, every unique event must be regarded as uncaused. An unexampled biological sport could not even be set down as miracle since miracles are supposed to be caused; it would have to be an explosion of chance. (2) No human action would ever spring from a self or from a motive; there is no intrinsic connection between volition and behaviour, character and conduct, motive and performance. Strictly speaking, no one murders anyone, though in some cases homicide has unhappily and quite inexplicably associated itself with certain elements of a person's constitution. This association is the more unfortunate because, though wholly irrational, it is also permanent. Such a view conflicts at a thousand points with our everyday judgements about practical action and moral accountability; and though all these judgements may be mistaken, the fact that the sequence view would *require* that they be mistaken is enough to impose on it a heavy burden of proof. (3) Note that we used the word "require." It was natural to use it, and those who hold the regularity view do frequently use it. Yet, as we have seen, if they hold any belief that is said to be required by their theory, its being required can have nothing to do with their holding it. (4) Nor is their explanation of how we came to suppose that causality involved more than association at all convincing. The usual explanation is Hume's, that the regular repetition of *a* and *b* together produced a habit of conjoining them in thought. But apart from the difficulty that a habit or even a thought of uniform conjunction is clearly different from the thought of necessity, what is meant here by "produced"? When one says that regular repetition produces a habit, does one mean only that there is a regular repetition of regular-repetition's-being-followed-by-a-habit? It does not seem likely. . . .

For all these reasons we believe that the view which would deny to causality any intrinsic connection and reduce it to conjunction may be dismissed. *Some* intrinsic connection there must be. But of what sort? Does the insight that between cause and effect there is an intrinsic connection suffice to show that this is also a *necessary* connection? We believe that it does. . . . When anything is said to have a consequent or a consequence in virtue of its special nature, necessity is part of our meaning, and what follows can not be denied except in pain of self-contradiction. Note that in this we have made no such unredeemable claim as that we can see *why* a particular hammer-stroke should drive a particular nail. Despite all the changes in physics since the turn of the century, we are very far from the sort of insight into physical things that would enable us to isolate the nerve of a given physical interaction. But unless there is such a nerve, the principle is illusory on which all practice is conducted and all causal argument is based. . . .

With this result we have reached the natural end of our inquiry. We have sketched the ideal of thought, and shown, so far as we could, that it is applicable to the real. If any reader is disposed to complain that the idea of a completely coherent system is still obscure, we may point out that in our present position there are two kinds of obscurity. One is the kind that comes of relaxing logical tension in the face of ultimate difficulty, of letting all holds go, surrendering to "wishful thinking," and plunging blindly into the mist. As one nears so high a conclusion, and one so much to be desired, as the intelligibility of the world, the temptation to relapse into a milky mysticism is strong. If there has been any compromise with this sort of thing, we are culpable; we hope there has not. On the other hand, there is a kind of vagueness whose condemnation, on such an issue, would be far less reasonable. If thought is what we hold it is, namely the pursuit of an end whose character can be realized only as the pursuit advances, a full and clear account of that end must in the nature of the case be impossible at any point along the journey. An account that was really adequate would not now be intelligible; an account that was quite simple, neat and plain could only be suspicious. The tale we have told of the concrete universal, and concrete necessity, and a system of parts such that none can be or be known without the others, cannot be rendered entirely clear from the level of a logic of mosaics. And of this particular kind of obscurity we trust we have been adequately guilty.

H. H. Joachim: THE IDEALIST POSITION

> JOACHIM *undertakes the task of answering two major criticisms that have been brought against Idealism. The first of these is that the idealist cannot provide an adequate theory of error and the second is that the idealist contradicts him-*

self by sometimes speaking of knowledge as a system in the process of completing itself and, at other times, speaking of it as a complete and all-inclusive system.

After elaborating on these criticisms, he points out that non-idealists as well as idealists find it difficult to account for error. He then proceeds to sketch an idealist theory of error which is based on the distinction between the partial truth of a judgment which fits consistently into our web of human knowledge and erroneousness of a judgment which fails to meet such a test of coherence. Joachim refuses to accept the critics' premise that to say a judgment can only give us partial knowledge (since human knowledge is always limited) is to admit the judgment is erroneous and thereby indistinguishable from any random judgment. As to the second criticism, he responds by appealing to a distinction somewhat like the one utilized in his theory of error. It is the distinction between the limited knowledge of a finite thinker and the total knowledge of an infinite mind. From a temporal point of view, the first seems to be a futile attempt to proceed from the imperfection of the part to the perfection of the whole. It is manifest the we can never capture the timelessness of the whole through the continuing processes of human thought. From a logical point of view, however, the human part of knowledge is both integral to, and a genuine expression of, the whole of knowledge. Joachim is charging that his critics in their search for contradiction have become insensitive to this basic distinction, a distinction which is analogous to that of inference and implication. Inference is a psychological process, whereas implication is a logical relation.

"The Idealist Position" was published in H. H. Joachim's Logical Studies in 1948, pp. 265–278. It is reprinted here with the kind permission of the Oxford University Press.

If we are to maintain a position of this kind [Idealism], we must be prepared to encounter many difficulties—some really formidable, others formidable only in appearance, but all certain to be urged by critics of various schools. Two of the most serious criticisms—based upon difficulties which lie at the root of all the rest—may be set out briefly as follows.

(i) *The fact of error*—so the first of these criticisms will insist—*is fatal to the idealist position.* For if one could assume that there is no difference between falsity and partial truth, between error and incomplete knowledge, then doubtless every judgment—and every group and subordinate system of judgments—would be both true and false, part only of knowledge and *eo ipso* an error. On that assumption—but not otherwise—every judgement, or group of judgements, being less than the available totality of knowledge, is knowledge incomplete and therefore erroneous; or must be false, because only a phase or stretch (or, at the most, a stage) in "the self-development of reality in the form of truth"—or, to use simpler language, because only a step in the advance of knowledge, a grade in the evolution of truth. But such an assumption conflicts with the plainest facts. Incomplete knowledge of geometry, for example, cannot be identified with geometrical error. The knowledge, say, of the beginner, who has mastered no more than the first proposition of Euclid, is totally different in character from, for example, the error that the diagonal of the square is commensurate with its side. There is a radical difference between a partial truth and a falsity—between (say) the true, but vague and indeterminate, judgement that "Charles I met a violent death," and the false judgement that "the end came peacefully to him in his bed."

And with the recognition that falsity and error have, so to speak, a positive character of their own; are radically different from, and irreducible to, partial truth and incomplete knowledge—the idealist position seems utterly to collapse. For that falsities and errors occur, it does not—and indeed could not—dispute. Yet what account could possibly be given of them within its outlines? They stand out, it seems, in irreconcilable hostility to that "self-fulfilment of the theoretical spirit" which according to the idealist position, is knowledge-or-truth.

And (ii) this first criticism will be reinforced by a second. For, the critic will say, there is a fundamental inconsistency in the idealist position. Knowledge-or-truth, we are told on the one hand, is a *discursus* or a dialectic; and our single judgements, our groups and subordinate systems of judgements, are respectively phases, stretches, stages of its continuous, onward-sweeping flow. To put it broadly, knowledge-or-truth is essentially *in fieri*; a process or growth in time, advancing, evolving, fulfilling, completing itself—but never finished or complete, never finally developed or fulfilled. But, on the other hand, we are also told that knowledge-or-truth is a "realm" or "world," a self-fulfilment of spirit in one of its essential modalities; a spiritual reality which affirms and keeps its concrete unity and self-identity; a *total* self-development; a dialectic which is "infinite"— not because unending, but because all-inclusive, self-supporting, and timelessly complete.

Now, the critic will insist, between these two ways of conceiving knowledge-or-truth the idealist logician must make his choice. He cannot be allowed to shift from one to the other; for most certainly they are mutually incompatible. Is knowledge-or-truth essentially *in fieri*—a never-ending advance, an evolution pointing always to a fuller stage beyond? Then, clearly, knowledge is of necessity always incomplete, truth always partial. For there is no stage in the advance which will not give place to a fuller and more coherent successor— even if every stage is relatively complete and whole, by contrast with the stages it succeeds or with the mere stretches and phases of itself. Knowledge-or-truth, therefore, being by its very nature always incomplete and partial, is—according to the idealist logician's own theory—error as well as knowledge, false in some degree as well as true. The dialectic, in short, the self-fulfilling *discursus*, is nothing but a procession of errors. Viewed as moments in the continuous advance, its successive phases, stretches, and stages may be said, no doubt, to contribute to "the truth"—i.e. to a knowledge more inclusive and more coherent than themselves. But this "truth," to which they contribute, is destined to be merged and superseded in the next stage of the advance; it is part only of a fuller truth that is to be. Hence they must equally be said to contribute always to a falsity and an error larger and more misleading than themselves.

Perhaps, then, the idealist logician will choose, and hold fast to, the other alternative. Perhaps he will maintain that the temporal character of knowledge-or-truth is a mere appearance, belying the real nature of that which is here appearing; that, essentially and in reality, knowledge-or-truth is a timeless whole—an infinite dialectic, eternally self-fulfilling and eternally self-fulfilled. Let us assume, the critic will say, that it is possible so to conceive knowledge-or-truth—a very large and generous assumption. The timeless whole, the infinite dialectic, would doubtless, in its absolute completeness, be knowledge in no sense erroneous or error; and, in its absolute self-supporting coherence, be true wholly and utterly—*the* truth without a trace of falsity. But so to conceive knowledge-or-truth will leave the idealist logician powerless to offer any intelligible account of the "apparent facts"—of the judgements that seem both true and false; of the knowledge (or the error) that appears to be a growth in time; of the *discursus* which seems to pass in part through temporally existent minds; of the self-development and self-manifestation of fact, in which the finite judging subjects seem to co-operate and play their part. For, measured against the eternal and absolute completeness of the whole (the timeless whole which knowledge-or-truth essentially is), every phase and stretch and stage of the so-called advance of knowledge is equally and utterly worthless and condemned. All, measured by such a standard, are sheerly false. They contribute not at all to knowledge or to truth; for knowledge-or-truth, *ex hypothesi*, is timelessly self-supporting and timelessly complete.

Lines of Defence. The formidable nature of the difficulties, which lie behind these criticisms, must at once be admitted. A complete solution of them is not to be found in any of the theories which conform to the idealist position. "Then," the critic will say, "the common opinion is right. These difficulties *are* fatal to the idealist position. The conclusion of the whole matter is scepticism; and that, in philosophy, is the confession of bankruptcy." But the difficulties are formidable, not to the idealist logician alone, but to theories conforming to any and every conceivable philosophical position. They are formidable, because they are real—i.e. inherent in the very nature of knowledge-or-truth. And if the idealist logician is no more able than any other philosopher to offer a "complete solution," he is able at least to show that a "complete solution" is, in the nature of the case, impossible. For a "complete solution" would mean the achievement and possession of absolute knowledge-or-truth here and now and by a particular mind. It would mean the compression and concentration of the infinite dialectic, of the *discursus* in its infinitude and wholeness, within an infinitesimal and transient phase of itself.

The idealist logician, then, will be the first to recognize that, behind these criticisms, lie difficulties which are, and must remain, insoluble. Nevertheless, he has open to him certain lines of defence against the criticisms themselves—i.e. against the special formulation given to the difficulties by the supposed critic. Thus, the fact of error constitutes in one sense a difficulty which no theory of knowledge-or-truth—logic—can solve. In one sense; but not precisely in the sense represented in the preceding criticism. Against that formulation, the idealist logician has every right to protest. And though there is in error a feature which remains to the end insoluble, the idealist logician is not so helpless as the critic supposes. His theory does not "utterly collapse." On the contrary: within limits, which he recognizes and rightly recognizes to be inevitable, he does in fact succeed in offering an intelligible account even of error. Similarly, what, borrowing a phrase from Bradley and applying it in our own manner, we may conveniently call the "twofold nature" of knowledge-or-truth, constitutes in one sense an insoluble difficulty. In one sense; but, once again, not in the sense represented by our imaginary critic. For the real difficulty is not that the idealist logician is bound to choose one or the other of two alternative views of knowledge-or-truth—both of which ignore or deny its twofold nature—and that, whichever he chooses, his failure is inevitable and ludicrous. The real difficulty is, on the contrary, that he is bound to recognize and accept this "twofold nature"; and, in doing so, to recognize that no intelligible account is possible of its "how" or "why." For knowledge-or-truth—like every form of spiritual reality, like every modality of self-expression or self-fulfilment of spirit—is eternal and yet appears in time, is infinite and yet displayed in and through the self-limitation by spirit of its infinitude. The fact of this union of contrasted and seemingly incompatible characters is forced upon our recognition throughout the whole range, and in every detail, of our experience; but the whole of our philosophical speculation presupposes it, moves within it, and can hardly be said, perhaps, to render it fully intelligible.

(i) *Against the first criticism*, then, the lines of the idealist logician's defence may be traced as follows:

He will refuse to be bluffed into accepting either of the alternatives, which the critic tacitly assumes to be exclusive; or to be deceived by the superficial plausibility of his examples. He is not bound to choose—here, or anywhere—between blank identity and utter difference. A judgement, *qua* false, has a character it does not possess *qua* true; and yet, unless it were true in some degree, unless it were a partial truth, it would not be a judgement at all. Nothing but a partial truth can be a false judgement; though mere deficiency of truth is not of itself enough to constitute its falsity. And knowledge at every stage is incomplete, and nothing but incomplete knowledge can ever be an error; though in the knowledge, which is an error, there is a further feature, there is a positive qualification, besides the mere absence of completeness.

What is this further feature, this positive qualification, which distinguishes the falsity of a judgement from its mere deficiency of truth, the erroneousness of every stage of knowledge from its falling short of being complete? It is bound up with that "subjective assurance of thinking truly" to which I referred before as the *differentia* of judgement viewed on the side of the judging subject, viewed as his personal experience. If there is to be falsity, in the full and proper sense of the term, there must be a partial truth affirmed (believed) as truth absolute and whole. And if there is to be error, the incomplete knowledge, which now passes through and possesses some particular mind, must be *for* that mind, *as* its experience, complete and final, or absolute.

Now up to a certain point there is nothing in this characterization of error or falsity, which does not harmonize with the idealist logician's general conception of knowledge and of judgement. For, according to the idealist position, it will be remembered, knowledge is a two-sided *discursus*, "objective" and "subjective" in one; and every single judgement, as a constituent phase of that *discursus*, shares its two-sided character. Nothing, therefore, is a judgement unless two essential conditions are both fulfilled. If there is to be a judgement, (*a*) there must be a phase of the "objective *discursus*." There must be a "self-development of fact"—a synthetic-analysis in which an "object" constitutes itself, and makes itself known, as what it really is, i.e. as a "spiritual fact" or a "truth." And (*b*) this phase of the "objective *discursus*"—this phase of the activity of a power of thought impersonal or rooted in the nature of things—must have a "personal" or "subjective" side. It must *pass through* a finite mind, must be present in, and appear as a phase of, its conscious flow. A judgement, that is, is a self-development of fact; yet this self-development requires—somehow, and in some measure—the co-operation of a particular mind. It is the emergence of a truth which is also—somehow and in some measure—being elicited by the contributory act of this or that judging subject, who, in the eliciting, experiences it and is subjectively assured that what he experiences is true.

"But, if so," the critic will object, "it follows that, according to the idealist position, every judgement is a falsity, and not true at all; every stage of the *discursus* error, and in no sense knowledge. For, on the one hand, every judgement and every system of judgements (or stage of the *discursus*) must be experienced by a finite knower, by a particular mind—and experienced in the assurance that what is experienced is absolute truth; and yet, on the other hand, no judgement, nor even any system of judgements, can be true except relatively. Its truth is partial and imperfect, subject to conditions it implies but does not include. In order to be true wholly—in order to be and embody absolute truth—every judgement, and every system of judgements—would have to be indefinitely supplemented; to be expanded, to be corrected; to be transformed, perhaps, into we know not what. Hence, according to the idealist position, every judgement, taken as it actually is (taken, that is, in the concrete unity of its twofold character as a spiritual fact), is, it seems, false utterly and without qualification; and, taken similarly in its concreteness, every system of judgements (every so-called 'stage in the advance of knowledge') is a mass of errors, error unadulterated."

This objection betrays a misunderstanding of *the precise scope* of the "subjective assurance" which, according to the idealist position, is an ineliminable moment in the judgement. My former account, perhaps, was not sufficiently guarded; at all events, what must (as I think) be maintained, is less than the critic supposes. If I am to judge, I must feel absolutely certain that what I judge is true; i.e. that in the given situation, in the actual context which provokes my judgement, any and every judging subject must think *so* and not otherwise. But if I am to judge, I need not feel absolutely certain that what I judge is absolutely true; i.e. true in all situations and contexts, true unconditionally and without respect to any determinate stage of knowledge, an absolute item of absolute truth.

Thus (to take one of the critic's examples) nobody can judge that "Charles I met a violent death," except in the absolute assurance (the unhesitating feeling of certainty) that, in the given situation, any and every judging subject must think *so* and not otherwise. He must feel absolutely certain that what he thus judges is relatively true; i.e. that it is demanded by, fits in with, indispensably supplements, "the whole" (as it would be called) "of his present and actual knowledge of English history." The judgement, as he thus makes it, is a partial truth—a truth provisional and relative—but not (in the full and positive sense) a falsity or an error. It would be a falsity or an error only if he affirmed it in the unhesitating assurance of its absolute truth—affirmed it stubbornly as true: wholly, and finally, and without reserve. And such an assurance of absolute truth is not an essential condition of our judgements; nor even, fortunately, a very common accompaniment of them.

(ii) "But," the critic will insist, "what, according to the idealist position, is this so-called 'whole' of the judging subject's present and actual knowledge of English history? It is a mere stretch or mutilated stage of the *discursus* as it happens to pervade and inform a particular mind. It is, therefore, fragmentary and relative, provisional and shifting—*at most* a whole in the making; a whole, moreover, such that it can never be finally made. Even as it now possesses and informs the judging subject's mind, this so-called 'whole of knowledge' is in the very act of expanding and transforming itself into a more inclusive and more coherent system of more precisely defined constituent judgements—a system, in which the judgement that 'Charles I met a violent death' will be displaced by the more accurate judgement 'was beheaded at Whitehall in 1649.' The given situation, the relevant context, of the judgement is, in short, a 'situation' of error as much as of knowledge—a 'context' conferring upon its constituents (upon the judgements which imply and supplement it) falsity as well as truth."

In trying to meet this objection, we shall at the same time be tracing our lines of defence against the second of the two criticisms that were set out just now; for indeed the difficulties, which lie behind these criticisms, are too closely connected to be kept apart. What in the end remains insoluble, *in the fact of error*, is precisely that it involves a stubborn feeling of assurance, on the part of this or that judging subject, that what he judges is absolute truth. How is it possible or conceivable that this or that finite mind—i.e. this or that transient concentration of the infinite mind, of the *potentia infinita cogitandi*—should ever thus seem to itself to possess, within the compass of its present experiencing, absolute knowledge-or-truth? And what in the end remains insoluble, *in regard to the "twofold nature" of knowledge-or-truth*, is the same difficulty in a more ultimate and universal form. How is it possible or conceivable that the *potentia infinita cogitandi*, which fulfils itself in knowledge-or-truth, should divide and distribute itself into, and over, a plurality of limited and transient minds—and should eternally have achieved, eternally maintain, the infinite fulfilment of itself *only* by this self-division and self-limitation, *only* through the co-operation of these finite thinkers, and through the temporal (and essentially never complete or final) processes of their thinking?

"My whole present knowledge of English history"—to return to the critic's objection—is, undoubtedly, a mutilated stretch or stage of the *discursus*; not complete, not self-supporting; in short, if the term is to be pressed, not "a whole" of knowledge-or-truth at all. It is, however, a "whole," *first*, by contrast with the still more fragmentary phases it includes, and the still more rudimentary and imperfect stretches and stages it has superseded and absorbed; and, *secondly*, in virtue also of its tendency towards wholeness. For—as the critic himself rightly emphasizes—"my present knowledge" (whether of history, or of geometry, or of any subject) is in the very act of expanding and transforming itself; but the trend of this self-development is towards completeness and coherence. The principle, or the mainspring, of the *discursus* is a *"nisus towards totality"* inherent in every phase and stretch and stage of itself.

"My present knowledge as a whole," then, in spite of its manifest imperfection and instability, is the criterion and the measure of the truth of every constituent phase of itself. For me at least, as I make my present judgement, it is the sole and the sufficient criterion. There is nothing *"for"* me—nothing within my actual experience—on which I could base a reasoned doubt or criticism of "my present knowledge as a whole"—however provisional and incomplete its "wholeness" must (on the general principles of the "idealist position") be admitted to be. Every judgement, therefore, which contributes essentially to constitute this relatively complete and relatively coherent system of judgements—to constitute (say) my present "total" knowledge of English history, or of plane geometry —is, *for me as I judge,* true in proportion to the amount, the value or significance, and the indispensability (the irreplaceableness) of its contribution. From this point of view—the point of view not of practice only, but of theory at all its levels short of philosophical speculation—every judgement (in the context in which alone it is, and can be, made) is "true" *and not false;* and the whole, to which it contributes (the context which provokes it and which it supplements), is "knowledge" *and not error.* And if here the critic objects "But *is* it, then, *not* false that 'the diagonal is commensurate with the side' or that 'Charles I died peacefully in his bed'? Is it really contended by the idealist logician that these judgements are true?," the line of defence is plain. *Either* they are implied by, and contribute essentially to, some present and actual whole of knowledge—and so contributing, and within that context, are indeed "true" and not false. *Or* they are not judgements, not actual beliefs, at all. For as we have already tried to explain, nothing is a "judgement," according to the theory of the idealist logician, unless in it a fact develops itself through the co-operation of the actual thinking of a particular mind. The mere grammatical form of the statement does not in the least guarantee that the thought expressed in it is a judgement—or even that any thought is expressed in it at all. The plausibility of the critic's examples, therefore, need not disturb us. For, on a closer scrutiny, it is plain they are not examples of *judgement* at all. No sane and intelligent person could *judge*—i.e. could affirm or believe in the absolute assurance of the relative truth of the "affirmed" or "believed"—that "Charles I died peacefully in his bed" or that "the diagonal is commensurate with the side."

That, then, is the first line of defence for the idealist logician; but behind it, supporting and supplementing it, he must trace another. For he has admitted (or rather, insisted) that "the whole of any judging subject's present knowledge" stretched to its uttermost compass—interpreted even, if that be possible, as all the knowledge possessing and possessed by, or available to, the human spirit as it exists and is embodied at a given period of the world's history—remains still a mere section or stage of the *discursus* which is "knowledge-or-truth." Indeed, what he has admitted seems even more damaging than that. For the *discursus*, on his view, must be conceived as timelessly whole, as eternally complete. It is the infinite dialectic; it is reality self-shaping and eternally self-shaped, fulfilling itself and eternally self-fulfilled, in the form of absolute knowledge or absolute truth. Now, as we saw before, he cannot be called upon to show *how* the infinite dialectic affirms and maintains its infinite and eternal completeness by appearing as an incompletable advance in time. He cannot be challenged by the critic to explain *how* the *potentia infinita cogitandi*, by the inherent necessity of its own nature, divides and distributes itself into a plurality of finite subjects, affirming and sustaining its timeless actuality only through their co-operation, i.e. only in, and by means of, the temporal processes of their thinking. But he must be prepared to answer one very obvious question: Why must the *discursus* be conceived as timelessly whole, as eternally complete?

The answer he will make to this question is simple and familiar.

We are forced to conceive the *discursus* (of which our actual cognizant experiences are fragmentary phases) as timelessly whole and eternally complete—we are forced, in other words, to identify it with the infinite dialectic, which is reality, half-showing and half-concealing itself in the form of a temporal development—because (1) "to perceive imperfection is to judge by the perfect," and because (2), when we set out the character of *this* "perfect," of the ideal implied in our criticism of our cognizant experiences, we shall find it takes no other form than that of a dialectic, which is infinite—which is the eternal synthetic-analysis of spirit in, and by, and for itself.

(1) When we reflect philosophically upon our cognizant experiences—upon any of those experiences, no matter what, in which, while we live in them, we feel assured that we are preaching fact or affirming truth—they show themselves (in various degrees, but one and all) intrinsically "imperfect." Intrinsically "imperfect": i.e. because falling short of an ideal, which they themselves suggest. The awareness of fact, i.e. the adequate apprehension of an actual constituent of the "external" world;—*this* is the perfection, the ideal, which every actual perception "sets" (so to speak) "to itself"—and fails to achieve. It is what it "has in it" to be, what it aims at being and professes to be; and it is also precisely what, in various degrees, it falls short of being. Or again: to affirm and embody truth, the whole truth, neither more nor less, in respect to some matter-of-fact or complex object—*this* is the perfection, the ideal, which every

actual judgement "sets to itself" (so to speak), which it "has in it" to be, which by its very form it professes to be. And *this* is the ideal, by which it is condemned—the perfection, which (in various degrees, but always and manifestly in *some* degree) it fails to attain.

So far, in the endeavour to simplify the issue, I have been speaking as though each several cognizant experience brought with it its own distinct ideal, its own separate standard of perfection, by which it criticized and condemned itself. But this is to misrepresent the actual situation. For according to the "idealist" position—the position which is to be defended—there are no *several* cognizant experiences, i.e. none that are isolable, and self-contained or complete in their isolation. There are, always and only, phases, grades, stages of a *single* —infinitely differentiated and endlessly developing—*discursus*. It is this single, continuous and continuing, *discursus*, which philosophical reflection shows to be "imperfect"—"imperfect" throughout, and in each of the distinguishable phases of its continuous development, because "coming short" of an ideal which it implies; i.e. which, in that sense, it "sets to itself" and suggests to the philosopher as the standard of perfection by which he criticizes and condemns it.

(2) What, then, is this ideal? What is this standard of perfection, which the idealist logician, in reflecting upon the *discursus*, recognizes that each and all its phases *imply*, but fail in various degrees to achieve?

"When we set out its character," I asserted, "we shall find it takes no other form than that of the eternal synthetic-analysis of spirit in, and by, and for itself." In making this assertion, I was thinking primarily of Hegel's treatment of the matter—for Hegel is the originator of the "idealism" I have been trying to maintain. The dialectic, as which (on Hegel's theory) the Absolute displays itself to speculative thought—to thought at its best and cleverest, to the thought which is philosophy—is not a temporal development. It is not a coming-into-being of the Whole, nor its development to a fuller state of itself: it is the timeless self-analysis and self-synthesis, in which the "being" of the Whole—its spiritual actuality—consists. The Absolute (*die Idee, das Wahre, das Gute,* &c.), Hegel constantly insists, is timelessly perfect, eternally self-fulfilled: the inclusive whole of all the moments and stages of the dialectic "process," in which it is displayed. No doubt, in calling the dialectic a "process" or a "movement," as Hegel constantly does, he exposes himself to misunderstanding, in spite of the care he takes to guard himself against it. But the "process" in this case (we must remember) *is* the Whole. And the "movement" is not a passage *towards* perfection, not a movement of transition [a *kinesis*]; but the living self-expression of the perfect Whole [an *energeia akinesias*]. The order of the terms in this "process"—in the Hegelian dialectic—is not temporal, but logical; and the logical nexus throughout is determined by the immanence of the Whole in each and all of them, by the immanence of the Absolute in every moment and stage of the dialectic "movement."

"But," it will be objected, "the fact (if it be a fact) that Hegel took this view is not sufficient to justify what was asserted. An appeal to authority is here irrelevant. Granted that Hegel was a great philosopher; granted, further, that Hegel, reflecting upon our actual cognizant experience, conceived it to imply a timeless dialectic as the ideal—as the absolute and perfect reality—of which it is the imperfect temporal appearance. Still, Hegel may have been mistaken. And, apart from that, the point at issue is not how this or that philosopher in fact conceives the ideal, the 'perfect,' by which he judges the 'imperfection' of our actual knowledge in all its phases. It was asserted not that the ideal *has been*, but that it *must be*, thus conceived: that it *must*, when set out explicitly, take the form of a dialectic timelessly self-fulfilling and timelessly self-fulfilled."

Beyond all question this objection would hold against an attempt to justify what was asserted by Hegel's, or by anyone's authority. But the reference to Hegel's treatment of the subject was intended as an appeal not to his "authority"—which would have been absurd—but to the substance of his doctrine. And the reference was suggested by what seems a not unreasonable reflection. For to maintain that the idea *must* be conceived in such and such a manner is, in effect, to maintain that such and such is the most adequate conception that can be formed, the truest account that can be given, of it. And it is not unreasonable to presume that this "truest account" will be found, if anywhere, in the works of those, who have thought most deeply on the subject. . . .

GUIDE TO FURTHER READINGS IN CONTEMPORARY IDEALISM

IDEALISM AND HISTORY

Benedetto Croce (1866–1952), the most influential Italian idealist, insisted that reality manifests itself solely in the thought and experience of human minds. While rejecting that part of Hegelian doctrine which pertains to the Absolute and its associated nontemporal categories, Croce retained that part which identifies reality with historical process and its associated dynamic categories of evolution, creativity, and freedom. For

Croce, history is identified with the workings of the human mind, and philosophy is simply a description of the operative principles of history. See especially *History as the Story of Liberty,* trans. S. Sprigge (New York: Norton, 1941).

R. G. Collingwood (1889–1943), a British philosopher and historian, believed with Croce that the philosopher ought to look to history rather than natural science as the model of genuine knowledge. Collingwood insisted that natural science itself constitutes one form of historical knowledge. "Natural science as a form of thought exists and has always existed in a context of history, and depends upon historical thought for its existence. . . . No one can understand natural science unless he understands history and no one can answer the question what nature is unless he knows what history is." [16] His *The Idea of History* (Oxford: Clarendon, 1946) constitutes the fullest expression of this view.

Additional Readings

Collingwood, R. G., *Autobiography.* New York: Oxford University Press, 1939.

———, *An Essay on Philosophical Method.* Oxford: Clarendon Press, 1933.

———, *The Idea of Nature.* Oxford: Clarendon Press, 1945.

Croce, B., *The Philosophy of G. B. Vico.* Trans. by R. G. Collingwood. New York: Macmillan, 1913.

IDEALISM AND KNOWLEDGE

W. T. Stace (1886–   ) has aggressively defended Berkeley's *esse est percipi* against the criticisms of the Realists, pointing out that the burden of disproof falls on them. On the positive side, he suggests that "belief in an external world is a mental construction." The unexperienced entities about which scientists and philosophers speak in their accounts of things are introduced by the mind for the sake of convenience and clarity. See especially "The Refutation of Realism," *Mind,* 43 (1934): 145–55.

Additional Readings

"Russell's Neutral Monism," in *The Philosophy of Bertrand Russell,* ed. P. Schilpp. Evanston and Chicago: Northwestern University Press, 1944.

Stace, W. T., *The Theory of Knowledge and Existence.* New York: Oxford University Press, 1932.

Wood, L., *The Analysis of Knowledge*. Princeton: Princeton University Press, 1940.

IDEALISM AND METAPHYSICS

In the spirit of Plato, W. E. Hocking (1873–   ) emphasizes the moral and religious significance of the universe. He opposes materialistic and positivistic philosophies on the grounds that at best they impose a false dichotomy between objective facts and subjective values and at worst deny values altogether. In general, he recommends that the philosopher follow the lead of poets and mystics, and seek to enlarge his vision of things; in particular, he underscores the importance of the self as the "center of value." See especially *Human Nature and Its Remaking* (New Haven: Yale University Press, 1918).

E. S. Brightman (1884–1953), like Hocking, believed that the universe is essentially spiritual and purposive in nature. However, following B. P. Bowne (1847–1910) and other American personalists, he rejected the neo-Hegelian view that individual selves are but aspects of the Absolute, on the ground that it cannot account for the uniqueness and moral freedom of the individual. According to the personalists, the individual monads or selves are, however, dependent on a supreme monad or God, both as the source of their being and nature and as the provider of a meaningful context in which they may fully realize themselves. See especially *Personality and Religion* (New York: Abingdon-Cokesbury, 1934).

Additional Readings

Bowne, B. P., *Personalism*. Boston: Houghton Mifflin, 1908.
Flewelling, R. T., *Creative Personalism*. New York: Macmillan, 1926.
Hocking, W., *The Meaning of God in Human Experience*. New Haven: Yale University Press, 1912.
Werkmeister, W. H., *The Basis and the Structure of Knowledge*. New York: Harper, 1948.

IDEALISM AND LANGUAGE

Wilbur M. Urban (1873–1952) was an idealist to the extent that he regarded as real only that which is intelligible. For him, however, only what can be stated in terms of ordinary language passes the test of intelligibility. After an extensive investigation of the categories of natural language he concludes that a supraempirical concept such as God or the Absolute is indeed meaningful; however, he warns that the language in which such a thought is expressed is not to be taken literally. On his view, the mistake of the positivistic opponents of idealism is that they declare all metaphysical (and religious) statements unintelligible and thereby ignore all the important nonliteral (symbolic and analogical) meanings. See especially *Language and Reality* (New York: Macmillan, 1939).

Ernst Cassirer (1874–1945), a neo-Kantian and, incidentally, Urban's successor at Yale, continued to stress the importance of language in knowledge. The rudiments of the symbolic process are to be found even in the "direct" experiences of primitive men, since these experiences have at least a minimum of order; the highest culmination to date of the symbolic process occurs in the great systematizations of science, art, religion, and other cultural fields. The measure of human progress is the degree to which man has moved from the chaos in which his experience was barely structured to a world intelligibly organized through the creative use of symbols. See especially *The Philosophy of Symbolic Forms*, 3 vols., trans. R. Manheim (New Haven: Yale University Press, 1953–57).

Additional Readings

Cassirer, E., *An Essay on Man*. New Haven: Yale University Press, 1944.

———, *The Myth of the State*. New Haven: Yale University Press, 1946.

Langer, S. K., *Philosophy in a New Key*. Cambridge: Harvard University Press, 1942.

Urban, W., *Beyond Realism and Idealism*. London: Allen and Unwin, 1949.

———, *The Intelligible World*. London: Allen and Unwin, 1929.

NOTES FOR CHAPTER II

1 Plato, *Laws*, Book X, *The Dialogues of Plato*, trans. B. Jowett (New York: Oxford University Press, 1892), V, 274.
2 M. Nahm, *Selections from Early Greek Philosophy* (New York: Crofts, 1940), pp. 114–115. The italics in the quotation are ours. A follower of Parmenides, Zeno (490–430 B.C.), applied the same kind of reasoning to the problem of motion and rest, showing that motion is illusory. The paradoxes that he posed have remained items for serious discussion to this very day, especially in philosophy and mathematics.
3 *Dialogues of Plato*, trans. Jowett, II, 215–216.
4 *Republic*, Book VII, *Dialogues of Plato*, trans. Jowett, III, 517. In Plato's philosophy it is inaccurate to identify either the Idea of the Good or the realm of Ideas with a divine being. Particularly in the *Timaeus*, which

was written late in his career, Plato characterizes God as an uncreated entity who, out of his goodness, creates order out of chaos. It is to be noted, however, that God acts from love of the Good and employs the universals as his architectural model.

5   Aristotle, *Metaphysics*, trans. R. Hope (Ann Arbor: University of Michigan Press, 1960), pp. 36–38.
6   *Ibid.*, pp. 259–260.
7   M. Calkins (ed.), *George Berkeley: Principles of Human Knowledge* (Boston: Scribner's, 1929), pp. 105–107.
8   *Ibid.*, pp. 108–9.
9   John Wild (ed.), *Spinoza Selections* (Boston: Scribner's, 1930), p. 94.
10 See Immanuel Kant, *Critique of Pure Reason*, trans. N. K. Smith (London: Macmillan, 1933), pp. 244–7.
11 *Ibid.*, p. 68.
12 Perhaps Kant's position is not as defenseless as it appeared to his idealist successors. It is true that there can be no empirical knowledge of things-in-themselves; for example, it is a misapplication of the category "cause" to say that things-in-themselves cause the data of experience. If, indeed, our account of phenomena and the conditions for their occurrence exhaust knowledge, then it is absurd to speak of knowing things-in-themselves. However, this may make the Kantian restriction more stringent than he intended. We may regard him as having held that every positive concept is limited by a negative one. For instance, in applying the positive concept *red* to an object, it must be realized simultaneously that the negative concept *nonred* does not apply. Looking at the matter in this way, we may say that in entertaining the concept *phenomena*, Kant was necessarily thinking of its limiting concept, *non-phenomena*, or *noumena*, as well.
13 Nahm, *Selections*, p. 115.
14 The difficulty may be stated as follows: The Absolute Idea is the upper limit of the categories of the *mind* precisely because it contains no contradiction within itself. How then can it have an antithesis in a final triad?
15 Bradley did grant, however, that the intelligibility of the real is manifest in discursive thought to the limited extent that such thought can be made consistent, and he conceded that our direct experiences, though disparate and diverse, provide us with some nonrelational feeling for the continuity and unity of the real. Nevertheless, neither discursive thought nor immediate apprehension is sufficient in itself or in combination to disclose reality wholly. Yet, together, they indicate that reality, the Absolute, is "superrelational" in nature.
16 R. G. Collingwood, *The Idea of Nature* (Oxford: Clarendon Press, 1945), p. 177.

III · Pragmatism

WHAT IS the most effective way for man to resolve his problems? Some people rely almost exclusively on reason, while others seem to depend entirely on animal instinct. But doesn't each of these by itself represent an unsatisfactory approach to problem solving? On the one hand, it is doubtful whether total intellectualization of a problem initiates the decisive action required for its solution in the life situation. On the other, it is doubtful as well whether entirely nonrational responses to a problem provide the reliable guidance essential to its solution. Is there no middle ground between reflective nonparticipation and unreflective participation, between life observed in timeless detachment and life reacted to in frenzied involvement, between a withdrawal from life and an engulfment by it? The answer to our initial question would seem to be that reason should provide a framework within which and by which impulses can be controlled and guided. The pragmatist argues that such coordination between reason and impulse is within man's capabilities and, moreover, that the degree of success he enjoys as a competent problem-solver in a complex environment depends on the measure of harmony existing between the rational and nonrational components of his nature.

The literature of pragmatism abounds with descriptions of effective thinking. For example, John Dewey (1859–1952) writes:

> A man travelling in an unfamiliar region comes to a branching of the road. Having no sure knowledge to fall back upon, he is brought to a standstill of hesitation and suspense. Which road is right? And how shall his perplexity be resolved? There are but two alternatives: He must either blindly or arbitrarily take his course, trusting to luck

for the outcome, or he must discern grounds for the conclusion that a given road is right. An attempt to decide the matter by thinking will involve inquiring into other facts, whether brought to mind by memory, or by further observation, or by both. The perplexed wayfarer must carefully scrutinize what is before him and he must cudgel his memory. He looks for evidence. He may climb a tree; he may go first in this direction, then in that. He wants something in the nature of a signboard or a map, and his reflection is aimed at the discovery of facts that will serve his purpose.[1]

Such a description appeals to the ordinary man because it "makes sense," because it calls attention to the practical, problem-solving activities in which he engages daily. But the question arises immediately whether mundane problem solving is analogous to the complex thought processes of the scientist, mathematician, philosopher, or, indeed, any individual in his most rational moments. Clearly, a philosophy centering around such a view of thought must have roots that go deeper than a mere appeal to our immediate and practical concerns. A method of knowing, for example, cannot be dealt with in isolation from a consideration of the nature of that which we know. It was precisely in the context of debate over the nature of the objects of knowledge that the issue of the proper method of knowing emerged clearly for the first time.

SOPHISTS

During the fifth century B.C. many Greek thinkers began to lose confidence in the philosophic quest to discover objective truth and absolute reality. One group of philosophers—of whom the best known was Parmenides—claimed that the objects of knowledge are non-sensible and that they are to be discovered only by rational means. However, this view, which tended to set the realm of knowledge apart from the realm of sense experience and in its extreme form to reduce the latter to mere appearance, failed to satisfy those who look to philosophy for effective guidance in daily affairs. On the other hand, another group of philosophers—of whom the best known was Heraclitus—maintained that the objects of knowledge are sensible and discoverable solely by empirical means (see pages 64–65, for a more accurate account). But this type of philosophy, which tended to identify the objects of knowledge with the objects of sense experience, also failed those who seek guidance from philosophy, because it did not provide stable and unifying principles for dealing effectively with the confusing, ever-changing data of the senses.

The ontological speculations engaged in and epistemological methods prescribed by the early Greek philosophers increasingly lost their hold on the minds of men because they seemed irrelevant to human problems. A group of thinkers, the Sophists, ranging from mere verbalizers to enlightened skeptics, came into prominence during this period of disenchantment. They developed numerous arguments debunking the possibility of absolute and objective knowledge. For example, when a Pythagorean defines reality as number (that is, with respect to its mathematical properties), a Sophist might counter as follows: Since number itself is derived from sense experience by abstraction, it cannot adequately explain that from which it is derived. Or again, when an atomist or pluralist accounts for the world of visible things on the basis of a world of invisible particles or "seeds," a Sophist might respond thus: Since one is attempting to explain the visible by reference to the invisible through its resemblances to the visible, one does no more than beg the question.

Most Sophistic arguments, however, do presuppose a set of positive beliefs. They presume that the test of any philosophy is always its ability to explain the world of our senses. This suggests that Sophists regarded what sense experience reveals as real. Furthermore, since they recognized sense experience as differing from person to person, they were forced to conclude that reality is as it appears to each individual. This view was expressed by Protagoras (481–411 B.C.) in the maxim "Man is the measure of all things, of existing things that they exist, and of nonexisting things that they exist not." In conceiving reality as relative to the perceiver, they obliterated the distinction between the real and the apparent, and the basis for the distinction between knowledge and opinion. Moreover, since each person can judge what is real for him, he can decide when his beliefs are true and when they are false. In short, what one perceives to be real, *is* real, and what one believes or feels to be true, *is* true.

Partly because of circumstances that existed in Greece at the time and partly because of their subjectivism and relativism, the Sophists posed the following question: If there are no objectively true beliefs and no certain guiding principles, what, if any, basis can there be for the state? Some Sophists answered, in effect, that the state was merely a matter of happenstance. Others, like Thrasymachus (*fl. c.* 427 B.C.), maintained that society is based on the subservience of the weak to the will of the strong. But more relevant to the tradition of pragmatism, Sophists such as Protagoras held that society is based on convention. They argued that following the prevailing patterns of behavior proves less frustrating than opposing them and is therefore more productive of personal happiness. The ground for taking Protagoras' advice rather than ignoring it, for saying it's true in some sense rather than false, is solely expediency. Generalizing this Protagorean point of view, the Sophists' claim for any statement being true rather than false was identical with the claim that experience shows it to be a successful guiding principle for satisfying our personal desires.

PLATO AND ARISTOTLE

The Socratic-Platonic and the Aristotelian traditions were barriers to all forms of subjectivism and relativism, and, thereby, to essential features of pragmatism. Nevertheless both Plato and Aristotle contributed much to the background of pragmatism. For example, in focusing on experience as a necessary constituent of knowledge and on the concrete particular as the real, Aristotle redirected many subsequent thinkers toward common sense and away from the extreme transcendentalism associated with Plato. Again, Plato anticipated the role of prediction in knowledge, much stressed in contemporary pragmatism, in his dialogue *Theaetetus*. Placing himself within the Protagorean framework, he showed that the radical relativism expressed in the "man is the measure" doctrine cannot properly be combined with the expediency theory of truth:

> SOCRATES: Whatever be the term used, the good or expedient is the aim of legislation, and as far as she has an opinion, the state imposes all laws with a view to the greatest expediency; can legislation have any other aim?
> THEOD.: Certainly not.
> SOCRATES: But is the aim attained always? Do not mistakes often happen?
> THEOD.: Yes, I think that there are mistakes.
> SOCRATES: The possibility of error will be more distinctly recognized, if we put the question in reference to the whole class under which the good or expedient falls. That whole class has to do with the future, and laws are passed under the idea that they will be useful in after-time; which, in other words, is the future.
> THEOD.: Very true.
> SOCRATES: Suppose now, that we ask Protagoras, or one of his disciples, a question:—O, Protagoras, we will say to him, man is, as you declare, the measure of all things—white, heavy, light: of all such things he is the judge; for he has the criterion of them in himself, and when he thinks that things are such as he experiences them to be, he thinks what is and is true to himself. Is it not so?
> THEOD.: Yes.
> SOCRATES: And do you extend your doctrine, Protagoras (as we

shall further say), to the future as well as to the present; and has he the criterion not only what in his opinion is but of what will be, and do things always happen to him as he expected? For example, take the case of heat:—When an ordinary man thinks that he is going to have a fever, and that this kind of heat is coming on, and another person, who is a physician, thinks the contrary, whose opinion is likely to prove right?—he will have a heat and fever in his own judgment, and not have a fever in the physician's judgment?

THEOD.: How ludicrous! . . .

SOCRATES: And the cook will be a better judge than the guest, who is not a cook, of the pleasure to be derived from the dinner which is in preparation; for of present or past pleasure we are not arguing; but can we say that every one will be to himself the best judge of the pleasure which will seem to be and will be to him in the future?—Nay, would not you, Protagoras, better guess which arguments in a court would convince any one of us than the ordinary man?

THEOD.: Certainly, Socrates, he used to profess in the strongest manner that he was the superior of all men in this respect.

SOCRATES: To be sure, friend: who would have paid a large sum for the privilege of talking to him, if he had really persuaded his visitors that neither a prophet nor any other man was better able to judge what will be and seem to be in the future than every one could for himself?

THEOD.: Quite true.

SOCRATES: Then we may fairly argue against your master, that he must admit one man to be wiser than another, and that the wiser is a measure. . . .[2]

EPICURUS

Epicurus (341–270 B.C.) and his disciples drew heavily on Democritean atomism, an alternative cosmology (theory about the structure of the universe) to the cosmologies developed by Plato and Aristotle, in constructing a philosophy of life. As a set of maxims to promote the happy life, this philosophy is elegant in its simplicity, though commonplace in that it merely reflects the best thought of ordinary men. However, as a systematic philosophy, it is a radical departure from the traditional quest for absolute truth. For the Epicurean, a philosophical truth is one that performs the practical function of improving the lot of its believer by minimizing pain and maximizing pleasure. The application of the above definition to a maxim such as "Limit your desires to those which are natural and necessary" may be satisfactory. But Epicurus was willing to rest an entire cosmology on the foundation of calculated pleasure and pain. He accepted the cosmology of Democritus, properly amended, rather than any more factually adequate account of nature, solely on the grounds that it functioned successfully in removing fears and frustrations, the chronic causes of human unhappiness. Thus the Epicureans conceived of philosophizing on all levels of sophistication as a practical activity, as the skillful selections of means to ends; in this respect they stand as direct ancestors of pragmatism.

But Epicureanism contributed to pragmatism in additional ways. It insisted on naturalistic rather than supernaturalistic explanation: general principles were selected on the basis of their own plausibility and their ability in combination with sense observations to account for the world of our experience. Superficially this point constituted no more than a rudimentary anticipation of the contemporary conception of a hypothesis. But, more fundamentally, it represented an extremely skillful effort to bridge the gap between the ancient rationalists and empiricists, between those who insisted that knowledge begins with self-evident principles and proceeds in a solely deductive way and those who insisted that knowledge begins with sense observations and proceeds inductively. The Epicureans criticized the first group for providing only contentless explanation and the second for providing only unexplained content. Their blend of rationalism and empiricism is evident in the pattern their basic philosophic arguments take: universal, self-evident principles (for example, "Where there is motion, there is empty space"), conjoined with particular, empirical assertions (for example, "This ball is in motion"), result in general truths about the real world (for example, "There is empty space"). We find here an insistence that all *a priori* judgments must be combined with empirical statements in order to apply to the sensible realm. But a tension develops even within the Democritean-Epicurean method of knowing. It appears in their methodological position concerning celestial phenomena: What are we to think when we are confronted with a situation in which several principles suggest themselves, none of which seems self-evident and none of which is inconsistent with our accepted principles, and all of which might be applicable to our daily lives? Epicurus comments as follows:

> We must not try to force an impossible explanation nor employ a method of inquiry like our reasoning either about the modes of life or with respect to the solution of other physical problems: witness such propositions as that the universe consists of bodies and the in-

tangible, or that "the elements are indivisible," and all such statements in circumstances where there is only one explanation which harmonizes with phenomena. For this is not so with the things above us: they admit of more than one cause of coming into being and more than one account of their nature which harmonizes with our sensations. For we must not conduct scientific investigations by means of empty assumptions and arbitrary principles, but follow the lead of phenomena: For our life has not now any place for irrational belief and groundless imaginings, but we must live free from trouble. Now all goes on without disturbance as far as regards each. Those things which may be explained in several ways so as to harmonize with what we perceive, when one admits, as we are bound to do, probable theories about them. But when one accepts one theory and rejects another, which harmonizes just as well with the phenomenon, it is obvious that he altogether leaves the path of scientific inquiry and has recourse to myth. Now we can obtain inductions of what happens above from some of the phenomena on earth: for we can observe how they come to pass, though we cannot observe the phenomena in the sky: for they may be produced in several ways. Yet we must never desert the appearance of each of these phenomena, and further, as regards what is associated with it, must distinguish those things whose production in several ways is not contradicted by phenomena on earth.[3]

From a practical point of view this passage seems adequate, and it is surprisingly modern in tone. But philosophically, it contains a tension between one conception of truth and another. When a terrestrial hypothesis is true, it is regarded as the sole possible account of a given aspect of reality; it is regarded as true in the sense of being a unique account because of its self-evident nature. In contrast, a true celestial hypothesis is regarded as merely one of a number of possible accounts of a given aspect of reality; it is regarded as a true but not necessarily unique account, because it is not self-evident. The latter definition of "hypothesis," that is, the definition which reflects the Epicurean loss of confidence in self-evidence as the sole test of truth—or even as a criterion in combination with application—is the veritable seed of modern pragmatism. When considerations of self-evidence are no longer effective in distinguishing among several hypotheses, each of which may account for present experience, it becomes necessary to find another test. One is already at hand for the Epicureans, although it is made barely explicit by them. Hypotheses are to account not only for present phenomena but also for future events—that is, they are to be tested additionally by their power of prediction. It is but a small step from this to the pragmatic view that these very properties of present and future applicabilities constitute the test of hypotheses *being true.*

AUGUSTINE AND DUNS SCOTUS

Confidence in both self-evident knowledge and empirical knowledge continued to waver, but there was no lessening of the demand for certitude. The leading thinkers of the medieval period sought to meet this demand through religious faith: Tertullian (c. 160–230) regarded revelation as the exclusive source of certain knowledge; Augustine (354–430) regarded divine faith as the indispensable precondition of certain knowledge; and Aquinas (1225–1274) regarded divine faith and natural reason as complementary sources of certain knowledge.

Tertullian is reputed to have said, *Credo quia absurdum est* [I believe it because it is absurd], a dictum which implies that reason must be rejected in favor of faith in all matters of ultimate concern. Man's quest for certainty can be realized only through divine revelation; he must come to realize the futility of seeing the world as ordered in accordance with his own finite reason. While Augustine and Aquinas both rejected Tertullian's view as too extreme, Aquinas accepted Tertullian's sharp distinction between faith and reason. However, while Tertullian rejected reason, Thomas Aquinas regarded it as complementing faith as a source of knowledge. Following Aristotle's empirical emphasis—there is nothing "in" the intellect that was not first "in" the senses—Aquinas accepted the primacy of reason in the natural realm, but insisted that the natural realm is ultimately subordinate to the supernatural realm in which faith is primary. However, to a limited extent, these two methods of knowing overlap and establish coincident truths. For example, God's existence may be established by rational argument as well as by revelation. On the other hand, the knowledge that God is triune is exclusively an article of faith and is not a demonstrable truth of natural theology.

The tradition of pragmatism is more closely related to the Augustinian tradition with its treatment of the faith-reason relationship than to either the Tertullian or Thomistic traditions. Augustine asserted *credo ut intelligam* [I believe so as to understand]. That is, he insisted that only faith—the willingness to believe—makes possible our understanding of ultimate things. A person cannot receive divine illumination unless he is receptive to it; moreover, it is only with the help of such illumination that man with his finite reason can distinguish genuine knowledge from mere opinion. In the eyes of the pragmatists, Augustine's emphasis on faith amounts to underscoring the role of volition in knowing. Yet this feature, so important for certain pragmatists, does not obviate the basic difference between Augustine and all pragmatists: his objects of knowledge are universal and eternal whereas theirs are particular and temporal.

Although generally identified with the Augustinian tradition, Duns Scotus (1270–1308) diverged from it in several ways. In the first place, he rejected the Augustinian doctrine that knowledge depends on divine illumination in favor of the Aristotelian-Thomistic view that knowledge depends on experience. Second, he rejected the Platonic-Augustinian doctrine that we can know only universals in favor of the view that we can also know particulars. At the same time he reprimanded those philosophers who speak loosely of universals is being abstractions from particulars. The correct thing to say is that *universal ideas are abstracted from particular ideas;* this is so because abstraction is a mental process and as such can only move from the *idea* of a particular to the *idea* of a universal. Thus the very notion of our acquiring knowledge of universals presupposes that we begin with knowledge of particulars. Further, he found that the capacity of the intellect is severely limited in theological matters. For example, in contrast with Aquinas, Scotus argued that it is impossible to establish by reason alone the proposition that the soul is immortal. Yet he pointed out that our belief in theological propositions such as this is commensurate with our belief in scientific propositions and concludes therefrom that reason cannot be the necessary condition for belief. Rather, it is the case that belief is a function of will. As he moved from the human level to the cosmic level, Scotus' voluntarism led him to the primacy of God's will. An important ramification of his view of God's nature—one that was to be exploited by pragmatists and others—is that the divine creation, the universe, is logically contingent in its structure rather than logically necessary, because it derives from His will and not from His reason.

BACON, COPERNICUS, AND GALILEO

We have been able to find many of the ingredients of pragmatism latent in ancient and medieval philosophy. However, it was to be a long time before these features were utilized in the construction of a full pragmatist position. For example, we observed that the Epicureans were on the brink of a modern view of the role of hypothesis and that Duns Scotus emphasized volitional activity as a prerequisite to knowledge. But, for the most part, ancient philosophers regarded the Epicurean employment of hypothesis merely as an obstacle diverting them from their quest for first principles, and medieval philosophers viewed Duns Scotus' emphasis on volition over reason simply as a mistake in priority brought about through failure to distinguish adequately between what is psychologically prior and what is logically prior. (But to admit that no divine intellection precedes God's volitional acts does not imply that God is able to will what is unintelligible.)

In moving from a consideration of the medieval to the Renaissance world view, we find thinkers in significant numbers who were concerned to overthrow rather than to emend. Francis Bacon (1561–1626) was one such man. Bacon was convinced that the deductive, intuitive, and even "primitive" empirical approaches to knowledge inherited from the Greek and medieval thinkers were productive of mere pseudoknowledge. For example, those who advocated strict deduction were so preoccupied with the logical arrangement of what they already presumably knew, that they failed to face up to the necessity of providing a method for discovering truths. Bacon insisted that only the method of induction, the method followed by contemporary natural scientists such as Harvey with his investigations of the circulation of the blood and Gilbert with his studies of magnetism, allowed one to come to grips with concrete reality. It seemed to Bacon that these men were, for the first time in the history of thought, carefully avoiding the imposition of their prejudices and predilections on the world of experience and observing nature systematically and open-mindedly. He gave elaborate directions for acquiring the objectivity essential for reliable observations and for making accurate generalizations and classifications. Although he acknowledged that men can learn only by submitting themselves to nature in this sense, he also proclaimed that their motive for doing so was to make nature submit to human ends: "the end ought to be . . . to separate and reject vain speculations and whatsoever is empty and void, and to preserve and augment whatsoever is solid and fruitful; that knowledge may not be as a curtesan, for pleasure and vanity only, or as a bond-woman, to acquire and gain to her master's use; but as a spouse, for generation, fruit and comfort." [4]

We find in Francis Bacon several of the themes of modern pragmatism clearly expressed: he underscored the basic role of observation in knowledge; he rejected all forms of rationalism as futile attempts to comprehend nature by fancies concocted by the human mind; and he emphasized that "knowledge is power," that knowledge allows us to bring nature under our control so that human ends will be served. Though Bacon regarded knowledge as primarily of practical value, he did not fully anticipate modern pragmatism. He differs from all pragmatists in his view that the observer is a passive rather than an active agent in the acquisition of knowledge and from some pragmatists in providing no role for will and feeling in his account of knowing. While Bacon caught the spirit of modern science, he failed to capture its letter. In his own way he still subscribed to the Aristotelian doctrine that the proper objects of knowledge are the essential forms or qualities that we come to know by direct observation of objects. He missed the following all-important point about science as it was being developed by scholars at the University of Paris and by the great Galileo: the objects of scientific knowledge are only those qualities of things that are capable of quantitative expression. The difference here is roughly the difference between science conceived as classificatory and descriptive and science viewed as mathematical and predictive. Like almost all thinkers of his period, he failed to grasp the directive role of hypothesis in scientific method.

During Bacon's time a spectacular dispute arose over the status of hypotheses in the field of astronomy, a field in which it was already obvious that explanation must involve more than astronomical observations. Copernicus (1473–1543) challenged the established geocentric (earth-centered) theory of Ptolemy by reviving and revising the heliocentric (sun-centred) theory. This produced a situation in which, from a mathematical point of view, there were alternative and conflicting theories capable of accounting for all available astronomical observations of the solar system. However, because of the ease of calculation, the practical advantage was largely on the side of the Copernican theory. If no more than mathematical elegance had been at stake, there would have been no serious objection to the Copernican theory. Indeed, to help him avoid difficulties with Catholic and Protestant thinkers, the theologian Osiander advised Copernicus that the proper view of such a hypothesis was to consider it solely as a "basis for calculation," a "convenient fiction." "For it is the part of the astronomer to record a picture of celestial motion with diligence and scientific observation. And then, since he can in no way perceive the true causes of these movements, it becomes his part to contrive and to invent some sort of hypotheses by which these movements can be calculated by geometric principles." [5]

But the prevailing view about conflicting hypotheses was that, although more than one might be mathematically without error, only one could be true "in reality." For the criteria for a genuine or true hypothesis must include not only mathematical soundness and agreement with observation, but also consistency with propositions about reality known to be true either theologically or philosophically. Copernicus could follow neither Osiander in viewing *all* astronomical theories as mere convenient fictions nor the majority of thinkers in viewing mathematical elegance as unrelated to the philosophical truth of a theory. Because Copernicus would not renounce the claim that his theory was relevant to reality and because his view was incompatible with the dominant world view, he was denounced.

The debate about the status of hypotheses intensified and increased in significance as the role of hypotheses in the developing sciences grew. Even the great Galileo (1564–1642), so deeply identified with the new sciences, vacillated in his judgment of the status of hypotheses. He resisted thinking about theories, in the manner of Osiander, as mere fictions concocted to account for appearances. Far from being free inventions of the mind, hypotheses seemed to him to be gleaned from controlled observations: they originate in careful experimentation, are generalized mathematically, and terminate in sense verification. But Galileo came to see that scientific method, as he practiced it, could not guarantee us genuine knowledge about the nature of reality, since, strictly speaking, it deals with mathematical regularities of the observable world and has no way of coming in contact with transempirical reality.

PASCAL

There was another response to the developing method of science that was important to the pragmatic movement. The mathematician and physicist Blaise Pascal (1623–1662), though impressed with the new sciences' mechanistic account of the universe, insisted that they were limited by their methods to the observable realm and, as a consequence, provided us with no knowledge about the ultimate principles governing the universe. He regarded it as a mistake to think that science, any more than speculative philosophy, provides us with a way to answer such questions as "Does God exist?" and "What is the nature of the human soul?" In his negative account, then, Pascal warned us against becoming totally preoccupied with scientific knowledge. But there is also a positive aspect to Pascal's position. If our feelings are encouraged rather than suppressed in the domain of ultimate or religious principles—that domain wherein reason is impotent—we may yet establish true beliefs about the ultimate nature of things. Pascal's famous wager can help us illustrate his position:

> You must either believe or not believe that God is—which will you do? Your human reason cannot say. A game is going on between you and the nature of things which at the day of judgment will bring out either heads or tails. Weigh what your gains and your losses would be if you should stake all you have on heads, or God's exis-

tence: if you win in such a case, you gain eternal beatitude; if you lose, you lose nothing at all. If there were an infinity of chances, and only one for God in this wager, still you ought to stake your all on God; for though you surely risk a finite loss by this procedure, any finite loss is reasonable, even a certain one is reasonable, if there is but the possibility of infinite gain. Go, then, and take holy water, and have masses said; belief will come and stupefy your scruples—*Cela vous fera croire et vous abêtira.* Why should you not? At bottom, what have you to lose? [6]

It is to be noted first that Pascal dismissed the possibility of providing conclusive demonstration of God's existence. Second, and more important, Pascal shows that although the consequences of believing in God's existence or nonexistence can be rationally understood, the decision to believe or not to believe falls outside the domain of reason. He suggests that this nonrational decision must be made "passionally"—that is, must be based on will rather than intellect.

The historical importance of Pascal for pragmatism is more indirect than direct. In characterizing scientific knowledge as rational (in the broad sense of deriving from mathematico-inductive techniques) and religious knowledge as primarily nonrational, he denied any attempts, on the one hand, to reduce all knowledge to scientific knowledge and, on the other, to dismiss the knowledge claims of religion as mere speculation. In a word, we may say that Pascal suggested an additional model of genuine knowledge to be placed alongside that provided by science. Thus Pascal opened up the possibility of a countermovement—a movement pursued by romanticists such as Rousseau (1712–1778) and voluntarists (those who emphasize the primacy of will) such as Schopenhauer (1788–1860) —against the extreme claims of science-oriented methodologists. This movement connects with the modern pragmatist's view that we are faced with alternative methods for belief in science and religion, and that more radical still, even within the domain of scientific inquiry belief in one theory rather than another may represent an act of volition.

KANT, COMTE, AND MILL

The theme that we have just observed in Pascal is related to aspects of Kantian philosophy. Kant's central contribution was to spell out the legislative role of mind in both sense experience and understanding. On the first of these levels, he insisted that sense experience depends not only on the nature of the given phenomena but also on the a priori (universal and necessary) forms of the sensibilia. On the second level, he insisted, in an analogous way, that theoretical or scientific knowledge depended not only on organized sense experience but also on a priori concepts which he termed "the categories of the understanding." Scientific knowledge was doubly limited: on the one hand, without the structuring framework of mind, there could be no knowledge of experience; on the other, without the content of experience, there would be no object of knowledge. Kant charged that many notable philosophers and theologians had failed to recognize the second limitation and had tried to establish by the use of reason devoid of any sensible content what is beyond the domain of understanding. Kant discussed the futility of such efforts to transcend the phenomenal realm under the title of Transcendental Dialectic. He claimed that error is inevitable when we attempt to account for the nature of the soul, the nature of the universe, and the nature and existence of God.

Furthermore, Kant insisted that the theoretical knowledge provided by pure reason is inadequate to the task of guiding us in the practical sphere, the sphere of morality. Insofar as men seek to be reasonable in *doing* as well as knowing, they must turn from pure reason to practical reason. The test of rational conduct is the *categorical imperative*, a test of the logical consistency of that which we *will*. Thus, Kant in his first formulation of the categorical imperative states: "Act on that maxim whereby you can *will* it to be a universal law." But it is clear that we can apply such a test only if we presuppose that man is morally free. Once again it is evident that a self which is to be regarded as free to choose between alternative courses of action must be distinguished from a self which, like other phenomenal events, is conceived to be governed by causal laws. This free self, the autonomous self of Kant's moral theory, falls in the noumenal rather than phenomenal realm and thus cannot be an object of theoretical knowledge. But if this is the case, recalling Kant's own warning against speculative metaphysics, we may ask, "What is the status of the autonomous will or self?" Kant's resolution of the problem is reminiscent of Pascal: the autonomous will is an item of belief or article of faith poised precariously between being an object of knowledge and being merely a fiction. Belief in such a will does not depend on its being demonstrably real or unreal but rather on our commitment to it as rational creatures who claim to be moral agents.

Kant was a precursor of pragmatism in many ways, even though it is clear that he would have opposed pragmatism as a basic philosophical position. First, as we have just seen in distinguishing between the activities of pure reason and practical reason, he acknowledged, in the latter domain, for example, that moral behavior can be accounted for only through ideas such as the autonomy of the will. The pragmatists enlarge the sphere of practical reason to the point of equating the meaning of all ideas with the functions they perform. Second, the pragmatist acknowledges the major Kantian insight of the importance of mind as an active agent in the interpretation of experience. This is not to say, however, that he acknowledges the fixed categories of mind which are basic to the Kantian epistemology. Third, although it may seem out of phase with the first point, the pragmatist acknowledges the Kantian critique of speculative metaphysics: he too insists that ideas cannot properly refer to objects outside of sense experience.

This third point, Kant's warning against speculative metaphysics, became the dominant theme of the nineteenth-century positivists, a group that directly influenced modern pragmatism. Auguste Comte (1798–1857), early positivism's most important figure, was convinced that in the most advanced disciplines such as mathematics, physics, and astronomy, man's efforts to explain and understand the universe had proceeded through three stages or modes of explanation. In the initial stage, men accounted for the physical world first as magical and later as somehow related to a supernatural being; in the second stage they substituted cosmic principles for appeals to the supernatural in their explanations and in developing a mechanistic physics based largely on the concept of force; in the final stage (now being achieved in physics) all animistic, supernaturalistic, cosmological, and causal principles are replaced with observable correlations of sense data. Comte labeled these three stages—each of which admits of substages—the "theological," "metaphysical," and "positive." With the exception of the most advanced sciences, man remains in either the first or second stage in his efforts to comprehend himself and the universe.

Comte was unwavering in his belief that the evolutionary movement through these stages represented progress, not only in knowledge proper, but also in individual and social well-being. On the assumption that there is an intimate connection between knowing and doing, he notes that our failures in promoting individual and social welfare stem from the fact that the common man has remained in the theological stage. Even the educated class has not advanced much beyond the metaphysical stage. He exhorts us, in the name of both pure knowledge and humanity, to advance the most comprehensive science of them all, the science of society ("sociology").

As a forerunner of pragmatism, Comte was important for the following reasons. (1) While following Kant's rejection of speculative metaphysics, he nevertheless viewed it as an unavoidable stage in man's endeavor to know. (2) He suggested that thought and action are unified, that both men and man are perfectible, and that evolution is not merely movement but progress. (3) With respect to the method of science, he was an extreme empiricist—that is, he believed that all knowledge is reducible to hypotheses about objects of sense and their observable relations.

John Stuart Mill (1806–1873) was also convinced that we must turn to extreme empiricism to adequately account for scientific knowledge. In contrast with Comte, however, he defended this thesis on philosophical grounds rather than by an appeal to the historical record of progress in the sciences. His argument consisted of an attack on all forms of apriorism, including not only the type that Kant called "speculative metaphysics" but also the type that Kant accepted as the very precondition of science. Mill denied the need for any innate principles or laws to make experience intelligible. Roughly speaking, we may say that on the Kantian analysis, sense experience turned out to be a necessary condition for the pervasive principles of science but was not a sufficient condition for them. Mill, on the other hand, regarded sense experience as both the necessary and sufficient condition for such principles. For example, both thinkers would agree that there are no uncaused events. Kant would do so because the causal principle is a logical precondition of intelligible experience, while Mill would do so because it is a highly confirmed empirical generalization. According to Mill, the reason for Kant's error is the difficulty in tracing a universal generalization back to its particular sources. The causal principle is the result of abstraction from multitudinous specific generalizations, each of which is itself the result of induction based on specific statements such as "This moving stone broke the window" and "That piece of iron expanded when heated." It is the hallmark of the human mind to collate and associate sense events; the conviction we have about the reliability of a given belief is a function of the frequency with which the sense events occur.

Mill argued that not even mathematical truths are *a priori*. An arithmetical proposition such as "$7 + 5 = 12$" is a generalization abstracted from the empirical process of counting, and a geometrical axiom such as "Two straight lines cannot enclose a space" is merely a statement of an experimental truth:

> Whether the axiom needs confirmation or not, it receives confirmation in almost every instant of our lives, since we cannot look at any two straight lines which intersect one another without seeing that from that point they continue to diverge more and more. Experimental proof crowds in upon us in such endless profusion, and

without one instance in which there can be even a suspicion of an exception to the rule, that we should soon have stronger ground for believing the axiom even as an experimental truth, than we have for almost any of the general truths which we confessedly learn from the evidence of our senses: . . . Where, then, is the necessity for assuming that our recognition of these truths has a different origin from the rest of our knowledge when its existence is perfectly accounted for by supposing its origin to be the same? . . . The burden of proof lies on the advocates of the contrary opinion; it is for them to point out some fact inconsistent with the supposition that this part of our knowledge of nature is derived from the same sources as every other part.[7]

NIETZSCHE

The intense attack allegedly on *a priori* knowledge that we have traced from Kant's and Comte's denial of speculative metaphysics to Mill's total rejection of the *a priori* presaged, on the technical level, the pragmatists' position on absolute and objective truth, and, on the general level, their concern to reestablish man's central position in his natural and cultural environment. During the last quarter of the nineteenth century, most philosophers were convinced that their task was to extend the principles of idealism to all fields of knowledge; most scientists—excepting those responding to theories of evolution—were convinced that their task was to extend the principles of mechanics to all phenomena. Although there was a manifest disagreement between philosopher and scientist as to the ultimate principles of knowledge, both were equally guilty, in the eyes of a minority of thinkers, of having ignored the uniqueness of the individual —his idiosyncratic actions, his creative efforts, his tragic moments—in the interest of rigid systems of thought.

Perhaps no minority voice was more strident than that of Friedrich Nietzsche (1844–1900). Influenced equally by his studies of the early heroic literature of the Greeks and by the intense philosophy of Arthur Schopenhauer, who held that the processes of nature and life express a blind ceaseless striving rather than the workings of a rationally ordered system, Nietzsche focused his full philosophical attention on man as a dynamic individual striving not only to survive but also to exploit his environment for his own ends. For Nietzsche the basic fact about any organism is that it is an objectification of the *will to power,* the will to dominate; man is essentially volitional rather than rational. However, even though man's past evolutionary success and future development are primarily functions of the intensity and priority of the will, Nietzsche does recognize that reason is valuable as an instrument of the will. In keeping with his volitional emphasis, Nietzsche goes on to depict philosophical theories, whether technical or popular, as no more than articulations of the individual temperaments of those who subscribe to them. A philosophy is for him more revelatory of human idiosyncrasies than of the nature of the world:

> Gradually I have come to realize what every great philosophy up to now has been; the personal confession of its originator, a type of involuntary and unaware memoirs; also that the moral (or amoral) intentions of each philosophy constitute the protoplasm from which each entire plant has grown. Indeed, one will do well (and wisely), if one wishes to explain to himself how on earth the more remote metaphysical assertions of a philosopher ever arose, to ask each time: what sort of morality is this (is *he*) aiming at? Thus I do not believe that a "desire for comprehension" is the father of philosophy, but rather that a quite different desire has here as elsewhere used comprehension (together with miscomprehension) as tools to serve its own ends.[8]

PEIRCE

Others among late nineteenth-century thinkers who were concerned to deny that there is a systematic body of truths, which man may somehow hope to discover, avoided Nietzsche's anti-intellectualism. Henri Poincaré (1854–1912) developed a well-reasoned position called *conventionalism* in the area of philosophy of science. He argued that scientific laws and theories are mere conventions rather than statements about reality, and that, as such, we need demand of them only that they form a logically consistent set of statements, provide the simplest possible explanation of diverse sense phenomena, and permit successful prediction. Again, Hans Vaihinger (1852–1933) may be described as having developed the doctrine of conventionalism within the framework of Kantian philosophy. Admitting that Kant's fixed categories of mind are indeed successful guides for understanding the arts and sciences, he insisted that they are real in the sense that they serve us well. However, he cautioned that their reality is no more than the reality of a convenient fiction.

While men such as these contributed to the general climate in which modern pragmatism was to develop, the actual foundations for the specific movement were being laid by the American philosopher-mathematician-scientist Charles Sanders Peirce (1839–1914). He was a many-faceted philosopher who dealt with a wide variety of problems ranging from logic and science to metaphysics and value theory. His solutions to the problems of clarifying the meaning of an intellectual concept and of justifying belief provided certain of the methodological principles designated by the name "pragmatism." [9]

Peirce's statement of the pragmatic maxim indicates his solution to the first of the two problems mentioned: "In order to ascertain the meaning of an intellectual conception one should consider what practical consequences might conceivably result by necessity from the truth of that conception; and the sum of these consequences will constitute the entire meaning of the conception." [10] The immediate implications of this statement are:

(1) To speak of the meaning of a concept is to speak of the totality of of "practical anticipations" to which it leads;
(2) To speak of a "practical anticipation" is to speak of a future event that may be empirically verified;
(3) Any idea which is not empirically verifiable (that is, without "practical anticipations") is without meaning;
(4) When we use two apparently disparate ideas that carry the same practical consequences, we are in fact employing only one idea.

The pragmatic maxim provides radically new directions for philosophical inquiry. First, it turns us away from metaphysical speculation. Henceforth, the initial and often decisive act in any philosophical dispute will be to determine whether or not apparently alternative beliefs result in different sets of empirical consequences. If they do not, then the issue is purely verbal and the philosopher's work is completed. If they do, then the issue is genuine and sufficiently clarified to permit further inquiry. In the second place, as suggested by implications (1) and (2) above, it leads us to an altered view of logic. Since all universal propositions are anticipatory of events or predictive in nature, their proper form is that of conditional rather than categorical statements. Thus, to say, "All diamonds are hard" is really to say "If something is a diamond, then it will remain unaltered under specifiable conditions of scratching, attempts at deforming, and the like."

Regarding the problem of justifying belief, Peirce insisted that inquiry is a psychological or even a biological process, initiated by the irritation of doubt that we wish to avoid and issuing into the calm of belief that we wish to achieve. "Inquiry" refers to the process by which the human organism responds to the difficulties of his social and physical environment when his instinctive and habitual responses fail. Thus man is equally engaged in inquiry whether he is Plato attempting to resolve troublesome intellectual problems or Hannibal bent on overcoming a practical difficulty.

But what method of inquiry is most effective? How may we distinguish between effective and ineffective guiding beliefs that suggest themselves when we are confronted with a problem? Peirce reviewed the various possibilities: he dismissed the "method of tenacity"—a method in which we meet the future by blindly adhering to inherited convictions—because its only defense against competing ideas is the intensity with which it is held; he dismissed the "method of authority"—a method in which we submit to an institutionally regulated set of beliefs—because it encourages the suspension of man's natural process of inquiry, and like all artifices, leads to its own dissolution; he dismisses the *"a priori* method"—a method whereby we seek to base all our beliefs on a few self-evident principles—because there are no criteria for self-evidence that insulate us from the whimsy of our underlying tastes and preferences. He accepts only the general method of science—a method that employs hypotheses but requires their empirical verification—because it guides us to relevant and objective solutions to our concrete problems. Furthermore, the scientific method alone is self-corrective in the sense that it stakes its claim on continuing rather than past success.

WILLIAM JAMES

As we have noted, Peirce's treatment of the problem of inquiry begins with a pronounced psychological orientation. It was not surprising, therefore, that William James (1842–1910), who had already distinguished himself as America's foremost psychologist, was acutely receptive to the psychological emphases in Peirce's thought. James' philosophy involved, in the first place, recasting the methodological features of Peirce's philosophy in such a way as to emphasize their psychological basis, and in the second, appending to this methodology a theory of truth that allowed for subjective as well as objective factors. The overall consequences of such a philosophical reconstruction were startling. For example, whereas Peirce supported the realist view that "there are real things whose characters are entirely independent of our opinions about them . . . ,"[11] James—and subsequently most other pragmatists—shifted to the phenomenalist view that the real world *is* as it is experienced.

Each of James' philosophical essays and books is characterized by an appeal to personal thought. The reader finds himself intimately concerned with the problem to which James is addressing himself and actively working with James toward its resolution. In this regard, his captivating literary style is well suited to his conception of philosophy: "For the philosophy which is so important in each of us is not a technical matter; it is our more or less dumb sense of what life honestly and deeply means. It is only partly got from books; it is our individual way of just seeing and feeling the total push and pressure of the cosmos." [12]

James represents the method of pragmatism as one which may be utilized by any philosophical view or position. The pragramtic method "lies in the midst of our theories, like a corridor in a hotel." [13] What James is suggesting is that no matter how expert we may become at abstract thinking and no matter what direction such thought may take, it remains the case both that the origin of our thought is always to be found in a set of concrete problematic situations, and that such theorizing is completed only through resolving these concrete issues. Furthermore, as a good empiricist, he is reminding us that concrete experience is a necessary condition of abstract thought, and that unless we are abstracting from the stream of actual experience, our ideas are without meaning. James is expanding Peirce's method for establishing belief to include the most comprehensive questions of life. Just as, in the final analysis, an engineer engages in abstract calculation because he is faced with a decision as to which beams will properly support a bridge, so, too, a speculative metaphysician develops abstractions because he encounters frustration in understanding the world about him. The difference here is one of degree rather than of kind.

But can any view as tolerant as this be of service to the philosopher? Is it not precisely his task to distinguish between genuine knowledge and pseudoknowledge? Is there to be no critical evaluation of the intellectual performances going on in the various rooms that the "corridor" of pragmatism links? James assures us that such evaluation is indeed pertinent but maintains that it is accomplished by the pragmatic theory of truth rather than by the pragmatic method as such. The latter is an appeal for open-mindedness sufficient to prevent us from prejudging the results of anyone's intellectual labor and from inhibiting anyone's creative efforts to solve problems. The former comes into play only after human inventiveness issues into creations.

The central insight of James' theory of truth is that *the truth of any hypothesis is measured by its success in resolving the problem which occasioned it.* Quite obviously, any such theory of truth must provide criteria by which to assess successful performance or successful resolution. Of all pragmatists, perhaps William James is the most sensitive to the diverse contexts in which such a theory is expected to apply. He is acutely aware of the fact that even for a given individual, thought arises from, and has consequences for, divergent aspects of his experience. For example, when I am engaged in a mathematical problem, the conditions which I lay down for a satisfactory solution to this problem differ considerably from those which I impose in attempting to resolve an artistic problem. This accounts, in part at least, for the varying formulations of the criteria of truth to be found in James' writings. Let us examine three such statements:

- (a) "Ideas (which themselves are but parts of our experience) become true just in so far as they help us to get into satisfactory relation with other parts of our experience." [14]
- (b) "True ideas are those that we can assimilate, validate, corroborate and verify. False ideas are those that we can not." [15]
- (c) "The true is the name of whatever proves itself to be good in the way of belief, and good, too, for definite, assignable reasons." [16]

Formulation (a) emphasizes that experience is continuous and organic in its nature rather than discrete and atomistic, and that true ideas are those which facilitate our entering into a harmonious relationship with the continuum of experience, as both participants and observers. In this perspective, James appears most sympathetic to disciplines such as mathematics, logic, and idealistic metaphysics, in which the primary criterion of truth is logical consistency. In formulation (b), although James is not denying that experience is a continuum and that we may respond to it conceptually at certain stages, he reminds us that our typical circumstances place us in direct perceptual relationships with concrete and specific situations. As we might expect, James here draws on the method of the experimental sciences. He portrays this method as the basic way of relating concepts to percepts: concepts or hypotheses function as predictors of percepts or concrete experiences. Truth is then constituted by the perceptual fulfillment of conceptual foresight—that is, the test of the truth of a scientific hypothesis is its verification in direct experience. In formulation (c), he stresses experience as uniquely human—that is, he does not preclude as irrelevant to our problems or to truth private experiences such as emotion, feeling, pleasure, and pain. According to James, not all problems can be resolved by either logic or experiment. Indeed, by their very nature, some of the fundamental problems in the domains of religion and morality—problems that are of utmost concern to many of us as individuals—must be settled on a nonrational basis. For example, the conditions accounting for my concern about the reality of God are emotional and volitional in character rather than logical or experimental, and, accordingly, demand an adjustment of my "passional" nature. Jamesian pragmatism calls for us to risk, solely on a volitional basis, believing or disbelieving in the hypothesis about God's reality to achieve a change in our personalities. If our volitional actions in such a circumstance result in emotional satisfaction, then our beliefs are true.

Two quite general comments seem to be in order. The first is that James' philosophy accommodates remarkably well a great variety of apparently diverse philosophical insights. Not only does it accommodate the wide-ranging ideas of mankind in the sense that it makes them effective constituents of experience (the "corridor" simile), but also and what is more significant, at the level of fundamental philosophical debate it represents a response to numerous philosophical demands. Let us indicate some of these demands. Protagoras' demand that man acknowledge himself as the measure of knowledge; Mill's denial that knowledge is rooted in anything but experience; Peirce's enunciation that a concept means what it does; Pascal's insistence that our moral and religious problems cannot be ministered to by science; Augustine's affirmation that belief necessarily precedes knowledge; the modern scientist's conviction that hypotheses are the *sine qua non* of knowledge; and the modern humanist's reminder that in the last analysis, since the purpose of knowledge is solely to serve human beings, it, like any other tool, should be judged by its performance.[17]

Our second comment is that although James' theory of truth exhibits a sensitivity to the demands of reason, it is ultimately a voluntaristic theory. For James, the mathematician's view of logical consistency as the chief criterion of truth and the scientist's view of experimental verification as the final test of truth are themselves rooted in personal preferences:

> Our belief in truth itself, for instance, that there is a truth, and that our needs and it are made for each other—What is it but a passionate affirmation of desire, in which our social system backs us up? We want to have a truth; we want to believe that our experiments and studies and discussions must put us in a continually better and better position towards it; and on this line we agree to fight out our thinking lives. But if a pyrrhonistic sceptic asks us *how we know* all this, can our logic find a reply? No! certainly it cannot. It is just one volition against another—we willing to go in for life upon a trust or assumption which he, for his part, does not care to make.[18]

John Dewey, a younger contemporary of William James, became the dominant figure in the pragmatic movement for a quarter of a century.

His influence was great not only among philosophers but also among educators and social scientists.

On Dewey's interpretation, the significance of James' pragmatism resides less in his ultimate acknowledgment of will than in his recognition of reason as the creative instrument which "helps to make the world other than it would have been without it." Dewey's pragmatism, which he preferred to all *instrumentalism*, is a "precise logical theory of concepts, of judgments and inferences in their various forms by considering primarily how thought functions in the experimental determinations of future consequences." [19] *Experience and Nature*, from which our first reading is selected, provides a clear and fully developed statement of this view.

Impressed both by Dewey's logic and by developments in formal logic and axiomatic theory that are quite independent of the pragmatic movement, C. I. Lewis (1883–1965) argued that in combination, these two approaches provide an adequately sophisticated account of knowledge. He develops this thesis in the essay "The Pragmatic Conception of the *A Priori*," which we include in its entirety.

John Dewey: NATURE, MEANS, AND KNOWLEDGE

> DEWEY *sets the stage for an appreciation of the modern scientific method of inquiry by reviewing the essential features of the Greek approach to knowledge. He charges that the Greeks typically disparaged the instrumentalities of change—that is, the means whereby ends are achieved—on the grounds that change is symptomatic of imperfection. To say that something is changing in any way is to assert that it is in the process of rectifying its deficiencies, that the stage from which it changes is inferior to the ultimate form which it can fulfill. Furthermore, the Greeks presuppose that the proper objects of knowledge are these ultimate ends; that is, the objects of knowledge are regarded as unchanging and therefore as different in kind from the features of ordinary experience. The method of modern science stands as a repudiation of the Greek assumption that knowledge is both unchanging in its nature and detached from experience.*

The passages below come from Dewey's Experience and Nature, *1925, pp. 123–146, 149–151. They are reprinted here by kind permission of Open Court Publishing Co., La Salle, Illinois.*

Classic philosophy was conceived in wonder, born in leisure and bred in consummatory contemplation. Hence it noted the distinction between objects consummatory or final in the fine arts and instrumental and operative in the industrial. It then employed the distinction to interpret nature in terms of a dialectical physics. Useful arts are *possible* because things have observable efficiencies; but they are *necessary* because of lack, privation, imperfection, Non-being. This deficiency is manifest in sensation and appetite; the very transitiveness of materials which renders them capable of transformation into serviceable forms is evidence that they too lack fullness of Being. Things have potentialities or are instrumental because they are not Being, but rather Being in process of becoming. They lend themselves to operative connections that fulfill them because they are not themselves Real in an adequate sense. This point of view protected Greek thought from that modern onesidedness which conceives tools as mere subjective conveniences. But the safeguard was at the expense of the introduction into nature of a split in Being itself, its division into some things which are inherently defective, changing, relational, and other things which are inherently perfect, permanent, self-possessed. Other dualisms such as that between sensuous appetite and rational thought, between the particular and universal, between the mechanical and the telic, between experience and science, between matter and mind, are but the reflections of this primary metaphysical dualism.

The counterpart of the conversion of esthetic objects into objects of science, into the one, true and good, was the conversion of operative and transitive objects into things which betray absence of full Being. This absence causes their changing instability which is, none the less, after the model of materials of the useful arts, potentially useful for ends beyond themselves. The social division into a laboring class and a leisure class, between industry and esthetic contemplation, became a metaphysical division into things which are mere means and things which are ends. Means are menial, subservient, slavish; and ends liberal and final; things as means testify to inherent defect, to dependence, while ends testify to independent and intrinsically self-sufficing being. Hence the former can never be known in themselves but only in their subordination to objects that are final, while the latter can be known in and through themselves by self-enclosed reason. Thus the identification of knowledge with esthetic contemplation and the exclusion from science of trial, work, manipulation and administration of things, comes full circle.

The ingratitude displayed by thinkers to artists, who by creation of harmoniously composed objects supplied idealistic philosophy with empirical models of their ultimately real objects, was shown in even greater measure to artisans. The accumulated results of the observations and procedures of farmers, navigators, builders furnished matter-of-fact information about natural events, and also supplied the pattern of logical and metaphysical subordination of change to directly possessed and enjoyed fulfillments. While thinkers condemned the industrial class and despised labor, they borrowed from them the facts and the conceptions that gave form and substance to their own theories. For apart from processes of art there was no basis for introducing the idea of fulfillment, realization, into the notion of end nor for interpreting antecedent operations as potentialities.

Yet we should not in turn exhibit ingratitude. For if Greek thinkers did not achieve science, they achieved the idea of science. This accomplishment was beyond the reach of artist and artisan. For no matter how solid the content of their own observations and beliefs about natural events, that content was bound down to occasions of origin and use. The relations they recognized were of local areas in time and place. Subject-matter underwent a certain distortion when it was lifted out of this context, and placed in a realm of eternal forms. But the idea of knowledge was thereby liberated, and the scheme of logical relationships among existences held up as an ideal of inquiry. Thinking was uncovered as an enterprise having its own objects and procedures; and the discovery of thought as method of methods in all arts added a new dimension to all subsequent experience. It would be an academic matter to try to balance the credit items due to the discovery of thought and of logic as a free enterprise, against the debit consequences resulting from the hard and fast separation of the instrumental and final.

A great change took place in Greek experience between the time of Homer and Hesiod and the fifth century before Christ. The earlier period evinces a gloomy temper of life. The sense of the sovereignty of fortune, largely ill-fortune, is prevalent. The temper is shown by such quotations as the following: "Thus the gods have decided for unhappy mortals that men should live misery while they themselves live free from suffering." "A thousand woes traverse the abode of man; the earth is gorged with them and the sea filled; day and night bring grief. They come in silence for prudent Zeus has taken away their voice." "Men favored by Hecate have no need for knowledge, memory or effort to achieve success; she acts alone without the assistance of her favorites." Divination of the intent of unseen powers and pious sacrifice are man's only resource, but this is of no avail. Reckon no man happy till after his death. The gods have indeed bestowed arts on man to ameliorate his hard lot, but their issue is uncertain. The end rests with the gods and with fate who rules even the gods, a fate to be neither bribed with offerings nor yet compelled by knowledge and art.

By the days of the Sophists and their great Athenian successors there is marked change in mood. The conditions then existed that have occasioned the myth of Greek serenity. The Sophists taught that man could largely control the fortunes of life by mastery of the arts. No one has exceeded Plato in awareness of present ills. But since they are due to ignorance and opinion, they are remediable, he holds, by adequate knowledge. Philosophy should terminate in an art of social control. The great rival of Plato taught that fortune "is a fantom which men have invented to excuse their own imprudence. Fortune does not easily resist thought and for the most part an instructed and far-seeing soul will attain its goal." In short, arts based on knowledge cooperate with nature and render it amenable to human happiness. The gods recede into twilight. Divination has a powerful competitor. Worship becomes moral. Medicine, war, and the crafts desert the temple and the altar of the patron-god of the guild, as inventions, tools, techniques of action and works multiply.

This period of confident expansion did not endure. It soon gave way; it was succeeded by what Gilbert Murray has so well named the failure of nerve, and a return to the supernatural, philosophy changing from a supreme art into a way of access to the supernatural. Yet the episode even if brief is more than historically significant. It manifests another way open to man in the midst of an uncertain, incomplete and precarious universe; another way, that is, in addition to that of celebrating such moments of respite and festal joy as occur in the troubled life of man. Through instrumental arts, arts of control based on study of nature, objects which are fulfilling and good may be multiplied and rendered secure. This road after almost two millennia of obscuration and desertion was refound and retaken; its rediscovery marks what we call the modern era. Consideration of the significance of science as a resource in a world of mixed uncertainty, peril, and of uniformity, stability, furnishes us with the theme of this chapter of experience.

That the sciences were born of the arts, the physical sciences of the crafts and technologies of healing, navigation, war and the working of wood, metals, leather, flax and wool; the mental sciences of the arts of political management, is I suppose, an admitted fact. The distinctively intellectual attitude which marks scientific inquiry was generated in efforts at controlling persons and things so that consequences, issues, outcomes would be more stable and assured. The first step away from oppression by immediate things and events was taken when man employed tools and appliances, for manipulating things so as to render them contributory to desired objects. In responding to things not in their immediate qualities but for the sake of ulterior results, immediate qualities are dimmed, while those features which are signs, indices of something else, are distinguished. A thing is more significantly what it makes possible than what it immediately is. The very conception of cognitive meaning, intellectual significance, is that things in their immediacy are subordinated to what they portend and give evidence of. An intellectual sign denotes that a thing is not taken immediately but is referred to something that may come in consequence of it. Intellectual meanings may themselves be appropriated, enjoyed and appreciated; but the character of intellectual meaning is instrumental. Fortunate for us is it that tools and their using can be directly enjoyed; otherwise all work would be drudgery. But this additive fact does not alter the definition of a tool; it remains a thing used as an agency for some concluding event.

The first groping steps in defining spatial and temporal qualities, in transforming purely immediate qualities of local things into generic relationships, were taken through the arts. The finger, the foot, the unit of walking were used to measure space; measurements of weight originated in the arts of commercial exchange and manufacture. Geometry, beginning as agricultural art, further emancipated space from being a localized quality of immediate extensity. But the radically different ways of conceiving geometry found in ancient and in modern science is evidence of the slowness of the process of emancipation of even geometrical forms from direct or esthetic traits. In Greek astronomy the intrinsic qualities of figures always dominated their instrumental significance in inquiry; they were forms to which phenomena had to conform instead of means of indirect measurements. Hardly till our own day did spatial relations get emancipated from esthetic and moral qualities, and become wholly intellectual and relational, abstracted from immediate qualifications, and thereby generalized to their limit.

Anything approaching a history of the growth of recognition of things in their intellectual or instrumental phase is far beyond our present scope. We can only point out some of its net results. In principle the step is taken whenever objects are so reduced from their status of complete objects as to be treated as signs or indications of other objects. Enter upon this road and the time is sure to come when the appropriate object-of-knowledge is stripped of all that is immediate and qualitative, of all that is final, self-sufficient. Then it becomes an anatomized epitome of just and only those traits which are of indicative or instrumental import. Abstraction is not a psychological incident; it is a following to its logical conclusion of interest in those phases of natural existence which are dependable and fruitful signs of other things; which are means of prediction by formulation in terms implying other terms. Self-evidence ceases to be a characteristic trait of the fundamental objects of either sensory or noetic objects. Primary propositions are statements of objects in terms which procure the simplest and completest forming and checking of other propositions. Many systems of axioms and postulates are possible, the more the merrier, since new propositions as consequences are thus brought to light. Genuine science is impossible as long as the object esteemed for its own intrinsic qualities is taken as the object of knowledge. Its completeness, its immanent meaning, defeats its use as indicating and implying.

Said William James, "Many were the ideal prototypes of rational order: teleological and esthetic ties between things . . . as well as logical and mathematical relations. The most promising of these things at first were of course the richer ones, the more sentimental ones. The baldest and least promising were mathematical ones; but the history of the latter's application is a history of steadily advancing successes, while that of the sentimentally richer ones is one of relative sterility and failure. Take those aspects of phenomena which interest you as a human being most . . . and barren are all your results. Call the things of nature as much as you like by sentimental moral and esthetic names, no natural consequences follow from the naming. . . . But when you give the things mathematical and mechanical names and call them so many solids in just such positions, describing just such paths with just such velocities, all is changed. . . . Your 'things' realize the consequences of the names by which you classed them."

A fair interpretation of these pregnant sentences is that as long as objects are viewed telically, as long as the objects of the truest knowledge, the most real forms of being, are thought of as ends, science does not advance. Objects are possessed and appreciated, but they are not known. To know, means that men have become willing to turn away from precious possessions; willing to let drop what they own, however precious, in behalf of a grasp of objects which they do not as yet own. Multiplied and secure ends depend upon letting go existent ends, reducing them to indicative and implying means. The great historic obstacle to science was unwillingness to make the surrender, lest moral, esthetic and religious objects suffer. To large groups of persons, the bald and dry objects of natural science are still objects of fear. The mechanical or mathematical-logical object presents itself as a rival of the ideal and final object. Then philosophy becomes a device for conserving "the spiritual values of the universe" by devices of interpretation which converts the material and mechanical into mind. By means of a dialectic of the implications of the possibility of knowledge, the physical is transformed into something mental, psychic—as if psychic existence were sure to be inherently more ideal than the physical.

The net result of the new scientific method was conception of nature as a mathematical-mechanical object. If modern philosophy, reflecting the tendencies of the new science, abolished final causes from nature, it was because concern with qualitative ends, already existing objects of possession and enjoyment, blocked inquiry, discovery and control, and ended in barren dialectical disputes about definitions and classifications. A candid mind can hardly deny that sensory qualities, colors, moist and dry, hard and soft, light and heavy are genuine natural ends. In them the potentialities of the body are brought into functioning, while the activity of the body thus achieved brings in turn to completion potentialities in nature outside of the body. Nevertheless the theory that final objects are the appropriate objects of knowledge, in assimilating knowledge to esthetic contemplation had fatal consequences for science. All natural phenomena had to be known in terms of qualities. Hot and cold, wet and dry, up and down, light and heavy were things to know with and by. They were essential forms, active principles of nature. But Galileo and his scientific and philosophical followers (like Descartes and Hobbes) reversed the method by asserting that these sensory forms are things to be known, challenges to inquiry, problems, not solutions nor terms of solution. The assertion was a general one; it necessitated search for objects of knowledge. Dependable material with which to know was found in a different realm of being; in spatial relations, positions, masses, mathematically defined, and in motion as change of space having direction and velocity. Qualities were no longer things to do with; they were things already done, effects, requiring to be known by statement and description in mathematical and mechanical relations. The only world which defines and describes and explains was a world of masses in motion, arranged in a system of Cartesian coordinates.

When we view experientially this change, what occurs is the kind of thing that happens in the useful arts when natural objects, like crude ores, are treated as materials for getting something else. Their character ceases to lie in their immediate qualities, in just what they are and as directly enjoyed. Their character is now representative; some pure metal, iron, copper, etc. is their essence, which may be extracted as their "true" nature, their "reality." To get at this reality many existent constituents have to be got rid of. From the standpoint of the object, pure metal, these things to be eliminated are "false," irrelevant and obstructive. They stand in the way, and in the existent thing those qualities are alone significant which indicate the ulterior objective and which offer means for attaining it.

Modern science represents a generalized recognition and adoption of the point of view of the useful arts, for it proceeds by employment of a similar operative technique of manipulation and reduction. Physical science would be impossible without the appliances and procedures of separation and combinations of the industrial arts. In useful arts, the consequence is increase of power, multiplication of ends appropriated and enjoyed, and an enlarged and varied flexibility and economy in means used to achieve ends. Metal can be put to thousands of uses, while the crude ore can only be beheld for whatever esthetic qualities it happens to present, or be hurled bodily at game or an enemy. Reduction of natural existences to the status of means thus presents nothing inherently adverse to possessed and appreciated ends, but rather renders the latter a more secure and extensive affair.

Why then has it been so often assumed in modern philosophy that the advance of physical science has created a serious metaphysical problem; namely, that of the relation of a mechanical world as the object of knowledge to ends; the reconciliation of antithetical worlds of description and appreciation? In empirical fact, the advance of mechanistic science has multiplied and diversified ends, has increased wants and satisfactions, and has multiplied and diversified the means of attaining them. Why the problem? There are two historical empirical reasons to be given in answer. In the first place, the Aristotelian metaphysics of potentiality and actuality, of objects consummatory of natural processes, was intricately entangled with an astronomy and physics which had become incredible. It was also entangled with doctrines and institutions in politics and economics which were fast getting out of relationship to current social needs. The simplest recourse was to treat the classic tradition as the Jonah of science and throw it bodily overboard. The method was imperious and impatient, but it served a need. By a single act it relieved scientific inquiries of notions that were hampering, even paralyzing investigation into nature and that were limiting new practices by outworn sanctions.

By itself alone, however, this cause would hardly have created more than a passing historic episode. The reason that rendered the abandonment of any theory of natural ends something more than a gesture of impatient haste lies in the persistence of the classic theory of knowledge. Greek thought regarded possession, contemplation as the essence of science, and thought of the latter as such a complete possession of reality as incorporates it with mind. The notion of knowledge as immediate possession of Being was retained when knowing as an actual affair radically altered. Even when science had come to include a method of experimental search and finding, it was still defined as insight into, grasp of, real being as such, in comparison with which other modes of experience are imperfect, confused and perverted. Hence a serious problem. If the proper object of science is a mathematico-mechanical world (as the achievements of science have proved to be the case) and if the object of science defines the true and perfect reality (as the perpetuation of the classic tradition asserted), then how can the objects of love, appreciation— whether sensory or ideal—and devotion be included within true reality?

Efforts to answer this question constitute a large part of the technical content of modern metaphysical thought. Given the premises, its import covers almost everything from the problem of freedom, ideals and ideas to the relation of the physical and the mental. With respect to the latter, there is the causal problem of their existential relation; and there is the cognitive problem of how one order of existence can refer to the other in such a way as to know it. We are not concerned here with the voluminous literature and various (controversial and controverted) points of view that have emerged. It is pertinent, however, to recall the source of the problems; and to register the statement that without the underlying dubious assumption, we are not called upon to find solutions; they cease to be perplexities as soon as certain premises are surrendered. The premise which concerns us here is that science is grasp of reality in its final self-sufficing form. If the proper object of knowledge has the character appropriate to the subject matter of the useful arts, the problem in question evaporates. The objects of science, like the direct objects of the arts, are an order of relations which serve as tools to effect immediate havings and beings. Goods, objects with qualities of fulfillment are the natural fruition of the discovery and employment of means, when the connection of ends with a sequential order is determined. Immediate empirical things are just what they always were: endings of natural histories. Physical science does not set up another and rival realm of antithetical existence; it reveals the state or order upon which the occurrence of immediate and final qualities depends. It adds to casual having of ends an ability to regulate the date, place and manner of their emergence. Fundamentally, the assertion that this condition of ordered relationships is mathematic, mechanical, is tautology; that is, the meaning of anything which is such that perception and use of it enables us to regulate consequences or attain terminal qualities is a mathematical, mechanical—or if you please—logical order. If we did not discover those which we have found, we should have to find another, if deliberate planning and execution are to occur.

If science be perfect grasp, or envisagement of being, and if science terminate with a mathematico-mechanical world, then, in the second place, we have upon our hands the problems of reality and appearance. In ancient thought, the problem occurred in a simple form. There were higher and lower forms of knowledge; but all stages of knowledge were alike realizations of some level of Being, so that appearance in contrast with reality meant only a lower degree of Being, being imperfect or not fully actualized. In modern science, with its homogeneous natural world, this contrast of perfect and defective Being is meaningless. It is a question of knowledge or error, not of differences of cognitive grasp in one to one correspondence with different levels of Being. In the ancient view, sensation and opinion are good forms of knowledge in their place; what they know, their place, is just an inferior grade of Being. To the modern mind, they are not knowledge of anything unless they are brought to agree with the deliverances of science. Is matter an appearance of mind as true reality? Or is the mental only an appearance of the physical as the final reality? Or are both of them appearances of some still more ultimate reality?

Such questions are as necessary as they are unanswerable, given the premise which defines knowledge as direct grasp and envisagement. They vanish if the proper objects of science are nature in its instrumental characters. Any immediate object then becomes for inquiry, as something to be known, an appearance. To call it "appearance" denotes a functional status, not a kind of existence. Any quality in its immediacy is doubly an appearance. In the first place it appears; it is evident, conspicuous, outstanding, it is, to recur to language already used, had. A thing appears in the sense in which a bright object appears in a dark room, while other things remain obscure, hidden. The affair is one of physical and physiological limits of vision and audition, etc. We see islands floating as it were upon the sea; we call them islands because of their apparent lack of continuity with the medium that immediately surrounds them. But they are projections of the very earth upon which we walk; the connecting links do not ordinarily appear; they are there, but are not had. The difference between the appearing and the unappearing is of immense practical and theoretical import, imposing upon us need for inference, which would not exist if things appeared to us in their full connections, instead of with sharply demarcated outlines due to limits of perceptibility. But the ground of the difference is as physical as that between solid, liquid and gas. The endings of organic events, seeing, hearing, etc. are for the time being, or immediately, endings of the history of all natural events. To re-establish a connection of histories within a longer course of events and a more inclusive state of affairs, requires delving, probing, and extension by artifice beyond the apparent. To link the things which are immediately and apparitionally had with one another by means of what is not immediately apparent and thus to create new historic successions with new initiations and new endings depends in turn upon the system of mathematical-mechanical systems which form the proper objects of science as such.

The empirical basis of the distinction between the apparent and the nonapparent thus lies in the need for inference. When we take the outstandingly evident as evidence, its status is subordinate to that of unperceived things. For the nonce, it is a way of establishing something more fundamental than it is itself with respect to the object of inquiry. If we conceive of the world of immediately apparent things as an emergence of peaks of mountains which are submerged except as to their peaks or endings, and as a world of initial climbings whose subsequent career emerges above the surface only here and there and by fits and starts; and if we give attention to the fact that any ability of control whatever depends upon ability to unite these disparate appearances into a serial history, and then give due attention to the fact that connection into a consecutive history can be effected only by means of a scheme of constant relationships (a condition met by the mathematical-logical-mechanical objects of physics), we shall have no difficulty in seeing why it is that the immediate things from which we start lend themselves to interpretation as signs or appearances of the objects of physics; while we also recognize that it is only with respect to the function of instituting connection that the objects of physics can be said to be more "real." In the total situation in which they function, they are means to weaving together otherwise disconnected beginnings and endings into a consecutive history. Underlying "reality" and surface "appearance" in this connection have a meaning fixed by the function of inquiry, not an intrinsic metaphysical meaning.

To treat therefore the object of science—which in effect is the object of physics—as a complete and self-sufficient object, the end of knowing, is to burden ourselves with an unnecessary and insoluble problem. It commits us on one side to a realm of immediately apparent things, the socalled perceptual order which is an order only by courtesy, and on the other to a realm of inferred and logically constructed real objects. These two realms are rivals of each other. If knowledge is possession or grasp, then there are two incompatible kinds of knowledge, one sensible, the other rational. Which is the genuine article and which the counterfeit? If we say sensible knowledge is the genuine, then we are committed to phenomenalism of a somewhat chaotic kind, unless we follow Berkeley and invoke deity to hold the immediate things together.

If we say rational knowledge is the genuine article, then true reality becomes the reality of materialism or of logical realism or of objective idealism, according to training and temperament. To follow the clues of experience is to see that the socalled sensible world is a world of immediate beginnings and endings; not at all an affair of cases of knowledge but a succession of qualitative events; while the socalled conceptual order is recognized to be the proper object of science, since it constitutes the scheme of constant relationships by means of which spare, scattered and casual events are bound together into a connected history. These emergent immediate events remain the beginning and the end of knowledge; but since their occurrence is one with their being sensibly, affectionally and appreciatively had, they are not themselves things known. That the qualities and characters of these immediate apparitions are tremendously modified when they are linked together by "physical objects"—that is, by means of the mathematical-mechanical objects of physics—is a fact of the same nature as that a steel watch-spring is a modification of crude iron ore. The objects of physics subsist precisely in order to bring about this transformation—to change, that is, casual endings into fulfillments and conclusions of an ordered series, with the development of meaning therein involved.

Practically all epistemological discussion depends upon a sudden and unavowed shift to and fro from the universe of having to the universe of discourse. At the outset, ordinary empirical affairs, chairs, tables, stones, sticks, etc., are called physical objects—which is obviously a term of theoretical interpretation when it so applied, carrying within itself a complete metaphysical commitment. Then physical objects are defined as the objects of physics, which is, I suppose, the only correct mode of designation. But such objects are clearly very different things from the plants, lamps, chairs, thunder and lightning, rocks, etc. that were first called physical objects. So another transformation phantasmagoria in the tableau is staged. The original "physical things," ordinary empirical objects, not being the objects of physics, are not physical at all but mental. Then comes the grand dissolving climax in which objects of physics are shown as themselves hanging from empirical objects now dressed up as mental, and hence as themselves mental.

Everything now being mental, and the term having lost its original contrasting or differential meaning, a new and different series of transformation scenes is exhibited. Immediate empirical things are resolved into hard sensory data, which are called the genuine physical things, while the objects of physical science are treated as are logical constructions; all that remains to constitute mental existence is images and feelings. It is not necessary to mention other permutations and combinations, familiar to the student of theories of the possibility of knowledge. The samples mentioned are illustrations of the sort of thing which happens when the having of immediate objects, whether sensible, affectional or appreciatoral, is treated as a mode of knowledge.

If objects which are colored, sonorous, tactile, gustatory, loved, hated, enjoyed, admired, which are attractive and repulsive, exciting, indifferent and depressive, in all their infinitely numerous modes, are beginnings and endings of complex natural affairs, and if physical objects (defined as objects of physical science) are constituted by a mathematical-mechanical order; then physical objects instead of involving us in the predicament of having to choose between opposing claimants to reality, have precisely the characters which they should have in order to serve effectively as means for securing and avoiding immediate objects. Four of these characters may be noted. First, immediate things come and go; events in the way of direct seeing, hearing, touching, liking, enjoying, and the rest of them are in rapid change; the subject-matter of each has a certain uniqueness, unrepeatedness. Spatial-temporal orders, capable of mathematical formulation are, by contrast, constant. They present stability, recurrence at its maximum, raised to the highest degree. Qualitative affairs like red and blue, although in themselves unlike, are subject to comparison in terms of objects of physics; on the basis of connection with orders of sequence, a qualitative spectrum or scale becomes a scheme of numerable variations of a common unit.

The second character of objects of science follows from this feature. The possibility of regulating the occurrence of any event depends upon the possibility of reconstituting substitutions. By means of the latter, a thing which is within grasp is used to stand for another thing which is not immediately had, or which is beyond control. The technique of equations and other functions characteristic of modern science is, taken generically, a method of thoroughgoing substitutions. It is a system of exchange and mutual conversion carried to its limit. The cognitive result is the homogeneous natural world of modern science, in its contrast with the qualitatively heterogeneous world of ancient science; the latter being made up of things different in inherent kinds and in qualities of movement, such as up and down, lateral and circular, and heterogeneous according to periods of time, such as earlier and later. These become amenable to transformations in virtue of reciprocal substitutions.

In the third place, objects of knowledge as means explain the importance attached to elements, or numerically discrete units. Control of beginnings and ends by means is possible only when the individual, the unique, is treated as a composite of parts, made by sequential differentiations and integrations. In its own integrity an immediate thing just exists as it exists; it stays or it passes; it is enjoyed or suffered. That is all that can be said. But when it is treated as the outcome of a complex convergence or coincidence of a large number of elementary independent variables, points, moments, numerical units, particles of mass and energy or more elementary space-times (which in spite of their independence are capable of one to one correspondence with one another), the situation changes. The simples or elements are in effect the last pivots upon which regulation of conditions turns; last, that is to say, as far as present appliances permit.

Preoccupation with elementary units is as marked in logic, biology, and psychology, as in physics and chemistry. Sometimes it seems to have resulted in taking merely dialectical entities for actual unitary elements; but that is not logically necessary. Such an outcome signifies only that the right units were not found. Serious objection holds when the instrumental character of the elements is forgotten; and they are treated as independent, ultimate; when they are treated as metaphysical finalities, insoluble epistemological problems result. Whatever are designated as elements, whether logical, mathematical, physical or mental, depend especially upon the existence of immediate, qualitatively integral objects. Search for elements starts with such empirical objects already possessed. Sensory data, whether they are designated psychic or physical, are thus not starting points; they are the products of analysis. Denial of the primary reality of immediate empirical objects logically terminates in an abrogation of the reality of elements; for sensory data, or sensa and sensibilia, are the residua of analysis of these primary things. Moreover every step of analysis depends upon continual reference to these empirical objects. Drop them from mental view for a moment and any clew in the search for elements is lost. Unless macroscopic things are recognized, cells, electrons, logical elements become meaningless. The latter have meaning only as elements *of*. Since, for example, only propositions have implications, a proposition cannot be a mere conjunction of terms; terms having no implications, a proposition so formed would have no significance. Terms must have a significance and since that they have only in a proposition, they depend upon some prior unity. In similar fashion, a purely unitary physical element would have no efficacy; it could not act or be acted upon.

Lastly, the instrumental nature of objects of knowledge accounts for the central position of laws, relations. These are the formulations of the regularities upon which intellectual and other regulation of things as immediate apparitions depends. Variability of elements in mathematical science is specious; elements vary independently of one another, but not independently of a relation to others, the relation of law being the constancy among variations. It is a truism that mathematics is the method by which elements can be stated as terms in constant relations, and be subjected to equations and other functions of transformation and substitution. An element is appropriately represented by a mathematical variable; for since any variable falls within some equation, it is treated as a constant function of other variables. The shift from variability to constancy is repeated as often as is needed. It is thus only *pro forma* that the variable is variable. It is not variable in the sense in which unique individualized existences are variable. The inevitable consequence is the subsection of individuals or unique modes of external relations, to laws of uniformity; that is to say, the elimination of individuality. Bear in mind the instrumental nature of the relation of elements, and this abrogation of individuality merely means a temporary neglect—as abstracted gaze—in behalf of attending to conditions under which individualities present themselves. Convert the objects of knowledge into real things by themselves, and individuals become anomalous or unreal; they are not individualized for science but are instances, cases, specimens, of some generical relation or law. . . .

The entire discussion has but a single point. It aims to show that the problems which constitute modern epistemology with its rival, materialistic, spiritualistic, dualistic doctrines, and rival realistic, idealistic, representational theories; and rival doctrines of relation of mind and matter occasionalism, pre-established harmony, parallelism, panpsychism, etc., have a single origin in the dogma which denies temporal quality to reality as such. Such a theory is bound to regard things which are causally explanatory as superior to results and outcomes; for the temporal dependence of the latter cannot be disguised, while "causes" can be plausibly converted into independent beings, or laws, or other non-temporal forms. As has been pointed out, this denial of change to true Being had its source in bias in favor of objects of contemplative enjoyment, together with a theory that such objects are the adequate subject-matter of science.

The bias is spontaneous and legitimate. The accompanying theory of knowledge and reality is a distortion. The legitimate implication of the preference for worthy objects of appreciation is the necessity of art, or control of the sequential order upon which they depend; a necessity which carries with it the further implication that this order, which is to be discovered by inquiry and confirmed by experimental action, is the proper object of knowledge. Such a recognition would, however, have conceded the dependence of the contemplative functions of the leisure class upon the appliances and technique of artisans—among whom all artists were included. And since in olden time the practice of the arts was largely routine, fixed by custom and ready-made patterns, such a recognition would have carried with it the need of transforming the arts themselves, if the occurrence of ends was to be a real fulfillment, a realization, and not a contingent accident. The introduction of inventive thought into the arts and the civil emancipation of the industrial class at last made the transformation possible.

When the appliances of a technology that had grown more deliberate were adopted in inquiry, and the lens, pendulum, magnetic needle, lever were used as tools of knowing, and their functions were treated as models to follow in interpreting physical phenomena, science ceased to be identified with appreciative contemplation of noble and ideal objects, was freed from subjection to esthetic perfections, and became an affair of time and history intelligently managed. Ends were in consequence no longer determined by physical accident and social traditions. Anything whatsoever for which means could be found was an end to be averted or to be secured. Liberation from a fixed scheme of ends made modern science possible. In large affairs, practice precedes the possibility of observation and formulation; the results of practice must accumulate before mind has anything to observe. There is little cause for wonder therefore that long after the objects of science had become instrumentalities rather than things in their own rights, the old theory persisted, and philosophy spent much of its effort in the effort to reconcile the traditional theory of knowledge as immediate possession with the terms and conclusions of the new method of practice. . . .

John Dewey: THE QUESTION OF METHOD

> ACCORDING to Dewey, modern science represents a systematic employment of ideas as hypotheses with which to initiate and direct activities toward ends which we, as participants in the natural environment, seek. The Greek notion of "science" as a system in which each particular object can be classified as an inferior instance of an essential form is entirely abandoned. Dewey depicts the scientist as a man who exhibits intelligence through intentionally controlling the environment of which he is a dynamic part, as a man who has outgrown the dream that he can be an earthly spectator of an eternal order.
>
> "The Question of Method" was published in Dewey's Experience and Nature in 1925 (pp. 152–165) and is reprinted here with the kind permission of Open Court Publishing Co., La Salle, Illinois.

We are brought to the question of method. In ancient science the essence of science was demonstration; the life blood of modern science is discovery. In the former, reflective inquiry existed for the sake of attaining a stable subject-matter; in the latter systematized knowledge exists in practice for the sake of stimulating, guiding and checking further inquiries. In ancient science, "learning" belonged in the realm of inferior being, of becoming, change; it was transitive, and ceased in the actualization of final and fixed objects. It was thought of after the analogy of master and disciple; the former was already in possession of the truth, and the learner merely appropriated what already is there in the store house of the master. In modern science, learning is finding out what nobody has previously known. It is a transaction in which nature is teacher, and in which the teacher comes to knowledge and truth only through the learning of the inquiring student.

Characteristic differences in logic thus accompany the change from "knowledge" whose subject-matter is final affairs to knowledge dealing with instrumental objects. Where the objects of knowledge are taken to be final, perfect, complete, metaphysical fulfillments of nature, proper method consists in definition and classification; learning closes with demonstration of the rational necessity of definitions and classifications. Demonstration is an exhibition of the everlasting, universal, final and fixed nature of objects. Investigation denoted merely the accumulation of material with which to fill in gaps in an antecedent ready-made hierarchy of species. Discovery was merely the perception that some particular material hitherto unclassified by the learner came under a universal form already known. The universal is already known because given to thought; and the particular is already known, because given to perception; learning merely brings these two given forms into connection, so that what is "discovered" is the subsumption of particular under its universal.

Apart from their theories, or in spite of them, the Greeks were possessed by a lively curiosity, and their practice was better than their logic. In the medieval Christian period, the logic was taken literally. Revelation, scriptures, church fathers and other authentic sources, increased the number of given universal truths, and also of given particular facts and events. The master-teacher was God, who taught not through the dim instrumentality of rational thought alone, but directly through official representatives. The form of apprehension of truth remained the demonstrative syllogism; the store of universal truths was supplemented by the gracious gift of revelation, and the resources of the minor premise extended by divinely established historic facts. Truth was given to reason and faith; and the part of the human mind was to humble itself to hearken, accept and obey.

The scheme was logically complete; it carried out under new circumstances the old idea that the highest end and good of man is knowledge of true Being, and that such knowledge in the degree of its possession effects an assimilation of the mind to the reality known. It added to old theoretical premises such institutions and practices as were practically required to give them effect, so that the humblest of human creatures might at least start on the road to that knowledge the possession of which is salvation and bliss. In comparison, most modern theories are an inconsistent mixture; dialectically the modernist is easy prey to the traditionalist; he carries so many of the conceptions of the latter in his intellectual outfit that he is readily confuted. It is his practice not his theory that gets him ahead. His professed logic is still largely that of antecedent truths, demonstration and certitude; his practice is doubting, forming hypotheses, conducting experiments. When he surrenders antecedent truths of reason it is usually only to accept antecedent truths of sensation. Thus John Stuart Mill conceives of an inductive logic in which certain canons shall bear exactly the same relation to inquiry into fact that the rules of the syllogism bore to classic "deductive" proof or dialectic. He recognizes that science is a matter of inference, but he is as certain as was Aristotle that inference rests upon certain truths which are immediately possessed, differing only about the organ through which they come into our possession.

But in the practice of science, knowledge is an affair of making sure, not of grasping antecedently given sureties. What is already known, what is accepted as truth, is of immense importance; inquiry could not proceed a step without it. But it is held subject to use, and is at the mercy of the discoveries which it makes possible. It has to be adjusted to the latter and not the latter to it. When things are defined as instruments, their value and validity reside in what proceeds from them; consequences not antecedents supply meaning and verity. Truths already possessed may have practical or moral certainty, but logically they never lose a hypothetic quality. They are true if: if certain other things eventually present themselves; and when these latter things occur they in turn suggest further possibilities; the operation of doubt-inquiry-finding recurs. Although science is concerned in practice with the contingent and its method is that of making hypotheses which are then tried out in actual experimental change of physical conditions, its traditional formulation persists in terms of necessary and fixed objects. Hence all kinds of incoherences occur. The more stubbornly the traditional formulation is clung to, the more serious become these inconsistencies.

Leonardo virtually announced the birth of the method of modern science when he said that true knowledge begins with opinion. The saying involves a revolution; no other statement could be so shocking to the traditional logic. Not that opinion as such is anything more than opinion or an unconfirmed and unwarranted surmise; but that such surmises may be used; when employed as hypotheses they induce experimentation. They then become forerunners of truth, and mind is released from captivity to antecedent beliefs. Opinion, in the classic conception, was concerned with what was inherently contingent and variable as to possibility and probability, in contrast with knowledge concerned with the inherently necessary and everlasting. It therefore was as ultimate and unquestionable in its proper sphere as science was in its place. But opinion as a venture, as an "it seems to me probable," is an occasion of new observations, an instigator of research, an indispensable organ in deliberate discovery. Taken in this fashion, opinion was the source of new histories, the beginning of operations that terminated in new conclusions. Its worth lay neither in itself nor in a peculiar realm of objects to which it was applied, but in the direction of inquiries which it set agoing. It was a starting point, and like any beginning of any history was altered and displaced in the history of which it was the initiation.

Sometimes discovery is treated as a proof of the opposite of which it actually shows. It is viewed as evidence that the object of knowledge is already there in full-fledged being and that we just run across it; we uncover it as treasure-hunters find a chest of buried gold. That there is existence antecedent to search and discovery is of course admitted; but it is denied that as such, as other than the conclusion of the historical event of inquiry in its connection with other histories, it is already the object of knowledge. The Norsemen are said to have discovered America. But in what sense? They landed on its shores after a stormy voyage; there was discovery in the sense of hitting upon a land hitherto untrod by Europeans. But unless the newly found and seen object was used to modify old beliefs, to change the sense of the old map of the earth, there was no discovery in any pregnant intellectual sense, any more than mere stumbling over a chair in the dark is discovery till used as basis of inference which connects the stumbling with a body of meanings. Discovery of America involved insertion of the newly touched land in a map of the globe. This insertion, moreover, was not merely additive, but transformative of a prior picture of the world as to its surfaces and their arrangements. It may be replied that it was not the world which was changed but only the map. To which there is the obvious retort that after all the map is part of the world, not something outside it, and that its meaning and bearings are so important that a change in the map involves other and still more important objective changes.

It was not simply states of consciousness or ideas inside the heads of men that were altered when America was actually discovered; the modification was one in the public meaning of the world in which men publicly act. To cut off this meaning from the world is to leave us in a situation where it makes no difference what change takes place in the world; one wave more or less in a puddle is of no account. Changing the meaning of the world effected an existential change. The map of the world is something more than a piece of linen hung on a wall. A new world does not appear without profound transformations in the old one; a discovered America was a factor interacting with Europe and Asia to produce consequences previously impossible. A potential object of further exploration and discoveries now existed in Europe itself; a source of gold; an opportunity for adventure; an outlet for crowded and depressed populations, an abode for exiles and the discounted, an appeal to energy and invention: in short, an agency of new events and fruitions, at home as well as abroad. In some degree, every genuine discovery creates some such transformation of both the meanings and the existences of nature.

Modern idealistic theories of knowledge have displayed some sense of the method and objective of science. They have apprehended the fact that the object of knowledge implies that the found rather than the given is the proper subject matter of science. Recognizing the part played by intelligence in this finding, they have framed a theory of the constitutive operation of mind in the determination of real objects. But idealism, while it has had an intimation of the constructively instrumental office of intelligence, has mistranslated the discovery. Following the old tradition, in its exclusive identification of the object of knowledge with reality, equating truth and Being, it was forced to take the work of thought absolutely and wholesale, instead of relatively and in detail. That is, it took re-constitution to be constitution; re-construction to be construction. Accepting the premise of the equivalence of Reality with the attained object of knowledge, idealism had no way of noting that thought is intermediary between some empirical objects and others. Hence an office of transformation was converted into an act of original and final creation. A conversion of actual immediate objects into better, into more secure and significant, objects was treated as a movement from merely apparent and phenomenal Being to the truly Real. In short, idealism is guilty of neglect that thought and knowledge are histories.

To call action of thought in constituting objects direct is the same as to say that it is miraculous. For it is not thought as idealism defines thought which exercises the reconstructive function. Only action, interaction, can change or remake objects. The analogy of the skilled artist still holds. His intelligence is a factor in forming new objects which mark a fulfillment. But this is because intelligence is incarnate in overt action, using things as means to affect other things. "Thought," reason, intelligence, whatever word we choose to use, is existentially an adjective (or better an adverb), not a noun. It is disposition of activity, a quality of that conduct which foresees consequences of existing events, and which uses what is foreseen as a plan and method of administering affairs.

This theory, explicitly about thought as a condition of science, is actually a theory about nature. It involves attribution to nature of three defining characteristics. In the first place, it is implied that some natural events are endings whether enjoyed or obnoxious, which occur, apart from reflective choice and art, only casually, without control. In the second place, it implies that events, being events and not rigid and lumpy substances, are ongoing and hence as such unfinished, incomplete, indeterminate. Consequently they possess a possibility of being so managed and steered that ends may become fulfillments not just termini, conclusions not just closings. Suspense, doubt, hypotheses, experiment with alternatives are exponents of this phase of nature. In the third place, regulation of ongoing and incomplete processes in behalf of selected consequences, implies that there are orders of sequence and coexistence involved; these orders or relations when ascertained are intellectual means which enable us to use events as concrete means of directing the course of affairs to forecast conclusions. The belief that these orders of relations, which are the appropriate object of science, are therefore the sole ultimately "real" objects is the source of that assertion of a symmetrical dovetailed and completed universe made by both traditional materialism and idealism. The belief is due to neglect of the fact that such relations are always relations of ongoing affairs characterized by beginnings and endings which mark them off into unstable individuals. Yet this neglected factor is empirically so pervasive and conspicuous that it has to be acknowledged in some form; it is usually acknowledged in a backhanded way—and one which confuses subsequent reflection—by attributing all qualities inconsistent with nature thus defined to "finite" mind, in order to account for ignorance, doubt, error and the need of inference and inquiry.

If nature is as finished as these schools have defined it to be, there is no room or occasion in it for such a mind; it and the traits it is said to possess are literally supernatural or at least extra-natural.

A realist may deny this particular hypothesis that, existentially, mind designates an instrumental method of directing natural changes. But he cannot do so in virtue of his realism; the question at issue is what the real is. If natural existence is qualitatively individualized or genuinely plural, as well as repetitious, and if things have both temporal quality and recurrence or uniformity, then the more realistic knowledge is, the more fully it will reflect and exemplify these traits. Science seizes upon whatever is so uniform as to make the changes of nature rhythmic, and hence predictable. But the contingencies of nature make discovery of these uniformities with a view to prediction needed and possible. Without the uniformities, science would be impossible. But if they alone existed, thought and knowledge would be impossible and meaningless. The incomplete and uncertain gives point and application to ascertainment of regular relations and orders. These relations in themselves are hypothetical, and when isolated from application are subject-matter of mathematics (in a non-existential sense). Hence the ultimate objects of science are guided processes of change.

Sometimes the use of the word "truth" is confined to designating a logical property of propositions; but if we extend its significance to designate character of existential reference, this is the meaning of truth: processes of change so directed that they achieve an intended consummation. Instrumentalities are actually such only in operation; when they operate, an end-in-view is in process of actualization. The means is fully a means only in its end. The instrumental objects of science are completely themselves only as they direct the changes of nature toward a fulfilling object. Thus it may be said intelligibly and not as mere tautology that the end of science is knowledge, implying that knowledge is more than science, being its fruit.

Knowledge is a word of various meanings. Etymologically, "science" may signify tested and authentic instance of knowledge. But knowledge has also a meaning more liberal and more humane. It signifies events understood, events so discriminately penetrated by thought that mind is literally at home in them. It means comprehension, or inclusive reasonable agreement. What is sometimes termed "applied" science, may then be more truly science than is what is conventionally called pure science. For it is directly concerned with not just instrumentalities, but instrumentalities at work in effecting modifications of existence in behalf of conclusions that are reflectively preferred. Thus conceived the characteristic subject-matter of knowledge consists of fulfilling objects, which as fulfillments are connected with a history to which they give character. Thus conceived, knowledge exists in engineering, medicine and the social arts more adequately than it does in mathematics, and physics. Thus conceived, history and anthropology are scientific in a sense in which bodies of information that stop short with general formulae are not.

"Application" is a hard word for many to accept. It suggests some extraneous tool ready-made and complete, which is then put to uses that are external to its nature. To call the arts applications of science is then to introduce something foreign to the sciences which the latter irrelevantly and accidentally serve. Since the application is in human use, convenience, enjoyment and improvement, this view of application as something external and arbitrary reflects and strengthens the theories which detach man from nature, which, in the language of philosophy, oppose subject and object. But if we free ourselves from preconceptions, application of "science" means application in, not application to. Application in something signifies a more extensive interaction of natural events with one another, an elimination of distance and obstacles; provision of opportunities for interactions that reveal potentialities previously hidden and that bring into existence new histories with new initiations and endings. Engineering, medicine, social arts realize relationships that were unrealized in actual existences. Surely in their new context the latter are understood or known as they are not in isolation. Prejudice against the abstract, as something remote and technical, is often irrational; but there is sense in the conviction that in the abstract there is something lacking which should be recovered. The serious objection to "applied" science lies in limitation of the application, as to private profit and class advantage.

"Pure" science is of necessity relational and abstract: it fulfills its meaning and gains full truth when included within a course of concrete events. The proposition that "pure" science is non-existential is a tacit admission that only "applied" science is existential. Something else than history and anthropology lose all scientific standing when standards of "purity" are set up as ultimate; namely, all science of existential events. There is superstitious awe reflected in the current estimate of science. If we could free ourselves from a somewhat abject emotion, it would be clear enough that what makes any proposition scientific is its power to yield understanding, insight, intellectual at-homeness, in connection with any existential state of affairs, by filling events with coherent and tested meanings. The case of history is typical and basic. Upon the current view, it is a waste of time to discuss whether there can be such a thing as a science of history. History and science are by definition at opposite poles. And yet if all natural existences are histories, divorce between history and the logical-mathematical schemes which are the appropriate objects of pure science, terminates in the conclusion that of existences there is no science, no adequate knowledge. Aside from mathematics, all knowledge is historic; chemistry, geology, physiology, as well as anthropology and those human events to which, arrogantly, we usually restrict the title of history. Only as science is seen to be fulfilled and brought to itself in intelligent management of historical processes in their continuity can man be envisaged as with nature, and not as a supernatural extrapolation. Just because nature is what it is, history is capable of being more truly known—understood, intellectually realized—than are mathematical and physical objects. Do what we can, there always remains something recondite and remote in the latter, until they are restored in the course of affairs from which they have been sequestrated. While the humanizing of science contributes to the life of humanity, it is even more required in behalf of science, in order that it may be intelligible, simple and clear; in order that it may have that correspondence with reality which true knowledge claims for itself.

One can understand the sentiment that animates the bias of scientific inquirers against the idea that all science is ultimately applied. It is justified in the sense in which it is intended; for it is directed against two conceptions which are harmful, but which, also, are irrelevant to the position here taken. One of these conceptions is that the concern or personal motive of the inquirer should be in each particular inquiry some specific practical application. This is just as it happens to be. Doubtless many important scientific discoveries have been thus instigated, but that is an incident of human history rather than of scientific inquiry as such. And upon the whole, or if this animating interest were to become general, the undoubted effect is limitation of inquiry and thereby in the end of the field of application. It marks a recurrence to the dogma of fixed predetermined ends, while emancipation from the influence of this dogma has been the chief service rendered modern scientific methods.

The evil thus effected is increased by the second notion, namely, that application is identical with "commercialized" use. It is an incident of human history, and a rather appalling incident, that applied science has been so largely made an equivalent of use for private and economic class purposes and privileges. When inquiry is narrowed by such motivation or interest, the consequence is in so far disastrous both to science and to human life. But this limitation does not spring from nor attach to the conception of "application" which has been just presented. It springs from defects and perversions of morality as that is embodied in institutions and their effects upon personal disposition. It may be questioned whether the notion that science is pure in the sense of being concerned exclusively with a realm of objects detached from human concerns has not conspired to reinforce this moral deficiency. For in effect it has established another class-interest, that of intellectuals and aloof specialists. And it is of the nature of any class-interest to generate and confirm other class-interests, since division and isolation in a world of continuities are always reciprocal. The institution of an interest labelled ideal and idealistic in isolation tends of necessity to evoke and strengthen other interests lacking ideal quality. The genuine interests of "pure" science are served only by broadening the idea of application to include all phases of liberation and enrichment of human experience.

C. I. Lewis: A PRAGMATIC CONCEPTION OF THE A PRIORI

C. I. LEWIS *seeks to defend pragmatists against the charge that they regard the* a priori *components of knowledge as mere functions of human interest and that these principles accordingly are subject to human whim. On his analysis, any hypothesis or theory must ultimately depend on unquestioned submission to* a priori *conventions such as the rules of a certain logic. Furthermore, short of falling into a typical contradiction, no grounds can be established within the theory for refuting its* a priori *components.*

In claiming that the a priori *in this way transcends man's volition, however, Lewis is not disclaiming the pragmatic thesis that one set of* a priori *features may be supplanted by another set. In final analysis our selection of a set of* a priori *principles will, just as our selection of theories does, depend on the verdict of experience.*

The article reprinted here was originally published in the Journal of Philosophy, Vol. 20, pp. 169–177, *and is reproduced with the kind permission of that journal. The article is also available in Feigl and Sellars,* Readings in Philosophical Analysis (New York: Appleton-Century-Crofts, 1949), pp. 286–294.

The conception of the *a priori* points up two problems which are perennial in philosophy; the part played in knowledge by the mind itself, and the possibility of "necessary truth" or of knowledge "independent of experience." But traditional conceptions of the *a priori* have proved untenable. That the mind approaches the flux of immediacy with some godlike foreknowledge of principles which are legislative for experience, that there is any natural light or any innate ideas, it is no longer possible to believe.

Nor shall we find the clue to the *a priori* in any compulsion of the mind to incontrovertible truth or any peculiar kind of demonstration which establishes first principles. All truth lays upon the rational mind the same compulsion to belief; as Mr. Bosanquet has pointed out, this character belongs to all propositions or judgments once their truth is established.

The difficulties of the conception are due, I believe, to two mistakes: whatever is *a priori* is necessary, but we have misconstrued the relation of necessary truth to mind. And the *a priori* is independent of experience, but in so taking it, we have misunderstod its relation to empirical fact. What is *a priori* is necessary truth not because it compels the mind's acceptance, but precisely because it does not. It is given experience, brute fact, the *a posteriori* element in knowledge which the mind must accept willy-nilly. The *a priori* represents an attitude in some sense freely taken, a stipulation of the mind itself, and a stipulation which might be made in some other way if it suited our bent or need. Such truth is necessary as opposed to contingent, not as opposed to voluntary. And the *a priori* is independent of experience not because it prescribes a form which the data of sense must fit, or anticipates some preestablished harmony of experience with the mind, but precisely because it prescribes nothing to experience. That is *a priori* which is true, *no matter what*. What it anticipates is not the given, but our attitude toward it: it concerns the uncompelled initiative of mind or, as Josiah Royce would say, our categorical ways of acting.

The traditional example of the *a priori par excellence* is the laws of logic. These can not be derived from experience since they must first be taken for granted in order to prove them. They make explicit our general modes of classification. And they impose upon experience no real limitation. Sometimes we are asked to tremble before the spectre of the "alogical," in order that we may thereafter rejoice that we are saved from this by the dependence of reality upon mind. But the "alogical" is pure bogey, a word without a meaning. What kind of experience could defy the principle that everything must either be or not be, that nothing can both be and not be, or that if x is y and y is z, then x is z? If anything imaginable or unimaginable could violate such laws, then the ever-present fact of change would do it every day. The laws of logic are purely formal; they forbid nothing but what concerns the use of terms and the corresponding modes of classification and analysis. The law of contradiction tells us that nothing can be both white and not-white, but it does not and can not tell us whether black is not white or soft or square is not-white. To discover *what contradicts what* we must always consult the character of experience. Similarly the law of the excluded middle formulates our decision that whatever is not designated by a certain term shall be designated by its negative. It declares our purpose to make, for every term, a complete dichotomy of experience, instead—as we might choose—of classifying on the basis of a tripartite division into opposites (as black and white) and the middle ground between the two. Our rejection of such tripartite division represents only our penchant for simplicity.

Further laws of logic are of similar significance. They are principles of procedure, the parliamentary rules of intelligent thought and speech. Such laws are independent of experience because they impose no limitations whatever upon it. They are legislative because they are addressed to ourselves—because definition, classification, and inference represent no operations of the objective world, but only our own categorical attitudes of mind.

And further, the ultimate criteria of the laws of logic are pragmatic. Those who suppose that there is, for example, *a* logic which everyone would agree to if he understood it and understood himself, are more optimistic than those versed in the history of logical discussion have a right to be. The fact is that there are several logics, markedly different, each self-consistent in its own terms and such that whoever, using it, avoids false premises, will never reach a false conclusion. Mr. Russell, for example, bases *his* logic on an implication relation such that if twenty sentences be cut from a newspaper and put in a hat, and then two of these be drawn at random, one of them will certainly imply the other, and it is an even bet that the implication will be mutual. Yet upon a foundation so remote from ordinary modes of inference the whole strucure of *Principia Mathematica* is built. This logic—and there are others even more strange—is utterly consistent and the results of it entirely valid. Over and above all question of consistency, there are issues of logic which can not be determined—nay, can not even be argued—except on pragmatic grounds of conformity to human bent and intellectual convenience. That we have been blind to this fact, itself reflects traditional errors in the conception of the *a priori*.

We may note in passing one less important illustration of the *a priori*—the proposition "true by definition." Definitions and their immediate consequences, analytic propositions generally, are necessarily true, true under all possible circumstances. Definition is legislative because it is in some sense arbitrary. Not only is the meaning assigned to words more or less a matter of choice—that consideration is relatively trivial—but the manner in which the precise classifications which definition embodies shall be effected, is something not dictated by experience. If experience were other than it is, the definition and its corresponding classification might be inconvenient, fantastic, or useless, but it could not be false. Mind makes classifications and determines meanings; in so doing it creates the *a priori* truth of analytic judgments. But that the manner of this creation responds to pragmatic considerations, is so obvious that it hardly needs pointing out.

If the illustrations so far given seem trivial or verbal, that impression may be corrected by turning to the place which the *a priori* has in mathematics and in natural science. Arithmetic, for example, depends *in toto* upon the operation of counting or correlating, a procedure which can be carried out at will in any world containing identifiable things—even identifiable ideas—regardless of the further characters of experience. Mill challenged this *a priori* character of arithmetic. He asked us to suppose a demon sufficiently powerful and maleficent so that every time two things were brought together with two other things, this demon should always introduce a fifth. The implication which he supposed to follow is that under such circumstances $2 + 2 = 5$ would be a universal law of arithmetic. But Mill was quite mistaken. In such a world we should be obliged to become a little clearer than is usual about the distinction between arithmetic and physics, that is all. If two black marbles were put in the same urn with two white ones, the demon could take his choice of colors, but it would be evident that there were more black marbles or more white ones than were put in. The same would be true of all objects in any wise identifiable. We should simply find ourselves in the presence of an extraordinary physical law, which we should recognize as universal in our world, that whenever two things were brought into proximity with two others, an additional and similar thing was always created by the process. Mill's world would be physically most extraordinary. The world's work would be enormously facilitated if hats or locomotives or tons of coal could be thus multiplied by anyone possessed originally of two pairs. But the laws of mathematics would remain unaltered. It is because this is true that arithmetic is *a priori*. Its laws prevent *nothing*; they are compatible with anything which happens or could conceivably happen in nature. They would be true in any possible world. Mathematical addition is not a physical transformation. Physical changes which result in an increase or decrease of the countable things involved are matters of everyday occurrence. Such physical processes present us with phenomena in which the purely mathematical has to be separated out by abstraction. Those laws and those laws only have necessary truth which we are prepared to maintain, no matter what. It is because we shall always separate out that part of the phenomenon not in conformity with arithmetic and designate it by some other category —physical change, chemical reaction, optical illusion—that arithmetic is *a priori*.

The *a priori* element in science and in natural law is greater than might be supposed. In the first place, all science is based upon definitive concepts. The formulation of these concepts is, indeed, a matter determined by the commerce between our intellectual or our pragmatic interests and the nature of experience. Definition is classification. The scientific search is for such classification as will make it possible to correlate appearance and behavior, to discover law, to penetrate to the "essential nature" of things in order that behavior may become predictable. In other words, if definition is unsuccessful, as early scientific definitions mostly have been, it is because the classification thus set up corresponds with no natural cleavage and does not correlate with any important uniformity of behavior. A name itself must represent *some* uniformity in experience or it names nothing. What does not repeat itself or recur in intelligible fashion is not a thing. Where the definitive uniformity is a clue to other uniformities, we have successful scientific definition. Other definitions can not be said to be false; they are merely useless. In scientific classification the search is, thus, for *things worth naming*. But the naming, classifying, defining activity is essentially prior to investigation. We can not interrogate experience in general. Until our meaning is definite and our classification correspondingly exact, experience can not conceivably answer our questions.

In the second place, the fundamental laws of any science—or those treated as fundamental—are *a priori* because they formulate just such definitive concepts or categorical tests by which alone investigation becomes possible. If the lightning strikes the railroad track at two places, A and B, how shall we tell whether these events are simultaneous? "We . . . require a definition of simultaneity such that this definition supplies us with the method by means of which . . . we can decide whether or not both the lightning strokes occurred simultaneously. As long as this requirement is not satisfied, I allow myself to be deceived as a physicist (and of course the same applies if I am not a physicist), when I imagine that I am able to attach a meaning to the statement of simultaneity. . . .

"After thinking the matter over for some time you then offer the following suggestion with which to test simultaneity. By measuring along the rails, the connecting line AB should be measured up and an observer placed at the mid-point M of the distance AB. This observer should be supplied with an arrangement (e.g., two mirrors inclined at 90°) which allows him visually to observe both places A and B at the same time. If the observer perceives the two flashes at the same time, then they are simultaneous.

"I am very pleased with this suggestion, but for all that I can not regard the matter as quite settled, because I feel constrained to raise the following objection: 'Your definition would certainly be right, if I only knew that the light by means of which the observer at M perceives the lightning flashes travels along the length A—M with the same velocity as along the length B—M. But an examination of this supposition would only be possible if we already had at our disposal the means of measuring time. It would thus appear as though we were moving here in a logical circle.'

"After further consideration you cast a somewhat disdainful glance at me—and rightly so—and you declare: 'I maintain my previous definition nevertheless, because in reality it assumes absolutely nothing about light. There is only *one* demand to be made of the definition of simultaneity, namely, that in every real case it must supply us with an empirical decision as to whether or not the conception which has to be defined is fulfilled. That light requires the same time to traverse the path A—M as for the path B—M is in reality *neither a supposition nor a hypothesis* about the physical nature of light, but a *stipulation* which I can make of my own free-will in order to arrive at a definition of simultaneity.' . . . We are thus led also to a definition of 'time' in physics" [A. Einstein, *Relativity*, pp. 26–27].

As this example from the theory of relativity well illustrates, we can not even ask the questions which discovered law would answer until we have first by *a priori* stipulation formulated definitive criteria. Such concepts are not verbal definitions, nor classifications merely; they are themselves laws which prescribe a certain uniformity of behavior to whatever is thus named. Such definitive laws are *a priori*; only so can we enter upon the investigation by which further laws are sought. Yet it should also be pointed out that such *a priori* laws are subject to abandonment if the structure which is built upon them does not succeed in simplifying our interpretation of phenomena. If, in the illustration given, the relation "simultaneous with," as defined, should not prove transitive—if event A should prove simultaneous with B, and B with C, but not A with C—this definition would certainly be rejected.

And thirdly, there is that *a priori* element in science—as in other human affairs—which constitutes the criteria of the real as opposed to the unreal in experience. An object itself is a uniformity. Failure to behave in certain categorical ways marks it as unreal. Uniformities of the type called "natural law" are the clues to reality and unreality. A mouse which disappears where no hole is, is no real mouse; a landscape which recedes as we approach is but illusion. As the queen remarked in the episode of the wishing-carpet, "If this were real, then it would be a miracle. But miracles do not happen. Therefore I shall wake presently." That the uniformities of natural law are the only reliable criteria of the real, is inescapable. But such a criterion is *ipso facto a priori*. No conceivable experience could dictate the alteration of a law so long as failure to obey that law marked the content of experience as unreal.

This is one of the puzzles of empiricism. We deal with experience: what any reality may be which underlies experience, we have to learn. What we desire to discover is natural law, the formulation of those uniformities which obtain amongst the real. But experience as it comes to us contains not only the real but all the content of illusion, dream, hallucination, and mistake. The *given* contains both real and unreal, confusingly intermingled. If we ask for uniformities of this unsorted experience, we shall not find them. Laws which characterize all experience, of real and unreal both, are non-existent and would in any case be worthless. What we seek are the uniformities of the *real*; but *until we have such laws, we can not sift experience and segregate the real.*

The obvious solution is that the enrichment of experience, the separation of the real from the illusory or meaningless, and the formulation of natural law, all grow up together. If the criteria of the real are *a priori*, that is not to say that no conceivable character of experience would lead to alteration of them. For example, spirits can not be photographed. But if photographs of spiritistic phenomena, taken under properly guarded conditions, should become sufficiently frequent, this *a priori* dictum would be called in question. What we should do would be to redefine our terms. Whether "spook" was spirit or matter, whether the definition of "spirit" or of "matter" should be changed; all this would constitute one interrelated problem. We should reopen together the question of definition or classification, of criteria for this sort of real, and of natural law. And the solution of one of these would mean the solution of all. Nothing could *force* a redefinition of spirit or of matter. A sufficiently fundamental relation to human bent, to human interests, would guarantee continuance unaltered even in the face of unintelligible and baffling experiences. In such problems, the mind finds itself uncompelled save by its own purposes and needs. I *may* categorize experience as I will; but *what* categorical distinctions will best serve my interests and objectify my own intelligence? What the mixed and troubled experience shall be—that is beyond me. But what I shall do with it—that is my own question, when the character of experience is sufficiently before me. I am coerced only by my own need to understand.

It would indeed be inappropriate to characterize as *a priori* a law which we are wholly prepared to alter in the light of further experience, even though in an isolated case we should discard as illusory any experience which failed to conform. But the crux of the situation lies in this; beyond such principles as those of logic, which we seem fully prepared to maintain no matter what, there must be further and more particular criteria of the real prior to any investigation of nature whatever. We can not even interrogate experience without a network of categories and definitive concepts. And we must further be prepared to say what experimental findings will answer what questions, and how. Without tests which represent anterior principle, there is no question which experience could answer at all. Thus the most fundamental laws in any category—or those which we regard as most fundamental—are *a priori*, even though continued failure to render experience intelligible in such terms might result eventually in the abandonment of that category altogether. Matters so comparatively small as the behavior of Mercury and of starlight passing the sun's limb may, if there be persistent failure to bring them within the field of previously accepted modes of explanation, result in the abandonment of the independent categories of space and time. But without the definitions, fundamental principles, and tests, of the type which constitute such categories, no experience whatever could prove or disprove anything. And to that mind which should find independent space and time absolutely necessary conceptions, no possible experiment could prove the principles of relativity. "There must be some error in the experimental findings, or some law not yet discovered," represents an attitude which can never be rendered impossible. And the only sense in which it could be proved unreasonable would be the pragmatic only of comparison with another method of categorical analysis which more successfully reduced all such experience to order and law.

At the bottom of all science and all knowledge are categories and definitive concepts which represent fundamental habits of thought and deep-lying attitudes which the human mind has taken in the light of its total experience. But a new and wider experience may bring about some alteration of these attitudes, even though by themselves they dictate nothing as to the content of experience, and no experience can conceivably prove them invalid.

Perhaps some will object to this conception on the ground that only such principles should be designated *a priori* as the human mind *must* maintain, no matter what; that if, for example, it is shown possible to arrive at a consistent doctrine of physics in terms of relativity, even by the most arduous reconstruction of our fundamental notions, then the present conceptions are by that fact shown not to be *a priori*. Such objection is especially likely from those who would conceive the *a priori* in terms of an absolute mind or an absolutely universal human nature. We should readily agree that a decision by popular approval or a congress of scientists or anything short of such a test as would bring to bear the full weight of human capacity and interest, would be ill-considered as having to do with the *a priori*. But we wish to emphasize two facts: first, that in the field of those conceptions and principles which have altered in human history, there are those which could neither be proved nor disproved by any experience, but represent the uncompelled initiative of human thought—that without this uncompelled initiative no growth of science, nor any science at all, would be conceivable. And second, that the difference between such conceptions as are, for example, concerned in the decision of relativity versus absolute space and time, and those more permanent attitudes such as are vested in the laws of logic, there is only a difference of degree. The dividing line between the *a priori* and the *a posteriori* is that between principles and definitive concepts which can be maintained in the face of all experience and those genuinely empirical generalizations which might be proven flatly false. The thought which both rationalism and empiricism have missed is that there are principles, representing the initiative of mind, which impose upon experience no limitations whatever, but that such conceptions are still subject to alteration on pragmatic grounds when the expanding boundaries of experience reveal their infelicity as intellectual instruments.

Neither human experience nor the human mind has a character which is universal, fixed, and absolute. "The human mind" does not exist at all save in the sense that all humans are very much alike in fundamental respects, and that the language habit and the enormously important exchange of ideas has greatly increased our likeness in those respects which are here in question. Our categories and definitions are peculiarly social products, reached in the light of experiences which have much in common, and beaten out, like other pathways, by the coincidence of human purposes and the exigencies of human cooperation. Concerning the *a priori* there need be neither universal agreement nor complete historical continuity. Conceptions, such as those of logic, which are least likely to be affected by the opening of new ranges of experience, represent the most stable of our categories; but none of them is beyond the possibility of alteration.

Mind contributes to experience the element of order, of classification, categories, and definition. Without such, experience would be unintelligible. Our knowledge of the validity of these is simply consciousness of our own fundamental ways of acting and our own intellectual intent. Without this element, knowledge is impossible, and it is here that whatever truths are necessary and independent of experience must be found. But the commerce between our categorical ways of acting, our pragmatic interests, and the particular character of experience, is closer than we have realized. No explanation of any one of these can be complete without consideration of the other two.

Pragmatism has sometimes been charged with oscillating between two contrary notions; the one, that experience is "through and through malleable to our purpose," the other, that facts are "hard" and uncreated by the mind. We here offer a mediating conception: through all our knowledge runs the element of the *a priori*, which is indeed malleable to our purpose and responsive to our need. But throughout, there is also that other element of experience which is "hard," "independent," and unalterable to our will.

GUIDE TO FURTHER READINGS IN CONTEMPORARY PRAGMATISM

PRAGMATISM AND SOCIAL PHILOSOPHY

Sidney Hook (1902–   ), a student and colleague of John Dewey, is an acknowledged expert in the study of comparative political systems, having written extensively about the contrasts between totalitarian and democratic theories. He has been particularly concerned to appraise the conditions favorable and unfavorable to democracy. He views the institutions of modern democracy as uniquely suited to, and essential for, men who have the attitude of open-mindedness and who approach their problems pragmatically. With this orientation it becomes possible for men to retain their freedom without losing their ability for effective, collective action. See especially his "Naturalism and Democracy," in *Naturalism and the Human Spirit*, Y. H. Krikorian (ed.) (New York: Columbia University Press, 1944).

T. V. Smith (1890–1964), a philosopher who was equally familiar with the theoretical and practical aspects of politics, concerned himself with the problem of how our "democratic way of life" works. He asks the following question: How can a nonconformist society, in which each man is allowed to hold and develop his own ideals, manage to arrive at binding decisions without becoming either fanatical or submissive on the one hand or apathetic on the other? Smith's answer is that the citizens in a democracy commit themselves to the processes whereby they effect compromises within the context of fair-mindedness. Translated into political terms, this means that an institution of democracy is a good one if and only if it permits and encourages an accommodation between individual ideals and interests. See especially his *The Democratic Way of Life*, with E. C. Lindeman (New York: New American Library, 1951).

Additional Readings
Dewey, J., *Individualism, Old and New*. New York: Minton, 1930.
Mead, G. H., *Mind, Self and Society*. Chicago: University of Chicago Press, 1934.
Smith, T. V., *The Legislative Way of Life*. Chicago: University of Chicago Press, 1940.

PRAGMATISM AND VALUE THEORY

R. B. Perry (1876–1957) moved from pragmatism to neorealism in his theory of knowledge but retained a close affinity to his teacher, William James, in value theory. It is not too great an exaggeration to say that Perry's extensive work in value theory constitutes an elaboration of James' notable essay, "The Moral Philosopher and the Moral Life." Seeking first to understand the general problem of value, Perry concludes that values, whether ethical or aesthetic, derive from an organism's interest in objects. In the most important domain of value, namely the moral, Perry's chief concept is that of moral good; he defines it as "the fulfillment of an organization of interests." See especially his *General Theory of Value* (New York: Longmans, Green, 1926).

Ray Lepley (1903–   ), a disciple of John Dewey, is of interest because he attempts to work through, in detail, two theses in the instrumentalist theory of value. The first is the belief that value judgments are translatable into assertions of fact and that they are, accordingly, subject to empirical verification. The second thesis is that the pattern of inquiry which obtains in resolving value issues is no different in kind from that employed in problem solving generally. See especially *Verifiability of Value* (New York: Columbia University Press, 1944).

Additional Readings

    Dewey, J., "Theory of Valuation," in *International Encyclopedia of Unified Science*. Chicago: University of Chicago Press, 1939, Vol. II, No. 4.

    Lepley, Ray, *Value: A Cooperative Inquiry*. New York: Columbia University Press, 1949.

    Lewis, C. I., *An Analysis of Knowledge and Valuation*. La Salle: Open Court, 1947.

    Otto, M., *The Human Enterprise*. New York: Crofts, 1940.

PRAGMATISM AND PHILOSOPHY OF SCIENCE

Percy W. Bridgman (1882–1961), a Nobel prize winner in physics and a philosopher of science, has been the chief proponent of the operationalist view of science, a view that is related to both positivism and pragmatism. He was impressed with Peirce's theory of meaning as setting forth the essential feature of concept determination. Bridgman holds that, far from proceeding on the basis of abstract definitions, the practicing scientist is guided by concepts or definitions that are constituted by sets of "operations." Thus, for example, the concept of length is properly defined as nothing more than a special set of measuring operations. See especially *The Logic of Modern Physics* (New York: Macmillan, 1927).

Ernest Nagel (1901–   ), a logician and philosopher of science, is noted for his penetrating analyses of the underlying logical problems of science. Although he agrees with Dewey that logic can be conceived only as a functioning part of inquiry, he moves away from the Deweyan preoccupation with it as a biological or psychological phenomenon. Logic is constituted by a set of habits of inference which not only guide empirical inquiry but which also are justified by the success of that inquiry. In recent centuries, the area in which logic has achieved its most fruitful and sophisticated development is that of the sciences. See especially *The Structure of Science* (New York: Harcourt, Brace and World, 1961).

Additional Readings

    Benjamin, A. C., *Operationism*. Springfield: Charles C Thomas, 1955.

    Bridgman, P., *The Way Things Are*. Cambridge: Harvard University Press, 1959.

Churchman, C. W., *Theory of Experimental Inference*. New York: Macmillan, 1948.

Nagel, E., *Sovereign Reason*. Glencoe: Free Press, 1954.

ALLIED MOVEMENTS: PRAGMATICS AND NATURALISM

C. W. Morris (1901–   ) attempts to refine and extend Peirce's theory of signs. He proceeds by drawing a threefold linguistic distinction: the science of syntactics (sign as related to signs), the science of semantics (sign as related to referent), and the science of pragmatics (sign as related to interpreter). The science of pragmatics, as the name suggests, is an empirical, objective study of the way in which men employ signs as instruments of environmental adjustment. Morris does not attempt to reduce either syntactics or semantics to pragmatics. See especially his "Foundations of the Theory of Signs," in *International Encyclopedia of Unified Science* (Chicago: University of Chicago Press, 1938), Vol. I, No. 1.

William R. Dennes (1898–   ), like realistic naturalists such as Woodbridge (see p. 61) and pragmatic naturalists such as Dewey, is an opponent of idealism, materialism, and all metaphysical reductionisms. Although he is willing to accept the world with all of the qualitative distinctions that our experience reveals, he insists that there is one and only one method of inquiry, that of science. It is the philosopher's abiding task to protect us from those who would claim that since there are various kinds of subject matters there are also various methods of inquiry. See especially "The Categories of Naturalism," in *Naturalism and the Human Spirit* (New York: Columbia University Press, 1944).

Additional Readings

Krikorian, Y. H. (ed.), *Naturalism and the Human Spirit*. New York: Columbia University Press, 1944.

Morris, C. W., *Signs, Language and Behavior*. New York: Prentice-Hall, 1946.

Schneider, H. W., *Ways of Being*. New York: Columbia University Press, 1962.

NOTES FOR CHAPTER III

1 John Dewey, *How We Think*, rev. ed. (Boston: Heath, 1933), pp. 13–14.
2 *The Dialogues of Plato*, trans. B. Jowett (New York: Random House, 1937), I, 180–181.
3 W. Oates, *The Stoic and Epicurean Philosophers* (New York: Random House, 1940), pp. 19–20.

4   M. McClure (ed.), *Bacon: Selections* (New York: Scribner's, 1928), p. 80.
5   Cited in R. Blake, C. Ducasse, and E. Madden, *Theories of Scientific Method* (Seattle: University of Washington Press, 1960), p. 28.
6   Cited in W. James, *The Will to Believe* (New York: Longmans, Green, 1896), pp. 5–6.
7   J. S. Mill, *A System of Logic* (New York: Harper, 1895), p. 173.
8   F. Nietzsche, *Beyond Good and Evil*, trans. M. Cowan (Chicago: Regnery, 1955), p. 6.
9   It was Peirce who coined the term "pragmatism." At a later point in his career, he renounced the affinity of his philosophy with that of William James and other pragmatists and adopted the word "pragmaticism" to refer to the pragmatic features of his own philosophy.
10 C. S. Peirce, *Collected Papers*, ed. C. Hartshorne and P. Weiss (Cambridge: Harvard University Press, 1931–35), V, para. 9.
11 J. Buchler, *The Philosophy of Peirce* (London: Routledge and Kegan Paul, 1940), p. 18.
12 W. James, *Pragmatism* (New York: Longmans, Green, 1907), p. 4.
13 *Ibid.*, p. 54.
14 *Ibid.*, p. 58.
15 *Ibid.*, p. 201.
16 *Ibid.*, p. 76.
17 The English philosopher, F. C. S. Schiller (1864–1937), influenced James somewhat in underscoring the humanistic aspect of pragmatism; however, he is far more subjective in his account of knowledge. For him, the facts of experience are to a great extent free private creations, and the so-called public facts are scarcely more than socially agreed-to private facts.
18 James, *Will to Believe*, pp. 9–10.
19 D. Runes (ed.), *Twentieth Century Philosophy* (New York: Philosophical Library, 1947), p. 464.

IV · Existentialism

MAN ASKS himself three questions: Who am I? What is my relation to the physical and social world? How do I achieve true beliefs? The average man's answers tend to be muddled. On the one hand, he conceives himself—as do scientists and many philosophers—to be representatively *Homo sapiens*, an object subject to natural and social laws, and an objective investigator employing public methods for the discovery of truth. On the other hand, he conceives himself—as do artists and a strident minority of philosophers, including existentialists—to be uniquely individual, an autonomous agent transcending his environment, and a subjective creator committed to the private realization of truth.

Perhaps the two opposed groups would agree to the following: the failure of the average man to be decisive leaves him emasculated. Because of his tendency to adopt both positions, he forfeits the possibility of achievement. At the very point where a disciplined scientist, say, seeks to solve a hard problem by applying his mind to it persistently and consistently, the average man takes the path of least resistance by turning to his passions and feelings as a form of escape. Again, at the juncture where a creative artist, for example, seeks to express the depths of a human predicament by first experiencing it tenaciously and relentlessly, the average man retreats to a rationally detached position.

Like most of us, the representatives of each extreme are aware that life and thought seem to contain both rational and nonrational components. Neither group would deny that life as we experience it is filled with both regularities and contingencies, with necessary and accidental occurrences, and that thought contains both certainty and probability, both reasoning and "rationalization." However, philosophers maintain that the features they emphasize are primary. The man of reason maintains that mathematical certainty and experimental predictability alone satisfy his curiosity and provide an adequate basis for dealing with the world. To the extent that he is unsuccessful in his efforts to resolve all problems rationally, he claims either that he has insufficient evidence and mental acuity, or that he can be concerned only with the things he can make intelligible. The man who acknowledges the primacy of nonrational components such as his will and passions, however, is impressed with himself as a unique agent, a contingent force in the world about him, and an intensely personal and subjective participant in this world.

Two facts help sustain the existentialist in his attitude: first, many philosophers who turned to reason exclusively have had to admit that it is limited; second, even rationalists who have most nearly succeeded in understanding nature have failed conspicuously to grasp the "human situation." The existentialist sees those who acknowledge the limits of reason and fail to seek alternatives as consigned to a debilitating scepticism; and he sees those who militantly demand rational accounts of man's behavior as having submitted to a dehumanized view. The contemporary existentialist insists we come to the painful realization that reason cannot cope with the particular, the contingent, and the transcendent; as a consequence, reason can deal neither with the individual as a unique person nor with his freedom and inner commitments. In the words of Karl Jaspers (1883–   ), the moral to be drawn from twenty-five centuries of philosophy is that the "non-rational is found in the opacity of the here and now; in matter, it is what is only enveloped but never consumed by rational form; it is an actual empirical existence which is just as it is and not otherwise, which is subsumed under just those regularities we experience and not otherwise; it is in the contents of faith for religious revelation. All philosophizing which would like to dissolve Being into pure rationality retains in spite of itself the non-rational. . . ."[1]

SOCRATES, PLATO, AND ARISTOTLE

Socrates (469–399 B.C.) showed his concern for personal existence when he recommended to every man, "know thyself," for "the unexamined life is not worth living." On closer scrutiny, we discover that his efforts to meet his own recommendation are characterized by a strange tension. On the one hand, he appeared to know himself by living a life in which he overcame the tyranny of convention and in which he achieved thereby a higher level of personal existence. On the other, his self-knowledge was attained by disciplined reflection in which characterizing himself he characterized all men. History proclaims two Socrates: the participant in life and the spectator of life. Which bears the message of Socratic truth? Is it the inner-directed, self-determining creator, a personage who stands unique among men? Or is it the dispassionate, passive observer of that which unifies all men? Even in the Socratic dialogues in which Plato's concern is predominantly conceptual, the courageous and audacious figure of Socrates as a man with a moral mission fed by his own energies and faithful to his own convictions emerges. Plato explicitly represents Socrates as turning to an inner voice (*daimon*)—a voice that is a product neither of social conditioning nor of reason—at crucial moments of decision. For example, in the *Apology*, the dialogue concerning his trial, Socrates expressed loyalty to the voice of conscience without regard for his own life:

> If you say to me, Socrates, this time . . . you shall be let off, but upon one condition, that you are not to enquire and speculate in this way any more, and that if you are caught doing so again you shall die;—if this was the condition on which you let me go, I shall reply: Men of Athens I honour and love you; but I shall obey God rather than you, and while I have life and strength I shall never cease from the practice and teaching of philosophy. . . .[2]

In the Platonic tradition, the emphasis is on Socrates playing the role of philosopher rather than on Socrates the person who has committed himself to playing such a role. According to the existentialists, this amounts to a cardinal philosophical error. What the Platonists and, indeed, the majority of traditional philosophers have done is to assume that all of an individual's problems can and must be formulated in such a way that they are resolvable rationally. Furthermore, the existentialists point out that even if you grant the Platonist's initial move of referring to human problems in this way, there is no prospect of final success because the domain of reason is limited, as Plato himself asserted. For example, when Plato talked about the highest form, the Good, which stands as the ultimate ground of knowledge and value, he had to switch from the careful language of reason to that of metaphor. It is only through the devices of myth and literary analogy that he could communicate at all about this ultimate reality. Thus the existentialist feels vindicated by a passage such as the following, which occurs in Plato's *Republic*, a dialogue presumed to be a paradigm of rational inquiry:

> My opinion is that in the world of knowledge the idea of good appears last of all, and is seen only with an effort; and, when seen, is

also inferred to be the universal author of all things beautiful and right, parent of light and of the lord of light in this visible world, and the immediate source of reason and truth in the intellectual; and this is the power upon which he who would act rationally either in public or private life must have his eye fixed.[3]

The existentialists also take comfort in the difficulties that they claim the other great proponent of reason, Aristotle, had. Accepting his analysis of the limitations of demonstrable knowledge, they feel that his efforts to extend reason so as to include nondemonstrable knowledge represent merely a desperate attempt to smuggle nonrational components into the realm of reason. For the existentialists, such passages as the following become compelling accounts of reason's limitations:

> Some hold that, owing to the necessity of knowing the primary premisses, there is no scientific knowledge. Others think there is, but that all truths are demonstrable. Neither doctrine is either true or a necessary deduction from the premisses. The first school, assuming that there is no way of knowing other than by demonstration, maintain that an infinite regress is involved, on the ground that if behind the prior stands no primary, we could not know the posterior though the prior (wherein they are right, for one cannot traverse an infinite series): If on the other hand—they say—the series terminates and there are primary premisses, yet these are unknowable because incapable of demonstration, which according to them is the only form of knowledge. And since thus one cannot know the primary premisses, knowledge of the conclusions which follow from them is not pure scientific knowledge nor properly knowing at all, but rests on the mere supposition that the premisses are true. The other party agree with them as regards knowing, holding that it is only possible by demonstration, but they see no difficulty in holding that all truths are demonstrated, on the ground that demonstration may be circular and reciprocal. . . . Our own doctrine is that not all knowledge is demonstrative: on the contrary, knowledge of the immediate premisses is independent of demonstration. (The necessity of this is obvious; for since we must know the prior premisses from which the demonstration is drawn, and since the regress must end in immediate truths, those truths must be undemonstrable.) [4]

AUGUSTINE AND PASCAL

The transition from the views of the major Greek philosophers to those of the early Christian thinkers involved a gradually diminishing claim for the power of reason to resolve human difficulties. Perhaps the most perceptive critique of its efficacy was that given by St. Augustine. In one of the most poignant and sincere autobiographies ever written, *The Confessions,* Augustine faced up to the limitations of his capacities as a human being and to the fleeting nature of his achievements. With a finite understanding of things, subject to enslavement to his desires, swept by conflicting winds of passion, corrupted even by his own standards of morality and unsure of the principles that ought to guide him through life, man stands revealed as a depraved creature. More alarming still, Augustine discovered that man is unable to extricate himself from this depraved and helpless condition through his own capacities. Moreover, man's need to escape his depravity grows in intensity as he comes to recognize himself for what he is. The despair becomes total when he realizes that reason alone—man's highest and most celebrated faculty—is as unequal to the task of extricating man from his predicament as are any of the other human capacities:

> For what flood of eloquence can suffice to detail the miseries of this life? . . . For where, when, how, in this life can these primary objects of nature be possessed so that they may not be assailed by unforeseen accidents? Is the body of the wise man exempt from any pain which may dispel pleasure, from any disquietude which may banish repose? The amputation or decay of the members of the body puts an end to its integrity, deformity blights its beauty, weakness its health, lassitude its vigour, sleepiness or sluggishness its activity,— and which of these is it that may not assail the flesh of the wise man? [5]

The claim of a philosopher like Epicurus that reason is a sufficiently practical instrument to select appropriate means for achieving happiness has a hollow ring for Augustine because happiness of this sort is not lasting. The Epicurean doctrine of happiness depends on the truth of the claim that only the desires which reason can serve are essential to happiness. For example, Epicurus dismisses man's basic desire for immortality; he plays fast and loose with the yearning for immortality that characterizes most men. Still more discouraging is Augustine's recognition that—Plato and Aristotle's views notwithstanding—even when one exercises reason in its purest and noblest form, one does not partake thereby of the eternal truths as he comes to comprehend them. Man's greatest rational efforts are significant precisely because they attest to his need to identify with the eternal; paradoxically, however, they remain mere exercises in pointing out the goal of immortality rather than being stages of advance toward it. The situation is further complicated by the fact that the very success of reason in recognizing the eternal may lead us falsely to identify reason with the eternal; this breeds in us an intellectual pride that blocks the acknowledgment of our own predicament and blinds us to our limitations.

Augustine counsels us to *know ourselves*, that is, to recognize that we are imperfect, dependent creatures seeking the perfection of the eternal. In his terms, this full acknowledgment constitutes the basis of faith and stands as a necessary prelude to an escape from our predicament, through the liberating intervention of "God's grace." It is in God alone that human despair comes to rest.

The Augustinian appraisal of the human situation was forcefully reasserted by Pascal (1623-1662):

> What a chimera then is man! What a novelty! What a monster, what a chaos, what a contradiction, what a prodigy! Judge of all things, imbecile worm of the earth; depository of truth, a sink of uncertainty and error; the pride and refuse of the universe! . . . When I consider the short duration of my life, swallowed up in the eternity before and after, the little space which I fill, and even can see, engulfed in the infinite immensity of spaces of which I am ignorant, and which knows me not, I am frightened. . . . Know then, proud man, what a paradox you are to yourself. Humble yourself, weak reason; be silent, foolish nature; learn that man infinitely transcends man, and learn from your Master your condition, of which you are ignorant. Hear God.[6]

In these passages, man is represented as a "frail reed" to whom the universe remains incomprehensible despite his effort to grasp it through reason, and beyond this, as a creature with an absolute desire to establish a measure of rapport with an otherwise hostile or indifferent universe. If this desire is left unsatisfied, any man is condemned to a solitary life of terror.

Whereas Augustine was concerned with the difficulties that stand in the way of man coming to *know* God, Pascal directed his attention to the problem of coming to *believe* in God. Impressed with the Augustinian point that belief in God precedes knowledge of God, Pascal was most concerned to investigate the basis of such belief. He concluded that only belief in God will assuage man's need to be in harmony with the universe. Whether or not God's existence can be established conclusively through empirical or rational methods is basically unimportant; what Pascal declared is important, rather, is that solely through our belief in God can we move to a state in which we are no longer alienated from the rest of the universe.

HEGEL

Of all the modern philosophers, perhaps George W. F. Hegel stands in the most interesting relationship to the existentialists. Paradoxically, he is an object of their derision since he made unlimited claims for reason, while at the same time he provided them with important philosophical insights and to a great extent established the philosophical framework within which existentialism functions.

The Hegelian concept of "alienation" or "estrangement" illustrates his direct contribution to contemporary existentialism. As we noted, both Augustine and Pascal provided us with descriptions of the human situation to which these terms are relevant. They did not, however, supply us with an adequate philosophical account of these concepts.

In his *Philosophy of Mind* Hegel used the term "experience" to describe the conscious process of alienation in which simultaneously we not only distinguish between datum and pure thought but also externalize both of them. This flow of experience finally reaches a critical point at which the two kinds of alienation become acute. The first type might be termed Platonic: that is, the datum and pure thought, the particular existent and the essence, the table and the Idea of the table are so totally divorced from one another that on principle there can be no connection or mediation between them. In the second type of alienation, of more interest to the existentialist, both the datum and the pure thought seem to exist independent of our consciousness: that is, the perceiver appears to be related only accidentally or externally to the perceived, and the thinker, a mere instrument of thought. For Hegel, these developing dichotomies occasion a new phase in the evolution of mind or consciousness, one in which the process of experience is toward unity in both senses, that is, toward synthesizing data and thoughts and toward obliterating the distinction between the objective and subjective components of experience. As Hegel said:

> Since it is in the medium of consciousness that mind is developed and brings out its various moments, this opposition between the factors of conscious life is found at each stage in the evolution of mind, and all the various moments appear as modes or forms of consciousness. . . . Consciousness knows and comprehends nothing but what falls within its experience. . . . And experience is called this very process by which the element that is immediate, unexperienced, *i.e.*, abstract—whether it be in the form of sense or of a bare thought

—externalizes itself and then comes back to itself from this stage of estrangement, and by so doing is at length set forth in its concrete nature and real truth, and becomes too a possession of consciousness.[7]

Just as the existentialists interpret Aristotle's account of reason as testimony to the primacy of nonreason, so too they interpret Hegel's account of rational experience as a description of the tensions that reason produces but that reason cannot dissipate. Thus, they accept his view of the cognitive origin of alienation but deny his claim that reason is capable of uniting that which it has separated. In a word, the existentialists subscribe to the thesis that reason is an instrument suitable only for analyzing and abstracting; according to them, it is fanciful to expect the instrument of analysis and abstraction to synthesize and concretize, the instrument of divorce to effect a reconciliation. Furthermore, the existentialists view the Hegelian cognitive alienation as critical not because of the intellectual problem it poses, but because of the emotional problem it generates.

It is worth repeating, however, that although the existentialists are preoccupied with criticizing Hegel and his successors, they nevertheless agree with him on certain cardinal points: most conspicuously, they agree— as the majority of contemporary British philosophers would not—that the immediate, raw data of our experience are chaotic and that man cannot avoid being preoccupied with this fact. Furthermore, the existentialists can agree with Hegel that reason in and of itself is powerless to deal with raw data. For Hegel, however, such immediate experience is made increasingly intelligible, and therefore real, as reason fulfills its unified function of categorizing experience. In sharp contrast, the existentialists claim that the unifying function of reason is limited rather than unlimited, productive of appearance rather than of reality. It is their view that the application of reason to the world of immediate, particular experience serves only as an insidious mechanism for escaping from reality.

KIERKEGAARD

The existentialists' unqualified protest against the traditional ways in which philosophers have tended to depict man began with Sören Kierkegaard (1813–1855). As a strict Christian moralist who felt the stultifying effects of the political, social, and religious institutions of his time and the post-Hegelian atmosphere, Kierkegaard launched a crusade to make men renounce their identification with state, society, church, and, most insidious of all, speculative metaphysical systems. He lashed out at the social institutions of his time, just as many sensitive observers do today, because these institutions demanded that the individual conform rather than exercise his freedom and because they reduced him to an anonymous entity rather than acknowledged him as a person valuable as an end in himself. Kierkegaard saw not only the institutions such as the modern state and church as denigrating enemies of man's dignity, but also their respective supporting ideologies and theologies. For example, the view is put forward by classical economists that man is essentially an acquisitive creature, basically describable with reference to his economic interests. To view man in this way is to attribute to him as his essential characteristic one that he exhibits in certain types of societies, and thereby to perpetuate those kinds of societies by diverting man from exercising his basic freedom.

But most threatening to the uniqueness of man, according to Kierkegaard, is the penchant of philosophers for employing abstract reasoning in building grandiose metaphysical systems in which the nature of man is viewed as irrevocably fixed; man is shown in preestablished relationships to the cosmos. Such speculative philosophers offer men the narcotic of self-delusion that inhibits them from gaining self-knowledge. As the contemporary existentialist Karl Jaspers (1883–   ) put it, following Kierkegaard: "The philosopher of systems is, as a man, like someone who builds a castle, but lives next door in a shanty. Such a fantastical being does not himself live within what he thinks; but the thought of a man must be the house in which he lives or it will become perverted." [8]

Kierkegaard rejected as futile Hegel's attempt to conceptualize all things through the dialectical method. The error that Kierkegaard sees in such a rationalistic effort can be comprehended by contrasting Kierkegaard's ultimate datum, personal existence, with a representative Hegelian concept, say the concept of unity. If personal existence is to be regarded in the way that Hegel viewed unity, then it is a concept, since concepts enter into deduction and become thereby knowable. Thus, if personal existence were a concept, we would have to grasp it through an exercise of reason. But Kierkegaard pointed out that our awareness of personal existence comes about by a transrational act, a special kind of "encounter"; that is, it comes about through a direct feeling rather than through the abstracting activity of the intellect. This means then that the Kierkegaardian "personal existence" cannot be accounted for within the Hegelian system. Our perception of contrast between Kierkegaard and Hegel is sharpened additionally when we note that, for Kierkegaard, personal existence stands in *absolute* opposition to nonpersonal existence. This means that each individual man is faced with the inexorable situation of either being or not being himself. The mediating and synthesizing forces of reason are not effective at this fundamental level.

For Kierkegaard and his successors, exhibit A in their case against extreme rationalism might well be Hegel's view of the self. They would feel that a passage such as the following must be rejected by anyone who aspires, who loves, who suffers, who struggles—in short, who lives:

> By the term "I" I mean myself, a single and altogether determinate person. And yet I really utter nothing peculiar to myself, for everyone else is an "I" or "Ego," and when I called myself "I," though I indubitably mean the single person myself, I express a thorough universal. "I," therefore, is mere being-for-self, in which everything peculiar or marked is renounced and buried out of sight; it is as it were the ultimate and unanalyzable point of consciousness. We may say [that] "I" and thought are the same, or, more definitely, [that] "I" is thought as a thinker.[9]

But it is one thing to demand that the subjective side of man be considered rather than eliminated by Hegelian magic, and quite another to communicate intelligently about it. The opponents of existentialism insist that Kierkegaard and, indeed, all his followers, face the dilemma either of conceptualizing that which cannot be conceptualized or of failing altogether to communicate. While sensitive to the dilemma, the existentialist seeks to escape it by the use of language that induces feelings comparable to his in others. His mode of communication is far more like that of the artist than that of the scientist. Thus we find him writing diaries, plays, novels, and, in any event, avoiding direct, precise forms of communication.

Through the masterly use of evocative language, Kierkegaard attempted to make each of us aware of our primal subjectivity, so that we may live authentically, without the crutch of antecedent social and intellectual guides. He conveyed the message that one can only live authentically—become a person—by bearing the sole responsibility for his decisions rather than by appealing to the authority of custom or even of one's own past patterns of thought. Perhaps some realization of our lives as *crisis* may be captured by giving a list of false statements about the basis for making decisions: (1) such decisions are the necessary result of cultural patterns; (2) such decisions are products of rational deliberation; (3) such decisions are based on relative strengths of desires; (4) such decisions are habitual responses; (5) such decisions are forced by motives. Kierkegaard's "freedom of choice" must not be understood as in any sense involving deliberation among alternatives; our freedom to choose can have no limits. Some suggestion of what is intended by this meaning of freedom is captured by the phrase "a free act of imagination." What we imagine does not result from selecting among things that we might imagine; rather, it is the result of a spontaneous act of creation.

Kierkegaard attempted to make us dramatically aware of the path we must travel if we are to achieve genuine personal existence—a path that involves us in nothing less than a leap across a bottomless chasm. This awareness of the conditions for becoming authentic constitutes a part of self-knowledge. But the full truth, that is, the completion of self-knowledge, is the "intensified awareness" of an encounter with God in the person of the Christ. What is stressed in Kierkegaard's and all other Christian existentialists' accounts is, just as it is in Augustine's *Confessions*, that an individual can truly know himself only through an encounter with God.

Kierkegaard did not provide, nor did he intend to provide, objective grounds for a belief in God's existence or even a conceptual account of God's nature. Since, as we have just suggested, "existing" for the existentialist involves temporal engagement or encounter, it would seem strange to ascribe existence to God, the eternal. For Kierkegaard, man's relationship to God becomes extremely perplexing. How is it possible for a temporal being to encounter an eternal one? Am I not, because of my temporality, cut off from any relation whatsoever with the Divine? Kierkegaard insisted that this paradox about the man-God relationship can be resolved only by faith in the incarnation; that is, it can be resolved only through believing in the conceptual absurdity that God, the eternal, enters into a relationship with individual men through the person of Christ, the temporal. But the demands of faith do not end here. How do we know that the God to which we are led by our intense inwardness is the Christian God? Might it not be Satan, a nameless something, or even an imaginative projection? Kierkegaard answered that we cannot know, that the religious commitment must proceed without any objective certainty about the nature of God. Of greatest importance is not the external, rationally appraised *what* to which we relate, but rather the inward felt *how*. "*An objective uncertainty held fast in an appropriation-process of the most passionate inwardness is the truth*, the highest truth attainable for an existing individual." [10]

NIETZSCHE AND BERGSON

During the latter portion of the nineteenth and the beginning of the twentieth century, a number of writers created a favorable cultural climate for the growth of existentialism. Dostoyevsky (1821–1881) probed deeply into human subjectivity and freedom in his works. Poets such as Hölderlin (1770–1843) and Rilke (1875–1926) addressed themselves to the problem of man overcoming his alienation from God. But the most conspicuous figure among the catalysts of existentialism was Friedrich Nietzsche (1844–1900).

Nietzsche, no less than Kierkegaard, was appalled by the insidious subversion of the individual resulting from the modern state, orthodox religion, and all-embracing philosophical systems. While Kierkegaard's response to the tragedy of modern man was one of dread and despair, Nietzsche's response was one of anger and disgust. He saw everywhere a civilization slowly dying from glorifying the past rather than appreciating it as an earlier portion of a continuing adventure: The philosophers so honor Aristotle that they become Aristotelians rather than thinking for themselves; disciples are so taken up adoring Jesus that they become Christians rather than individuals seeking a proper relationship to God; and the politicians are so busy celebrating the achievements of past heroes that they fail to lead. For Nietzsche, the brute facts were that the accomplishments of a civilization are a function of the courage, audacity, and creative genius of individuals and that the health of a civilization is measured, not by its homogeneity, but by the continued appearance of genuine men who insist on establishing and seeking to achieve their own norms or standards.

He took it to be the basic fact of nature that every living form strives not only to survive but also to remake and overpower its environment. Biological evolution and human history derive their meaning and course from organic nature as a myriad manifestation of the Will to Power. Nietzsche warned that the life principle, this Will to Power that needs always to be affirmed by the individual, was in danger of being subverted by the modern institutions of conformity. The hour is late for all those who can still feel the pulse of life! Nothing short of a complete "transvaluation of values" will suffice if men are to regain their creative freedom.

Again Nietzsche, like Kierkegaard, advocated "authentic living" and insisted that the individual must make his decisions entirely on his own, without regard for social and religious mores or for speculative rational systems. That is to say, Nietzsche too insisted that we can become ourselves only by stripping away all externalities. But in contrast with Kierkegaard, Nietzsche portrayed freedom as dynamic rather than as static. Unfettered by conventions of behavior and thought, Nietzschean man achieves immediate and joyous release of his creative energies, in contrast with Kierkegaardian man who is left helplessly suffering the agony of intense inwardness. Furthermore, whereas a free man, according to Kierkegaard, unqualifiedly rejects reason and institutionalized society, Nietzsche's free man at least accepts them insofar as he can manipulate them for his own ends.

Denying his account of freedom, contemporary existentialists nevertheless find Nietzsche full of suggestive portrayals of the human situation. For example, he advanced the thesis that for modern man "God is dead." The existentialists seize upon this theme as a dramatic way of capturing and communicating the awesome fact that the individual is thrust into a dreadful situation in which he alone is responsible for his choices. However, they remain unimpressed with Nietzsche's optimistic view that in removing this barrier to freedom, man moves toward that stage in which he becomes capable of genuine accomplishment.

Henri Bergson (1859–1941), a French philosopher of immense popularity at the end of the nineteenth and beginning of the twentieth century, also contributed notably to the anti-intellectual climate that supported existentialism. While it is inaccurate to refer to him as an opponent of reason to the degree that Nietzsche was, he still warns against all who regard intellect as more than a practical instrument. He deplored the mechanistic and static view of reality that seemingly drew its support from science; instead, reality was radically organic and dynamic. The mechanist mistakes scientific for metaphysical inquiry, and the follower of "scientism" mistakes the sign or symbol for that which is signified. Bergson defined metaphysics as "the science which claims to dispense with symbols." [11] He held that insofar as there are realities, we must seize them, as it were, from within, by intuition, rather than by intellectual analysis. He insisted that intuition is the sole direct means for apprehending reality; symbols irrevocably distort reality by representing interpenetrated things as separated, and collections of distinctively individual things as wholes characterized by a multiplicity of attributes. Furthermore, he maintained that any attempted analysis of the symbols we use serves only to spell out the very distortions inherent in the symbols themselves. While symbols "may be abstracted by our thought from mobile reality . . . there are no means of reconstructing the mobility of the real with fixed concepts." [12]

Yet Bergson could not completely dispense with symbols—particularly those of the scientist. He admitted, somewhat grudgingly in some of his writings, that metaphysics must use the knowledge of objective affairs that derives from science as a rough guide, or better, as a catalytic agent to activate intuition. However, our intuitions, whatever their origin, provide us with our knowledge of reality. It is in this sense that we have referred to Bergson as anti-intellectual.

Bergson's opposition to the tyranny of scientific concepts in the area of human existence illustrates his kinship with the existentialist. He warned us that any effort to "know thyself" through conceptualization is tragically foredoomed. In representing himself as a spatiotemporal object, capable of being subsumed under the deterministic categories of science, the individual systematically rejects the inner life with its uniqueness, freedom, and growth that intuition alone can discern. Approached scientifically, an individual remains indistinguishable from all other individuals, since the object of science is precisely that which is common to the species *Homo sapiens*. The message of Bergson's philosophy is that the price we pay for excessive dependence on intellectual analysis is the loss of our very identities.

HUSSERL AND HEIDEGGER

Edmund Husserl (1859–1938) had and continues to have a great influence on existentialism, though his avowed interests and sympathies lay elsewhere. Although he was critical of the major intellectual accomplishments of his day—logic, mathematics, the natural sciences, rationalistic and empirical philosophies—he did not seek to minimize their importance in the manner of an enemy of reason; he rather sought to correct them.

The central insight in the Husserlian philosophy can be indicated most readily by examining his remarks on Descartes. On the one hand, he applauded Descartes for challenging the epistemological assumption of the objectivists that we may know the external world *directly* through experience and agreed with Descartes that the data of experience alone do not demonstrate the existence of the external world. On the other hand, he criticized Descartes for yielding to a subjectivism in which the data of experience are shorn of all reference to the external world. Husserl contended that to succumb to this subjectivism is to miss the essential feature of our awareness, namely, its intending, its referring beyond itself. In brief, for him, the items of our experience are, in and of themselves, *signs* or phenomenological objects and as such have meaning or signification, quite independent of the experiencing self on the one hand and the existence of the external world on the other.

We are now in a position to glimpse the chief influence that Husserl exerted on the existentialists. Descartes' critical doubt led him finally to conceive the self or human ego as a "thinking thing" that is radically different from all extended things. However, this leads us to the question: How is it possible for a disembodied self to stand in any kind of relationship with its physical environment? According to Husserl, no amount of ingenious metaphysical manipulation by a dualist can provide us with a satisfactory answer. In contrast with Descartes, Husserl's method of doubt led him to depict the human ego as that which is always related to the world, however much doubt we may cast on the world's existence. His analysis of the human ego as inextricably "leading" beyond itself provides an attractive philosophical basis for those among the existentialists who attempt to answer the charge that they are merely engaged in the literary expression of some form of subjectivism. However, this is not the main conclusion of the Husserlian analysis. He proceeded to isolate the "transcendental ego," which is constituted by our pure consciousness of what it is to be a human ego thus engaged in the world. This ego, this passive observer, of which Husserl spoke in the final phase of his analysis, is itself totally removed from the world of human involvements with which the existentialists are preoccupied. Thus, Husserl's philosophy, like Hegel's, is viewed by the existentialists as a source of important insights, even though they do not accept it as a system.

Husserl's most direct influence on existentialism was through his student Martin Heidegger (1889–   ). The Husserlian depiction of the human ego in its "intending" relationships afforded Heidegger a philosophical basis for his concept of "concern," a concept that he employed to show the individual as outward—rather than inward—oriented. It was Husserl's "natural ego" rather than his "transcendental ego" that became the focal point of Heidegger's philosophy. Husserl and Heidegger warned against regarding the "natural ego" as no more than an isolated component of the formula "man-having-experience, the experiences themselves, and that-which-is-experienced." Husserl's antidote to this atomistic analysis was to seek understanding of our-being-in-the-world by becoming spectators of ourselves-in-the-world. Heidegger, however, regarded any such effort to transcend ourselves as a retreat from being-in-the-world and as fatal even for appreciating the human situation. It is only when we are deeply engaged, when we are in the world in the fullest sense, that *Dasein* —the proper mode of human existence—is revealed, and, beyond this, that we discern Being itself, that ultimate ground of all modes of being, including the human mode.

By *Dasein*, Heidegger meant man responsibly creating himself through choice; more specifically, he seemed to be characterizing my human existence as authentic only when I face up to the world in all its particularity and concreteness. When I deal with the world through abstractions, that is, when I regard its objects as mere congeries of universals, I deceive myself and live inauthentically. Like Kierkegaard before him, Heidegger depicted authentic man as eschewing the palliatives of either socially directed responses or intellectualized acts in favor of responsibly, albeit painfully, committing himself to act without social precedence or rational guidance. He then was insisting that the human situation is a succession of unique confrontations demanding unique responses. Thus, for example, when I deal authentically with another human being, I am in the agonizing situation of having to deal with a unique individual in a unique circumstance offering an unlimited range of possible courses of action for which there can be no guidelines as to choice; yet the situation demands that I choose and fully accept the burdensome responsibility for that choice.

Speaking quite generally, Heidegger's answer to why people tend toward inauthentic rather than authentic existence is that we do so to avoid *dread*. To understand this answer and place it in perspective, we must analyze this emotion. Of all the human emotions, it is at once the least specific with regard to its source and purpose and at the same time the most fundamental, because it is a necessary concomitant of authentic living. Consider another important emotion—fear. We ordinarily have very little difficulty tracing fear to a specific cause and taking specific steps to remove it. However, we find that dread ultimately has its origin in our very mode of being. No particular object or event causes dread, and no change in the course of events can eliminate it. Yet there is a possibility of gaining limited relief from this fundamental human emotion. Through ignoring or postponing or seeking to reform or understand the human situation, we lose ourselves in some form of anonymity. But membership in any "human beings anonymous" club is a temporary expedient that cannot remedy the basic condition of life.

The normative feature of Heidegger's philosophy manifests itself at this point. The painful human condition—a condition in which accomplishment is a mere illusion and happiness an evasion—permits only one value, the value of recognizing and bearing the nothingness of human existence. Human dignity rests on the heroic acknowledgment of this dreadful truth. The sole imperative is: live authentically.

The thinkers we speak of as existentialists may be described more properly as men sharing a way of viewing things than as men contributing to a systematic philosophical movement. Any attempt at forming existentialists into schools is likely to hinder rather than to help us in understanding them. For example, we may say, as is sometimes said, that Jean-Paul

Sartre (1905–   ) is the leader of atheistic existentialism while Paul Tillich (1886–1966) is the outstanding spokesman of religious or Christian existentialism. But these classifications tend to detract from the basic importance of their common approach to philosophy. It is not a distortion to claim that Tillich has far less in common with many of the theologians, say, of the Anglican church than he has with Sartre. Our first selection, from Sartre, reveals the existential situation and depicts its essential hopelessness. Our second selection, from Tillich, characterizes the human situation and finds there a basis for religious hope.

Jean-Paul Sartre: NAUSEA

> IN HIS NOVEL Nausea, *Jean-Paul Sartre is concerned to introduce his reader to existentialism by immersing him in an emotional situation. The general point he wishes to make is that the world is radically contingent, that is, we cannot account for existence on any rational basis. Attempting to know things through such devices of reason as definitions, classifications, and theories is at best a philosophically superfluous and fruitless endeavor, and at its worst an escape from owning up to the absurdity of existence. Sartre's message is not entirely negative: a person can, with a measure of relief, confront the brute reality without recourse to the illusions provided by reason and thereby enter into authentic existence.*
>
> *The following passages are reprinted by kind permission of New Directions (Laughlin), who published the English translation by L. Alexander of Sartre's* Nausea, *and represent pp. 170–182.*

I can't say I feel relieved or satisfied; just the opposite, I am crushed. Only my goal is reached: I know what I wanted to know; I have understood all that has happened to me since January. The Nausea has not left me and I don't believe it will leave me so soon; but I no longer have to bear it, it is no longer an illness or a passing fit: it is I.

Existentialism: Jean-Paul Sartre

So I was in the park just now. The roots of the chestnut tree were sunk in the ground just under my bench. I couldn't remember it was a root any more. The words had vanished and with them the significance of things, their methods of use, and the feeble points of reference which men have traced on their surface. I was sitting, stooping forward, head bowed, alone in front of this black, knotty mass, entirely beastly, which frightened me. Then I had this vision.

It left me breathless. Never, until these last few days, had I understood the meaning of "existence." I was like the others, like the ones walking along the seashore, all dressed in their spring finery. I said, like them, "The ocean *is* green; that white speck up there *is* a seagull," but I didn't feel that it existed or that the seagull was an "existing seagull"; usually existence hides itself. It is there, around us, in us, it is *us*, you can't say two words without mentioning it, but you can never touch it. When I believed I was thinking about it, I must believe that I was thinking nothing, my head was empty, or there was just one word in my head, the word "to be." Or else I was thinking . . . how can I explain it? I was thinking of belonging, I was telling myself that the sea belonged to the class of green objects, or that the green was a part of the quality of the sea. Even when I looked at things, I was miles from dreaming that they existed: they looked like scenery to me. I picked them up in my hands, they served me as tools, I foresaw their resistance. But that all happened on the surface. If anyone had asked me what existence was, I would have answered, in good faith, that it was nothing, simply an empty form which was added to external things without changing anything in their nature. And then all of a sudden, there it was, clear as day: existence had suddenly unveiled itself. It had lost the harmless look of an abstract category: it was the very paste of things, this root was kneaded into existence. Or rather the root, the park gates, the bench, the sparse grass, all that had vanished: the diversity of things, their individuality, were only an appearance, a veneer. This veneer had melted, leaving soft, monstrous masses, all in disorder—naked, in a frightful, obscene nakedness.

I kept myself from making the slightest movement, but I didn't need to move in order to see, behind the trees, the blue columns and the lamp-posts of the bandstand and the Velleda, in the midst of a mountain of laurel. All these objects . . . how can I explain? They inconvenienced me; I would have liked them to exist less strongly, more dryly, in a more abstract way, with more reserve. The chestnut tree pressed itself against my eyes. Green rust covered it half-way up; the bark, black and swollen, looked like boiled leather. The sound of the water in the Masqueret Fountain sounded in my ears, made a nest there, filled them with signs; my nostrils overflowed with a green, putrid odour. All things, gently, tenderly, were letting themselves drift into existence like those relaxed women who burst out laughing and say: "It's good to laugh," in a wet voice; they were parading, one in front of the other, exchanging abject secrets about their existence. I realized that there was no half-way house between non-existence and this flaunting abundance. If you existed, you had to *exist all the way*, as far as mouldiness, bloatedness, obscenity were concerned. In another world, circles, bars of music keep their pure and rigid lines. But existence is a deflection. Trees, night-blue pillars, the happy bubbling of a fountain, vital smells, little heat-mists floating in the cold air, a red-haired man digesting on a bench: all this somnolence, all these meals digested together, had its comic side. ... Comic ... no: it didn't go as far as that, nothing that exists can be comic; it was like a floating analogy, almost entirely elusive, with certain aspects of vaudeville. We were a heap of living creatures, irritated, embarrassed at ourselves, we hadn't the slightest reason to be there, none of us, each one, confused, vaguely alarmed, felt in the way in relation to the others. *In the way:* it was the only relationship I could establish between these trees, these gates, these stones. In vain I tried to *count* the chestnut trees, to *locate* them by their relationship to the Velleda, to compare their height with the height of the plane trees: each of them escaped the relationship in which I tried to enclose it, isolated itself, and overflowed. Of these relations (which I insisted on maintaining in order to delay the crumbling of the human world, measures, quantities, and directions) —I felt myself to be the arbitrator; they no longer had their teeth into things. *In the way,* the chestnut tree there, opposite me, a little to the left. *In the way,* the Velleda. ...

And I—soft, weak, obscene, digesting, juggling with dismissal thoughts—I, too, was *In the way.* Fortunately, I didn't feel it, although I realized it, but I was uncomfortable because I was afraid of feeling it (even now I am afraid—afraid that it might catch me behind my head and lift me up like a wave). I dreamed vaguely of killing myself to wipe out at least one of these superfluous lives. But even my death would have been *In the way. In the way,* my corpse, my blood on these stones, between these plants, at the back of this smiling garden. And the decomposed flesh would have been *In the way* in the earth which would receive my bones, at last, cleaned, stripped, peeled, proper and clean as teeth, it would have been *In the way:* I was in the way for eternity.

The word absurdity is coming to life under my pen; a little while ago, in the garden, I couldn't find it, but neither was I looking for it, I didn't need it: I thought without words, *on* things, *with* things. Absurdity was not an idea in my head, or the sound of a voice, only this long serpent dead at my feet, this wooden serpent. Serpent or claw or root or vulture's talon, what difference does it make. And without formulating anything clearly, I understood that I had found the key to Existence, the key to my Nauseas, to my own life. In fact, all that I could grasp beyond that returns to this fundamental absurdity. Absurdity: another word; I struggle against words; down there I touched the thing. But I wanted to fix the absolute character of this absurdity here. A movement, an event in the tiny coloured world of men is only relatively absurd: by relation to the accompanying circumstances. A madman's ravings, for example, are absurd in relation to the situation in which he finds himself, but not in relation to his delirium. But a little while ago I made an experiment with the absolute or the absurd. Oh, how can I put it in words? Absurd: in relation to the stones, the tufts of yellow grass, the dry mud, the tree, the sky, the green benches. Absurd, irreducible; nothing—not even a profound, secret upheaval of nature—could explain it. Evidently I did not know everything, I had not seen the seeds sprout, or the tree grow. But faced with this great wrinkled paw, neither ignorance nor knowledge was important: the world of explanations and reasons is not the world of existence. A circle is not absurd, it is clearly explained by the rotation of a straight segment around one of its extremities. But neither does a circle exist. This root, on the other hand, existed in such a way that I could not explain it. Knotty, inert, nameless, it fascinated me, filled my eyes, brought me back unceasingly to its own existence. In vain to repeat: "This is a root"—it didn't work any more. I saw clearly that you could not pass from its function as a root, as a breathing pump, to that, to this hard and compact skin of a sea lion, to nothing: it allowed you to understand generally that it was a root, but not *that one* at all. This root, with its colour, shape, its congealed movement, was . . . below all explanation. Each of its qualities escaped it a little, flowed out of it, half solidified, almost became a thing; each one was *in the way* in the root and the whole stump now gave me the impression of unwinding itself a little, denying its existence to lose itself in a frenzied excess. I scraped my heel against this black claw: I wanted to peel off some of the bark. For no reason at all, out of defiance, to make the bare pink appear absurd on the tanned leather: to *play* with the absurdity of the world. But, when I drew my heel back, I saw that the bark was still black.

 Black? I felt the word deflating, emptied of meaning with extraordinarily rapidity. Black? The root *was not* black, there was no black on this piece of wood—there was . . . something else: black, like the circle, did not exist. I looked at the root: was it *more than* black or *almost* black? But I soon stopped questioning myself because I had the feeling of knowing where I was. Yes, I had already tried—vainly—to think something *about* them: and I had already felt their cold, inert qualities elude me, slip through my fingers. Adolphe's suspenders, the other evening in the "Railwaymen's Rendezvous." They *were not* purple. I saw the two inexplicable stains on the shirt. And the stone—the well-known stone, the origin of this whole business: it was not . . . I can't remember exactly just what it was that the stone refused to be. But I had not forgotten its passive resistance. And the hand of the Self-Taught Man; I held it and shook it one day in the library and then I had the feeling that it wasn't quite a hand. I had thought of a great white worm, but that wasn't it either. And the suspicious transparency of the glass of beer in the Cafe Mably. Suspicious: that's what they were, the sounds, the smells, the tastes. When they ran quickly under your nose like startled hares and you didn't pay too much attention, you might believe them to be simple and reassuring, you might believe that there was real blue in the world, real red, a real perfume of almonds or violets. But as soon as you held on to them for an instant, this feeling of comfort and security gave way to a deep uneasiness: colours, tastes, and smells were never real, never themselves and nothing but themselves. The simplest, most indefinable quality had too much content, in relation to itself, in its heart. That black against my foot, it didn't look like black, but rather the confused effort to imagine black by someone who had never seen black and who wouldn't know how to stop, who would have imagined an ambiguous being beyond colours. It *looked* like a colour, but also . . . like a bruise or a secretion, like an oozing—and something else, an odour, for example, it melted into the odour of wet earth, warm, moist wood, into a black odour that spread like varnish over this sensitive wood, in a flavour of chewed, sweet fibre. I did not simply *see* this black: sight is an abstract invention, a simplified idea, one of man's ideas. That black, amorphous, weakly presence, far surpassed sight, smell and taste. But this richness was lost in confusion and finally was no more because it was too much.

This moment was extraordinary. I was there, motionless and icy, plunged in a horrible ecstasy. But something fresh had just appeared in the very heart of this ecstasy; I understood the Nausea, I possessed it. To tell the truth, I did not formulate my discoveries to myself. But I think it would be easy for me to put them in words now. The essential thing is contingency. I mean that one cannot define existence as necessity. To exist is simply *to be there*; those who exist let themselves be encountered, but you can never deduce anything from them. I believe there are people who have understood this. Only they tried to overcome this contingency by inventing a necessary, causal being. But no necessary being can explain existence: contingency is not a delusion, a probability which can be dissipated; it is the absolute, consequently, the perfect free gift. All is free, this park, this city and myself. When you realize that, it turns your heart upside down and everything begins to float, as the other evening at the "Railwaymen's Rendezvous": here is Nausea; here there is what those bastards—the ones on the Coteau Vert and others—try to hide from themselves with their idea of their rights. But what a poor lie: no one has any rights; they are entirely free, like other men, they cannot succeed in not feeling superfluous. And in themselves, secretly, they are *superfluous*, that is to say, amorphous, vague, and sad.

How long will this fascination last? I *was* the root of the chestnut tree. Or rather I was entirely conscious of its existence. Still detached from it—since I was conscious of it—yet lost in it, nothing but it. An uneasy conscience which, notwithstanding, let itself fall with all its weight on this piece of dead wood. Time had stopped: a small black pool at my feet; it was impossible for something to come *after* that moment. I would have liked to tear myself from that atrocious joy, but I did not even imagine it would be possible; I was inside; the black stump did *not move*, it stayed there, in my eyes, as a lump of food sticks in the windpipe. I could neither accept nor refuse it. At what a cost did I raise my eyes? Did I raise them? Rather did I not obliterate myself for an instant in order to be reborn in the following instant with my head thrown back and my eyes raised upward? In fact, I was not even conscious of the transformation. But suddenly it became impossible for me to think of the existence of the root. It was wiped out, I could repeat in vain: it exists, it is still there, under the bench, against my right foot, it no longer meant anything. Existence is not something which lets itself be thought of from a distance: it must invade you suddenly, master you, weigh heavily on your heart like a great motionless beast—or else there is nothing more at all.

There was nothing more, my eyes were empty and I was spellbound by my deliverance. Then suddenly it began to move before my eyes in light, uncertain motions: the wind was shaking the top of the tree.

It did not displease me to see a movement, it was a change from these motionless beings who watched me like staring eyes. I told myself, as I followed the swinging of the branches: movements never quite exist, they are passages, intermediaries between two existences, moments of weakness, I expected to see them come out of nothingness, progressively ripen, blossom: I was finally going to surprise beings in the process of being born.

No more than three seconds, and all my hopes were swept away. I could not attribute the passage of time to these branches groping around like blind men. This idea of passage was still an invention of man. The idea was too transparent. All these paltry agitations, drew in on themselves, isolated. They overflowed the leaves and branches everywhere. They whirled about these empty hands, enveloped them with tiny whirlwinds. Of course a movement was something different from a tree. But it was still an absolute. A thing. My eyes only encountered completion. The tips of the branches rustled with existence which unceasingly renewed itself and which was never born. The existing wind rested on the tree like a great bluebottle, and the tree shuddered. But the shudder was not a nascent quality, a passing from power to action; it was a thing; a shudder-thing flowed into the tree, took possession of it, shook it and suddenly abandoned it, going further on to spin about itself. All was fullness and all was active, there was no weakness in time, all, even the least perceptible stirring, was made of existence. And all these existents which bustled about this tree came from nowhere and were going nowhere. Suddenly they existed, then suddenly they existed no longer: existence is without memory; of the vanished it retains nothing—not even a memory. Existence everywhere, infinitely, in excess, for ever and everywhere; existence—which is limited only by existence. I sank down on the bench, stupefied, stunned by this profusion of beings without origin: everywhere blossomings, hatchings out, my ears buzzed with existence, my very flesh throbbed and opened, abandoned itself to the universal burgeoning. It was repugnant. But why, I thought, why so many existences, since they all look alike? What good are so many duplicates of trees? So many existences missed, obstinately begun again and again missed—like the awkward efforts of an insect fallen on its back? (I was one of those efforts.) That abundance did not give the effect of generosity, just the opposite. It was dismal, ailing, embarrassed at itself. Those trees, those great clumsy bodies. . . . I began to laugh because I suddenly thought of the formidable springs described in books, full of crackings, burstings, gigantic explosions. There were those idiots who came to tell you about will-power and struggle for life. Hadn't they ever seen a beast or a tree? This plane-tree with its scaling bark, this half-rotten oak, they wanted me to take them for rugged youthful endeavour surging towards the sky. And that root? I would have undoubtedly had to represent it as a voracious claw tearing at the earth, devouring its food?

Impossible to see things that way. Weaknesses, frailties, yes. The trees floated. Gushing towards the sky? Or rather a collapse; at any instant I expected to see the tree-trunks shrivel like weary wands, crumple up, fall on the ground in a soft, folded, black heap. They *did not want* to exist, only they could not help themselves. So they quietly minded their own business; the sap rose up slowly through the structure, half reluctant, and the roots sank slowly into the earth. But at each instant they seemed on the verge of leaving everything there and obliterating themselves. Tired and old, they kept on existing, against the grain, simply because they were too weak to die, because death could only come to them from the outside: strains of music alone can proudly carry their own death within themselves like an internal necessity: only they don't exist. Every existing thing is born without reason, prolongs itself out of weakness and dies by chance. I leaned back and closed my eyes. But the images, forewarned, immediately leaped up and filled my closed eyes with existences: existence is a fullness which man can never abandon.

Strange images. They represented a multitude of things. Not real things, other things which looked like them. Wooden objects which looked like chairs, shoes, other objects which looked like plants. And then two faces: the couple who were eating opposite to me last Sunday in the Brasserie Vezelize. Fat, hot, sensual, absurd, with red ears. I could see the woman's neck and shoulders. Nude existence. Those two—it suddenly gave me a turn—those two were still existing somewhere in Bouville; somewhere—in the midst of smells?—this soft throat rubbing up luxuriously against smooth stuffs, nestling in lace; and the woman picturing her bosom under her blouse . . . then I shouted and found myself with my eyes wide open.

Had I dreamed of this enormous presence? It was there, in the garden, toppled down into the trees, all soft, sticky, soiling everything, all thick, a jelly. And I was inside, I with the garden. I was frightened, furious, I thought it was so stupid, so out of place, I hated this ignoble mess. Mounting up, mounting up as high as the sky, spilling over, filling everything with its gelatinous slither, and I could see depths upon depths of it reaching far beyond the limits of the garden, the houses, and Bouville, as far as the eye could reach. I was no longer in Bouville, I was nowhere, I was floating. I was not surprised, I knew it was the world, the naked World suddenly revealing itself, and I choked with rage at this gross, absurd being. You couldn't even wonder where all that sprang from, or how it was that a world came into existence, rather than nothingness. It didn't make sense, the World was everywhere, in front, behind. There had been nothing *before* it. Nothing. There had never been a moment in which it could not have existed. That was what worried me: of course there was no *reason* for this flowing larva to exist. *But it was impossible* for it not to exist. It was unthinkable: to imagine nothingness you had to be there already, in the midst of the World, eyes wide open and alive; nothingness was only an idea in my head, an existing idea floating in this immensity: this nothingness had not come *before* existence it was an existence like any other and appeared after many others. I shouted "Filth! what rotten filth!" and shook myself to get rid of this sticky filth, but it held fast and there was so much, tons and tons of existence, endless: I stifled at the depths of this immense weariness. And then suddenly the park emptied as though a great hole, the World disappeared as it had come, or else I woke up—in any case, I saw no more of it; nothing was left but the yellow earth around me, out of which dead branches rose upward.

I got up and went out. Once at the gate, I turned back. Then the garden smiled at me. I leaned against the gate and watched for a long time. The smile of the trees, of the laurel, *meant* something; that was the real secret of existence. I remembered one Sunday, not more than three weeks ago, I had already detected everywhere a sort of conspiratorial air. Was it in my intention? I felt with boredom that I had no way of understanding. No way. Yet it was there, waiting, looking at one. It was there on the trunk of the chestnut tree . . . it was *the* chestnut tree. Things—you might have called them—thoughts—which stopped halfway, which were forgotten, which forgot what they wanted to think and which stayed like that, hanging about with an odd little sense which was beyond them. That little sense annoyed me: I *could not* understand it, even if I could have stayed leaning against the gate for a century; I had learned all I could know about existence. I left, I went back to the hotel and I wrote.

Paul Tillich: TYPES OF ANXIETY

TILLICH is concerned to discuss three types of anxiety which are genuinely existential rather than merely psychological aberrations. He calls the *first* of these the threat to "ontic self-affirmation" and is referring to our anxiety about death which permeates all human situations; he calls the *second* the threat to "spiritual self-affirmation" and is referring to our anxiety about the meaninglessness which accompanies an inability to participate in any cultural creation; he calls the third the threat to "moral self-affirmation" and is referring to our anxiety of guilt about what we have made of ourselves. Placing his emphasis on the first of these, Tillich points out that the fear of death is universal and absolutely inescapable. It underscores for the individual his finitude and contingency. Homeless and insecure, no matter how courageously he faces his challenges, he can be rewarded with no more than partial victories. To go to the obvious, in recovering from a disease, a man succeeds only in postponing his own ultimate defeat. There is no escape from the human predicament itself. Even though, for example, we are not consciously aware of death at every moment of our lives, our concern about death is of decisive importance in "the interpretation of existence as a whole."

Tillich's words come from his The Courage to Be, 1952, pp. 40–57, and are reprinted by kind permission of the Yale University Press.

THE THREE TYPES OF ANXIETY AND THE NATURE OF MAN

Nonbeing is dependent on the being it negates. "Dependent" means two things. It points first of all to the ontological priority of being over nonbeing. The term nonbeing itself indicates this, and it is logically necessary. There could be no negation if there were no preceding affirmation to be negated. Certainly one can describe being in terms of non-nonbeing; and one can justify such a description by pointing to the astonishing prerational fact that there is something and not nothing. One could say that "being is the negation of the primordial night of nothingness." But in doing so one must realize that such an aboriginal nothing would be neither nothing nor something, that it becomes nothing only in contrast to something; in other words, that the ontological status of nonbeing as nonbeing is dependent on being. Secondly, nonbeing is dependent on the special qualities of being. In itself nonbeing has no quality and no difference of qualities. But it gets them in relation to being. The character of the negation of being is determined by that in being which is negated. This makes it possible to speak of qualities of nonbeing and, consequently, of types of anxiety.

Up to now we have used the term nonbeing without differentiation, while in the discussion of courage several forms of self-affirmation were mentioned. They correspond to different forms of anxiety and are understandable only in correlation with them. I suggest that we distinguish three types of anxiety according to the three directions in which nonbeing threatens being. Nonbeing threatens man's ontic self-affirmation, relatively in terms of fate, absolutely in terms of death. It threatens man's spiritual self-affirmation, relatively in terms of emptiness, absolutely in terms of meaninglessness. It threatens man's moral self-affirmation, relatively in terms of guilt, absolutely in terms of condemnation. The awareness of this threefold threat is anxiety appearing in three forms, that of fate and death (briefly, the anxiety of death), that of emptiness and loss of meaning (briefly, the anxiety of meaninglessness), that of guilt and condemnation (briefly, the anxiety of condemnation). In all three forms anxiety is existential in the sense that it belongs to existence as such and not to an abnormal state of mind as in neurotic (and psychotic) anxiety. The nature of neurotic anxiety and its relation to existential anxiety will be discussed in another chapter. We shall deal now with the three forms of existential anxiety, first with their reality in the life of the individual, then with their social manifestations in special periods of Western history. However, it must be stated that the difference of types does not mean mutual exclusion. In the first chapter we have seen for instance that the courage to be as it appears in the ancient Stoics conquers not only the fear of death but also the threat of meaninglessness. In Nietzsche we find that in spite of the predominance of the threat of meaninglessness, the anxiety of death and condemnation is passionately challenged. In all representatives of classical Christianity death and sin are seen as the allied adversaries against which the courage of faith has to fight. The three forms of anxiety (and of courage) are immanent in each other but normally under the dominance of one of them.

THE ANXIETY OF FATE AND DEATH

Fate and death are the way in which our ontic self-affirmation is threatened by nonbeing. "Ontic," from the Greek *on*, "being," means here the basic self-affirmation of a being in its simple existence. (Onto-logical designates the philosophical analysis of the nature of being.) The anxiety of fate and death is most basic, most universal, and inescapable. All attempts to argue it away are futile. Even if the so-called arguments for the "immortality of the soul" had argumentative power (which they do not have) they would not convince existentially. For existentially everybody is aware of the complete loss of self which biological extinction implies. The unsophisticated mind knows instinctively what sophisticated ontology formulates: that reality has the basic structure of self-world correlation and that with the disappearance of the one side the world, the other side, the self, also disappears, and what remains is their common ground but not their structural correlation. It has been observed that the anxiety of death increases with the increase of individualization and that people in collectivistic cultures are less open to this type of anxiety. The observation is correct yet the explanation that there is no basic anxiety about death in collectivist cultures is wrong. The reason for the difference from more individualized civilizations is that the special type of courage which characterizes collectivism . . . , as long as it is unshaken, allays the anxiety of death. But the very fact that courage has to be created through many internal and external (psychological and ritual) activities and symbols shows that basic anxiety has to be overcome even in collectivism. Without its at least potential presence neither war nor the criminal law in these societies would be understandable. If there were no fear of death, the threat of the law or of a superior enemy would be without effect—which it obviously is not. Man as man in every civilization is anxiously aware of the threat of nonbeing and needs the courage to affirm himself in spite of it.

The anxiety of death is the permanent horizon within which the anxiety of fate is at work. For the threat against man's ontic self-affirmation is not only the absolute threat of death but also the relative threat of fate. Certainly the anxiety of death overshadows all concrete anxieties and gives them their ultimate seriousness. They have, however, a certain independence and, ordinarily, a more immediate impact than the anxiety of death. The term "fate" for this whole group of anxieties stresses one element which is common to all of them: their contingent character, their unpredictability, the impossibility of showing their meaning and purpose. One can describe this in terms of the categorical structure of our experience. One can show the contingency of our temporal being, the fact that we exist in this and no other period of time, beginning in a contingent moment, ending in a contingent moment, filled with experiences which are contingent themselves with respect to quality and quantity. One can show the contingency of our spatial being (our finding ourselves in this and no other place, and the strangeness of this place in spite of its familiarity); the contingent character of ourselves and the place from which we look at our world; and the contingent character of the reality at which we look, that is, our world. Both could be different: this is their contingency and this produces the anxiety about our spatial existence. One can show the contingency of the causal interdependence of which one is a part, both with respect to the past and to the present, the vicissitudes coming from our world and the hidden forces in the depths of our own self. Contingent does not mean causally undetermined but it means that the determining causes of our existence have no ultimate necessity. They are given, and they cannot be logically derived. Contingently we are put into the whole web of causal relations. Contingently we are determined by them in every moment and thrown out by them in the last moment.

Fate is the rule of contingency, and the anxiety about fate is based on the finite being's awareness of being contingent in every respect, of having no ultimate necessity. Fate is usually identified with necessity in the sense of an inescapable causal determination. Yet it is not causal necessity that makes fate a matter of anxiety but the lack of ultimate necessity, the irrationality, the impenetrable darkness of fate.

The threat of nonbeing to man's ontic self-affirmation is absolute in the threat of death, relative in the threat of fate. But the relative threat is a threat only because in its background stands the absolute threat. Fate would not produce inescapable anxiety without death behind it. And death stands behind fate and its contingencies not only in the last moment when one is thrown out of existence but in every moment within existence. Nonbeing is omnipresent and produces anxiety even where an immediate threat of death is absent. It stands behind the experience that we are driven, together with everything else, from the past toward the future without a moment of time which does not vanish immediately. It stands behind the insecurity and homelessness of our social and individual existence. It stands behind the attacks on our power of being in body and soul by weakness, disease, and accidents. In all these forms fate actualizes itself, and through them the anxiety of nonbeing takes hold of us. We try to transform the anxiety into fear and to meet courageously the objects in which the threat is embodied. We succeed partly, but somehow we are aware of the fact that it is not these objects with which we struggle that produce the anxiety but the human situation as such. Out of this the question arises: Is there a courage to be, a courage to affirm oneself in spite of the threat against man's ontic self-affirmation?

THE ANXIETY OF EMPTINESS AND MEANINGLESSNESS

Nonbeing threatens man as a whole, and therefore threatens his spiritual as well as his ontic self-affirmation. Spiritual self-affirmation occurs in every moment in which man lives creatively in the various spheres of meaning. Creative, in this context, has the sense not of original creativity as performed by the genius but of living spontaneously, in action and reaction, with the contents of one's cultural life. In order to be spiritually creative one need not be what is called a creative artist or scientist or statesman, but one must be able to participate meaningfully in their original creations. Such a participation is creative insofar as it changes that in which one participates, even if in very small ways. The creative transformation of a language by the interdependence of the creative poet or writer and the many who are influenced by him directly or indirectly and react spontaneously to him is an outstanding example. Everyone who lives creatively in meanings affirms himself as a participant in these meanings. He affirms himself as receiving and transforming reality creatively. He loves himself as participating in the spiritual life and as loving its contents. He loves them because they are his own fulfillment and because they are actualized through him. The scientist loves both the truth he discovers and himself insofar as he discovers it. He is held by the content of his discovery. This is what one can call "spiritual self-affirmation." And if he has not discovered but only participates in the discovery, it is equally spiritual self-affirmation.

Such an experience presupposes that the spiritual life is taken seriously, that it is a matter of ultimate concern. And this again presupposes that in it and through it ultimate reality becomes manifest. A spiritual life in which this is not experienced is threatened by nonbeing in the two forms in which it attacks spiritual self-affirmation: emptiness and meaninglessness.

We use the term meaninglessness for the absolute threat of nonbeing to spiritual self-affirmation, and the term emptiness for the relative threat to it. They are no more identical than are the threat of death and fate. But in the background of emptiness lies meaninglessness as death lies in the background of the vicissitudes of fate.

The anxiety of meaninglessness is anxiety about the loss of an ultimate concern, of a meaning which gives meaning to all meanings. This anxiety is aroused by the loss of a spiritual center, of an answer, however symbolic and indirect, to the question of the meaning of existence.

The anxiety of emptiness is aroused by the threat of nonbeing to the special contents of the spiritual life. A belief breaks down through external events or inner processes: one is cut off from creative participation in a sphere of culture, one feels frustrated about something which one had passionately affirmed, one is driven from devotion to one object to devotion to another and again on to another, because the meaning of each of them vanishes and the creative eros is transformed into indifference or aversion. Everything is tried and nothing satisfies. The contents of the tradition, however excellent, however praised, however loved once, lose their power to give content today. And present culture is even less able to provide the content. Anxiously one turns away from all concrete contents and looks for an ultimate meaning, only to discover that it was precisely the loss of a spiritual center which took away the meaning from the special contents of the spiritual life. But a spiritual center cannot be produced intentionally, and the attempt to produce it only produces deeper anxiety. The anxiety of emptiness drives us to the abyss of meaninglessness.

Emptiness and loss of meaning are expressions of the threat of nonbeing to the spiritual life. This threat is implied in man's finitude and actualized by man's estrangement. It can be described in terms of doubt, its creative and its destructive function in man's spiritual life. Man is able to ask because he is separated from, while participating in, what he is asking about. In every question an element of doubt, the awareness of not having, is implied. In systematic questioning systematic doubt is effective; e.g. of the Cartesian type. The threat to spiritual life is not doubt as an element but the total doubt. If the awareness of not having has swallowed the awareness of having, doubt has ceased to be methodological asking and has become existential despair. On the way to this situation the spiritual life tries to maintain itself as long as possible by clinging to affirmations which are not yet undercut, be they traditions, autonomous convictions, or emotional preferences. And if it is impossible to remove the doubt, one courageously accepts it without surrendering one's convictions. One takes the risk of going astray and the anxiety of this risk upon oneself. In this way one avoids the extreme situation—till it becomes unavoidable and the despair of truth becomes complete.

Then man tries another way out: Doubt is based on man's separation from the whole of reality, on his lack of universal participation, on the isolation of his individual self. So he tries to break out of this situation, to identify himself with something transindividual, to surrender his separation and self-relatedness. He flees from his freedom of asking and answering for himself to a situation in which no further questions can be asked and the answers to previous questions are

Existentialism: Paul Tillich 213

imposed on him authoritatively. In order to avoid the risk of asking and doubting he surrenders the right to ask and to doubt. He surrenders himself in order to save his spiritual life. He "escapes from his freedom" (Fromm) in order to escape the anxiety of meaninglessness. Now he is no longer lonely, not in existential doubt, not in despair. He "participates" and affirms by participation the contents of his spiritual life. Meaning is saved, but the self is sacrificed. And since the conquest of doubt was a matter of sacrifice, the sacrifice of the freedom of the self, it leaves a mark on the regained certitude: a fanatical self-assertiveness. Fanaticism is the correlate to spiritual self-surrender: it shows the anxiety which it was supposed to conquer, by attacking with disproportionate violence those who disagree and who demonstrate by their disagreement elements in the spiritual life of the fanatic which he must suppress in himself. Because he must suppress them in himself he must suppress them in others. His anxiety forces him to persecute dissenters. The weakness of the fanatic is that those whom he fights have a secret hold upon him; and to this weakness he and his group finally succumb.

It is not always personal doubt that undermines and empties a system of ideas and values. It can be the fact that they are no longer understood in their original power of expressing the human situation and of answering existential human questions. (This is largely the case with the doctrinal symbols of Christianity.) Or they lose their meaning because the actual conditions of the present period are so different from those in which the spiritual contents were created that new creations are needed. (This was largely the case with artistic expression before the industrial revolution.) In such circumstances a slow process of waste of the spiritual contents occurs, unnoticeable in the beginning, realized with a shock as it progresses, producing the anxiety of meaninglessness at its end.

Ontic and spiritual self-affirmation must be distinguished but they cannot be separated. Man's being includes his relation to meanings. He is human only by understanding and shaping reality, both his world and himself, according to meanings and values. His being is spiritual even in the most primitive expressions of the most primitive human being. In the "first" meaningful sentence all the richness of man's spiritual life is potentially present. Therefore the threat to his spiritual being is a threat to his whole being. The most revealing expression of this fact is the desire to throw away one's ontic existence rather than stand the despair of emptiness and meaninglessness. The death instinct is not an ontic but a spiritual phenomenon. Freud identified this reaction to the meaninglessness of the never-ceasing and never-satisfied libido with man's essential nature. But it is only an expression of his existential self-estrangement and of the disintegration of his spiritual life into meaninglessness. If, on the other hand, the ontic self-affirmation is weakened by nonbeing, spiritual indifference and emptiness can be the consequence, producing a circle of ontic and spiritual negativity. Nonbeing threatens from both sides, the ontic and the spiritual; if it threatens the one side it also threatens the other.

THE ANXIETY OF GUILT AND CONDEMNATION

Nonbeing threatens from a third side; it threatens man's moral self-affirmation. Man's being, ontic as well as spiritual, is not only given to him but also demanded of him. He is responsible for it; literally, he is required to answer, if he is asked, what he has made of himself. He who asks him is his judge, namely he himself, who, at the same time, stands against him. This situation produces the anxiety which, in relative terms, is the anxiety of guilt, in absolute terms, the anxiety of self-rejection or condemnation. Man is essentially "finite freedom"; freedom not in the sense of indeterminacy but in the sense of being able to determine himself through decisions in the center of his being. Man, as finite freedom, is free within the contingencies of his finitude. But within these limits he is asked to make of himself what he is supposed to become, to fulfill his destiny. In every act of moral self-affirmation man contributes to the fulfillment of his destiny, to the actualization of what he potentially is. It is the task of ethics to describe the nature of this fulfillment, in philosophical or theological terms. But however the norm is formulated man has the power of acting against it, of contradicting his essential being, of losing his destiny. And under the conditions of man's estrangement from himself this is an actuality. Even in what he considers his best deed nonbeing is present and prevents it from being perfect. A profound ambiguity between good and evil permeates everything he does, because it permeates his personal being as such. Nonbeing is mixed with being in his moral self-affirmation as it is in his spiritual and ontic self-affirmation. The awareness of this ambiguity is the feeling of guilt. The judge who is oneself and who stands against oneself, he who "knows with" (conscience) everything we do and are gives a negative judgment, experienced by us as guilt. The anxiety of guilt shows the same complex characteristics as the anxiety about ontic and spiritual nonbeing. It is present in every moment of moral self-awareness and can drive us toward complete self-rejection, to the feeling of being condemned—not to an external punishment but to the despair of having lost our destiny.

To avoid this extreme situation man tries to transform the anxiety of guilt into moral action regardless of its imperfection and ambiguity. Courageously he takes nonbeing into his moral self-affirmation. This can happen in two ways, according to the duality of the tragic and the personal in man's situation, the first based on the contingencies of fate, the second on the responsibility of freedom. The first way can lead to a defiance of negative judgments and the moral demands on which they are based; the second way can lead to a moral rigor and the self-satisfaction derived from it. In both of them—usually called anomism and legalism—the anxiety of guilt lies in the background and breaks again and again into the open, producing the extreme situation of moral despair.

Nonbeing in a moral respect must be distinguished but cannot be separated from ontic and spiritual nonbeing. The anxiety of the one type is immanent in the anxieties of the other types. The famous words of Paul about "sin as the sting of death" point to the immanence of the anxiety of guilt within the fear of death. And the threat of fate and death has always awakened and increased the consciousness of guilt. The threat of moral nonbeing was experienced in and through the threat of ontic nonbeing. The contingencies of fate received moral interpretation: fate executes the negative moral judgment by attacking and perhaps destroying the ontic foundation of the morally rejected personality. The two forms of anxiety provoke and augment each other. In the same way spiritual and moral nonbeing are interdependent. Obedience to the moral norm, i.e. to one's own essential being, excludes emptiness and meaninglessness in their radical forms. If the spiritual contents have lost their power the self-affirmation of the moral personality is a way in which meaning can be rediscovered. The simple call to duty can save from emptiness, while the disintegration of the moral consciousness is an almost irresistible basis for the attack of spiritual nonbeing. On the other hand, existential doubt can undermine moral self-affirmation by throwing into the abyss of skepticism not only every moral principle but the meaning of moral self-affirmation as such. In this case the doubt is felt as guilt, while at the same time guilt is undermined by doubt.

THE MEANING OF DESPAIR

The three types of anxiety are interwoven in such a way that one of them gives the predominant color but all of them participate in the coloring of the state of anxiety. All of them and their underlying unity are existential, i.e. they are implied in the existence of man as man, his finitude, and his estrangement. They are fulfilled in the situation of despair to which all of them contribute. Despair is an ultimate or "boundary-line" situation. One cannot go beyond it. Its nature is indicated in the etymology of the word despair: without hope. No way out into the future appears. Nonbeing is felt as absolutely victorious. But there is a limit to its victory; nonbeing is felt as victorious, and feeling presupposes being. Enough being is left to feel the irresistible power of nonbeing, and this is the despair within the despair. The pain of despair is that a being is aware of itself as unable to affirm itself because of the power of nonbeing. Consequently it wants to surrender this awareness and its presupposition, the being which is aware. It wants to get rid of itself—and it cannot. Despair appears in the form of reduplication, as the desperate attempt to escape despair. If anxiety were only the anxiety of fate and death, voluntary death would be the way out of despair. The courage demanded would be the courage not to be. The final form of ontic self-affirmation would be the act of ontic self-negation.

But despair is also the despair about guilt and condemnation. And there is no way of escaping it, even by ontic self-negation. Suicide can liberate one from the anxiety of fate and death—as the Stoics knew. But it cannot liberate from the anxiety of guilt and condemnation, as the Christians know. This is a highly paradoxical statement, as paradoxical as the relation of the moral sphere to ontic existence generally. But it is a true statement, verified by those who have experienced fully the despair of condemnation. It is impossible to express the inescapable character of condemnation in ontic terms, that is in terms of imaginings about the "immortality of the soul." For every ontic statement must use the categories of finitude, and "immortality of the soul" would be the endless prolongation of finitude and of the despair of condemnation (a self-contradictory concept, for "finis" means "end"). The experience, therefore, that suicide is no way of escaping guilt must be understood in terms of the qualitative character of the moral demand, and of the qualitative character of its rejection. Guilt and condemnation are qualitatively, not quantitatively, infinite. They have an infinite weight and cannot be removed by a finite act of ontic self-negation. This makes despair desperate, that is, inescapable. There is "No Exit" from it (Sartre). The anxiety of emptiness and meaninglessness participates in both the ontic and the moral element in despair. Insofar as it is an expression of finitude it can be removed by ontic self-negation: This drives radical skepticism to suicide. Insofar as it is a consequence of moral disintegration it produces the same paradox as the moral element in despair: there is no ontic exit from it. This frustrates the suicidal trends in emptiness and meaninglessness. One is aware of their futility.

In view of this character of despair it is understandable that all human life can be interpreted as a continuous attempt to avoid despair. And this attempt is mostly successful. Extreme situations are not reached frequently and perhaps they are never reached by some people. The purpose of an analysis of such a situation is not to record ordinary human experiences but to show extreme possibilities in the light of which the ordinary situation must be understood. We are not always aware of our having to die, but in the light of the experience of our having to die our whole life is experienced differently. In the same way the anxiety which is despair is not always present. But the rare occasions in which it is present determine the interpretation of existence as a whole.

Paul Tillich: COURAGE AND TRANSCENDENCE

> DESPITE *man's awareness of nonbeing—his confrontations with death, meaninglessness, and guilt—he can exhibit the courage to be, i.e., there can be a "self-affirmation of being in spite of nonbeing." Tillich calls the experience of this power, through which one can affirm himself, "faith," and goes on to detail its transcendent nature and to warn against falsely identifying it with such things as mystical experience and divine-human encounter.*
>
> *The question to which Tillich finally leads us is: What is the ultimate source of faith, of the courage to be? His answer is the "God above God." He insists that the rationally conceived God of the theologians cannot be the source of our faith, since no such God can possibly minister to the nonrational human condition. As the religion of the scriptures suggests, the courage to be is rooted in man's experience of a God who transcends the limits of reason. For example, the Bible in its full expression recognizes that God is neither a person akin to man nor an object alien to him. One can become aware of the true source of divine power when the symbols of traditional theism remain effective in combatting our anxieties even though belief in the God they symbolize is renounced as superstition.*

The following passages from The Courage to Be, *pp. 171–190, are reprinted with the kind permission of the Yale University Press.*

ABSOLUTE FAITH AND THE COURAGE TO BE

We have avoided the concept of faith in our description of the courage to be which is based on mystical union with the ground of being as well as in our description of the courage to be which is based on the personal encounter with God. This is partly because the concept of faith has lost its genuine meaning and has received the connotation of "belief in something unbelievable." But this is not the only reason for the use of terms other than faith. The decisive reason is that I do not think either mystical union or personal encounter fulfills the idea of faith. Certainly there is faith in the elevation of the soul above the finite to the infinite, leading to its union with the ground of being. But more than this is included in the concept of faith. And there is faith in the personal encounter with the personal God. But more than this is included in the concept of faith. Faith is the state of being grasped by the power of being-itself. The courage to be is an expression of faith and what "faith" means must be understood through the courage to be. We have defined courage as the self-affirmation of being in spite of nonbeing. The power of this self-affirmation is the power of being which is effective in every act of courage. Faith is the experience of this power.

But it is an experience which has a paradoxical character, the character of accepting acceptance. Being-itself transcends every finite being infinitely; God in the divine-human encounter transcends man unconditionally. Faith bridges this infinite gap by accepting the fact that in spite of it the power of being is present, that he who is separated is accepted. Faith accepts "in spite of"; and out of the "in spite of" of faith the "in spite of" of courage is born. Faith is not a theoretical affirmation of something uncertain, it is the existential acceptance of something transcending ordinary experience. Faith is not an opinion but a state. It is the state of being grasped by the power of being which transcends everything that is and in which everything that is participates. He who is grasped by this power is able to affirm himself because he knows that he is affirmed by the power of being-itself. In this point mystical experience and personal encounter are identical. In both of them faith is the basis of the courage to be.

This is decisive for a period in which, as in our own, the anxiety

Existentialism: Paul Tillich   219

of doubt and meaninglessness is dominant. Certainly the anxiety of fate and death is not lacking in our time. The anxiety of fate has increased with the degree to which the schizophrenic split of our world has removed the last remnants of former security. And the anxiety of guilt and condemnation is not lacking either. It is surprising how much anxiety of guilt comes to the surface in psychoanalysis and personal counseling. The centuries of puritan and bourgeois repression of vital strivings have produced almost as many guilt feelings as the preaching of hell and purgatory in the Middle Ages.

But in spite of these restricting considerations one must say that the anxiety which determines our period is the anxiety of doubt and meaninglessness. One is afraid of having lost or of having to lose the meaning of one's existence. The expression of this situation is the Existentialism of today.

Which courage is able to take nonbeing into itself in the form of doubt and meaninglessness? This is the most important and most disturbing question in the quest for the courage to be. For the anxiety of meaninglessness undermines what is still unshaken in the anxiety of fate and death and of guilt and condemnation. In the anxiety of guilt and condemnation doubt has not yet undermined the certainty of an ultimate responsibility. We are threatened but we are not destroyed. If, however, doubt and meaninglessness prevail one experiences an abyss in which the meaning of life and the truth of ultimate responsibility disappear. Both the Stoic who conquers the anxiety of fate with the Socratic courage of wisdom and the Christian who conquers the anxiety of guilt with the Protestant courage of accepting forgiveness are in a different situation. Even in the despair of having to die and the despair of self-condemnation meaning is affirmed and certitude preserved. But in the despair of doubt and meaninglessness both are swallowed by nonbeing.

The question then is this: Is there a courage which can conquer the anxiety of meaninglessness and doubt? Or in other words, can the faith which accepts acceptance resist the power of nonbeing in its most radical form? Can faith resist meaninglessness? Is there a kind of faith which can exist together with doubt and meaninglessness? These questions lead to the last aspect of the problem . . . and the one most relevant to our time: How is the courage to be possible if all the ways to create it are barred by the experience of their ultimate insufficiency? If life is as meaningless as death, if guilt is as questionable as perfection, if being is no more meaningful than nonbeing, on what can one base the courage to be?

There is an inclination in some Existentialists to answer these questions by a leap from doubt to dogmatic certitude, from meaninglessness to a set of symbols in which the meaning of a special ecclesiastical or political group is embodied. This leap can be interpreted in different ways. It may be the expression of a desire for safety; it may be as arbitrary as, according to Existentialist principles, every decision is; it may be the feeling that the Christian message is the answer to the questions raised by an analysis of human existence; it may be a genuine conversion, independent of the theoretical situation. In any case it is not a solution of the problem of radical doubt. It gives the courage to be to those who are converted but it does not answer the question as to how such a courage is possible in itself. The answer must accept, as its precondition, the state of meaninglessness. It is not an answer if it demands the removal of this state; for that is just what cannot be done. He who is in the grip of doubt and meaninglessness cannot liberate himself from this grip; but he asks for an answer which is valid within and not outside the situation of his despair. He asks for the ultimate foundation of what we have called the "courage of despair." There is only one possible answer, if one does not try to escape the question: namely that the acceptance of despair is in itself faith and on the boundary line of the courage to be. In this situation the meaning of life is reduced to despair about the meaning of life. But as long as this despair is an act of life it is positive in its negativity. Cynically speaking, one could say that it is true to life to be cynical about it. Religiously speaking, one would say that one accepts oneself as accepted in spite of one's despair about the meaning of this acceptance. The paradox of every radical negativity, as long as it is an active negativity, is that it must affirm itself in order to be able to negate itself. No actual negation can be without an implicit affirmation. The hidden pleasure produced by despair witnesses to the paradoxical character of self-negation. The negative lives from the positive it negates.

The faith which makes the courage of despair possible is the acceptance of the power of being, even in the grip of nonbeing. Even in the despair about meaning being affirms itself through us. The act of accepting meaninglessness is in itself a meaningful act. It is an act of faith. We have seen that he who has the courage to affirm his being in spite of fate and guilt has not removed them. He remains threatened and hit by them. But he accepts his acceptance by the power of being-itself in which he participates and which gives him the courage to take the anxieties of fate and guilt upon himself. The same is true of doubt and meaninglessness. The faith which creates the courage to take them into itself has no special content. It is simply faith, undirected, absolute. It is undefinable, since everything defined is dissolved by doubt and meaninglessness. Nevertheless, even absolute faith is not an eruption of subjective emotions or a mood without objective foundation.

An analysis of the nature of absolute faith reveals the following elements in it. The first is the experience of the power of being which is present even in face of the most radical manifestation of nonbeing. If one says that in this experience vitality resists despair one must add that vitality in man is proportional to intentionality. The vitality that can stand the abyss of meaninglessness is aware of a hidden meaning within the destruction of meaning. The second element in absolute faith is the dependence of the experience of nonbeing on the experience of being and the dependence of the experience of meaninglessness on the experience of meaning. Even in this state of despair one has enough being to make despair possible. There is a third element in absolute faith, the acceptance of being accepted. Of course, in the state of despair there is nobody and nothing that accepts. But there is the power of acceptance itself which is experienced. Meaninglessness, as long as it is experienced, includes an experience of the "power of acceptance." To accept this power of acceptance consciously is the religious answer of absolute faith, of a faith which has been deprived by doubt of any concrete content, which nevertheless is faith and the source of the most paradoxical manifestation of the courage to be.

This faith transcends both the mystical experience and the divine-human encounter. The mystical experience seems to be nearer to absolute faith but it is not. Absolute faith includes an element of skepticism which one cannot find in the mystical experience. Certainly mysticism also transcends all specific contents, but not because it doubts them or has found them meaningless; rather it deems them to be preliminary. Mysticism uses the specific contents as grades, stepping on them after having used them. The experience of meaninglessness, however, denies them (and everything that goes with them) without having used them. The experience of meaninglessness is more radical than mysticism. Therefore it transcends the mystical experience.

Absolute faith also transcends the divine-human encounter. In this encounter the subject-object scheme is valid: a definite subject (man) meets a definite object (God). One can reverse this statement and say that a definite subject (God) meets a definite object (man). But in both cases the attack of doubt undercuts the subject-object structure. The theologians who speak so strongly and with such self-certainty about the divine-human encounter should be aware of a situation in which this encounter is prevented by radical doubt and nothing is left but absolute faith. The acceptance of such a situation as religiously valid has, however, the consequence that the concrete contents of ordinary faith must be subjected to criticism and transformation. The courage to be in its radical form is a key to an idea of God which transcends both mysticism and the person-to-person encounter.

NONBEING OPENING UP BEING

The courage to be in all its forms has, by itself, revelatory character. It shows the nature of being, it shows that the self-affirmation of being is an affirmation that overcomes negation. In a metaphorical statement (and every assertion about being-itself is either metaphorical or symbolic) one could say that being includes nonbeing but nonbeing does not prevail against it. "Including" is a spatial metaphor which indicates that being embraces itself and that which is opposed to it, nonbeing. Nonbeing belongs to being, it cannot be separated from it. We could not even think "being" without a double negation: being must be thought as the negation of the negation of being. This is why we describe being best by the metaphor "power of being." Power is the possibility a being has to actualize itself against the resistance of other beings. If we speak of the power of being-itself we indicate that being affirms itself against nonbeing. In our discussion of courage and life we have mentioned the dynamic understanding of reality by the philosophers of life. Such an understanding is possible only if one accepts the view that nonbeing belongs to being, that being could not be the ground of life without nonbeing. The self-affirmation of being without nonbeing would not even be self-affirmation but an immovable self-identity. Nothing would be manifest, nothing expressed, nothing revealed. But nonbeing drives being out of its seclusion, it forces it to affirm itself dynamically. Philosophy has dealt with the dynamic self-affirmation of being-itself wherever it spoke dialectically, notably in Neoplatonism, Hegel, and the philosophers of life and process. Theology has done the same whenever it took the idea of the living God seriously, most obviously in the trinitarian symbolization of the inner life of God. Spinoza, in spite of his static definition of substance (which is his name for the ultimate power of being), unites philosophical and mystical tendencies when he speaks of the love and knowledge with which God loves and knows himself through the love and knowledge of finite beings. Nonbeing (that in God which makes his self-affirmation dynamic) opens up the divine self-seclusion and reveals him as power and love. Nonbeing makes God a living God. Without the No he has to overcome in himself and in his creature, the divine Yes to himself would be lifeless. There would be no revelation of the ground of being, there would be no life.

Existentialism: Paul Tillich

But where there is nonbeing there is finitude and anxiety. If we say that nonbeing belongs to being-itself, we say that finitude and anxiety belong to being-itself. Wherever philosophers or theologians have spoken of the divine blessedness they have implicitly (and sometimes explicitly) spoken of the anxiety of finitude which is eternally taken into the blessedness of the divine infinity. The infinite embraces itself and the finite, the Yes includes itself and the No which it takes into itself, blessedness comprises itself and the anxiety of which it is the conquest. All this is implied if one says that being includes nonbeing and that through nonbeing it reveals itself. It is a highly symbolic language which must be used at this point. But its symbolic character does not diminish its truth; on the contrary, it is a condition of its truth. To speak unsymbolically about being-itself is untrue.

The divine self-affirmation is the power that makes the self-affirmation of the finite being, the courage to be, possible. Only because being-itself has the character of self-affirmation in spite of nonbeing is courage possible. Courage participates in the self-affirmation of being-itself, it participates in the power of being which prevails against nonbeing. He who receives this power in an act of mystical or personal or absolute faith is aware of the source of his courage to be.

Man is not necessarily aware of this source. In situations of cynicism and indifference he is not aware of it. But it works in him as long as he maintains the courage to take his anxiety upon himself. In the act of the courage to be the power of being is effective in us, whether we recognize it or not. Every act of courage is a manifestation of the ground of being, however questionable the content of the act may be. The content may hide or distort true being, the courage in it reveals true being. Not arguments but the courage to be reveals the true nature of being-itself. By affirming our being we participate in the self-affirmation of being-itself. There are no valid arguments for the "existence" of God, but there are acts of courage in which we affirm the power of being, whether we know it or not. If we know it, we accept acceptance consciously. If we do not know it, we nevertheless accept it and participate in it. And in our acceptance of that which we do not know the power of being is manifest to us. Courage has revealing power, the courage to be is the key to being-itself.

THEISM TRANSCENDED

The courage to take meaninglessness into itself presupposes a relation to the ground of being which we have called "absolute faith." It is without a special content, yet it is not without content. The content of absolute faith is the "God above God." [*God that other gods are but symbols of.*] Absolute faith and its consequence, the courage that takes the radical doubt, the doubt about God, into itself, transcends the theistic idea of God.

Theism can mean the unspecified affirmation of God. Theism in this sense does not say what it means if it uses the name of God. Because of the traditional and psychological connotations of the word God such an empty theism can produce a reverent mood if it speaks of God. Politicians, dictators, and other people who wish to use rhetoric to make an impression on their audience like to use the word God in this sense. It produces the feeling in their listeners that the speaker is serious and morally trustworthy. This is especially successful if they can brand their foes as atheistic. On a higher level people without a definite religious commitment like to call themselves theistic, not for special purposes but because they cannot stand a world without God, whatever this God may be. They need some of the connotations of the word God and they are afraid of what they call atheism. On the highest level of this kind of theism the name of God is used as a poetic or practical symbol, expressing a profound emotional state or the highest ethical idea. It is a theism which stands on the boundary line between the second type of theism and what we call "theism transcended." But it is still too indefinite to cross this boundary line. The atheistic negation of this whole type of theism is as vague as the theism itself. It may produce an irreverent mood and angry reaction of those who take their theistic affirmation seriously. It may even be felt as justified against the rhetorical-political abuse of the name God, but it is ultimately as irrelevant as the theism which it negates. It cannot reach the state of despair any more than the theism against which it fights can reach the state of faith.

Theism can have another meaning, quite contrary to the first one: it can be the name of what we have called the divine-human encounter. In this case it points to those elements in the Jewish-Christian tradition which emphasize the person-to-person relationship with God. Theism in this sense emphasizes the personalistic passages in the Bible and the Protestant creeds, the personalistic image of God, the word as the tool of creation and revelation, the ethical and social character of the kingdom of God, the personal nature of human faith and divine forgiveness, the historical vision of the universe, the idea of a divine purpose, the infinite distance between God and the world, the conflict between holy God and sinful man, the person-to-person character of prayer and practical devotion. Theism in this sense is the nonmystical side of biblical religion and historical Christianity. Atheism from the point of view of this theism is the attempt to escape the divine-human encounter. It is an existential—not a theoretical—problem.

Theism has a third meaning, a strictly theological one. Theological theism is, like every theology, dependent on the religious substance which it conceptualizes. It is dependent on theism in the first sense insofar as it tries to prove the necessity of affirming God in some way; it usually develops the so-called arguments for the "existence" of God. But it is more dependent on theism in the second sense insofar as it tries to establish a doctrine of God which transforms the person-to-person encounter with God into a doctrine about two persons who may or may not meet but have a reality independent of each other.

Now theism in the first sense must be transcended because it is irrelevant, and theism in the second sense must be transcended because it is one-sided. But theism in the third sense must be transcended because it is wrong. It is bad theology. This can be shown by a more penetrating analysis. The God of theological theism is a being beside others and as such a part of the whole of reality. He certainly is considered its most important part, but as a part and therefore as subjected to the structure of the whole. He is supposed to be beyond the ontological elements and categories which constitute reality. But every statement subjects him to them. He is seen as a self which has a world, as an ego which is related to a thou, as a cause which is separated from its effect, as having a definite space and an endless time. He is a being, not being-itself. As such he is bound to the subject-object structure of reality, he is an object for us as subjects. At the same time we are objects for him as a subject. And this is decisive for the necessity of transcending theological theism. For God as a subject makes me into an object which is nothing more than an object. He deprives me of my subjectivity because he is all-powerful and all-knowing. I revolt and try to make him into an object, but the revolt fails and becomes desperate. God appears as the invincible tyrant, the being in contrast with whom all other beings are without freedom and subjectivity. He is equated with the recent tyrants who with the help of terror try to transform everything into a mere object, a thing among things, a cog in the machine they control. He becomes the model of everything against which Existentialism revolted. This is the God Nietzsche said had to be killed because nobody can tolerate being made into a mere object of absolute knowledge and absolute control. This is the deepest root of atheism. It is an atheism which is justified as the reaction against theological theism and its disturbing implications. It is also the deepest root of the Existentialist despair and the widespread anxiety of meaninglessness in our period.

Theism in all its forms is transcended in the experience we have called absolute faith. It is the accepting of the acceptance without somebody or something that accepts. It is the power of being-itself that accepts and gives the courage to be. This is the highest point to which our analysis has brought us. It cannot be described in the way the God of all forms of theism can be described. It cannot be described in mystical terms either. It transcends both mysticism and personal encounter, as it transcends both the courage to be as a part and the courage to be as oneself.

THE GOD ABOVE GOD AND THE COURAGE TO BE

The ultimate source of the courage to be is the "God above God"; this is the result of our demand to transcend theism. Only if the God of theism is transcended can the anxiety of doubt and meaninglessness be taken into the courage to be. The God above God is the object of all mystical longing, but mysticism also must be transcended in order to reach him. Mysticism does not take seriously the concrete and the doubt concerning the concrete. It plunges directly into the ground of being and meaning, and leaves the concrete, the world of finite values and meanings, behind. Therefore it does not solve the problem of meaninglessness. In terms of the present religious situation this means that Eastern mysticism is not the solution of the problems of Western Existentialism, although many people attempt this solution. The God above the God of theism is not the devaluation of the meanings which doubt has thrown into the abyss of meaninglessness; he is their potential restitution. Nevertheless absolute faith agrees with the faith implied in mysticism in that both transcend the theistic objectivation of a God who is a being. For mysticism such a God is not more real than any finite being, for the courage to be such a God has disappeared in the abyss of meaninglessness with every other value and meaning.

The God above the God of theism is present, although hidden, in every divine-human encounter. Biblical religion as well as Protestant theology are aware of the paradoxical character of this encounter. They are aware that if God encounters man God is neither object nor subject and is therefore above the scheme into which theism has forced him. They are aware that personalism with respect to God is balanced by a transpersonal presence of the divine. They are aware that forgiveness can be accepted only if the power of acceptance is effective in man—biblically speaking, if the power of grace is effective in man. They are aware of the paradoxical character of every prayer, of speaking to somebody to whom you cannot speak because he is not "somebody," of asking somebody of whom you cannot ask anything because he gives or gives not before you ask, of saying "thou" to somebody who is nearer to the I than the I is to itself. Each of these paradoxes drives the religious consciousness toward a God above the God of theism.

The courage to be which is rooted in the experience of the God above the God of theism unites and transcends the courage to be as a part and the courage to be as oneself. It avoids both the loss of oneself by participation and the loss of one's world by individualization. The acceptance of the God above the God of theism makes us a part of that which is not also a part but is the ground of the whole. Therefore our self is not lost in a larger whole, which submerges it in the life of a limited group. If the self participates in the power of being-itself it receives itself back. For the power of being acts through the power of the individual selves. It does not swallow them as every limited whole, every collectivism, and every conformism does. This is why the Church, which stands for the power of being-itself or for the God who transcends the God of the religions, claims to be the mediator of the courage to be. A church which is based on the authority of the God of theism cannot make such a claim. It inescapably develops into a collectivist or semicollectivist system itself.

But a church which raises itself in its message and its devotion to the God above the God of theism without sacrificing its concrete symbols can mediate a courage which takes doubt and meaninglessness into itself. It is the Church under the Cross which alone can do this, the Church which preaches the Crucified who cried to God who remained his God after the God of confidence had left him in the darkness of doubt and meaninglessness. To be as a part in such a church is to receive a courage to be in which one cannot lose one's self and in which one receives one's world.

Absolute faith, or the state of being grasped by the God beyond God, is not a state which appears beside other states of the mind. It never is something separated and definite, an event which could be isolated and described. It is always a movement in, with, and under other states of the mind. It is the situation on the boundary of man's possibilities. It *is* this boundary. Therefore it is both the courage of despair and the courage in and above every courage. It is not a place where one can live, it is without the safety of words and concepts, it is without a name, a church, a cult, a theology. But it is moving in the depth of all of them. It is the power of being, in which they participate and of which they are fragmentary expressions.

One can become aware of it in the anxiety of fate and death when the traditional symbols, which enable men to stand the vicissitudes of fate and the horror of death have lost their power. When "providence" has become a superstition and "immortality" something imaginary that which once was the power in these symbols can still be present and create the courage to be in spite of the experience of a chaotic world and a finite existence. The Stoic courage returns but not as the faith in universal reason. It returns as the absolute faith which says Yes to being without seeing anything concrete which could conquer the nonbeing in fate and death.

And one can become aware of the God above the God of theism in the anxiety of guilt and condemnation when the traditional symbols that enable men to withstand the anxiety of guilt and condemnation have lost their power. When "divine judgment" is interpreted as a psychological complex and forgiveness as a remnant of the "father-image," what once was the power in those symbols can still be present and create the courage to be in spite of the experience of an infinite gap between what we are and what we ought to be. The Lutheran courage returns but not supported by the faith in a judging and forgiving God. It returns in terms of the absolute faith which says Yes although there is no special power that conquers guilt. The courage to take the anxiety of meaninglessness upon oneself is the boundary line up to which the courage to be can go. Beyond it is mere nonbeing. Within it all forms of courage are re-established in the power of the God above the God of theism. *The courage to be is rooted in the God who appears when God has disappeared in the anxiety of doubt.*

GUIDE TO FURTHER READINGS IN EXISTENTIALISM

EXISTENTIALISM AND RELIGION

Karl Barth (1886–   ), more than any other living theologian, has united Christianity and existentialism. In the tradition of Kierkegaard, he disclaims the authority of reason and insists that faith alone constitutes the precondition of the discovery of reality. For him, Kierkegaard's description of "crisis" is the proper account of that inner drama which can culminate in the disclosure of God. He is uncompromising in his biblical insistence that God manifests his word only at particular moments in history and to particular individuals. See especially *The Epistle to the Romans*, trans. E. Hoskyns (London: Oxford University Press, 1933).

Martin Buber (1878–1965) has dedicated his life to promoting the thesis that one's love of God must be expressed through his love of each particular man. Furthermore, it is the uniqueness in each particular man rather than generic "man" that is the proper object of respect. Thus the existentialist theme that "existence is prior to essence" is presupposed by Buber's philosophy; however, he does not pursue existentialism *per se*. Rather, it appears as an integral part of his interpretation of Hasidism, a latter-day blending of mysticism and Judaism. See especially *The Way of Man* (Chicago: Wilcox, 1951).

Additional Readings

Barth, K., *The Word of God and the Word of Man*. London: Hodder and Stoughton, 1928.

Brunner, E., *The Theology of Crisis*. New York: Scribner's, 1935.

Buber, M., *I and Thou*. Edinburgh: Clark, 1959.

Niebuhr, R., *The Nature and Destiny of Man*, 2 vols. New York: Scribner's, 1941–43.

EXISTENTIALISM AND SOCIETY

Karl Jaspers (1883–), one of the most distinguished and influential existentialists, seems to have been influenced by both Kierkegaard and Kant. His debt to Kierkegaard is indicated by his sensitivity to those "limit situations" that produce crisis and his belief that it is only through such an agonizing experience that contact can be made with unlimited reality. His dependence on Kant is clear in his accounts of the limitations of human knowledge. He is particularly skillful in evaluating our culture and society with respect to their tendency to reduce individuals to automatons. A distinctive claim in Jasper's philosophy is that symbolic communication about that which lies beyond what we may have limited knowledge of is possible. See especially *Man in the Modern Age*, trans. by E. Paul (London: Routledge, 1933).

Gabriel Marcel (1877–) comes to his position as a result of a reaction to such philosophical dualisms as thought and being, subject and object, self and God, the individual and society. Marcel insists that all such dichotomies are epistemological rather than ontological and, furthermore, even as epistemological distinctions, presuppose ontological unity. "Knowledge is seen to be contingent on a participation in being for which no epistemology can account because it continually presupposes it."

Thus he rejects the notion that we can know existent reality; he answers instead, in the spirit of Bergson, that we encounter reality through communion with it. For example, he would say that to have *knowledge* of another person involves us in reducing him to an impersonal "he"; we thereby lose contact with him as an individual. On the other hand, appreciating another person requires us to establish an "I-thou" relationship in which the other person's individuality remains inviolate. See especially G. Marcel, *The Philosophy of Existence*, trans. M. Harari (New York: Philosophical Library, 1949).

Additional Readings
   Marcel, G., *Metaphysical Journal*. London: Rockliff, 1952.
   ———, *The Mystery of Being*. London: Harvill, 1950.
   Jaspers, K., *Existentialism and Humanism*. New York: Moore, 1952.
   ———, *The Future of Mankind*. Chicago: University of Chicago Press, 1961.

EXISTENTIALISM AND LITERATURE

Albert Camus (1913–1960) was a celebrated literary figure who successfully captured existentialist themes in his novels and short stories. His work was reminiscent of Dostoyevsky in that he compelled us to acknowledge the essential absurdity of life through his skillful use of language and carefully drawn situations. In existentialist terminology, Camus' distinctive message was that neither reason nor faith can endow the "abyss of the absurd" with meaning. The only relief possible for those who live authentically is derived from acknowledging that there is no relief. See especially *The Myth of Sisyphus and Other Essays* (New York: Knopf, 1955).

Additional Readings
   Beauvoir, S. de, *The Ethics of Ambiguity*. New York: Philosophical Library, 1948.
   ———, *The Wanderers*. Cleveland: World, 1956.
   Camus, A., *The Fall*. New York: Knopf, 1960.
   ———, *The Plague*. New York: Knopf, 1954.
   Sartre, J. P., *The Wall and Other Stories*. New York: New Directions, 1948.

EXISTENTIALISM AND THOMISM

Although Etienne Gilson (1884–   ) is the outstanding defender of Thomistic philosophy, he does not equate Thomism and scholasticism as so many do. He is convinced that philosophy is a distinctive, open-ended discipline and that it is imperiled by philosophers who model it after science, mathematics, theology, or any other discipline. Accordingly, he argues that the true philosophers were Plato, Aristotle, and Aquinas, and not Descartes, Spinoza, and Hegel. In a period when man is suffering from the tyranny of science at both the practical and theoretical levels, Gilson, in the spirit of existentialism, emphasizes man's unique and creative role in nature. This is a countermovement to scientific reductionism. See especially *Being and Some Philosophers* (Toronto: Pontifical Institute of Medieval Studies, 1949).

Additional Readings

Gilson, E., *The Christian Philosophy of St. Augustine.* New York: Random House, 1960.

Maritain, J., *The Education of Man.* New York: Doubleday, 1962.

———, *Existence and The Existent.* New York: Pantheon, 1949.

NOTES FOR CHAPTER IV

1 K. Jaspers, *Reason and Existenz* (London: Routledge and Kegan Paul, 1956), pp. 19–20.
2 B. Jowett (trans.), *The Dialogues of Plato* (New York: Random House, 1937), I, 412.
3 *Ibid.*, p. 776.
4 R. McKeon (trans.), *The Basic Works of Aristotle* (New York: Random House, 1941), pp. 113–114.
5 St. Augustine, *The City of God*, trans. E. R. Dods (New York: Hafner, 1948), II, 302–303.
6 B. Pascal, *Pensées*, trans. W. F. Trotter (New York: Dutton, 1958), pp. 121, 61.
7 J. Loewenberg (ed.), *Hegel Selections* (New York: Scribner's, 1929), pp. 31–32.
8 K. Jaspers, *Reason and Existenz* (London: Routledge and Kegan Paul, 1956), p. 25.
9 G. W. F. Hegel, *The Logic of Hegel*, trans. W. Wallace (London: Oxford University Press, 1950), p. 48.
10 S. Kierkegaard, *Concluding Unscientific Postscript*, trans. D. F. Swenson (Princeton: Princeton University Press, 1944), p. 182.
11 H. Bergson, *An Introduction to Metaphysics*, trans. T. E. Hulme (New York: Library of Liberal Arts, 1949), p. 24.
12 *Ibid.*, p. 24.

V · Analysis

How can we be sure that another person truly is informing us about something when he speaks to us? A common answer is that we can know that we are being properly informed when we know that our informant is honest. But a moment's reflection reveals that while honesty may be a necessary condition, it is not sufficient. Suppose, for example, a friend tells me that he had been waiting for me at the station; suppose he meant the bus station, but I had understood him to mean the railroad station. I cannot attribute this failure in communication to his lack of honesty. Such a failure is due to the language. To avoid this misunderstanding the speaker should have made clear his sense of the term "station" by having said "bus station." Notice we assume that our would-be communicants are capable of distinguishing among various senses of the term "station."

The problem of communication is even more serious. Our language is characterized not only by those surface hazards that can be safeguarded against with good intentions and pocket dictionaries, but also by deep-seated hazards. Consider an exchange between a young pupil and his teacher about governmental action. In all likelihood, the child will understand "government" to mean a thing that acts in ways analogous to the ways a man acts; the teacher (let us hope) understands "government" to mean a system of functions. Thus, for example, the student might take the teacher's comment that "the government acted foolishly" as a literal statement rather than as a kind of metaphorical one. This suggests that there well may be systematic failures in communication, which can be corrected only by careful and detailed analyses of the ways in which language is used.

Let us consider, for example, the plight of the citizen Euthyphro in the

Platonic dialogue of the same name. Socrates asks Euthyphro to tell him the meaning of the term "piety" so that Socrates will know whether or not he ought to plead guilty to the charge of impiety that had been registered against him by certain Athenian citizens. He feels sure that Euthyphro, of all men, can provide this information because the latter has brought charges against his own father on the grounds of impiety. At Socrates' request, Euthyphro attempts to provide a definition for the term "piety," which is so crucial to both men:

> soc.: And what is piety and what is impiety?
> euth.: Piety is doing as I am doing; that is to say, prosecuting any one who is guilty of murder, sacrilege, or any similar crime—whether he be your father, or mother, or whoever he may be. . . .
> soc.: Remember that I did not ask you to give me two or three examples of piety, but to explain the general idea which makes all pious things to be pious. Do you not recollect that there was one idea which made the impious impious and the pious pious?
> euth.: I remember.
> soc.: Tell me what is the nature of this idea, and then I shall have a standard to which I may look, and by which I may measure actions, whether yours or those of any one else, and then I shall be able to say that such an action is pious, such another impious.
> euth.: I will tell you, if you like.
> soc.: I should very much like.
> euth.: Piety, then, is that which is dear to the gods, and impiety is that which is not dear to them.
> soc.: Very good, Euthyphro; you have now given me the sort of answers which I wanted. But whether what you say is true or not I cannot as yet tell, although I make no doubt that you will prove the truth of your words.
> euth.: Of course.
> soc.: Come, then, and let us examine what we are saying. That thing or person which is dear to the gods is pious, and that thing or person which is hateful to the gods is impious, these two being the extreme opposites of one another. Was not that said?
> euth.: It was.
> soc.: And well said?
> euth.: Yes, Socrates, I thought so; it was certainly said.
> soc.: And further, Euthyphro, the gods were admitted to have enmities and hatreds and differences?
> euth.: Yes, that was also said. . . .
> soc.: Then the same things are hated by the gods and loved by the gods, and are both hateful and dear to them?

EUTH.: True.

SOC.: And upon this view the same things, Euthyphro, will be pious and also impious?

EUTH.: So I should suppose.

SOC.: Then, my friend, I remark with surprise that you have not answered the question which I asked. For I certainly did not ask you to tell me what action is both pious and impious; but now it would seem that what is loved by the gods is also hated by them. And therefore, Euthyphro, in thus chastising your father you may very likely be doing what is agreeable to Zeus but disagreeable to Cronos or Uranus. . . .[1]

Throughout the increasingly complex dialogue Euthyphro is unable to provide an adequate definition of the term "piety," and he therefore can neither advise another nor even understand the nature of his own "pious" activities.

That language requires our continuing care and concern—that we must be prepared to analyze it to guard against communication failures—is granted by almost all philosophers, even though their attention to and skill with analysis vary widely. However, there is controversy as to whether linguistic analysis is itself philosophy or whether it is a method for safeguarding against fallacious thinking as we build our philosophical systems. The conception of philosophy as essentially analysis is generally a latter-day view, yet the roots of this view are as old as philosophy itself. The common core of the work of virtually all philosophers has been their analyses, no matter how diverse their positive speculations may have been.

EUBULIDES

Analyses from Zeno of Elea (490–430 B.C.) through the philosophers of Megara to the Stoics of Greece and Rome most frequently were distinctively logical in character and were intended to show that the opposing positions involved paradoxes or unacceptable patterns of reasoning. The Eleatics Parmenides and Zeno and their successors thought that such negative analysis led sometimes to reliable knowledge. Zeno's fame stemmed almost entirely from his mastery of such analytic procedures. Concerned to defend the monistic philosophy of Parmenides from the attacks of the pluralists, he first showed that the pluralist view entailed paradoxes or self-contradictions. Zeno then suggested that since pluralism had been shown to be logically impossible, its denial, monism, was necessarily true. This form of indirect argument, or *reductio ad absurdum*, first utilized by Zeno in philosophy and by Pythagoras (572–497 B.C.) in mathematics (the diagonal of a square is incommensurable with any side because the assumption of its commensurability proves self-contradictory) constitutes one of the most powerful and decisive patterns of inference.

Perhaps the paradoxes or antinomies that have come to be associated with the Megarian philosopher, Eubulides (360 B.C. *fl.*), best illustrate the spirit of the early Greek resistance to uncritical speculation. Although we cannot be sure that Eubulides or his contemporaries grasped the full implications of his puzzles, they have given rise to issues with which all subsequent philosophers have had to reckon. Thus, for example, consider The Heap. If two grains of wheat are a small number, can't we say the same about three? If about three, then why not about four? If about four, then why not about five, etc.? This being so, when is it clear that we have a heap of wheat rather than a small number of grains? This antinomy indicates how vague many of our normal terms are, and it suggests the folly of selecting a vague term to do precise work. Consider the practical confusion that would result from a king's demanding a heap of wheat from his subjects instead of requesting, say, a bushel! A more profound paradox is that of The Liar. If a man who is a liar says he lies, is he lying or telling the truth? It will be noted that if we believe he is lying, then we must believe he has just spoken the truth. If, on the other hand, we believe he's telling the truth, then we must believe he has just lied. This problem of a statement saying something about the condition under which it is itself true has been a challenge for philosophers and logicians from Chrysippus (280–209 B.C.) to Bertrand Russell (1872–   ).

The Electra Paradox of Eubulides involves the dramatic figure Electra, who appears in the plays of Sophocles, Euripides, and Aeschylus. If she is asked whether she knows or does not know her brother Orestes, who is at some distance from her and is dressed in unfamiliar garb, she will be answering incorrectly whether her reply is yes or no. If she says no, then she is denying that she has knowledge of her own brother, when it is well known that she is very much aware of her family relationships. If she says yes, then she is denying the realities of her senses, because it is quite clear that the man standing before her is so placed and dressed that she could not detect the clues to his identity as Orestes. The moral of this odd story is that we must acknowledge at least two uses of the term "know." Just how many uses the term "know" has is still being explored by contemporary philosophers!

A final example from the Megarians will serve to illustrate how an antinomy forces philosophers into drawing distinctions they might otherwise neglect. In The Initiate, it is proposed that one and the same sentence can be both true and false. Suppose that a man who is an initiate says "I am an initiate," and that a man who is not an initiate says "I am an initiate." Since they have both uttered the same words, that is, spoken the same sentence, and since one and the same thing cannot be both true and false, it is not the sentence itself to which the terms "true" and "false" are to be applied. It remains the case, however, that one man's assertion is true, and the other's, false. It would seem that the only way out of this predicament is to make a distinction between the sentence regarded as a repeatable physical occurrence and the sentence as a carrier of meanings that can vary with the specific circumstances under which the sentence is uttered. We can escape from the predicament, for example, by saying that truth and falsity do not apply to the sentence as an utterance but that they do apply to the meanings expressed. Almost all subsequent philosophers have regarded a distinction of this sort as essential.

PLATO

The analytic thrusts until the time of Plato tended to be isolated criticisms which, like fables, had morals the listener was expected to see and apply. In contrast, Plato employed analysis as an integral part of his total philosophy. If, indeed, we follow tradition and classify Plato as a speculative philosopher, then we should add immediately that he was preoccupied with safeguarding against speculative error through relentlessly demanding that we define our terms to draw distinctions and note implications, that we explicitly note the shifts from literal to metaphorical uses of language, that we strictly adhere to accepted patterns of inference, avoiding such things as circularity and being led into contradiction, that we recognize the difference between the objects about which we can have certain knowledge and those about which we can have only opinion, that we deal exhaustively with the alternative directions speculation may take. Thus, for example, in the following quotation from the *Theaetetus* we find Plato subjecting one of the views as to the nature of knowledge— the view of knowledge as perception—to a critical analysis:

> soc.: Someone will say, Can a man who has ever known anything, and still has and preserves a memory of that which he knows, not know that which he remembers at the time when he remembers? I have, I fear, a tedious way of putting a simple question, which is only, whether a man who has learned, and remembers, can fail to know?
>
> THEAET.: Impossible, Socrates; the supposition is monstrous.
>
> soc.: Am I talking nonsense, then? Think: is not seeing perceiving, and is not sight perception?

THEAET.: True.

SOC.: And if our recent definition holds, every man knows that which he has seen?

THEAET.: Yes.

SOC.: And you would admit that there is such a thing as memory?

THEAET.: Yes.

SOC.: And is memory of something or of nothing?

THEAET.: Of something, surely.

SOC.: Of things learned and perceived, that is?

THEAET.: Certainly.

SOC.: Often a man remembers that which he has seen?

THEAET.: True.

SOC.: And if he closed his eyes, would he forget?

THEAET.: Who, Socrates, would dare to say so?

SOC.: But we must say so, if the previous argument is to be maintained.

THEAET.: What do you mean? I am not quite sure that I understand you, though I have a strong suspicion that you are right.

SOC.: As thus: he who sees knows, as we say, that which he sees; for perception and sight and knowledge are admitted to be the same.

THEAET.: Certainly.

SOC.: But he who saw, and has knowledge of that which he saw, remembers, when he closes his eyes, that which he no longer sees.

THEAET.: True.

SOC.: And seeing is knowing, and therefore not-seeing is not-knowing?

THEAET.: Very true.

SOC.: Then the inference is, that a man may have attained the knowledge of something which he may remember and yet not know, because he does not see; and this has been affirmed by us to be a monstrous supposition.

THEAET.: Most true.

SOC.: Thus, then, the assertion that knowledge and perception are one, involves a manifest impossibility?

THEAET.: Yes.

SOC.: Then they must be distinguished?

THEAET.: I suppose that they must.[2]

The procedures of analysis themselves must be metaphysically neutral, in the sense that they involve the testing of philosophical proposals by universal standards of reason rather than on the basis of particular content. This feature of neutrality is well illustrated in the dialogues of Plato, who brings all his analytical skills to bear on the theory of Forms, the doctrine that beyond all others characterizes his systematic philosophy. In attempting to explain the precise relationship between forms and physical things, Plato spoke on numerous occasions of objects "partaking" of or "sharing" in the forms and provided various persuasive descriptions of the manner in which this was possible. Thus, in the *Republic* he portrayed this relationship of participation as being like the relationship between a physical object and its shadow and insisted that even as we say that the shadow of a man partakes of the man, so too we may say that a man partakes of the Form, Man. But in the *Parmenides* Plato spoke out against his own thesis:

> Then each individual partakes either of the whole of the idea or else of a part of the idea? Can there be any other mode of participation? There cannot be, he said.
> Then do you think the whole idea is one, and yet, being one, is in each one of the many?
> Why not, Parmenides? said Socrates.
> Because one and the same thing will exist as a whole at the same time in many separate individuals, and will therefore be in a state of separation from itself.
> Nay, but the idea may be like the day which is one and the same in many places at once, and yet continuous with itself; in this way each idea may be one and the same in all at the same time.
> I like your way, Socrates, of making one in many places at once. You mean to say, that if I were to spread out a sail and cover a number of men, there would be one whole including many—is not that your meaning?
> I think so.
> And would you say that the whole sail includes each man, or a part of it only, and different parts different men?
> The latter.
> Then, Socrates, the ideas themselves will be divisible, and things which participate in them will have a part of them only and not the whole idea existing in each of them?
> That seems to follow.
> Then would you like to say, Socrates, that the one idea is really divisible and yet remains one?
> Certainly not, he said. . . .
> Or suppose one of us to have a portion of smallness; this is but a part of the small, and therefore the absolutely small is greater; if the absolutely small be greater, that to which the part of the small is added will be smaller and not greater than before.

How absurd!

Then in what way, Socrates, will all things participate in the ideas, if they are unable to participate in them either as parts or wholes? Indeed, he said, you have asked a question which is not easily answered.[3]

Through such analyses, Plato came to realize that his statements about objects participating in their Forms are only apparently analogous to statements about shadows participating in objects. Indeed, he acknowledged that his previous statements about "participation" must be regarded as mere metaphors.

Philosophical analysis not only is a critical tool but also, perhaps indirectly, functions constructively. Analysis contributed to Plato's more sophisticated view expressed in the later dialogues such as the *Timaeus*, in which he insisted that we must assume that there is a cosmic psyche, or God, who connects the eternal forms on the one hand with the spatiotemporal world on the other.

ARISTOTLE

Perhaps no one in the history of philosophical thought has examined his predecessors more critically than Aristotle. He analyzed the works of his forerunners to disclose alternatives that they neglected and whose neglect led to abortive answers. No better example of constructive Aristotelian analysis can be given than his critique of earlier speculations on the phenomenon of change.

From the beginning, the Greek philosophers had been concerned with the opposition of qualities—that is, with the opposition of hot and cold, wet and dry, white and black—and with the fact that unlike, say, yellow and square these opposed pairs of qualities cannot exist in one object at the same time. It seemed obvious to Parmenides that any account of change must involve one in saying such contradictory things as hot becomes cold; accordingly, he insisted that, in the name of reason, we must deny change altogether. On the other hand, Heraclitus, perhaps sensitive to the same logical point, attempted to obviate the difficulty by postulating change as a brute, inexplicable fact. Aristotle began his analysis of this difficult problem by showing that his predecessors were the victims of linguistic confusion. The statement, "The iron poker has at one time the quality hot and at another time the quality cold" is a more natural translation of the expression, "The iron poker has changed from hot to cold" than is, "The hot quality of the iron poker at one time becomes the cold quality at another time." Having resolved the linguistic confusion, Aristotle discovered the problem of change to be as follows: How can something that has a certain quality at one time have an opposed quality at another? When the problem is stated in this fashion, a solution suggests itself which does not involve us in contradiction; namely, we may postulate that there is a substance or substratum—a something other than qualities —which can take on a variety of qualities.

Aristotle's sensitivity to and concern for language led him to formulate his *Organon*, the first systematic treatment of logic. In this work—actually a collection of several treatises—Aristotle deals with matters ranging from the identification of and a defense against fallacious reasoning to a positively developed formal calculus and from a doctrine concerning the source of our knowledge to rules for exfoliating such knowledge. Speaking generally, we may say that Aristotle studies judgments in their relationships to one another. A judgment is for him the basic unit of knowledge in which the subject of the proposition expressed stands for a substance and the predicate of the proposition stands for a form belonging to the substance. Aristotle holds that the propositions expressed by our judgments reflect the structure of reality and that therefore the various relations that obtain among the propositions provide us with the key for achieving a scientific body of knowledge. Thus, for example, the linguistic fact that we may apply a given predicate to an entire range of subjects, as in the instance, "All fish have gills," is paralleled by the ontological fact that a given form can recur as a property of various individual substances. And the linguistic fact that not all predicates apply to an entire range of subjects as in the instance, "Some fish are not edible," is paralleled by the ontological fact that a given form need not recur as a property of various individual substances. From a classification of judgments, each of which captures some aspect of reality in the propositions expressed, Aristotle moves to the study of the relations among these judgments.

Various propositions expressed by our judgments are linked together through common terms. It is precisely this fact of language and indeed, of nature, which makes it possible to account for, to explain, to make intelligible one judgment in terms of others. Suppose I think as a matter of fact that all perch have gills but that I wish (1) to be certain about this fact, and (2) to place this fact in relation to other facts, and to understand thereby why this fact is so. These ends may be achieved if I know both that all fish have gills and that all perch are fish. Reasoning of this sort is syllogistic; the abstract study of such patterns of reasoning which proceed through noting common terms is the science of formal logic.

The explanatory power of syllogistic reasoning depends not only on the truth of the propositions involved in an argument but also on its structure. An argument has the the capability of explaining, only if its structure is valid, that is, only if the truth of its premises necessitates the truth of its conclusion. Any argument which fails to satisfy this condition, the details of which constitute Aristotle's formal logic, is a pseudo-explanation. Thus we say that Aristotle provided an enlarged basis for the philosophical analysis of arguments—whether at the lowest practical level or highest theoretical level—by showing that mistakes in reasoning can arise not only because of linguistic but also because of purely formal inadequacies.

ROSCELLINUS, WILLIAM OF CHAMPEAUX, AND ABELARD

After Aristotle there was a significant but spasmodic concern for formal logic and a growing concern about the role of language in thought. The Stoics developed a logic of statements or propositions in contrast to Aristotle's logic of terms or classes. The Aristotelian and Stoic aspects of logic were not combined into a comprehensive scheme until the end of the nineteenth century, although there was much refinement and supplementation of both aspects by Hellenic and Christian thinkers.

An awareness that language can lead us into error and a concern to develop an adequate theory of the relation between language and reality were abundantly in evidence throughout the Greco-Roman and medieval periods. The nominalist-realist controversy concerning the status of universals provides many examples of analytic thought in medieval times. An opponent of the extreme realists such as the nominalist Roscellinus (1050–1122), might well have criticized extreme realism because it is committed to the view that only universals or essences are, in a strict sense, real and that particulars or individuals are real only in the sense that they exemplify collections of universals. That is, realism holds that class terms, such as "dog," stand for a *real* nonmaterial entity, a universal. An extreme realist, such as William of Champeaux (1070–1121), might well have stated and criticized the theory of Roscellinus' extreme nominalism because it holds that only particulars are real and that so-called "universals" are no more than general terms used to designate particulars. The only thing that is "real" about the universal is the name; only particular entities "exist."

Among the most perceptive and influential attempts to resolve the issue are the accounts of Abelard (1079–1142) and Ockham. A brief review of Abelard's thinking on this issue will pave the way for a study of the modern movement of philosophical analysis. Abelard, a student of Roscellinus, rejected his teacher's view but stopped short of accepting the realist view. Whereas Roscellinus maintained that a universal is no more than a general term to describe particulars, Abelard insisted that a general word also expresses a meaning or universal concept. Abelard's account of "a universal concept" varied; he held both that it is a confused mental image and that it is the result of a process of abstraction carried out by the mind. Thus, in the first instance he claimed that the universal concept "dog" is a blurred composite image of the various dogs I have seen, while in the second he claimed that it is the mentally abstracted characteristics that serve to distinguish dogs from "nondogs." It will be noticed that on both accounts the mind is a necessary condition for concept formation, but the concept, in and of itself, is *about* the common characteristics of a collection of individual entities. Thus, while Abelard held that the universal concept or meaning is the result of psychological processes, he was unwilling to equate it with the psychological processes themselves. Furthermore, while acknowledging that a universal concept or meaning is objective rather than subjective, he resisted the extreme realist thesis that it has an ontological status independent of the particulars out of which the mind has composed or abstracted it. In short, he would have insisted that whereas the proper names "Fido" and "Sport" denote discrete concrete particulars, and only concrete particulars are real, in saying of each that "He is a dog," we refer to his resemblance to other dogs with respect to certain universal concepts or meanings—concepts which are extramental in that they are abstracted from and applicable to concrete particulars and mental in that they are achieved through and employed by psychological processes.

LOCKE

It will be helpful in arriving at an understanding of contemporary philosophical analysis to pursue the problem of universals still further. It remains a perplexing problem for analysts, and the shifting treatment of the problem in the seventeenth and eighteenth centuries reflects the radically altered view as to the "objects of knowledge" which constitutes the direct heritage of the analysts. It is impossible to exaggerate the influence of John Locke's philosophy in bringing about the aforementioned epistemological shift, and the import and nature of this shift is most readily seen through a consideration of his treatment of the problem of universals.

Solutions to the problem of universals extend from the extreme realism of William of Champeaux (the universal exists independent of particulars and is discovered by the human mind) through the moderate realism of Abelard (the universal exists only in particulars which exemplify it and comes to be known through mental abstraction) to the extreme nominalism of Roscellinus (the universal is merely a term devised by the human mind to denote collections of particulars, which alone exist). Locke's solution, sometimes called "conceptualism," falls between the views of Abelard and Roscellinus. A universal is an abstract, general idea existing solely in the mind; a universal functions by signifying a common property of a collection of particular ideas. Our awareness of Locke's departure from both Roscellinus and Abelard is sharpened when we note that he confined us strictly to *particular ideas of the mind*: we can refer neither to particular things as Roscellinus does nor to properties common to particular things as Abelard does. Not only does Locke insist that our immediate knowledge is restricted to that of ideas rather than of objects and properties of objects, but he also insists that our words are mere symbols for ideas. For example, the word "man" is simply the agreed-upon symbol for the general, abstract idea "man." The impact of Locke's position (in conjunction with that of Descartes) on much of subsequent philosophy was to make the study of epistemology prior to that of ontology, that is, to make our answers to questions about the relation of language to things (of "man" to man) depend on our answers to questions about the relation of language to thought (of "man" to our idea of man).

Since Locke held that the nature of thought is decisive, he focused attention on this problem. It seemed natural to him to proceed by asking the question "What is the origin of our ideas?"—that is, from where do "the materials of reason and knowledge" come? As we shall see, his answer was that they come ultimately from experience. He insisted that his answer is the most plausible, not only because it is the most natural but also because the alternative claim that we have innate or inborn ideas cannot be defended. Locke reasoned that if indeed there were innate principles, then they would be known by all and beyond controversy; however, the fact is that every so-called "innate" principle—whether a metaphysical one such as "Nature abhors a vacuum" or a logical one such as "Whatever is, is"—seems novel to some and debatable to others. Moreover, Locke contended, even if there were universally acknowledged principles, it would still have to be shown that they could not be derived from experience, and he denied that any theorist of innate ideas had ever demonstrated this.[4] Assuming that he had disposed of the doctrine of innate ideas satisfactorily, Locke concluded that one could then distinguish between genuine knowledge and pseudoknowledge.

Locke began the exposition of his own position by insisting that all genuine ideas must have their origin in experience, either sensory or introspective:

> *All ideas come from sensation or reflection.*—Let us then suppose the mind to be, as we say, white paper, void of all characters, without any ideas: —How come it to be furnished? . . . Whence has it all the *materials* of reason and knowledge? To this I answer, in one word, from *experience*. In that all knowledge is founded; and from that it ultimately derives itself. Our observation employed either about external sensible objects, or about the internal operations of our minds perceived and reflected on by ourselves, is that which supplies our understandings with all the *materials* of thinking. These two are the fountains of knowledge, from whence all the ideas we have, or can naturally have, do spring.
>
> *The objects of sensation one source of ideas.*—First, our Senses, conversant about particular sensible objects, do convey into the mind several distinct perceptions of things, according to those various ways wherein those objects do affect them. And thus we come by those *ideas* we have of *yellow, white, heat, cold, soft, hard, bitter, sweet,* and all those which we call sensible qualities. . . .
>
> *The operations of our minds, the other source of them.*—Secondly, the other fountain from which experience furnisheth the understanding with ideas is,—the perception of the operations of our own mind within us, as it is employed about the ideas it has got;—which operations, when the soul comes to reflect on and consider, do furnish the understanding with another set of ideas, which could not be had from things without. And such are *perception, thinking, doubting, believing, reasoning, knowing, willing,* and all the different actings of our own minds. . . .[5]

The foregoing is an account of the acquisition of *simple ideas,* those ideas which the mind can neither create nor destroy. Locke went on to provide us with an account of *complex ideas* and to advance a doctrine concerning the ways in which simple ideas are "compounded." To characterize Locke roughly, he found that the mind engages in the processes of uniting, comparing, and abstracting ideas and that it is only through these processes that we pass beyond simple ideas. Ideas of substance, such as the idea of a man or of a dog, are produced by our uniting such simple ideas as those of a specific color, shape, and so on. Ideas of relation, such as the idea of a gray color patch A being "darker than" the gray color patch B, result from our comparing one idea with another. Ideas of abstraction, such as those of whiteness or humanity, have their origin in our sorting out common features in a multitude of ideas.

Details aside, the inescapable moral of Locke's philosophy is that our claim to knowledge must be radically limited. He found, for example, that such an honored philosophical phrase as "a space infinite" does not name any idea whatsoever, and, accordingly, all arguments that make use of the phrase—including several prominent arguments for the existence of God—are purely verbal nonsense. It frequently happens, according to Locke, that when we carefully distinguish among the alleged senses of a term, some of these will be without meaning. We may speak sensibly about the infinity of space, but not about an actual infinite space:

> The idea of the infinity of space . . . is nothing but a supposed endless progression of the mind over what repeated ideas of space it pleases; but to have actually in the mind the idea of a space infinite, is to suppose the mind already passed over, and actually to have a view of all those repeated ideas of space which an endless repetition can never totally represent to it.[6]

BERKELEY AND HUME

An important feature of the Lockean account of knowledge that his successors, Berkeley and Hume, found unsatisfactory was the notion of "abstract general ideas." Even Locke was indecisive regarding them, as is evident from the fact that he advanced several different theories about the origin and nature of such ideas. The theory he tended to favor most, however, and the one that his successors are most prone to criticize, is the view that we arrive at an abstract, general idea by eliminating from our ideas of particulars those characteristics that distinguish one idea from another. Berkeley and, in his wake, Hume, were quick to point out that, as Locke himself had maintained elsewhere, the only ideas a mind can entertain are particular ideas. This means, first, that our ideas have specific rather than generic characteristics. Thus, for example, to have a simple idea of a color is, say, to have an idea of a specific shade of red. Second, and even more drastic, to have a particular idea is to have a numerically singular idea rather than a "group" idea of a quality common to a class of particular ideas. Thus to have an idea of a specific red shade is to have in mind *this* distinct red image, say, of a three-inch tomato.

Berkeley and, again, Hume developed one of Locke's less developed lines of thought in their effort to remain consistent empiricists while giving the necessary account of general ideas. Their key insight was that we achieve generality by employing a particular idea as representative of a whole class of particulars. That is to say, a particular idea is singled out by the mind to be regarded, not for its own sake, but rather as the standard for classifying other particular ideas through their resemblance to it. This move is similar to that of a geometer when he says, "Let this triangle stand for any triangle." Note, again, that even if one were to accept Locke's theory of abstract, general ideas, one would still require some such account as Berkeley and Hume provided. For the abstractive process is being presupposed to range over a "class" of particular ideas, a "class" being a collection which in itself must be accounted for.

To put it another way, for Locke the basis for calling a term "abstract and general" is that it refers to an abstract, general idea. For Berkeley and Hume there is no parallel basis for calling a term "general"; a general term does not name a general idea, since there are only particular ideas. Rather, a term becomes "general" because of its capacity to evoke a particular idea that may be said to function loosely as representative of a group of resembling particular ideas.

Hume acknowledged that the general critique of Locke's theory and the outlines of an improved account were the contributions of Berkeley. However, it remained for Hume not only to polish Berkeley's account but also to complete it with a more detailed theory of meaning. Specifically, Hume held that a term is called "general" when it is associated with a custom of the mind, with a disposition to evoke any one of a set of resembling particular ideas gained from previous experience or to add a particular resembling idea from fresh experience to that set. What Berkeley started and Hume completed is the rejection of the traditional theory of meaning in which the meaning of a word is the single idea or object denoted by the word. Many contemporary analysts accept the Humean analysis and hold that general words, unlike proper names, do not stand in a one-to-one relationship with ideas or objects; at most these philosophers are willing to say, with Hume, that a general word stands in some sort of relationship to a disposition of mind to bring forth ideas which are similar.

Pursuing the task begun by Locke of confining the mind strictly to what it can know, Berkeley and Hume discovered the limitations of genuine knowledge to be far greater than Locke had supposed. This discovery was, in a small sense, the result of their rejection of the existence of abstract, general ideas and in a larger sense, the result of their concern to be consistent empiricists. For example, Berkeley was unwilling to follow Locke's view that we can speak meaningfully about unperceived objects:

> It is indeed an opinion strangely prevailing amongst men that houses, mountains, rivers, and, in a word, all sensible objects have an existence, natural or real, distinct from their being perceived by the understanding: . . . If we thoroughly examine this tenet it will, perhaps, be found at bottom to depend on the doctrine of abstract ideas. For can there be a nicer strain of abstraction than to distinguish the existence of sensible objects from their being perceived, so as to conceive them existing unperceived? Light and colors, heat and cold, extension and figures—in a word, the things we see and feel—what are they but so many sensations, notions, ideas, or impressions on the sense? And is it possible to separate, even in thought, any of these from perception? For my part, I might as easily divide a thing from itself. I may, indeed, divide in my thought, or conceive apart from each other, those things which, perhaps, I never perceived by sense so divided. Thus I imagine the trunk of a human body without the limbs, or conceive the smell of a rose without thinking on the rose itself. So far, I will not deny, I can abstract —if that may properly be called *abstraction* which extends beyond the possibility of real existence or perception. Hence, as it is impossible for me to see or feel anything without an actual sensation of that thing, so is it impossible for me to conceive in my thoughts any sensible thing or object distinct from the sensation or perception of it.[7]

The eighteenth-century drive to establish adequately and consistently the Lockean thesis that experience places a limit on what we may properly regard as knowledge culminated in Hume. Hume began by insisting that Locke failed to distinguish precisely between sensing something and thinking about it, between having an *impression* and having an *idea*. Because of this failure, Locke could not give a clear criterion for identifying genuine ideas. The test Hume provided is that every simple idea has as its necessary condition a simple impression to which the idea corresponds in every way except that (1) it is less vivid and forceful and (2) it must occur subsequent to the original impression. In addition to simple ideas there are complex ones that result from the play of the imagination as it is guided by the laws of association: resemblance, spatial and temporal contiguity, and cause and effect.

Having laid an epistemological groundwork of the sort we have indicated, Hume proceeded to apply the empiricist meaning criterion systematically to philosophical concepts in order to clarify those that are vague and to eliminate those that are meaningless. Hume claimed, for example, to have clarified the idea of "time." After having searched through his perceptions (ideas and impressions, simple and complex) in a futile quest for the origin of the idea, he concluded that the idea of "time" derives not from any single perception but from the *succession* of our perceptions.

Hume's utilization of the empiricist criterion for detecting meaningless ideas is significantly illustrated in his criticism of the idea of "necessary connection," an idea that philosophers traditionally believed characterized the cause-effect relationship. He began by reviewing the important uses to which the notion of causation is put, acknowledging, for example, that it is the basis of our inference from present experience to future events. He then proposed to reexamine the belief of many philosophers that causation is a complex idea analyzable into spatial juxtaposition, temporal succession, and necessary connection. Hume readily found the first two elements but failed completely to find a source in experience—either sensory or introspective—for the third element.

An essential feature of the Humean analysis is the rejection of the thesis that a proposition such as, "Billiard ball A causes billiard ball B to move" has the same status as the proposition, "$2 + 2 = 4$." That these propositions are not similar may be seen through an examination of their contradictories: To say that "$2 + 2 \neq 4$" is self-contradictory; to say that "Billiard ball A does not cause billiard ball B to move" may be false, but it is not self-contradictory. Thus, to admit that a mathematical relation implies a necessary connection is not to admit that a causal relation does.

Hume was drawing a sharp distinction—a distinction that was to play so decisive a role in subsequent philosophy that it cannot be overemphasized—between relations of the mathematical or logical variety and relations of the factual variety. Since, as we have seen, the causal relation is different in kind from the mathematicological relation, it must be factual; and this relation, like any other "matter of fact," must be verified experientially. Hume failed to discover any experiential relation corresponding to the notion of necessary connection; all he discovered was the relation of constant conjunction. At his most compromising, he was willing to say no more than that the mistake of conceiving causal relations as involving necessary connections results from a natural tendency to take a *psychological* habit of expectation about events to be indicative of a *logical* relation obtaining between the events themselves.

KANT

Strangely, the essential distinction between logical relations and factual relations, on which Hume had insisted, was given its most influential formulation by Immanuel Kant, the man most concerned to show that Hume's two categories of propositions were not exhaustive. Kant drew the following distinction: In every judgment of the subject-predicate form, the predicate term is either included in the subject term, explicitly or tacitly, or excluded from it. In the former case, the judgment is called "analytic," while in the latter, it is termed "synthetic." The judgment that "A bachelor is unmarried" is analytic, while the judgment that "The sun is shining today" is synthetic. It will be noticed that Hume's test for distinguishing between relations among ideas and matters of fact, which consists in showing that the contradictory of the former type of proposition is self-contradictory and the contradictory of the latter is not, was also utilized by Kant in distinguishing between "analytic" and "synthetic" judgments. For example, it is self-contradictory to deny that a bachelor is unmarried, but it is not self-contradictory to deny that the sun is shining today. It is also the case that every judgment is either *a priori* or *a posteriori*—that is, the verification of every judgment is either logically independent of or logically dependent on sense experience. Kant concluded that the distinction Hume made is that between *analytic a priori* and *synthetic a posteriori* judgments, but he denied Hume's claim that our knowledge is limited exclusively to judgments of one type or the other. While Kant eliminated the possibility of analytic *a posteriori* judgments because they would be required logically to be both independent of and dependent on experience for their verification, he insisted that there are no such grounds for eliminating the possibility of synthetic *a priori* judgments. He argued, first, that there is no contradiction in asserting that a true judgment may have a predicate term that is not included in the subject term and yet not depend on sense experience for its verification. He argued, second, that such important statements as "$7 + 5 = 12$" and "Every event has a cause" cannot be classified as either analytic *a priori* or synthetic *a posteriori*.

Beginning with Kant, then, there arose a strong movement in philosophy that may be characterized as an attempt to combat the sharp limitations of knowledge implicitly set by Hume's distinction. Kant argued somewhat as follows: (1) both analytic *a priori* and mathematical judgments are apodictic (absolutely certain truths); (2) synthetic *a posteriori* judgments fail to be apodictic; (3) analytic *a priori* judgments are such that their negations are self-contradictory, but this is not true of all mathematical judgments. Therefore, mathematical judgments are neither synthetic *a posteriori* nor (in some cases at least) analytic *a priori*. To put it positively, Kant believed that he had shown that there are synthetic *a priori* mathematical judgments and, by extending the argument, that there are also important synthetic *a priori* truths in such fields as ethics and epistemology.

RUSSELL

If Kant may be said to have made an elaborate attempt to distinguish, as different in kind, mathematical truths from logical truths, Bertrand Russell (1872–1969), as the culmination of a line of mathematically oriented philosophers from Leibniz through Boole (1815–1864), Frege (1848–1925) and Whitehead (1861–1947), has made an equally elaborate attempt to deny the distinction. Drawing together and enlarging immeasurably on the Aristotelian and Stoic logics, the men in this movement widened the domain of the analytic *a priori* to a degree which Kant could not possibly have foreseen. Armed with symbolic or mathematical logic, Russell sought to demonstrate that a mathematical proposition such as "$7 + 5 = 12$" was logically no different from a proposition such as "All tall men are tall."

Perhaps the most appropriate way to characterize the philosophizing of Russell is to say that he attempted to obviate or resolve philosophical problems by applying a principle known as Ockham's razor which commands, "Wherever possible, substitute constructions out of known entities for inferences to unknown entities." This principle in conjunction with the tools of the new logic led him both to reduce mathematics to logic and to sound a general philosophical alarm:

> As language grows more abstract, a new set of entities come into philosophy, namely, those represented by abstract words—the universals. I do not wish to maintain that there are no universals, but certainly there are many abstract words which do not stand for single universals—*e.g.* triangularity and rationality. In these respects language misleads us both by its vocabulary and by its syntax. We must be on our guard in both respects if our logic is not to lead to a false metaphysic.[8]

It is worthy of comment that although Russell does not adopt a strict nominalism, he nevertheless aligns himself with the nominalistic tradition in its long-standing effort to curtail fanciful excesses of realism. To a greater or lesser degree, his nominalizing tendency has been continued by a whole host of philosophical analysts. There is no better example of an analysis which undermines the unbridled metaphysical claims of realists than Russell's *theory of descriptions*.

Having accepted from classical logic the realist doctrine that all terms refer to something, Russell was confronted with a puzzle:

> Suppose we say; "The round square does not exist." It seems that this is a true proposition, yet we cannot regard it as denying the existence of a certain object called "the round square." For if there were such an object, it would exist: We cannot first assume that there is a certain object, and then proceed to deny that there is such an object.[9]

Russell attacked this problem by insisting that a distinction be drawn between two kinds of symbols which occur as grammatical subjects. In the first place, there are symbols which directly represent objects of our acquaintance. The meaning of a symbol of this kind is simply the object it represents and it has this meaning whether or not it occurs in a linguistic context. In the second place, there are symbols meaningful to use but not meaningful in isolation, viz., "incomplete" symbols. Direct representation is not the test of an incomplete symbol; the test is rather that a statement containing an incomplete symbol be analyzable into a form wherein each symbol does in fact represent something with which we can be acquainted, i.e., into a significant statement in which the incomplete symbol has completely disappeared.

> Thus when we say "the round square does not exist," we may, as a first attempt at such an analysis, substitute "it is false that there is an object x which is both round and square."[10]

Russell quickly recognized that his theory of descriptions was merely a striking instance of a distinctive form of analysis, "analysis as the resolution of incomplete symbols." In this, one proceeds by the replacement of symbols of dubious representation with apparently synonymous symbols which unquestionably do represent objects. He has always spoken about such analyses as straddling the borderline between logic and epistemology and metaphysics. For example, he comments that the theory of descriptions "clears up two millenia of muddle-headedness about 'existence.'"[11]

Flushed with the success of the philosophical application of logical techniques, Russell came to believe that the grammar of ordinary language with a happenstance vocabulary leading to muddle-headed metaphysical positions ought to be replaced by the strict syntax of logic combined with scientific terminology leading to a single but clear-headed metaphysics. This Russellian doctrine that an ideal language—a logico-scientific language—could be constructed and that it would directly and unambiguously reflect the nature of reality is called *logical atomism*.

MOORE AND WITTGENSTEIN

By far the most influential and fullest statement of logical atomism was worked out by Ludwig Wittgenstein (1889–1951), a student-colleague of Russell. His perfected statement of it in which the implications of an ideal language are carried out had a profound effect on numerous American and British philosophers, and also on a group of continental philosophers, the Vienna Circle, who were initiating a school of philosophy which has come to be known as logical positivism. Both the distinctive features of this philosophy and its persuasiveness are made manifest in an article which is to follow, written by Moritz Schlick (1882–1936), who more than any other man was the founder of the school.

We have mentioned the impact of Russell on the thinking of Wittgenstein. It was considerable but immediate. In the long run, Wittgenstein was more thoroughly impressed with the common-sensical endeavors of the philosopher whom he was to succeed at Cambridge University, G. E. Moore (1873–1958). In an age in which there was excitement about the power of abstract logic and in which there was deference shown to the methods of science because of its successes, G. E. Moore stood steadfast as a reminder that the problems of philosophy were not to be resolved either by logical manipulations or by merely increasing our scientific knowledge. He insisted instead that the key to solving philosophical problems lay in the quite different direction of paying close attention to common sense and its language, that is, ordinary language.

As early as 1903, Moore, in his *Principia Ethics*, set the modern fashion of viewing ethics as analysis. The key to his orientation was that before one wastes his efforts in attempting to answer an ethical question, he must clarify precisely what the question is that he is asking: Notice how easy it is to ask an impressive question without realizing that it is complex, and that as it stands, it is incapable of a precise answer. Philosophers, for example, have asked the question "What is good?" and then proceeded to search for an answer without even being clear as to whether they were dealing with "What things are good?" or "How is 'good' to be defined?" Because of his spectacular success in applying this simple methodological procedure, he influenced not only philosophers who worked in the field of ethics but also many working in other branches of philosophy.

By the time he wrote an essay entitled "A Defense of Common Sense" in 1925, he was willing to add to his original methodological principle another which equally appeals to our demand for basic simplicity. It may be stated as follows: We must distinguish between the statements which are known to be true with certainty and the analyses of such statements in which we endeavor to determine their full meaning. Speaking roughly, we may say that common sense provides us with a body of reliable but largely unanalyzed truths which, in turn, challenge philosophy to determine their meaning. From Moore's viewpoint, the philosopher's task is mainly that of coming to understand the truth rather than trying to discover it. He would, for example, be sympathetic with the fabled claim of Samuel Johnson that by kicking a stone and hurting his toe, he has refuted the conclusion, attributed (erroneously) to Berkeley, that philosophical analysis shows there can be no real objects. Again, Moore would be unsympathetic with David Hume's lament to the effect that as far as knowing the truth is concerned, we must turn from the comfort of everyday beliefs to the application of the methods of philosophic doubt.

When we take a close look at Moore's philosophy, it becomes difficult to determine whether it is better classified as a type of common-sense philosophy or as a philosophy of ordinary language. The correct interpretation aside, it remains the case that Ludwig Wittgenstein rather than G. E. Moore was the prime mover in the development of the *ordinary language school* which now dominates much of philosophy in the English-speaking world. A man reminiscent of Socrates in his ability to attract disciples and in his provocative style of expression, Wittgenstein was also effective in launching the new movement because of the authority he had gained in the earlier analytic movement of the logical positivists which he now renounced. It has been observed frequently that the Wittgenstein who wrote the *Tractatus* (1922) and the Wittgenstein whose span of work between 1929 and 1945 is captured in his *Philosophical Investigations* are two different philosophers.

Perhaps the difference between the earlier and later Wittgenstein, the difference between philosophical analysts such as Russell, the logical positivists and even G. E. Moore and the philosophical analysts such as J. Austin (1911–1960), G. Ryle (1900–   ) and A. J. Wisdom (1904–   ), is captured in the following observation: The later Wittgenstein is claiming that to ask for an analysis of a given statement is merely to ask how the statement is being used in a given context rather than to ask what the statement *really* means. He is objecting, in the first place, to the earlier analysts' article of faith that the meaning of a statement is the method of its verification; in the second place, to their practice of analyzing actual expressions of language by equating them with expressions which are more fully understandable. Wittgenstein insists that we appreciate the multiple uses of ordinary language, and that when, say, a statement is employed in such a way that it cannot possibly be verified, we are merely to conclude that it is not being used in a descriptive fashion. Our job in such a case is to be sensitive to the way it is being used rather than to be carried away by our discovery that it is non-referring and conclude dogmatically that it is meaningless. This sensitivity to the various ways in which statements are used leads the ordinary language philosopher to speak of each statement as having as its own "logic," its own function to perform. While there are, indeed, resemblances in the ways that various statements are used, we must not run the risk of arbitrarily imposing our own categories upon them by classifying them and by regarding them as units of on all-pervasive logical structure. Language is a subtle instrument in which many tasks are being performed at a variety of levels. This being so, we stand forewarned that unheeding analysis leads us not only to underestimate the power of language but also to deprive ourselves of much of the communication that it brings.

Many of the questions that the philosophers have asked from the earliest reflective period to the present have been unanswerable precisely because they make false presumptions about language. Wittgenstein suggests that this is the case with perennial puzzles which arise in connection with statements involving "meaning," "understanding," "believing," "true," "fact," "time," "space," "beautiful," "good," and the like. He suggests concerned in much of this chapter to trace historically an aspect of a actual language uses to which such words are and can be put, if we hope to escape the "bewitchment of our intelligence." Let us look a bit more closely at what Wittgenstein is advocating and what the trap is into which we have fallen. Consider the problem of *meaning*. We have been concerned in much of this chapter to trace historically an aspect of a celebrated problem, namely, to trace the conflict between nominalism and realism. We may say that many nominalists and realists have regarded themselves as irreconcilably opposed to each other. According to Wittgenstein, however, it remains that each has been presuming that words *name* —whether particular or universal—in a way completely analogous to the way in which a proper name or general noun refers to an individual or kind of individual, respectively. They have taken such conspicuous naming circumstances to be paradigms of the relationship of language to the world. Once conceived, such a thesis seemingly unifies the whole meaning issue; once adopted, it requires us to invent and dispute about a whole series of processes, entities, and categories, for which there is no other justification and which ultimately fails even to sustain our unitary account. To say, for example, that "five" denotes a number in the sense that "slab" denotes a building block is seen to be patently false when we remain alert to the various possible concrete language situations in which terms might occur. Let us suppose that a mason's assistant is told to fetch five slabs. Is it seriously open to him to complain that while he has found the slabs, he can't find the five? The absurdity of this situation points up the danger of imposing a unitary theory of meaning upon these terms. The Wittgensteinian point to see in this example is that "five" and "slab" have different roles to play in the effective language situation of a mason communicating with his apprentice. The language-sorting process that we have begun with this example must be extended by the philosopher, and once entered into, carries the case against any unitary theory of meaning.

In brief, the moral of Wittgenstein's writings bids us abandon our preoccupation with explaining the meaning of language and concentrate on describing the rich variety of ways in which language functions. Whether Wittgenstein is ultimately prepared to identify meaning and use is a moot question. However, that he has stimulated a legion of philosophers to undertake the task of describing the actual and possible uses of language is undebatable.

We have selected articles from two important philosophical analysts. Moritz Schlick was a founder of logical positivism and one of the ablest proponents of its central doctrine, the verifiability theory of meaning. His article is entitled "Meaning and Verification." The second philosopher is John Austin, an extremely influential pioneer in the ordinary-language wing of analysis. His article, "Other Minds," illustrates the distinctive ways in which ordinary-language philosophers may be said to reinterpret age-old problems and to seek their solution.

Moritz Schlick: MEANING AND VERIFICATION

> MORITZ SCHLICK *is examining the verification criterion of meaning, that is, the thesis that "The meaning of a proposition is the method of its verification." This view that we can only understand the meaning of a sentence if we are able to*

specify the empirical conditions under which it can be verified has been criticized on the grounds that it would preclude much that is normally regarded as philosophically significant. How, for example, can statements about the future be meaningful? Schlick's answer is simply that we must wait for the events to take place, that is, that such statements are verifiable and hence meaningful. In addition to the distinction between the verified and verifiable, he also distinguishes between the empirically and logically verifiable. It will be noticed in each of these pairs, the second concept is inclusive of the former and that therefore the most inclusive of them all is logical verifiability. Schlick is contending that the verifiability principle does not require us to know all of the laws of nature in order to determine what statements are and what statements are not meaningful. He is demanding instead only that our statements conform to a set of stipulations governing their verification.

The article reprinted here with the kind permission of the Philosophical Review *originally appeared in the pages of that quarterly, in Volume 45, pp. 339–369.*

I

Philosophical questions, as compared with ordinary scientific problems, are always strangely paradoxical. But it seems to be an especially strange paradox that the question concerning the meaning of a proposition should constitute a serious philosophical difficulty. For is it not the very nature and purpose of every proposition to express its own meaning? In fact, when we are confronted with a proposition (in a language familiar to us) we usually know its meaning immediately. If we do not, we can have it explained to us, but the explanation will consist of a new proposition; and if the new one is capable of expressing the meaning, why should not the original one be capable of it? So that a snippy person when asked what he meant by a certain statement might be perfectly justified in saying, "I meant exactly what I said!"

It is logically legitimate and actually the normal way in ordinary life and even in science to answer a question concerning the meaning of a proposition by simply repeating it either more distinctly or in slightly different words. Under what circumstances, then, can there be any sense in asking for the meaning of a statement which is well before our eyes or ears?

Evidently the only possibility is that we have not *understood* it. And in this case what is actually before our eyes or ears is nothing but a series of words which we are unable to handle; we do not know how to use it, how to "apply it to reality." Such a series of words is for us simply a complex of signs "without meaning," a mere sequel of sounds or a mere row of marks on paper, and we have no right to call it "a proposition" at all; we may perhaps speak of it as "a sentence."

If we adopt this terminology we can now easily get rid of our paradox by saying that we cannot inquire after the meaning of a proposition, but can ask about the meaning of a sentence, and that this amounts to asking, "What proposition does the sentence stand for?" And this question is answered either by a proposition in a language with which we are already perfectly familiar; or by indicating the logical rules which will make a proposition out of the sentence, i.e., will tell us exactly in what circumstances the sentence is to be *used*. These two methods do not actually differ in principle; both of them give meaning to the sentence (transform it into a proposition) by locating it, as it were, within the system of a definite language; the first method making use of a language which is already in our possession, the second one building it up for us. The first method represents the simplest kind of ordinary "translation"; the second one affords a deeper insight into the nature of meaning, and will have to be used in order to overcome philosophical difficulties connected with the understanding of sentences.

The source of these difficulties is to be found in the fact that very often we do not know how to handle our own words; we speak or write without having first agreed upon a definite logical grammar which will constitute the signification of our terms. We commit the mistake of thinking that we know the meaning of a sentence (i.e., understand it as a proposition) if we are familiar with all the words occurring in it. But this is not sufficient. It will not lead to confusion or error as long as we remain in the domain of everyday life by which our words have been formed and to which they are adapted, but it will become fatal the moment we try to think about abstract problems by means of the same terms without carefully fixing their signification for the new purpose. For every word has a definite signification only within a definite context into which it has been fitted; in any other context it will have no meaning unless we provide new rules for the use of the word in the new case, and this may be done, at least in principle, quite arbitrarily.

Let us consider an example. If a friend should say to me, "Take me to a country where the sky is three times as blue as in England!" I should not know how to fulfill his wish; his phrase would appear nonsensical to me, because the word "blue" is used in a way which is not provided for by the rules of our language. The combination of a numeral and the name of a color does not occur in it; therefore my friend's sentence has no meaning, although its exterior linguistic form is that of a command, or a wish. But he can, of course, give it a meaning. If I ask him, "What do you mean by 'three times as blue'?," he can arbitrarily indicate certain definite physical circumstances concerning the serenity of the sky which he wants his phrase to be the description of. And then, perhaps, I shall be able to follow his directions; his wish will have become meaningful for me.

Thus, whenever we ask about a sentence, "What does it mean?," what we expect is instruction as to the circumstances in which the sentence is to be used; we want a description of the conditions under which the sentence will form a *true* proposition, and of those which will make it *false*. The meaning of a word or a combination of words is, in this way, determined by a set of rules which regulate their use and which, following Wittgenstein, we may call the rules of their *grammar*, taking this word in its widest sense.

(If the preceding remarks about meaning are as correct as I am convinced they are, this will, to a large measure, be due to conversations with Wittgenstein which have greatly influenced my own views about these matters. I can hardly exaggerate my indebtedness to this philosopher. I do not wish to impute to him any responsibility for the contents of this article, but I have reason to hope that he will agree with the main substance of it.)

Stating the meaning of a sentence amounts to stating the rules according to which the sentence is to be used, and this is the same as stating the way in which it can be verified (or falsified). The meaning of a proposition is the method of its verification.

The "grammatical" rules will partly consist of ordinary definitions, i.e., explanations of words by means of other words, partly of what are called "ostensive" definitions, i.e., explanations by means of a procedure which puts the words to actual use. The simplest form of an ostensive definition is a pointing gesture combined with the pronouncing of the word, as when we teach a child the signification of the sound "blue" by showing a blue object. But in most cases the ostensive definition is of a more complicated form; we cannot point to an object corresponding to words like "because," "immediate," "chance," "again," etc. In these cases we require the presence of certain complex situations, and the meaning of the words is defined by the way we use them in these different situations.

It is clear that in order to understand a verbal definition we must know the signification of the explaining words beforehand, and that the only explanation which can work without any previous knowledge is the ostensive definition. We conclude that there is no way of understanding any meaning without ultimate reference to ostensive definitions, and this means, in an obvious sense, reference to "experience" or "possibility of verification."

This is the situation, and nothing seems to me simpler or less questionable. It is this situation and nothing else that we describe when we affirm that the meaning of a proposition can be given only by giving the rules of its verification in experience. (The addition, "in experience," is really superfluous, as no other kind of verification has been defined.)

This view has been called the "experimental theory of meaning"; but it certainly is no theory at all, for the term "theory" is used for a set of hypotheses about a certain subject-matter, and there are no hypotheses involved in our view, which proposes to be nothing but a simple statement of the way in which meaning is *actually* assigned to propositions, both in everyday life and in science. There has never been any other way, and it would be a grave error to suppose that we believe we have discovered a new conception of meaning which is contrary to common opinion and which we want to introduce into philosophy. On the contrary, our conception is not only entirely in agreement with, but even derived from, common sense and scientific procedure. Although our criterion of meaning has always been employed in practice, it has very rarely been formulated in the past, and this is perhaps the only excuse for the attempts of so many philosophers to deny its feasibility.

The most famous case of an explicit formulation of our criterion is Einstein's answer to the question, What do we mean when we speak of two events at distant places happening simultaneously? This answer consisted in a description of an experimental method by which the simultaneity of such events was actually ascertained. Einstein's philosophical opponents maintained—and some of them still maintain—that they knew the meaning of the above question independently of any method of verification. All I am trying to do is to stick consistently to Einstein's position and to admit no exceptions from it. (Professor Bridgman's book on *The Logic of*

Modern Physics is an admirable attempt to carry out this program for all concepts of physics.) I am not writing for those who think that Einstein's philosophical opponents were right.

II

Professor C. I. Lewis, in a remarkable address on "Experience and Meaning" [published in *The Philosophical Review*, March 1934], has justly stated that the view developed above (he speaks of it as the "empirical-meaning requirement") forms the basis of the whole philosophy of what has been called the "logical positivism of the Viennese Circle." He criticizes this basis as inadequate chiefly on the ground that its acceptance would impose certain limitations upon "significant philosophic discussion" which, at some points, would make such discussion altogether impossible and, at other points, restrict it to an intolerable extent.

Feeling responsible as I do for certain features of the Viennese philosophy (which I should prefer to call Consistent Empiricism), and being of the opinion that it really does not impose any restrictions upon significant philosophizing at all, I shall try to examine Professor Lewis' chief arguments and point out why I think that they do not endanger our position—at least as far as I can answer for it myself. All of my own arguments will be derived from the statements made in section I.

Professor Lewis describes the empirical-meaning requirement as demanding "that any concept put forward or any proposition asserted shall have a definite denotation; that it shall be intelligible not only verbally and logically but in the further sense that one can specify those empirical items which would determine the applicability of the concept or constitute the verification of the proposition" (*loc. cit.*, 125). Here it seems to me that there is no justification for the words "but in the *further sense* . . . ," i.e., for the distinction of two (or three?) senses of intelligibility. The remarks in section I show that, according to our opinion, "verbal and logical" understanding *consists in* knowing how the proposition in question could be verified. For, unless we mean by "verbal understanding" that we know how the words are actually used, the term could hardly mean anything but a shadowy feeling of being acquainted with the words, and in a philosophical discussion it does not seem advisable to call such a feeling "understanding." Similarly, I should not advise that we speak of a sentence as being "logically intelligible" when we just feel convinced that its exterior form is that of a proper proposition (if, e.g., it has the form, substantive—copula—adjective, and therefore appears to predicate a property of a thing). For it seems to me that by such a phrase we want to say much *more*, namely, that we are completely aware of the whole grammar of the sentence, i.e., that we know exactly the circumstances to which it is fitted. Thus knowledge of how a proposition is verified is not anything over and above its verbal and logical understanding, but is identical with it. It seems to me, therefore, that when we demand that a proposition be verifiable we are not adding a new requirement but are simply formulating the conditions which have actually always been acknowledged as necessary for meaning and intelligibility.

The mere statement that no sentence has meaning unless we are able to indicate a way of testing its truth or falsity is not very useful if we do not explain very carefully the signification of the phrases "method of testing" and "verifiability." Professor Lewis is quite right when he asks for such an explanation. He himself suggests some ways in which it might be given, and I am glad to say that his suggestions appear to me to be in perfect agreement with my own views and those of my philosophical friends. It will be easy to show that there is no serious divergence between the point of view of the pragmatist as Professor Lewis conceives it and that of the Viennese Empiricist. And if in some special questions they arrive at different conclusions, it may be hoped that a careful examination will bridge the difference.

How do we define verifiability?

In the first place I should like to point out that when we say that "a proposition has meaning only if it is verifiable" we are not saying ". . . if it is *verified*." This simple remark does away with one of the chief objections; the "here and now predicament," as Professor Lewis calls it, does not exist any more. We fall into the snares of this predicament only if we regard verification itself as the criterion of meaning, instead of "possibility of verification" ($=$ verifiability); this would indeed lead to a "reduction to absurdity of meaning." Obviously the predicament arises through some fallacy by which these two notions are confounded. I do not know if Russell's statement, "Empirical knowledge is confined to what we actually observe" (quoted by Professor Lewis, *loc. cit.*, 130), must be interpreted as containing this fallacy, but it would certainly be worth while to discover its genesis.

Let us consider the following argument which Professor Lewis discusses (131), but which he does not want to impute to anyone:

Suppose it maintained that no issue is meaningful unless it can be put to the test of decisive verification. And no verification can take place except in the immediately present experience of the subject. Then nothing can be meant except what is actually present in the experience in which that meaning is entertained.

This argument has the form of a conclusion drawn from two premisses. Let us for the moment assume the second premiss to be meaningful and true. You will observe that even then the conclusion does *not* follow. For the first premiss assures us that the issue has meaning if it *can* be verified; the verification does not have to take place, and therefore it is quite irrelevant whether it can take place in the future or in the present only. Apart from this, the second premiss is, of course, nonsensical; for what fact could possibly be described by the sentence "verification can take place only in present experience"? Is not verifying an act or process like hearing or feeling bored? Might we not just as well say that I can hear or feel bored only in the present moment? And what could I mean by this? The particular nonsense involved in such phrases will become clearer when we speak of the "egocentric predicament" later on; at present we are content to know that our empirical-meaning postulate has nothing whatever to do with the now-predicament. "Verifiable" does not even mean "verifiable here now"; much less does it mean "being verified now."

Perhaps it will be thought that the only way of making sure of the verifiability of a proposition would consist in its actual verification. But we shall soon see that this is not the case.

There seems to be a great temptation to connect meaning and the "immediately given" in the wrong way; and some of the Viennese positivists may have yielded to this temptation, thereby getting dangerously near to the fallacy we have just been describing. Parts of Carnap's [*Der logische*] *Aufbau der Welt*, for instance, might be interpreted as implying that a proposition about future events did not really refer to the future at all but asserted only the present existence of certain expectations (and, similarly, speaking about the past would really mean speaking about present memories). But it is certain that the author of that book does not hold such a view now, and that it cannot be regarded as a teaching of the new positivism. On the contrary, we have pointed out from the beginning that our definition of meaning does not imply such absurd consequences, and when someone asked, "But how can you verify a proposition about a future event?" we replied, "Why, for instance, by waiting for it to happen! 'Waiting' is perfectly legitimate method of verification."

* * *

Thus I think that everybody—including the Consistent Empiricist—agrees that it would be nonsense to say, "We can mean nothing but the immediately given." If in this sentence we replace the word "mean" by the word "know" we arrive at a statement similar to

Bertrand Russell's mentioned above. The temptation to formulate phrases of this sort arises, I believe, from a certain ambiguity of the verb "to know" which is the source of many metaphysical troubles and to which, therefore, I have often had to call attention on other occasions (see, e.g., *Allgemeine Erkenntnislehre*, 2nd ed. 1925 §12). In the first place the word may stand simply for "being aware of a datum," i.e., for the mere presence of a feeling, a color, a sound, etc.; and if the word "knowledge" is taken in this sense the assertion "Empirical knowledge is confined to what we actually observe" does not say anything at all, but is a mere tautology. (This case, I think, would correspond to what Professor Lewis calls "identity-theories" of the "knowledge-relation." Such theories, resting on a tautology of this kind, would be empty verbiage without significance.)

In the second place the word "knowledge" may be used in one of the significant meanings which it has in science and ordinary life; and in this case Russell's assertion would obviously (as Professor Lewis remarked) be false. Russell himself, as is well known, distinguishes between "knowledge by acquaintance" and "knowledge by description," but perhaps it should be noted that this distinction does not entirely coincide with the one we have been insisting upon just now.

* * *

III

Verifiability means possibility of verification. Professor Lewis justly remarks that to "omit all examination of the wide range of significance which could attach to 'possible verification,' would be to leave the whole conception rather obscure" (*loc. cit.*, 137). For our purpose it suffices to distinguish between two of the many ways in which the word "possibility" is used. We shall call them "empirical possibility" and "logical possibility." Professor Lewis describes two meanings of "verifiability" which correspond exactly to this difference; he is fully aware of it, and there is hardly anything left for me to do but carefully to work out the distinction and show its bearing upon our issue.

I propose to call "empirically possible" anything that does not contradict the laws of nature. This is, I think, the largest sense in which we may speak of empirical possibility; we do not restrict the term to happenings which are not only in accordance with the laws of nature but also with the actual state of the universe (where "actual" might refer to the present moment of our own lives, or to the condition of human beings on this planet, and so forth). If we chose the latter definition (which seems to have been in Professor Lewis' mind when he spoke of "possible experience as conditioned by the actual," *loc. cit.* 141) we should not get the sharp boundaries we need for our present purpose. So "empirical possibility" is to mean "compatibility with natural laws."

Now, since we cannot boast of a complete and sure knowledge of nature's laws, it is evident that we can never assert with certainty the empirical possibility of any fact, and here we may be permitted to speak of *degrees* of possibility. Is it possible for me to lift this book? Surely!—This table? I think so!—This billiard table? I don't think so!—This automobile? Certainly not!—It is clear that in these cases the answer is given by *experience,* as the result of experiments performed in the past. Any judgment about empirical possibility is based on experience and will often be rather uncertain; there will be no sharp boundary between possibility and impossibility.

Is the possibility of verification which we insist upon of this empirical sort? In that case there would be different degrees of verifiability, the question of meaning would be a matter of more or less, not a matter of yes or no. In many disputes concerning our issue it is the empirical possibility of verification which is discussed; the various examples of verifiability given by Professor Lewis, e.g., are instances of different empirical circumstances in which the verification is carried out or prevented from being carried out. Many of those who refuse to accept our criterion of meaning seem to imagine that the procedure of its application in a special case is somewhat like this: A proposition is presented to us ready made, and in order to discover its meaning we have to try various methods of verifying or falsifying it, and if one of these methods works we have found the meaning of the proposition; but if not, we say it has no meaning. If we really had to proceed in this way, it is clear that the determination of meaning would be entirely a matter of experience, and that in many cases no sharp and ultimate decision could be obtained. How could we ever know that we had tried long enough, if none of our methods were successful? Might not future efforts disclose a meaning which we were unable to find before?

This whole conception is, of course, entirely erroneous. It speaks of meaning as if it were a kind of entity inherent in a sentence and hidden in it like a nut in its shell, so that the philosopher would have to crack the shell or sentence in order to reveal the nut or meaning. We know from our considerations in section I that a proposition cannot be given "ready made"; that meaning does not inhere in a sentence where it might be discovered, but that it must be bestowed upon it. And this is done by applying to the sentence the rules of the logical grammar of our language, as explained in section I. These rules are not facts of nature which could be "discovered," but they are prescriptions stipulated by acts of definition. And these definitions have to be known to those who pronounce the sentence in question and to those who hear or read it. Otherwise they are not confronted with any proposition at all, and there is nothing they could try to verify, because you can't verify or falsify a mere row of words. You cannot even start verifying before you know the meaning, i.e., before you have established the possibility of verification.

In other words, the possibility of verification which is relevant to meaning cannot be of the empirical sort; it cannot be established *post festum*. You have to be sure of it before you can consider the empirical circumstances and investigate whether or no or under what conditions they will permit of verification. The empirical circumstances are all-important when you want to know if a proposition is *true* (which is the concern of the scientist), but they can have no influence on the *meaning* of the proposition (which is the concern of the philosopher). Professor Lewis has seen and expressed this very clearly (*loc. cit.* 142, first six lines), and our Vienna positivism, as far as I can answer for it, is in complete agreement with him on this point. It must be emphasized that when we speak of verifiability we mean *logical* possibility of verification, and nothing but this.

* * *

I call a fact or a process "logically possible" if it can be *described*, i.e., if the sentence which is supposed to describe it obeys the rules of grammar we have stipulated for our language. (I am expressing myself rather incorrectly. A fact which could not be described would, of course, not be any fact at all; *any* fact is logically possible. But I think my meaning will be understood.) Take some examples. The sentences, "My friend died the day after tomorrow"; "The lady wore a dark red dress which was bright green"; "The campanile is 100 feet and 150 feet high"; "The child was naked, but wore a long white nightgown," obviously violate the rules which, in ordinary English, govern the use of the words occurring in the sentences. They do not describe any facts at all; they are meaningless, because they represent *logical* impossibilities.

It is of the greatest importance (not only for our present issue but for philosophical problems in general) to see that whenever we speak of logical impossibility we are referring to a discrepancy between the definitions of our terms and the way in which we use them. We must avoid the severe mistake committed by some of the former Empiricists like Mill and Spencer, who regarded logical principles (e.g., the Law of Contradiction) as laws of nature governing the psychological process of thinking. The nonsensical statements alluded to above do not correspond to thoughts which, by a sort of psychological experiment, we find ourselves unable to think; they do not correspond to any thoughts at all. When we hear the words, "A tower which is both 100 feet and 150 feet high," the image of two towers of different heights may be in our mind, and we may find it psychologically (empirically) impossible to combine the two pictures into one image, but it is not this fact which is denoted by the words "logical impossibility." The height of a tower cannot be 100 feet and 150 feet at the same time; a child cannot be naked and dressed at the same time—not because we are unable to imagine it, but because our definitions of "height," of the numerals, of the terms "naked" and "dressed," are not compatible with the particular combinations of those words in our examples. "They are not compatible with such combinations" means that the rules of our language have not provided any use for such combinations; they do not describe any fact. We could change these rules, of course, and thereby arrange a meaning for the terms "both red and green," "both naked and dressed"; but if we decide to stick to the ordinary definitions (which reveal themselves in the way we actually use our words) we have decided to regard those combined terms as meaningless, i.e., not to use them as the description of *any* fact. Whatever fact we may or may not imagine, if the word "naked" (or "red") occurs in its description we have decided that the word "dressed" (or "green") cannot be put in its place in the same description. If we do not follow this rule it means that we want to introduce a new definition of the words, or that we don't mind using words without meaning and like to indulge in nonsense. (I am far from condemning this attitude under all circumstances; on certain occasions—as in *Alice in Wonderland*—it may be the only sensible attitude and far more delightful than any treatise on Logic. But in such a treatise we have a right to expect a different attitude.)

The result of our considerations is this: Verifiability, which is the sufficient and necessary condition of meaning, is a possibility of the logical order; it is created by constructing the sentence in accordance with the rules by which its terms are defined. The only case in which verification is (logically) impossible is the case where you have *made* it impossible by not setting any rules for its verification. Grammatical rules are not found anywhere in nature, but are made by man and are, in principle, arbitrary; so you cannot give meaning to a sentence by *discovering* a method of verifying it, but only by *stipulating* how it *shall* be done. Thus logical possibility or impossibility of verification is always *self-imposed*. If we utter a sentence without meaning it is always *our own fault*.

The tremendous philosophic importance of this last remark will be realized when we consider that what we said about the meaning of *assertions* applies also to the meaning of *questions*. There are, of course, many questions which can never be answered by human beings. But the impossibility of finding the answer may be of two different kinds. If it is merely empirical in the sense defined, if it is due to the chance circumstances to which our human existence is confined, there may be reason to lament our fate and the weakness of our physical and mental powers, but the problem could never be said to be absolutely insoluble, and there would always be some hope, at least for future generations. For the empirical circumstances may alter, human facilities may develop, and even the laws of nature may change (perhaps even suddenly and in such a way that the universe would be thrown open to much more extended investigation). A problem of this kind might be called practically unanswerable or technically unanswerable, and might cause the scientist great trouble, but the philosopher, who is concerned with general principles only, would not feel terribly excited about it.

But what about those questions for which it is *logically* impossible to find an answer? Such problems would remain insoluble under all imaginable circumstances; they would confront us with a definite hopeless *Ignorabimus*; and it is of the greatest importance for the philosopher to know whether there are any such issues. Now it is easy to see from what has been said before that this calamity could happen only if the question itself had no meaning. It would not be a genuine question at all, but a mere row of words with a question-mark at the end. We must say that a question is meaningful, if we can *understand* it, i.e., if we are able to decide for any given proposition whether, if true, it would be an answer to our question. And if this is so, the actual decision could only be prevented by empirical circumstances, which means that it would not be *logically* impossible. Hence no meaningful problem can be insoluble in *principle*. If in any case we find an answer to be logically impossible we know that we really have not been asking anything, that what sounded like a question was actually a nonsensical combination of words. A genuine question is one for which an answer is logically possible. This is one of the most characteristic results of our empiricism. It means that in principle there are no limits to our knowledge. The boundaries which must be acknowledged are of an empirical nature and, therefore, never ultimate; they can be pushed back further and further; there is no unfathomable mystery in the world.

* * *

The dividing line between logical possibility and impossibility of verification is absolutely sharp and distinct; there is no gradual transition between meaning and nonsense. For either you have given the grammatical rules for verification, or you have not; *tertium non datur*.

Empirical possibility is determined by the laws of nature, but meaning and verifiability are entirely independent of them. Everything that I can describe or define is logically possible—and definitions are in no way bound up with natural laws. The proposition "Rivers flow uphill" is meaningful, but happens to be false because the fact it describes is physically impossible. It will not deprive a proposition of its meaning if the conditions which I stipulate for its verification are incompatible with the laws of nature; I may prescribe conditions, for instance, which could be fulfilled only if the velocity of light were greater than it actually is, or if the Law of Conservation of Energy did not hold, and so forth.

An opponent of our view might find a dangerous paradox or even a contradiction in the preceding explanations, because on the one hand we insisted so strongly on what has been called the "*empirical-meaning requirement*," and on the other hand we assert most emphatically that meaning and verifiability do not depend on any empirical conditions whatever, but are determined by purely logical possibilities. The opponent will object: if meaning is a matter of experience, how can it be a matter of definition and logic?

In reality there is no contradiction or difficulty. The word "experience" is ambiguous. Firstly, it may be a name for any so-called "immediate data"—which is a comparatively modern use of the word —and secondly we can use it in the sense in which we speak, e.g., of an "experienced traveler," meaning a man who has not only seen a great deal but also knows how to profit from it for his actions. It is in this second sense (by the way, the sense the word has in Hume's and Kant's philosophy) that verifiability must be declared to be independent of experience. The possibility of verification does not rest on any "experiential truth," on a law of nature or any other true general proposition, but is determined solely by our definitions, by the rules which have been fixed for our language, or which we can fix arbitrarily at any moment. All of these rules ultimately point to ostensive definitions, as we have explained, and through them verifiability is linked to *experience* in the *first* sense of the word. No rule of expression presupposes any law or regularity in the world (which is the condition of "experience" as Hume and Kant use the word), but it does presuppose data and situations, to which names can be attached. The rules of language are rules of the application of language; so there must be something to which it can be applied. Expressibility and verifiability are one and the same thing. There is no antagonism between logic and experience. Not only can the logician be an empiricist at the same time; he *must* be one if he wants to understand what he himself is doing.

* * *

IV

Let us glance at some examples in order to illustrate the consequences of our attitude in regard to certain issues of traditional philosophy. Take the famous case of the reality of the other side of the moon (which is also one of Professor Lewis' examples). None of us, I think, would be willing to accept a view according to which it would be nonsense to speak of the averted face of our satellite. Can there be the slightest doubt that, according to our explanations, the conditions of meaning are amply satisfied in this case?

I think there can be no doubt. For the question, "What is the other side of the moon like?" could be answered, for instance, by a description of what would be seen or touched by a person located somewhere behind the moon. The question whether it be physically possible for a human being—or indeed any other living being—to travel around the moon does not even have to be raised here; it is entirely irrelevant. Even if it could be shown that a journey to another celestial body were absolutely incompatible with the known laws of nature, a proposition about the other side of the moon would still be meaningful. Since our sentence speaks of certain places in space as being filled with matter (for that is what the words "side of the moon" stand for), it will have meaning if we indicate under what circumstances a proposition of the form, "this place is filled with matter," shall be called true or false. The concept "physical substance at a certain place" is defined by our language in physics and geometry. Geometry itself is the grammar of our propositions about "spatial" relations, and it is not very difficult to see how assertions about physical properties and spatial relations are connected with "sense-data" by ostensive definitions. This connection, by the way, is *not* such as to entitle us to say that physical substance is "a mere construction put upon sense-data," or that a physical body is a "complex of sense-data"—unless we interpret these phrases as rather inadequate abbreviations of the assertion that all propositions containing the term "physical body" require for their verification the presence of sense-data. And this is certainly an exceedingly trivial statement.

In the case of the moon we might perhaps say that the meaning-requirement is fulfilled if we are able to "imagine" (picture mentally) situations which would verify our proposition. But if we should say in general that verifiability of an assertion implies possibility of "imagining" the asserted fact, this would be true only in a restricted sense. It would not be true in so far as the possibility is of the empirical kind, i.e., implying specific human capacities. I do not think, for instance, that we can be accused of talking nonsense if we speak of a universe of ten dimensions, or of beings possessing sense-organs and having perceptions entirely different from ours; and yet it does not seem right to say that we are able to "imagine" such beings and such perceptions, or a ten-dimensional world. But we *must* be able to say under what *observable* circumstances we should assert the existence of the beings or sense-organs just referred to. It is clear that I can speak meaningfully of the sound of a friend's voice without being able actually to recall it in my imagination. This is not the place to discuss the logical grammar of the word "to imagine"; these few remarks may caution us against accepting too readily a *psychological* explanation of verifiability.

We must not identify meaning with any of the psychological data which form the material of a mental sentence (or "thought") in the same sense in which articulated sounds form the material of a spoken sentence, or black marks on paper the material of a written sentence. When you are doing a calculation in arithmetic it is quite irrelevant whether you have before your mind the images of black numbers or of red numbers, or no visual picture at all. And even if it were empirically impossible for you to do any calculation without imagining black numbers at the same time, the mental pictures of those black marks could, of course, in no way be considered as constituting the meaning, or part of the meaning, of the calculation.

Carnap is right in putting great stress upon the fact (always emphasized by the critics of "psychologism") that the question of meaning has nothing to do with the psychological question as to the mental processes of which an act of thought may consist. But I am sure that he has seen with equal clarity that reference to ostensive definitions (which we postulate for meaning) does *not* involve the error of a confusion of the two questions. In order to understand a sentence containing, e.g., the words "red flag," it is indispensable that I should be able to indicate a situation where I could point to an object which I should call a "flag," and whose color I could recognize as "red" as distinguished from other colors. But in order to do this it is *not* necessary that I should actually call up the image of a red flag. It is of the utmost importance to see that these two things have nothing in common. At this moment I am trying in vain to imagine the shape of a capital G in German print; nevertheless I can speak about it without talking nonsense, and I know I should recognize it if I saw the letter. Imagining a red patch is utterly different from referring to an ostensive definition of "red." Verifiability has nothing to do with any images that may be associated with the words of the sentence in question.

* * *

No more difficulty than in the case of the other side of the moon will be found in discussing, as another significant example, the question of "immortality," which Professor Lewis calls, and which is usually called, a *metaphysical* problem. I take it for granted that "immortality" is not supposed to signify never-ending life (for that might possibly be meaningless on account of infinity being involved), but that we are concerned with the question of survival after "death." I think we may agree with Professor Lewis when he says about this hypothesis: "Our understanding of what would verify it has no lack of clarity." In fact, I can easily imagine, e.g., witnessing the funeral of my own body and continuing to exist without a body, for nothing is easier than to describe a world which differs from our ordinary world only in the complete absence of all data which I would call parts of my own body.

We must conclude that immortality, in the sense defined, should not be regarded as a "metaphysical problem," but is an empirical hypothesis, because it possesses logical verifiability. It could be verified by following the prescription: "Wait until you die!" Professor Lewis seems to hold that this method is not satisfactory from the point of view of science. He says (143):

The hypothesis of immortality is unverifiable in an obvious sense . . . if it be maintained that only what is scientifically verifiable has meaning, then this conception is a case in point. It could hardly be verified by science; and there is no observation or experiment which science could make, the negative result of which would disprove it.

I fancy that in these sentences the private method of verification is rejected as being unscientific because it would apply only to the individual case of the experiencing person himself, whereas a scientific statement should be capable of a *general* proof, open to any careful observer. But I see no reason why even this should be declared to be impossible. On the contrary, it is easy to describe experiences such that the hypothesis of an invisible existence of human beings after their bodily death would be the most acceptable explanation of the phenomena observed. These phenomena, it is true, would have to be of a much more convincing nature than the ridiculous happenings alleged to have occurred in meetings of the occultists—but I think there cannot be the slightest doubt as to the possibility (in the logical sense) of phenomena which would form a scientific justification of the hypothesis of survival after death, and would permit an investigation by scientific methods of that form of life. To be sure, the hypothesis could never be established as absolutely true, but it shares this fate with all hypotheses. If it should be urged that the souls of the deceased might inhabit some supercelestial space where they would not be accessible to our perception, and that therefore the truth or falsity of the assertion could never be tested, the reply would be that if the words "supercelestial space" are to have any meaning at all, that space must be defined in such a way that the impossibility of reaching it or of perceiving anything in it would be merely empirical, so that some means of overcoming the difficulties could at least be described, although it might be beyond human power to put them into use.

Thus our conclusion stands. The hypothesis of immortality is an empirical statement which owes its meaning to its verifiability, and it has no meaning beyond the possibility of verification. If it must be admitted that science could make no experiment the negative result of which would disprove it, this is true only in the same sense in which it is true for many other hypotheses of similar structure—especially those that have sprung up from other motives than the knowledge of a great many facts of experience which must be regarded as giving a high probability to the hypothesis. . . .

V

Let us now turn to a point of fundamental importance and the deepest philosophic interest. Professor Lewis refers to it as the "egocentric predicament," and he describes as one of the most characteristic features of logical positivism its attempt to take this predicament seriously. It seems to be formulated in the sentence (128), "Actually given experience is given in the first person," and its importance for the doctrine of logical positivism seems to be evident from the fact that Carnap, in his *Der logische Aufbau der Welt*, states that the method of this book may be called "methodological solipsism." Professor Lewis thinks, rightly, that the egocentric or solipsistic principle is not implied by our general principle of verifiability, and so he regards it as a second principle which, together with that of verifiability, leads, in his opinion, to the main results of the Viennese philosophy.

If I may be permitted to make a few general remarks here I should like to say that one of the greatest advantages and attractions of true positivism seems to me to be the antisolipsistic attitude which characterizes it from the very beginning. There is as little danger of solipsism in it as in any "realism," and it seems to me to be the chief point of difference between idealism and positivism that the latter keeps entirely clear of the egocentric predicament. I think it is the greatest misunderstanding of the positivist idea (often even committed by thinkers who called themselves positivists) to see in it a tendency towards solipsism or a kinship to subjective idealism. We may regard Vaihinger's *Philosophy of As If* as a typical example of this mistake (he calls his book a "System of Idealistic Positivism"), and perhaps the philosophy of Mach and Avenarius as one of the most consistent attempts to avoid it. It is rather unfortunate that Carnap has advocated what he calls "methodological solipsism," and that in his construction of all concepts out of elementary data the "eigenpsychische Gegenstände" (for-me entities) come first and form the basis for the construction of physical objects, which finally lead to the concept of other selves; but if there is any mistake here it is chiefly in the terminology, not in the thought. "Methodological solipsism" is *not* a kind of solipsism, but a *method* of building up concepts. And it must be borne in mind that the order of construction which Carnap recommends—beginning with "for-me entities"—is not asserted to be the only possible one. It would have been better to have chosen a different order, but in principle Carnap was well aware of the fact that original experience is "without a subject" (see Lewis, *loc cit.* 145).

The strongest emphasis should be laid on the fact that primitive experience is absolutely neutral or, as Wittgenstein has occasionally put it, that immediate data "have no owner." Since the genuine positivist denies (with Mach, etc.) that original experience "has that quality or status, characteristic of all given experience, which is indicated by the adjective 'first person'" (*loc. cit.* 145), he cannot possibly take the "egocentric predicament" seriously; for him this predicament does not exist. To see that primitive experience is *not* first-person experience seems to me to be one of the most important steps which philosophy must take towards the clarification of its deepest problems.

The unique position of the "self" is not a basic property of all experience, but is itself a fact (among other facts) of experience.

Idealism (as represented by Berkeley's "*esse = percipi*" or by Schopenhauer's "Die Welt ist meine Vorstellung") and other doctrines with egocentric tendencies commit the great error of mistaking the unique position of the ego, which is an empirical fact, for a logical, *a priori* truth, or, rather, substituting the one for the other. It is worth while to investigate this matter and analyse the sentence which seems to express the egocentric predicament. This will not be a digression, for without the clarification of this point it will be impossible to understand the basic position of our empiricism.

How does the idealist or the solipsist arrive at the statement that the world, as far as I know it, is "my own idea," that ultimately I know nothing but the "content of my own consciousness"?

Experience teaches that all immediate data depend in some way or other upon those data that constitute what I call "my body." All visual data disappear when the eyes of this body are closed; all sounds cease when its ears are stuffed up; and so on. This body is distinguished from the "bodies of other beings" by the fact that it always appears in a peculiar perspective (its back or its eyes, for instance, never appear except in a looking glass); but this is not nearly so significant as the other fact that the quality of *all* data is conditioned by the state of the organs of this particular body. Obviously these two facts—and perhaps originally the first one—form the only reason why this body is called "my" body. The possessive pronoun singles it out from among other bodies; it is an adjective which denotes the uniqueness described.

The fact that all data are dependent upon "my" body (particularly those parts of it which are called "sense-organs") induces us to form the concept of "perception." We do not find this concept in the language of unsophisticated, primitive people; they do not say, "I perceive a tree," but simply, "there is a tree." "Perception" implies the distinction between a subject which perceives and an object which is perceived. Originally the perceiver is the sense-organ or the body to which it belongs, but since the body itself—including the nervous system—is also one of the perceived things, the original view is soon "corrected" by substituting for the perceiver a new subject, which is called "ego" or "mind" or "consciousness." It is usually thought of as somehow residing *in* the body, because the sense-organs are on the surface of the body. The mistake of locating consciousness or mind inside the body ("in the head"), which has been called "introjection" by R. Avenarius, is the main source of the difficulties of the so-called "mind-body problem." By avoiding the error of introjection we avoid at the same time the idealistic fallacy which leads to solipsism. It is easy to show that introjection *is* an error. When I see a green meadow the "green" is declared to be a content of my consciousness, but it certainly is not inside my head. Inside my skull there is nothing but my brain; and if there should happen to be a green spot in my brain, it would obviously not be the green of the meadow, but the green of the brain.

But for our purpose it is not necessary to follow this train of thought; it is sufficient to restate the facts clearly.

It is a fact of experience that all data depend in some way or other upon the state of a certain body which has the peculiarity that its eyes and its back are never seen (except by means of a mirror). It is usually called "my" body; but here, in order to avoid mistakes, I shall take the liberty of calling it the body "M." A particular case of the dependence just mentioned is expressed by the sentence, "I do not perceive anything unless the sense-organs of the body M are affected." Or, taking a still more special case, I may make the following statement:

"I feel pain only when the body M is hurt." (P)

I shall refer to this statement as "proposition P."

Now let us consider another proposition (Q):

"I can feel only my pain." (Q)

The sentence Q may be interpreted in various ways. *Firstly*, it may be regarded as equivalent to P, so that P and Q would just be two different ways of expressing one and the same empirical fact. The word "can" occurring in Q would denote what we have called "empirical possibility," and the words "I" and "my" would refer to the body M. It is of the utmost importance to realize that in this first interpretation Q is the description of a fact of experience, i.e., a fact which we could very well imagine to be different.

We could easily imagine (here I am closely following ideas expressed by Mr. Wittgenstein) that I experience a pain every time the body of my friend is hurt, that I am gay when his face bears a joyful expression, that I feel tired after he has taken a long walk, or even that I do not see anything when his eyes are closed, and so forth. Proposition Q (if interpreted as being equivalent to P) denies that these things ever happen; but if they did happen, Q would be falsified. Thus we indicate the meaning of Q (or P) by describing facts which make Q true and other facts that would make it false. If facts of the latter kind occurred our world would be rather different from the one in which we are actually living; the properties of the "data" would depend on other human bodies (or perhaps only one of them) as well as upon the body M.

This fictitious world may be empirically impossible, because incompatible with the actual laws of nature—though we cannot at all be sure of this—but it is logically possible, because we were able to give a description of it. Now let us for a moment suppose this fictitious world to be real. How would our language adapt itself to it? It might be done in two different ways which are of interest for our problem.

Proposition P would be false. As regards Q, there would be two possibilities. The first is to maintain that its meaning is still to be the same as that of P. In this case Q would be false and could be replaced by the true proposition,

"I can feel somebody else's pain as well as my own." (R)

R would state the empirical fact (which for the moment we suppose to be true) that the datum "pain" occurs not only when M is hurt, but also when some injury is inflicted upon some other body, say, the body "O."

If we express the supposed state of affairs by the proposition R, there will evidently be no temptation and no pretext to make any "solipsistic" statement. *My* body—which in this case could mean nothing but "body M"—would still be unique in that it would always appear in a particular perspective (with invisible back, etc.), but it would no longer be unique as being the only body upon whose state depended the properties of all other data. And it was only this latter characteristic which gave rise to the egocentric view. The philosophic doubt concerning the "reality of the external world" arose from the consideration that I had no knowledge of that world except by perception, i.e., by means of the sensitive organs of *my* body. If this is no longer true, if the data depend also on other bodies O (which differ from M in certain empirical respects, but not in *principle*), then there will be no more justification in calling the data "*my* own"; other individuals O will have the same right to be regarded as owners or proprietors of the data. The sceptic was afraid that other bodies O might be nothing but images owned by the "mind" belonging to the body M, because everything seemed to depend on the state of the latter; but under the circumstances described there exists perfect symmetry between O and M; the egocentric predicament has disappeared.

You will perhaps call my attention to the fact that the circumstances we have been describing are fictitious, that they do not occur in our real world, so that in this world, unfortunately, the egocentric predicament holds its sway. I answer that I wish to base my argument only on the fact that the difference between the two worlds is merely empirical, i.e., proposition P just happens to be true in the actual world as far as our experience goes. Its denial does not even seem to be incompatible with the known laws of nature; the probability which these laws give to the falsity of P is not zero.

Now if we still agree that proposition Q is to be regarded as identical with P (which means that "my" is to be defined as referring to M), the word "can" in Q will still indicate *empirical* possibility. Consequently, if a philosopher tried to use Q as the basis of a kind of solipsism, he would have to be prepared to see his whole construction falsified by some future experience. But this is exactly what the true solipsist *refuses* to do. He contends that no experience whatever could possibly contradict him, because it would always necessarily have the peculiar for-me character, which may be described by the "egocentric predicament." In other words, he is well aware that solipsism cannot be based on Q as long as Q is, by definition, nothing but another way of expressing P. As a matter of fact, the solipsist who makes the statement Q attaches a different meaning to the same words; he does not wish merely to assert P, but he intends to say something entirely different. The difference lies in the word "my." He does not want to define the personal pronoun by reference to the body M, but uses it in a much more general way. This leads us to ask: What meaning does he give to the sentence Q?

Let us examine this *second* interpretation which may be given to Q.

The idealist or solipsist who says, "I can feel only my own pain," or, more generally, "I can be aware only of the data of my own consciousness," believes that he is uttering a necessary, self-evident truth which no possible experience can force him to sacrifice. He will have to admit the possibility of circumstances such as those we described for our fictitious world; but, he will say, even if I feel pain every time when another body O is hurt, I shall never say, "I feel O's pain," but always, "My pain is in O's body."

We cannot declare this statement of the idealist to be *false*; it is just a different way of adapting our language to the imagined new circumstances, and the rules of language are, in principle, arbitrary. But, of course, some uses of our words may recommend themselves as practical and well adapted; others may be condemned as misleading. Let us examine the idealist's attitude from this point of view.

He rejects our proposition R and replaces it by the other one:

"I can feel pain in other bodies as well as in my own." (S)

He wants to insist that any pain I feel must be called *my* pain, no matter where it is felt, and in order to assert this he says:

"I *can* feel only *my* pain." (T)

Sentence T is, as far as the words are concerned, the same as Q. I have used slightly different signs by having the words "can" and "my" printed in italics, in order to indicate that, when used by the solipsist, these two words have a signification which is different from the signification they had in Q when we interpreted Q as meaning the same as P. In T "my pain" no longer means "pain in body M," because, according to the solipsist's explanation, "my pain" may also be in another body O; so we must ask: what does the pronoun "my" signify here?

It is easy to see that it does not signify *anything*; it is a superfluous word which may just as well be omitted. "I feel pain" and "I feel my pain" are, according to the solipsist's definition, to have identical meaning; the word "my," therefore, has no function in the sentence. If he says, "The pain which I feel is my pain," he is uttering a mere tautology, because he has declared that whatever the empirical circumstances may be, he will never allow the pronouns "your" or "his" to be used in connection with "I feel pain," but always the pronoun "my." This stipulation, being independent of empirical facts, is a logical rule, and if it is followed, T becomes a tautology; the word "can" in T (together with "only") does not denote empirical impossibility, but *logical* impossibility. In other words it would not be false, it would be *nonsense* (grammatically forbidden) to say "I can feel somebody else's pain." A tautology, being the negation of nonsense, is itself devoid of meaning in the sense that it does not assert anything, but merely indicates a rule concerning the use of words.

We infer that T, which is the second interpretation of Q, adopted by the solipsist and forming the basis of this argument, is strictly meaningless. It does not say anything at all, does not express any interpretation of the world or view about the world; it just introduces a strange way of speaking, a clumsy kind of language, which attaches the index "my" (or "content of my consciousness") to everything without exception. Solipsism is nonsense, because its starting-point, the egocentric predicament, is meaningless.

The words "I" and "my," if we use them according to the solipsist's prescription, are absolutely empty, mere adornments of speech. There would be no difference of meaning between the three expressions, "I feel my pain"; "I feel pain"; and "there is pain." Lichtenberg, the wonderful eighteenth-century physicist and philosopher, declared that Descartes had no right to start his philosophy with the proposition "I think," instead of saying "it thinks." Just as there would be no sense in speaking of a white horse unless it were logically possible that a horse might *not* be white, so no sentence containing the words "I" or "my" would be meaningful unless we could replace them by "he" or "his" without speaking nonsense. But such a substitution is impossible in a sentence that would seem to express the egocentric predicament or the solipsistic philosophy.

R and S are not different explanations or interpretations of a certain state of affairs which we have described, but simply verbally different formulations of this description. It is of fundamental importance to see that R and S are not two propositions, but one and the same proposition in two different languages. The solipsist, by rejecting the language of R and insisting upon the language of S, has adopted a terminology which makes Q tautological, transforms it into T. Thus he has made it impossible to verify or falsify his own statements; he himself has deprived them of meaning. By refusing to avail himself of the opportunities (which we showed him) to make the statement "I can feel somebody else's pain" meaningful, he has at the same time lost the opportunity of giving meaning to the sentence "I can feel only my own pain."

The pronoun "my" indicates *possession*; we cannot speak of the "owner" of a pain—or any other datum—except in cases where the word "my" can be used meaningfully, i.e., where by substituting "his" or "your" we would get the description of a possible state of affairs. This condition is fulfilled if "my" is defined as referring to the body M, and it would also be fulfilled if I agree to call "my body" any body in which I can feel pain. In our actual world these two definitions apply to one and the same body, but that is an empirical fact which might be different. If the two definitions did not coincide and if we adopted the second one we should need a new word to distinguish the body M from other bodies in which I might have sensations; the word "my" would have meaning in a sentence of the form "A is one of my bodies, but B is not," but it would be meaningless in the statement "I can feel pain only in my bodies," for this would be a mere tautology.

The grammar of the word "owner" is similar to that of the word "my": it makes sense only where it is logically possible for a thing to *change* its owner, i.e., where the relation between the owner and the owned object is empirical, not logical ("external," not "internal"). Thus one could say "Body M is the owner of this pain," or "that pain is owned by the bodies M and O." The second proposition can, perhaps, never be truthfully asserted in our actual world (although I cannot see that it would be incompatible with the laws of nature), but both of them would make sense. Their meaning would be to express certain relations of dependence between the pain and the state of certain bodies, and the existence of such a relation could easily be tested.

The solipsist refuses to use the word "owner" in this sensible way.

He knows that many properties of the data do not depend at all upon any states of human bodies, viz., all those regularities of their behavior that can be expressed by "physical laws"; he knows, therefore, that it would be wrong to say "my body is the owner of everything," and so he speaks of a "self," or "ego," or "consciousness," and declares this to be the owner of everything. (The idealist, by the way, makes the same mistake when he asserts that we know nothing but "appearances.") This is nonsense because the word "owner," when used in this way, has lost its meaning. The solipsistic assertion cannot be verified or falsified, it will be true by definition, whatever the facts may be; it simply consists in the verbal prescription to add the phrase "owned by Me" to the names of all objects, etc.

Thus we see that unless we choose to call our body the owner or bearer of the data—which seems to be a rather misleading expression—we have to say that the data *have no owner* or bearer. This neutrality of experience—as against the subjectivity claimed for it by the idealist—is one of the most fundamental points of true positivism. The sentence "All experience is first-person experience" will either mean the simple empirical fact that all data are in certain respects dependent on the state of the nervous system of my body M, or it will be meaningless. Before this physiological fact is discovered, experience is not "my" experience at all, it is self-sufficient and does not "belong" to anybody. The proposition "The ego is the centre of the world" may be regarded as an expression of the same fact, and has meaning only if it refers to the body. The concept of "ego" is a construction put upon the same fact, and we could easily imagine a world in which this concept would not have been formed, where there would be no idea of an insurmountable barrier between what is inside the Me and what is outside of it. It would be a world in which occurrences like those corresponding to proposition R and similar ones were the rule, and in which the facts of "memory" were not so pronounced as they are in our actual world. Under those circumstances we should not be tempted to fall into the "egocentric predicament," but the sentence which tries to express such a predicament would be meaningless under *any* circumstances.

* * *

After our last remarks it will be easy to deal with the so-called problem concerning the existence of the external world. If, with Professor Lewis (143), we formulate the "realistic" hypothesis by asserting, "If all minds should disappear from the universe, the stars would still go on in their courses," we must admit the impossibility of verifying it, but the impossibility is merely *empirical*. And the empirical circumstances are such that we have every reason to believe the hypothesis to be true. We are as sure of it as of the best founded physical laws that science has discovered.

As a matter of fact, we have already pointed out that there are certain regularities in the world which experience shows to be entirely independent of what happens to human beings on the earth. The laws of motion of the celestial bodies are formulated entirely without reference to any human bodies, and *this is the reason* why we are justified in maintaining that they will go on in their courses after mankind has vanished from the earth. Experience shows no connection between the two kinds of events. We observe that the course of the stars is no more changed by the death of human beings than, say, by the eruption of a volcano, or by a change of government in China. Why should we suppose that there would be any difference if all living beings on our planet, or indeed everywhere in the universe, were extinguished? There can be no doubt that on the strength of empirical evidence the existence of living beings is no necessary condition for the existence of the rest of the world.

The question "Will the world go on existing after I am dead?" has no meaning unless it is interpreted as asking "Does the existence of the stars etc. depend upon the life or death of a human being?," and this question is answered in the negative by experience. The mistake of the solipsist or idealist consists in rejecting this empirical interpretation and looking for some metaphysical issue behind it; but all their efforts to construct a new sense of the question end only in depriving it of its old one.

It will be noticed that I have taken the liberty of substituting the phrase "if all living beings disappeared from the universe" for the phrase "if all *minds* disappeared from the universe." I hope it will not be thought that I have changed the meaning of the issue by this substitution. I have avoided the word "mind" because I take it to signify the same as the words "ego" or "consciousness," which we have found to be so dark and dangerous. By living beings I meant beings capable of perception, and the concept of perception had been defined only by reference to living *bodies*, to physical organs. Thus I was justified in substituting "death of living beings" for "disappearance of minds." But the arguments hold for any empirical definition one may choose to give for "mind." I need only point out that, according to experience, the motion of the stars, etc., is quite independent of all "mental" phenomena such as feeling joy or sorrow, meditating, dreaming, etc.; and we may infer that the course of the stars would not be affected if those phenomena should cease to exist.

But is it true that this inference could be verified by experience? Empirically it seems to be impossible, but we know that only logical possibility of verification is required. And verification without a "mind" is logically possible on account of the "neutral," impersonal character of experience on which we have insisted. Primitive experience, mere existence of ordered data, does not presuppose a "subject," or "ego," or "Me," or "mind"; it can take place without any of the facts which lead to the formation of those concepts; it is not an experience of anybody. It is not difficult to imagine a universe without plants and animals and human bodies (including the body M), and without the mental phenomena just referred to: it would certainly be a "world without minds" (for what else could deserve this name?), but the laws of nature might be exactly the same as in our actual world. We could describe this universe in terms of our actual experience (we would only have to leave out all terms referring to human bodies and emotions); and that is sufficient to speak of it as a world of possible experience.

The last considerations may serve as an example of one of the main theses of true positivism: that the naïve representation of the world, as the man in the street sees it, is perfectly correct; and that the solution of the great philosophical issues consists in returning to this original world-view, after having shown that the troublesome problems arose only from an inadequate description of the world by means of a faulty language.

John Austin: OTHER MINDS

As an ordinary-language philosopher, Austin contributes to the philosophical task of distinguishing between the various ways in which we ordinarily use such key terms as "know" and "believe." He notes, for example, that when someone reports that he knows something, he is speaking in a different way than when he reports that he believes it. In the first instance, it is fair to ask the person "How do you know?" but not "Why do you know?" However, in the second instance, the appropriate question is "Why do you believe?" and not "How do you believe?" Austin patiently pursues his inquiry into the uses of "know" by delineating several types of questions arising from knowledge claims. It may develop in con-

versation, for example, that in asking "How do you know?" one is really concerned to ask the more specific question "How are you in a position to know?" or again to ask the more specific question "How can you tell?"

In section I, Austin attempts to show that in establishing a knowledge claim, we can only be expected to respond to quite specific questions, not to questions of the general type which some metaphysicians ask. Thus, if someone says "I know that is a goldfinch" and he is asked, "Is it a real one?," he can only answer by presuming that the question, made more specific, is raised about his ability to identify this species of bird or his ability to see clearly at dusk or the like. Ordinary usage of the terms "know" or "real" do not provide us with a precedent for establishing a knowledge about goldfinches in any sense beyond those indicated by specific questions.

In sections II and III, the body of his paper, Austin turns to the problem of "other minds." He argues that the philosophical distinction between one's own feelings as direct, assured knowledge and those of others which can, at best, be known only indirectly and without assurance is the "original sin . . . by which the philosopher casts himself out from the garden of the world we live in." In the first place, we may make mistakes about our own feelings, e.g., a sensation may be so new to us that we misjudge it. Again the ordinary usages to which we put the term "know" do not support the above-mentioned distinction. This point indicates that knowledge of other minds is not second-rate knowledge in contrast to introspective knowledge, since the latter, like the former, is fallible.

Furthermore, Austin appeals to ordinary linguistic usage to show that the verb "know," like the verb "promise" has a performatory function. Saying that "I know something" does not imply that I could not possibly be mistaken, any more than saying that "I promise to do something" implies that I cannot conceivably fail to carry out my original intention.

Thus Austin is representing knowledge claims in a weaker form than philosophers have traditionally done. The effect of the foregoing two steps in his analysis is to make knowledge claims about other minds to be less incredible than many philosophers have assumed. He also advances the following positive argument: When we observe a person blinking his eye under certain conditions, we may take this as a sign of anger and as a basis for believing he is angry; however, when we see him pound the table and hear him curse, we are witnessing angry behavior—not a mere symptom of anger—and we know he is angry. Furthermore, Austin shows that the authority of linguistic practice supports this distinction. He is confident that although there may be special problems, knowledge of other minds is akin to knowledge of ourselves and material objects.

Austin's "Other Minds" was a lecture for the Aristotelian Society and was printed in the Proceedings of the Aristotelian Society, Supp. 20, 1946, pp. 148–187. *It is reprinted here with the kind permission of the Society.*

I feel that I agree with much, and especially with the more important parts, of what Mr. Wisdom has written, both in his present paper ["Other Minds"] and in his beneficial series of articles on "Other Minds" and other matters. I feel ruefully sure, also, that one must be at least one sort of fool to rush in over ground so well trodden by the angels. At best I can hope only to make a contribution to one part of the problem, where it seems that a little more industry still might be of service. I could only wish it was a more central part. In fact, however, I did find myself unable to approach the centre while still bogged down on the periphery. And Mr. Wisdom himself may perhaps be sympathetic toward a policy of splitting hairs to save starting them.

Mr. Wisdom, no doubt correctly, takes the "Predicament" to be brought on by such questions as "How do we know that another man is angry?" He also cites other forms of the question—"Do we (ever) know?," "Can we know?," "How can we know?" the thoughts, feelings, sensations, mind, etc., of another creature, and so forth. But it seems likely that each of these further questions is rather different from the first, which alone has been enough to keep me preoccupied, and to which I shall stick.

Mr. Wisdom's method is to go on to ask: *Is it like the way in which we know* that a kettle is boiling, or that there is a tea-party next door, or the weight of thistledown? But it seemed to me that perhaps, as he went on, he was not giving an altogether accurate account (perhaps only because too cursory a one) of what we should say if asked "How do you know?" these things. For example, in the case of the tea-party, to say we knew of it "by analogy" would at best be a very sophisticated answer (and one to which some sophisticates might prefer the phrase "by induction"), while in addition it seems incorrect because we don't, I think, claim to *know* by analogy, but only to *argue* by analogy. Hence I was led on to consider what sort of thing does actually happen when ordinary people are asked "How do you know?"

Much depends, obviously, on the sort of item it is about which we are being asked "How do you know?" and there are bound to be many kinds of case that I shall not cover at all, or not in detail. The sort of statement which seems simplest, and at the same time not, on the face of it, unlike "He is angry," is such a statement as "That is a goldfinch" ("The kettle is boiling")—a statement of particular, current, empirical fact. This is the sort of statement on making which we are liable to be asked "How do you know?" and the sort that, at least sometimes, we say we don't know, but only believe. It may serve for a stalking-horse as well as another.

When we make an assertion such as "There is a goldfinch in the garden" or "He is angry," there is a sense in which we imply that we are sure of it or know it ("But I took it you knew," said reproachfully), though what we imply, in a similar sense and more strictly, is only that we *believe* it. On making such an assertion, therefore, we are directly exposed to the questions (1) "Do you *know* there is?" "Do you *know* he is?" and (2) "*How* do you know?" If in answer to the first question, we reply "Yes," we may then be asked the second question, and even the first question alone is commonly taken as an invitation to state not merely *whether* but also *how* we know. But on the other hand, we may well reply "No" in answer to the first question: we may say "No, but I think there is," "No, but I believe he is." For the implication that I know or am sure is not strict: we are not all (terribly or sufficiently) strictly brought up. If we do this, then we are exposed to the question, which might also have been put to us without preliminaries, "Why do you believe that?" (or "What makes you think so?," "What induces you to suppose so?," etc.).

There is a singular difference between the two forms of challenge: "*How* do you know?" and "*Why* do you believe?" We seem never to ask "*Why* do you know?" or "*How* do you believe?" And in this, as well as in other respects to be noticed later, not merely such other words as "suppose," "assume," etc., but also the expressions "be sure" and "be certain," follow the example of "believe," not that of "know."

Either question, "How do you know?" or "Why do you believe?," may well be asked only out of respectful curiosity, from a genuine desire to learn. But again, they may both be asked as *pointed* questions, and, when they are so, a further difference comes out. "How do you know?" suggests that perhaps you *don't* know it at all, whereas "Why do you believe?" suggests that perhaps you *oughtn't* to believe it. There is no suggestion [12] that you *ought* not to know or that you *don't* believe it. If the answer to "How do you know?" or to "Why do you believe?" is considered unsatisfactory by the challenger, he proceeds rather differently in the two cases. His next riposte will be, on the one hand, something such as "Then you *don't* know any such thing," or "But that doesn't prove it: in that case you don't really know it at all," and on the other hand, something such as "That's very poor evidence to go on: you oughtn't to believe it on the strength of that alone." [13]

The "existence" of your alleged belief is not challenged, but the "existence" of your alleged knowledge *is* challenged. If we like to say that "I believe," and likewise "I am sure" and "I am certain," are descriptions of subjective mental or cognitive states or attitudes, or what not, then "I know" is not that, or at least not merely that: it functions differently in talking.

"But of course," it will be said, "'I know' is obviously more than that, more than a description of my own state. If I *know, I can't be wrong*. You can always show I don't know by showing I am wrong, or may be wrong, or that I didn't know by showing that I might have been wrong. *That's* the way in which knowing differs even from being as certain as can be." This must be considered in due course, but first we should consider the types of answer that may be given in answer to the question "How do you know?"

Suppose I have said "There's a bittern at the bottom of the garden," and you ask "How do you know?" my reply may take very different forms:
    (a) I was brought up in the fens
    (b) I heard it
    (c) The keeper reported it
    (d) By its booming

(e) From the booming noise
(f) Because it is booming.

We may say, roughly, that the first three are answers to the questions "How do you come to know?," "How are you in a position to know?" or "How do you know?" understood in different ways: while the other three are answers to "How can you tell?" understood in different ways. That is, I may take you to have been asking:

(1) How do I come to be in a position to know about bitterns?
(2) How do I come to be in a position to say there's a bittern here and now?
(3) How do (can) I tell bitterns?
(4) How do (can) I tell the thing here and now as a bittern?

The implication is that in order to know this is a bittern, I must have:

(1) been trained in an environment where I could become familiar with bitterns
(2) had a certain opportunity in the current case
(3) learned to recognize or tell bitterns
(4) succeeded in recognizing or telling this as a bittern.

(1) and (2) mean that my experience must have been of certain kinds, that I must have had certain opportunities: (3) and (4) mean that I must have had a certain kind and amount of acumen.[14]

The questions raised in (1) and (3) concern our past experiences, our opportunities and our activities in learning to discriminate or discern, and, bound up with both, the correctness or otherwise of the linguistic usages we have acquired. Upon these earlier experiences depends how *well* we know things, just as, in different but cognate cases of "knowing," it is upon earlier experience that it depends how *thoroughly* or how *intimately* we know: we know a person by sight or intimately, a town inside out, a proof backwards, a job in every detail, a poem word for word, a Frenchman when we see one. "He doesn't know what love (real hunger) is" means he hasn't had enough experience to be able to recognize it and to distinguish it from other things slightly like it. According to how well I know an item, and according to the kind of item it is, I can recognize it, describe it, reproduce it, draw it, recite it, apply it, and so forth. Statements like "I know *very well* he isn't angry" or "You know *very well* that isn't calico," though of course about the current case, ascribe the excellence of the knowledge to past experience, as does the general expression "You are old enough to know better." [15]

By contrast, the questions raised in (2) and (4) concern the circumstances of the current case. Here we can ask "How *definitely* do you know?" You may know it for certain, quite positively, officially, on his own authority, from unimpeachable sources, only indirectly, and so forth.

Some of the answers to the question "How do you know?" are, oddly enough, described as "reasons for knowing" or "reasons to know," or even sometimes as "reasons why I know," despite the fact that we do not ask "Why do you know?" But now surely, according to the Dictionary, "reasons" should be given in answer to the question "Why?" just as we do in fact give reasons for believing in answer to the question "Why do you believe?" However, there is a distinction to be drawn here. "How do you know that I. G. Farben worked for war?" "I have every reason to know: I served on the investigating commission": here, giving my reasons for knowing is stating how I come to be in a position to know. In the same way we use the expressions "I know *because* I saw him do it" or "I know *because* I looked it up only ten minutes ago": these are similar to "So it is: it *is* plutonium. How did you know?" "I did quite a bit of physics at school before I took up philology," or to "I ought to know: I was standing only a couple of yards away." Reasons for *believing* on the other hand are normally quite a different affair (a recital of symptoms, arguments in support, and so forth), though there are cases where we do give as reasons for believing our having been in a position in which we could get good evidence: "Why do you believe he was lying?" "I was watching him very closely."

Among the cases where we give our reasons for knowing things, a special and important class is formed by those where we cite authorities. If asked "How do you know the election is today?," I am apt to reply "I read it in *The Times*," and if asked "How do you know the Persians were defeated at Marathon?" I am apt to reply "Herodotus expressly states that they were." In these cases "know" is correctly used: we know "at second hand" when we can cite an authority who was in a position to know (possibly himself also only at second hand).[16] The statement of an authority makes me aware of something, enables me to know something, which I shouldn't otherwise have known. It is a source of knowledge. In many cases, we contrast such reasons for knowing with other reasons for believing the very same thing: "Even if we didn't know it, even if he hadn't confessed, the evidence against him would be enough to hang him."

It is evident, of course, that this sort of "knowledge" is "liable to be wrong," owing to the unreliability of human testimony (bias, mistake, lying, exaggeration, etc.). Nevertheless, the occurrence of a piece of human testimony radically alters the situation. We say "We shall never know what Caesar's feelings were on the field of the battle of Philippi," because he did not pen an account of them: *if he had*, then to say "We shall never know" won't do in the same way, even though we may still perhaps find reason to say "It doesn't read very plausibly: we shall never *really* know the *truth*" and so on. Naturally, we are judicious: we don't say we know (at second hand) if there is any special reason to doubt the testimony: but there has to be some reason. It is fundamental in talking (as in other matters) that we are entitled to trust others, except in so far as there is some concrete reason to distrust them. Believing persons, accepting testimony, is the, or one main, point of talking. We don't play (competitive) games except in the faith that our opponent is trying to win: if he isn't, it isn't a game, but something different. So we don't talk with people (descriptively) except in the faith that they are trying to convey information.[17]

It is now time to turn to the question "How can you tell?," i.e. to senses (2) and (4) of the question "How do you know?" If you have asked "How do you know it's a goldfinch?" then I may reply "From its behaviour," "By its markings," or, in more detail, "By its red head," "From its eating thistles." That is, I indicate, or to some extent set out with some degree of precision, those features of the situation which enable me to recognize it as one to be described in the way I did describe it. Thereupon you may still object in several ways to my saying it's a goldfinch, without in the least "disrupting my facts," which is a further stage to be dealt with later. You may object:

    (1) But goldfinches *don't* have red heads
    (1a) But that's not a *goldfinch*. From your own description I can recognize it as a gold*crest*
    (2) But that's not enough: plenty of other birds have red heads. What you say doesn't prove it. For all you know, it may be a woodpecker.

Objections (1) and (1a) claim that, in one way or another, I am evidently unable to recognize goldfinches. It may be (1a)—that I have not learned the right (customary, popular, official) name to apply to the creature ("Who taught you to use the word 'goldfinch'?"):[18] or it may be that my powers of discernment, and consequently of classification, have never been brought sharply to bear in these matter, so that I remain confused as to how to tell the various species of small British bird. Or, of course, it may be a bit of both. In making this sort of accusation, you would perhaps tend not so much to use the expression "You don't know" or "You oughtn't to say you know" as, rather, "But that *isn't* a goldfinch (*goldfinch*)," or you would of course deny the statement that I do know it is a goldfinch.

It is in the case of objection (2) that you would be more inclined to say right out "Then you don't know." Because it doesn't prove it, it's not enough to prove it. Several important points come out here:

(a) If you say "That's not enough," then you must have in mind some more or less definite lack. "To be a goldfinch, besides having a red head it must also have the characteristic eye-markings": or "How do you know it isn't a woodpecker? Woodpeckers have red heads too." If there is no definite lack which you are at least prepared to specify on being pressed, then it's silly (outrageous) just to go on saying "That's not enough."

(b) Enough is enough: it doesn't mean everything. Enough means enough to show that (within reason, and for present intents and purposes) it "can't" be anything else, there is no room for an alternative, competing, description of it. It does not mean, for example, enough to show it isn't a *stuffed* goldfinch.

(c) "*From* its red head," given as an answer to "How do you know?" requires careful consideration: in particular it differs very materially from "*Because* it has a red head," which is also sometimes given as an answer to "How do you know?," and is commonly given as an answer to "Why do you believe?" It is much more akin to such obviously "vague" replies as "From its markings" or "From its behaviour" than at first appears. Our claim, in saying we know, (i.e. that we can tell) is to *recognize:* and recognizing, at least in this sort of case, consists in seeing, or otherwise sensing, a feature or features which we are sure are similar to something noted (and usually named) before, on some earlier occasion in our experience. But, this that we see, or otherwise sense, is not necessarily describable in words, still less describable in detail, and in non-committal words, and by anybody you please. Nearly everbody can recognize a surly look or the smell of tar, but few can describe them non-committally, i.e. otherwise than as "surly" or "of tar": many can recognize, and "with certainty," ports of different vintages, models by different fashion houses, shades of green, motor-car makes from behind, and so forth, without being able to say "how they recognize them," i.e. without being able to "be more specific about it"—they can only say they can tell "by the taste," "from the cut," and so on. So, when I say I can tell the bird "from its red head," or that I know a friend "by his nose," I imply that there is something peculiar about the red head or the nose, something peculiar to goldfinches or to him, by which you can (always) tell them or him. In view of the fewness and crudeness of the classificatory words in any language compared with the infinite number of features which are recognized, or which could be picked out and recognized, in our experience, it is small wonder that we often and often fall back on the phrases beginning with "from" and "by," and that we are not able to *say*, further and precisely, *how* we can tell. Often we know things quite well, while scarcely able to say at all "from" what we know them, let alone what there is so very special about them. Any answer beginning "From" or "By" has, intentionally, this saving "vagueness." But on the contrary, an answer beginning "Because" is dangerously definite. When I say I know it's a goldfinch "Because it has a red head," that implies that all I have noted, or needed to note, about it is that its head is red (nothing special or peculiar about the shade, shape, etc. of the patch): so that I imply that there is no other small British bird that has any sort of red head except the goldfinch.

(d) Whenever I say I know, I am always liable to be taken to claim that, in a certain sense appropriate to the kind of statement (and to present intents and purposes), I am able to prove it. In the present, very common, type of case, "proving" seems to mean stating what are the features of the current case which are enough to constitute it one which is correctly describable in the way we have described it, and not in any other way relevantly variant. Generally speaking, cases where I can "prove" are cases where we use the "because" formula: cases where we "know but can't prove" are cases where we take refuge in the "from" or "by" formula.

I believe that the points so far raised are those most genuinely and normally raised by the question "How do you know?" But there are other, further, questions sometimes raised under the same rubric, and especially by philosophers, which may be thought more important. These are the worries about "reality" and about being "sure and certain."

Up to now, in challenging me with the question "How do you know?," you are not taken to have *queried my credentials as stated*, though you have asked what they were: nor have you *disputed my facts* (the facts on which I am relying to prove it is a goldfinch), though you have asked me to detail them. It is this further sort of challenge that may now be made, a challenge as to the *reliability* of our alleged "credentials" and our alleged "facts." You may ask:

(1) But do you know it's a *real* goldfinch? How do you know you're not dreaming? Or after all, mightn't it be a stuffed one? And is the head really red? Couldn't it have been dyed, or isn't there perhaps an odd light reflected on it?

(2) But are you certain it's the *right* red for a goldfinch? Are you quite sure it isn't too orange? Isn't it perhaps rather too strident a note for a bittern?

These two sorts of worry are distinct, though very probably they can be combined or confused, or may run into one another: e.g. "Are you sure it's really red?" may mean "Are you sure it isn't orange?" or again "Are you sure it isn't just the peculiar light?"

I REALITY

If you ask me, "How do you know it's a real stick?" "How do you know it's really bent?" ("Are you sure he's really angry?"), then you are querying my credentials or my facts (it's often uncertain which) in a certain special way. In various *special, recognized* ways, depending essentially upon the nature of the matter which I have announced myself to know, either my current experiencing or the item currently under consideration (or uncertain which) may be abnormal, *phoney*. Either I myself may be dreaming, or in delirium, or under the influence of mescal, etc.: or else the item may be stuffed, painted, dummy, artificial, trick, freak, toy, assumed, feigned, etc.: or else again there's an uncertainty (it's left open) whether *I* am to blame or *it* is—mirages, mirror images, odd lighting effects, etc.

These doubts are all to be allayed by means of recognized procedures (more or less roughly recognized, of course), appropriate to the particular type of case. There are recognized ways of distinguishing between dreaming and waking (how otherwise should we know how to use and to contrast the words?), and of deciding whether a thing is stuffed or live, and so forth. The doubt or question "But is it a *real* one?" has always (*must* have) a special basis, there must be some "reason for suggesting" that it isn't real, in the sense of some specific way, or limited number of specific ways, in which it is suggested that this experience or item may be phoney. Sometimes (usually) the context makes it clear what the suggestion is: the goldfinch might be stuffed but there's no suggestion that it's a mirage, the oasis might be a mirage but there's no suggestion it might be stuffed. If the context doesn't make it clear, then I am entitled to ask "How do you mean? Do you mean it may be stuffed or what? *What are you suggesting?*" The wile of the metaphysician consists in asking "Is it a real table?" (a kind of object which has no obvious way of being phoney) and not specifying or limiting what may be wrong with it, so that I feel at a loss "how to prove" it *is* a real one.[19] It is the use of the word "real" in this manner that leads us on to the supposition that "real" has a single meaning ("the real world" "material objects"), and that a highly profound and puzzling one. Instead, we should insist always on specifying with what "real" is being contrasted—not what I shall have to show it is, in order to show it is "real": and then usually we shall find some specific, less fatal, word, appropriate to the particular case, to substitute for "real."

Knowing it's a "real" goldfinch isn't in question in the ordinary case when I say I know it's a goldfinch: reasonable precautions only are taken. But when it *is* called in question, in *special* cases, then I make sure it's a real goldfinch in ways essentially similar to those in which I made sure it was a goldfinch, though corroboration by other witnesses plays a specially important part in some cases. Once again the precautions cannot be more than reasonable, relative to current intents and purposes. And once again, in the special cases just as in the ordinary cases, two further conditions hold good:

(a) I don't by any means *always* know whether it's one or not. It may fly away before I have a chance of testing it, or of inspecting it thoroughly enough. This is simple enough: yet some are prone to argue that because I *sometimes* don't know or can't discover, I *never* can.

(b) "Being sure it's real" is no more proof against miracles or outrages of nature than anything else is or, *sub specie humanitatis*, can be. If we have made sure it's a goldfinch, and a real goldfinch, and then in the future it does something outrageous (explodes, quotes Mrs. Woolf, or what not), we don't say we were wrong to say it was a goldfinch, *we don't know what to say*. Words literally fail us: "What would you have said?" "What are we to say now?" "What would *you* say?" When I have made sure it's a real goldfinch (not stuffed, corroborated by the disinterested, etc.) then I am *not* "predicting" in saying it's a real goldfinch, and in a very good sense I can't be proved wrong whatever happens. It seems a serious mistake to suppose that language (or most language, language about real things) is "predictive" in such a way that the future can always prove it wrong. What the future *can* always do, is to make us *revise our ideas* about goldfinches or real goldfinches or anything else.

Perhaps the normal procedure of language could be schematized as follows. First, it is arranged that, on experiencing a complex of features C, then we are to say "This is C" or "This is a C." Then subsequently, the occurrence either of the whole of C or of a significant and characteristic part of it is, on one or many occasions, accompanied or followed in definite circumstances by another special and distinctive feature or complex of features, which makes it seem desirable to revise our ideas: so that we draw a distinction between "This looks like a C, but in fact is only a dummy, etc." and "This is a real C (live, genuine, etc.)." *Henceforward,* we can only ascertain that it's a *real* C by ascertaining that the special feature or complex of features is present in the appropriate circumstances. The old expression "This is a C" will tend as heretofore to fail to draw any distinction between "real, live, etc." and "dummy, stuffed, etc." If the special distinctive feature is one which does not have to manifest itself in *any* definite circumstances (on application of some specific test, after some limited lapse of time, etc.) then it is not a suitable feature on which to base a distinction between "real" and "dummy, imaginary, etc." All we can then do is to say "Some Cs are and some aren't, some do and some don't: and it may be very interesting or important whether they are or aren't, whether they do or don't, but they're all Cs, real Cs, just the same." [20] Now if the special feature is one which must appear in (more or less) definite circumstances, then "This is a real C" is not necessarily predictive: we can, in favourable cases, make sure of it.[21]

II SURENESS AND CERTAINTY

The other way of querying my credentials and proofs ("Are you sure it's the *right* red?") is quite different. Here we come up against Mr. Wisdom's views on "the peculiarity of a man's knowledge of his own sensations," for which he refers us to "Other Minds VII" (*Mind,* vol. lii, N.S., no. 207), a passage with which I find I disagree.

Mr. Wisdom there says that, excluding from consideration cases like "being in love" and other cases which "involve prediction," and considering statements like "I am in pain" which, in the requisite sense, do *not* involve prediction, then a man *cannot* "be wrong" in making them, in the most favoured sense of being wrong: that is, though it is of course possible for him to *lie* (so that "I am in pain" may be false), and though it is also possible for him to *misname,* i.e. to use the word "pawn," say, instead of "pain," or because the use was momentary aberration, as when I call John "Albert" while knowing him quite well to be John—though it is possible for him to be "wrong" in these two senses, it is not possible for him to be wrong in the most favoured sense. He says again that, with this class of statement (elsewhere called "sense-statements"), to know directly that one is in pain is "to say that one is, and to say it on the basis of being in pain": and again, that the peculiarity of sense-statements lies in the fact that "when they are correct and made by X, then X knows they are correct."

This seems to me mistaken, though it is a view that, in more or less subtle forms, has been the basis of a very great deal of philosophy.

It is perhaps the original sin (Berkeley's apple, the tree in the quad) by which the philosopher casts himself out from the garden of the world we live in.

Very clearly detailed, this is the view that, at least and only in a certain favoured type of case, I can "say what I see (or otherwise sense)" almost quite literally. On this view, if I were to say "Here is something red," then I might be held to imply or to state that it is really a red thing, a thing which would appear red in a standard light, or to other people, or tomorrow too, and perhaps even more besides: all of which "involves prediction" (if not also a metaphysical substratum). Even if I were to say "Here is something which looks red," I might still be held to imply or to state that it looks red to others also, and so forth. If, however, I confine myself to stating "Here is something that looks red to me now," then at last I can't be wrong (in the most favoured sense).

However, there is an ambiguity in "something that looks red to me now." Perhaps this can be brought out by italics, though it is not really so much a matter of emphasis as of tone and expression, of confidence and hesitancy. Contrast "Here is something that (definitely) *looks to me* (anyhow) red" with "Here is something that looks to me (something like) *red* (I should say)." In the former case I am quite confident that, however it may look to others, whatever it may "really be," etc. it certainly does look red to me at the moment. In the other case I'm not confident at all: it looks reddish, but I've never seen anything quite like it before, I can't quite describe it—or, I'm not very good at recognizing colours, I never feel quite happy about them, I've constantly been caught out about them. Of course, this sounds silly in the case of "red": red is so *very* obvious, we all know red when we see it, it's *unmistakable*.[22] Cases where we should not feel happy about red are not easy (though not impossible) to find. But take "magenta": "It looks like magenta to me—but then I wouldn't be too sure about distinguishing magenta from mauve or from heliotrope. Of course I know in a way it's purplish, but I don't really know whether to say it's magenta or not: I just can't be sure." Here, I am not interested in ruling out consideration of how it looks to others (looks *to me*) or consideration about what its *real* colour is (*looks*): what I am ruling out is *my being sure or certain* what it looks to me. Take tastes, or take sounds: these are so much better as examples than colours, because we never feel so happy with our other senses as with our eyesight. Any description of a taste or sound or smell (or colour) or of a feeling, involves (is) saying that it is like one or some that we have experienced before: any descriptive word is classificatory, involves recognition and in that sense memory, and only when we use such words (or names or descriptions, which come down to the same) are we knowing anything, or believing anything. But memory and recognition are often uncertain and unreliable.

Two rather different ways of being hesitant may be distinguished.

(a) Let us take the case where we are tasting a certain taste. We may say "I simply don't know what it is: I've never tasted anything remotely like it before. . . . No, it's no use: the more I think about it the more confused I get: it's perfectly distinct and perfectly distinctive, quite unique in my experience." This illustrates the case where I can find nothing in my past experience with which to compare the current case: I'm certain it's not appreciably like anything I ever tasted before, not sufficiently like anything I know to merit the same description. This case, though distinguishable enough, shades off into the more common type of case where I'm not quite certain, or only fairly certain, or practically certain, that it's the taste of, say, laurel. In all cases, I am endeavouring to recognize the current item by searching in my past experience for something like it, some likeness in virtue of which it deserves, more or less positively, to be described by the same descriptive word:[23] and I am meeting with varying degrees of success.

(b) The other case is different, though it very naturally combines itself with the first. Here, what I try to do is to *savour* the current experience, to *peer* at it, to sense it vividly. I'm not sure it *is* the taste of pineapple: isn't there perhaps just *something* about it, a tang, a bite, a lack of bite, a cloying sensation, which isn't *quite* right for pineapple? Isn't there perhaps just a peculiar hint of green, which would rule out mauve and would hardly do for heliotrope? Or perhaps it is faintly odd: I must look more intently, scan it over and over: maybe just possibly there is a suggestion of an unnatural shimmer, so that it doesn't look quite like ordinary water. There is a lack of sharpness in what we actually sense, which is to be cured not, or not merely, by thinking, but by acuter discernment, by sensory discrimination (though it is of course true that thinking of other, and more pronounced, cases in our past experiences can and does assist our powers of discrimination).[24]

Cases (a) and (b) alike, and perhaps usually together, lead to our being not quite sure or certain what it is, what to say, how to describe it: what our feelings really are, whether the tickling is painful exactly, whether I'm really what you'd call angry with him or only something rather like it. The hesitation is of course, in a sense, over misnaming: but I am not so much or merely worried about possibly misleading others as about misleading myself (the most favoured sense of being wrong). I should suggest that the two expressions "being certain" and "being sure," though from the nature of the case they are often used indiscriminately, have a tendency to refer to cases (a) and (b) respectively. "Being certain" tends to indicate confidence in our memories and our past discernment, "being sure" to indicate confidence in the current perception. Perhaps this comes out in our use of the concessives "to be sure" and "certainly," and in our use of such phrases as "certainly not" and "surely not." But it may be unwise to chivvy language beyond the coarser nuances.

It may be said that, even when I don't know exactly how to describe it, I nevertheless *know* what I *think* (and roughly how confidently I think) it is mauve. So I do know *something*. But this is irrelevant: I *don't* know it's mauve, that it definitely looks to me now mauve. Besides, there are cases where I really don't know what I think: I'm completely baffled by it.

Of course, there are any number of "sense-statements" about which I can be, and am, completely sure. In ordinary cases ordinary men are nearly always certain when a thing looks red (or reddish, or anyhow reddish rather than greenish), or when they're in pain (except when that's rather difficult to say, as when they're being tickled): in ordinary cases an expert, a dyer or a dress designer, will be quite sure when something looks (to him in the present light) reseda green or [a shade of] . . . brown, though those who are not experts will not be so sure. Nearly always, if not quite always, we can be quite, or pretty, sure if we take refuge in a sufficiently *rough* description of the sensation: roughness and sureness tend to vary inversely. But the less rough descriptions, just as much as the rough, are all "sense-statements."

It is, I think, the problems of sureness and certainty, which philosophers tend (if I am not mistaken) to neglect, that have considerably exercised scientists, while the problem of "reality," which philosophers have cultivated, does not exercise them. The whole apparatus of measures and standards seems designed to combat unsureness and uncertainty, and concomitantly to increase the possible precision of language, which in science, pays. But for the words "real" and "unreal" the scientist tends to substitute, wisely, their cash-value substitutes, of which he invents and defines an increasing number, to cover an increasing variety of cases: he doesn't ask "Is it real?" but rather "Is it denatured?" or "Is it an allotropic form?" and so on.

It is not clear to me what the class of sense-statements is, nor what its "peculiarity" is. Some who talk of sense-statements (or sense data) appear to draw a distinction between talking about simple things like red or pain, and talking about complicated things like love or tables. But apparently Mr. Wisdom does not, because he treats "This looks to me now like a man eating poppies" as in the same case with "This looks to me now red." In this he is surely right: a man eating poppies may be more "complex" to recognize, but it is often not appreciably more difficult than the other. But if, again, we say that non-sense-statements are those which involve "prediction," why so? True, if I say, "This is a (real) oasis" without first ascertaining that it's not a mirage, then I do chance my hand: but if I *have* ascertained that it's not, and can recognize for sure that it isn't (as when I am drinking its waters), then surely I'm not chancing my hand any longer. I believe, of course, that it will continue to perform as (real) oases normally do: but if there's a *lusus naturae*, a miracle, and it doesn't, that wouldn't mean I was wrong, previously, to call it a real oasis.

With regard to Mr. Wisdom's own chosen formulae, we have seen already that it can't be right to say that the peculiarity of sense-statements is that "when they are correct, and made by X, then X knows they are correct": for X may *think*, without much confidence, that it tastes to him like Lapsang, and yet be far from certain, and then subsequently become certain, or more certain, that it did or didn't. The other two formulae were: "To know that one is in pain is to say that one is and to say it on the basis of being in pain" and that the only mistake possible with sense-statements is typified by the case where "knowing him to be Jack I call him 'Alfred,' thinking his name is Alfred or not caring a damn what his name is." The snag in both these lies in the phrases "on the basis of being in pain" and "knowing him to be Jack." "Knowing him to be Jack" means that I have recognized him as Jack, a matter over which I may well be hesitant and/or mistaken: it is true that I needn't recognize him *by name* as "Jack," (and hence I may call him "Alfred"), but at least I must be recognizing him correctly as, for instance, the man I last saw in Jerusalem, or else I *shall* be misleading *myself*. Similarly, if "on the basis of being in pain" only means "when I am (what would be correctly described as) in pain," then something more than merely *saying* "I'm in pain" is necessary for knowing I'm in pain: and this something more, as it involves recognition, may be hesitant and/or mistaken, though it is of course unlikely to be so in a case so comparatively obvious as that of pain.

Possibly the tendency to overlook the problems of recognition is fostered by the tendency to use a direct object after the word *know*. Mr. Wisdom, for example, confidently uses such expressions as "knowing the feelings of another (his mind, his sensations, his anger, his pain) in the way that *he* knows them." But, although we do correctly use the expressions "I know your feelings on the matter" or "He knows his own mind" or (archaically) "May I know your mind?," these are rather special expressions, which do not justify any general usage. "Feelings" here has the sense it has in "very strong feelings" in favour of or against something: perhaps it means "views" or "opinions" ("very decided opinions"), just as "mind" in this usage is given by the Dictionary as equivalent to "intention" or "wish." To extend the usage uncritically is somewhat as though, on the strength of the legitimate phrase "Knowing someone's tastes," we were to proceed to talk of "knowing someone's sounds" or "knowing someone's taste of pineapple." If, for example, it is a case of *physical* feelings such as fatigue, we do not use the expression "I know your feelings."

When, therefore, Mr. Wisdom speaks generally of "knowing his sensations," he presumably means this to be equivalent to "knowing *what* he is seeing, smelling, etc.," just as "knowing the winner of the Derby" means "knowing *what won* the Derby." But here again, the expression "know what" seems sometimes to be taken, unconsciously and erroneously, to lend support to the practice of putting a direct object after *know*: for "what" is liable to be understood as a relative, = "that which." This is a grammatical mistake: "what" *can* of course be a relative, but in "know what you feel" and " know what won" it is an interrogative (Latin *quid*, not *quod*). In this respect, "I can smell what he is smelling" differs from "I know what he is smelling." "I know what he is feeling" is not "There is an *x* which both I know and he is feeling," but "I know the answer to the question 'What is he feeling?'." And similarly with "I know what I am feeling": this does *not* mean that there is something which I am *both knowing and feeling.*

Expressions such as "We don't know another man's anger in the way he knows it" or "He knows his pain in a way we can't" seem barbarous. The man doesn't "know his pain": he feels (not knows) what he recognizes as, or what he knows to be, anger (not his anger), and he knows that he is feeling angry. Always assuming that he does recognize the feeling, which in fact, though feeling it acutely, he may not: "Now I know what it was, it was jealousy (or gooseflesh or angina). At the time I did not know at all what it was, I had never felt anything quite like it before: but since then I've got to know it quite well." [25]

Uncritical use of the direct object after *know* seems to be one thing that leads to the view that (or to talking as though) sensa, that is things, colours, noises, and the rest, speak or are labelled by nature, so that I can literally *say* what (that which) I *see*: it pipes up, or I read it off. It is as if sensa were *literally* to "announce themselves" or to "identify themselves," in the way we indicate when we say "It presently identified itself as a particularly fine white rhinoceros." But surely this is only a manner of speaking, a reflexive idiom in which the French, for example, indulge more freely than the English: sensa are dumb, and only previous experience enables *us* to identify them. If we choose to say that they "identify themselves" (and certainly "recognizing" is not a highly voluntary activity of ours), then it must be admitted that they share the birthright of all speakers, that of speaking unclearly and untruly.

III IF I KNOW I CAN'T BE WRONG

One final point about "How do you know?," the challenge to the user of the expression "I know," requires still to be brought out by consideration of the saying that "If you know you can't be wrong." Surely, if what has so far been said is correct, then we are often right to say we *know* even in cases where we turn out subsequently to have been mistaken—and indeed we seem always, or practically always, liable to be mistaken.

Now, we are perfectly, and should be candidly, aware of this liability, which does not, however, transpire to be so very onerous in practice. The human intellect and senses are, indeed, *inherently* fallible and delusive, but not by any means *inveterately* so. Machines are inherently liable to break down, but good machines don't (often). It is futile to embark on a "theory of knowledge" which denies this liability: such theories constantly end up by admitting the liability after all, and denying the existence of "knowledge."

"When you know you can't be wrong" is perfectly good sense. You are prohibited from saying "I know it is so, but I may be wrong," just as you are prohibited from saying "I promise I will, but I may fail." If you are aware you may be mistaken, you ought not to say you know, just as, if you are aware you may break your word, you have no business to promise. But of course, being aware that you are a fallible human being: it means that you have some concrete reason to suppose that you may be mistaken in this case. Just as "but I may fail" does not mean merely "but I am a weak human being" (in which case it would be no more exciting than adding "D.V."): it means that there is some concrete reason for me to suppose that I shall break my word. It is naturally *always* possible ("humanly" possible) that I may be mistaken or may break my word, but that by itself is no bar against using the expressions "I know" and "I promise" as we do in fact use them.

At the risk (long since incurred) of being tedious, the parallel between saying "I know" and saying "I promise" may be elaborated.[26]

When I say "S is P," I imply at least that I believe it, and, if I have been strictly brought up, that I am (quite) sure of it: when I say "I shall do A," I imply at least that I hope to do it, and, if I have been strictly brought up that I (fully) intend to. If I only believe that S is P, I can add "But of course I may (very well) be wrong": if I only hope to do A, I can add "But of course I may (very well) not." When I only believe or only hope, it is recognized that further evidence or further circumstances are liable to make me change my mind. If I say "S is P" and I don't even believe it, I am lying: if I say it when I believe it but am not sure of it, I may be misleading but I am not exactly lying. If I say "I shall do A" when I have not even any hope, not the slightest intention, of doing it, then I am deliberately deceiving: if I say it when I do not fully intend to, I am misleading but I am not deliberately deceiving in the same way.

But now, when I say "I promise," a new plunge is taken: I have not merely announced my intention, but, by using this formula (performing this ritual), I have bound myself to others, and staked my reputation, in a new way. Similarly, saying "I know" is taking a new plunge. But it is *not* saying "I have performed a specially striking feat of cognition, superior, in the same scale as believing and being sure, even to being merely quite sure": for there *is* nothing in that scale superior to being quite sure. Just as promising is not something superior, in the same scale as hoping and intending, even to merely fully intending: for there *is* nothing in that scale superior to fully intending. When I say "I know," I *give others my word: I give others my authority for saying* that "S is P."

When I have said only that I am sure, and prove to have been mistaken, I am not liable to be rounded on by others in the same way as when I have said "I know." I am sure *for my part*, you can take it or leave it: accept it if you think I'm an acute and careful person, that's your responsibility. But I don't know "for my part," and when I say "I know" I don't mean you can take it or leave it (though of course you *can* take it or leave it). In the same way, when I say I fully intend to, I do so for my part, and, according as you think highly or poorly of my resolution and chances, you will elect to act on it, whether or not you choose to do so. If I have said I know or I promise, you insult me in a special way by refusing to accept it. We all *feel* the very great difference between saying even "I'm *absolutely* sure" and saying "I know": it is like the difference between saying even "I firmly and irrevocably intend" and "I promise." If someone has promised me to do A, then I am entitled to rely on it, and can myself make promises on the strength of it: and so, where someone has said to me "I know," I am entitled to say *I* know too, at second hand. The right to say "I know" is transmissible, in the sort of way that other authority is transmissible. Hence, if I say it lightly, I may be *responsible* for getting *you* into trouble.

If you say you *know* something, the most immediate challenge takes the form of asking "Are you in a position to know?": that is, you must undertake to show, not merely that you are sure of it, but that it is within your cognisance. There is a similar form of challenge in the case of promising: fully intending is not enough—you must also undertake to show that "you are in a position to promise," that is, that it is within your power. Over these points in the two cases parallel series of doubts are apt to infect philosophers, on the ground that I cannot foresee the future. Some begin to hold that I should never, or practically never, say I know anything—perhaps only what I am sensing at this moment: others, that I should never, or practically never, say I promise—perhaps only what is actually within my power at this moment. In both cases there is an obsession: if I know I *can't be wrong*, so I can't have the right to say I know, and if I promise I *can't fail*, so I can't have the right to say I promise. And in both cases this obsession fastens on my inability to make *predictions* as the root of the matter, meaning by predictions claims to know the future. But this is doubly mistaken in both cases. As has been seen, we may be perfectly justified in saying we know or we promise, in spite of the fact that things "may" turn out badly, and it's a more or less serious matter for us if they do. And further, it is overlooked that the conditions which must be satisfied if I am to show that a thing is within my cognisance or within my power are conditions, not about the future, but about *the present and the past*: it is not demanded that I do more than *believe* about the future.[27]

We feel, however, an objection to saying that "I know" performs the same sort of function as "I promise." It is this. Supposing that things turn out badly, then we say, on the one hand "You're proved wrong, so you *didn't* know," but on the other hand "You've failed to perform, although you *did* promise." I believe that this contrast is more apparent than real. The sense in which you "did promise" is that you did *say* you promised (did say "I promise"): and you did *say* you knew. That is the gravamen of the charge against you when you let us down, after we have taken your word. But it may well transpire that you never fully intended to do it, or that you had concrete reason to suppose that you wouldn't be able to do it (it might even be manifestly impossible), and in another "sense" of promise you *can't* then have promised to do it, so that you *didn't* promise.

Consider the use of other phrases analogous to "I know" and "I promise." Suppose, instead of "I know," I had said "I swear": in that case, upon the opposite appearing, we should say, exactly as in the promising case, "You did swear, but you were wrong." Suppose again that, instead of "I promise," I had said "I guarantee" (e.g. to protect you from attack): in that case, upon my letting you down, you can say, exactly as in the knowing case "You *said* you guaranteed it, but you *didn't* guarantee it." [28] Can the situation perhaps be summed up as follows? In these "ritual" cases, the approved case is one where *in the appropriate circumstances,* I say a certain formula: e.g. "I do" when standing, unmarried or a widower, beside a woman, unmarried or a widow and not within the prohibited degrees of relationship, before a clergyman, registrar, etc., or "I give" when it is mine to give, etc., or "I order" when I have the authority to, etc. But now, if the situation transpires to have been in some way not orthodox (I was already married: it wasn't mine to give: I had no authority to order), then we tend to be rather hesitant about how to put it, as heaven was when the saint blessed the penguins. We call the man a bigamist, but his second marriage was not a marriage, is null and void (a useful formula in many cases for avoiding saying either "he did" or "he didn't"): he did "order" me: he did warn me it was going to charge, but it wasn't or anyway I knew much more about it than he did, so in a way he couldn't warn me, didn't warn me.[29] We hesitate between "He didn't order me," "He had no right to order me," "He oughtn't to have said he ordered me," just as we do between "You didn't know," "You can't have known," "You had no right to say you knew" (these perhaps having slightly different nuances, according to what precisely it is that has gone wrong). But the essential factors are (a) You said you knew: you said you promised. (b) You were mistaken: you didn't perform. The hesitancy concerns only the precise way in which we are to round on the original "I know" or "I promise."

To suppose that "I know" is a descriptive phrase, is only one example of the *descriptive fallacy,* so common in philosophy. Even if some language is now purely descriptive, language was not in origin so, and much of it is still not so. Utterance of obvious ritual phrases, in the appropriate circumstances, is not *describing* the action we are doing, but *doing* it ("I do"): in other cases it functions, like tone and expression, or again like punctuation and mood, as an intimation that we are employing language in some special way ("I warn," "I ask," "I define"). Such phrases cannot, strictly, *be* lies, though they can "imply" lies, as "I promise" implies that I fully intend, which may be untrue.

If these are the main and multifarious points that arise in familiar cases where we ask "How do you know that this is a case of so-and-so?," they may be expected to arise likewise in cases where we say "I know he is angry." And if there are, as no doubt there are, special difficulties in this case, at least we can clear ground a little of things which are not special difficulties, and get the matter in better perspective.

As a preliminary, it must be said that I shall only discuss the question of feelings and emotions, with special reference to anger. It seems likely that the cases where we know that another man thinks that 2 and 2 make 4, or that he is seeing a rat, and so on, are different in important respects from, though no doubt also similar to, the case of knowing that he is angry or hungry.

In the first place, we certainly do say sometimes that we know another man is angry, and we also distinguish these occasions from others on which we say only that we *believe* he is angry. For of course, we do not for a moment suppose that we *always* know, of *all* men, whether they are angry or not, or that we could discover it. There are many occasions when I realize that I can't possibly tell what he's feeling: and there are many *types* of people, and many individuals too, with whom I (they being what they are, and I being what I am) never can tell. The feelings of royalty, for example, or fakirs or bushmen or Wykehamists or simple eccentrics—these may be very hard to divine: unless you have had a prolonged acquaintance with such persons, and some intimacy with them, you are not in any sort of position to know what their feelings are especially if, for one reason or another, they can't or don't tell you. Or again, the feelings of some individual whom you have never met before—they might be almost anything: you don't know his character at all or his tastes, you have no experience of his mannerisms, and so on. His feelings are elusive and personal: people differ so much. It is this sort of thing that leads to the situation where we say "You never know" or "You never can tell."

In short, here even more than in the case of the goldfinch, a great deal depends on how familiar we have been in our past experience with this type of person, and indeed with this individual, in this type of situation. If we have no great familiarity, then we hesitate to say we know: indeed, we can't be expected to say (tell). On the other hand, if we *have* had the necessary experience, then we can, in favourable current circumstances, say we know: we certainly can recognize when some near relative of ours is angrier than we have ever seen him.

Further, we must have had experience also of the emotion or feeling concerned, in this case anger. In order to know what you are feeling, I must also apparently be able to imagine (guess, understand, appreciate) what you're feeling. It seems that more is demanded than that I shall have learned to discriminate displays of anger in others: I must also have been angry myself.[30] Or at any rate, if I have never felt a certain emotion, say ambition, then I certainly feel an *extra* hesitation in saying that his motive is ambition. And this seems to be due to the very special nature (grammar, logic) of feelings, to the special way in which they are related to their occasions and manifestations, which requires further elucidation.

At first sight it may be tempting to follow Mr. Wisdom, and to draw a distinction between (1) the physical symptoms and (2) the feeling. So that when, in the current case, I am asked "How can you tell he's angry?" I should answer "From the physical symptoms," while if *he* is asked how *he* can tell he's angry, he should answer "From the feeling." But this seems to be a dangerous over-simplification.

In the first place, "symptoms" (and also "physical") is being used in a way different from ordinary usage, and one which proves to be misleading.

"Symptoms," a term transferred from medical usage,[31] tends to be used only, or primarily, in cases where that of which there are symptoms is something undesirable (of incipient disease rather than of returning health, of despair rather than of hope, of grief rather than of joy): and hence it is more colourful than "signs" or "indications." This, however, is comparatively trivial. What is important is the fact that we never talk of "symptoms" or "signs" except *by way of implied contrast with inspection of the item itself*. No doubt it would often be awkward to have to say exactly where the signs or symptoms end and the item itself begins to appear: but such division is always implied to exist. And hence the words "symptom" and "sign" have no use except in cases where the item, as in the case of disease, is liable to be *hidden*, whether it be in the future, in the past, under the skin, or in some other more or less notorious casket: and when the item is itself before us, we no longer talk of signs and symptoms. When we talk of "signs of a storm," we mean signs of an impending storm, or of a past storm or of a storm beyond the horizon: we do *not* mean a storm on top of us.[32]

The words function like such words as "traces" or "clues." Once you know the murderer, you don't get any more clues, only what were or would have been clues: nor is a confession, or an eye-witness's view of the crime, a particularly good clue—these are something different altogether. When the cheese is not to be found or seen, then there may be traces of it: but not when it's there in front of us (though of course, there aren't, then, "no traces" of it either).

For this reason, it seems misleading to lump together, as a general practice, all the characteristic features of any casual item as "signs" or "symptoms" of it: though it is of course sometimes the case that some things which could in appropriate circumstances be called characteristics or effects or manifestations or parts or sequelae or what not of certain items may *also* be called signs or symptoms of those items in the appropriate circumstances. It seems to be this which is really wrong with Mr. Wisdom's paradox . . . about looking in the larder and finding "all signs" of bread, when we see the loaf, touch it, taste it and so on. Doing these things is not finding (some) signs of bread at all: the taste or feel of bread is not a sign or symptom of bread at all. What I might be taken to mean if I announced that I had found signs of bread in the larder seems rather doubtful, since the bread is not normally casketed (or if in the bin, leaves no traces), and not being a transient event (impending bread, etc.), does not have any normally accepted "signs": and signs, peculiar to the item, have to be more or less normally accepted. I might be taken to mean that I had found traces of bread, such as crumbs, or signs that bread had at one time been stored there, or something of the kind: but what I could *not* be taken to mean is that I had seen, tasted, or touched (something like) bread.

The sort of thing we do actually say, if the look is all right but we haven't yet tasted it, is "Here is something that looks like bread." If it turns out not to be bread after all, we might say "It tasted like bread, but actually it was only bread-substitute," or "It exhibited many of the characteristic features of bread, but differed in important respects: it was only a synthetic imitation." That is, we don't use the words "sign" or "symptom" at all.

Now, if "signs" and "symptoms" have this restricted usage, it is evident that to say that we only get at the "signs" or "symptoms" of anything is to imply that we never get at *it* (and this goes for "*all* the signs" too). So that, if we say that I only get at the *symptoms* of his anger, that carries an important implication. But *is* this the way we do talk? Surely we do not consider that we are never aware of more than *symptoms* of anger in another man?

"Symptoms" or "signs" of anger tend to mean signs of *rising* or of *suppressed* anger. Once the man has exploded, we talk of something different—of an expression or manifestation or display of anger, or an exhibition of temper, and so forth. A twitch of the eyebrow, pallor, a tremor in the voice, all these may be symptoms of anger: but a violent tirade or a blow in the face are not, they are the acts in which the anger is vented. "Symptoms" of anger are not, at least normally, contrasted with the man's own inner personal feeling of anger, but rather with the actual display of anger. Normally at least, where we have only symptoms to go upon, we should say only that we *believe* that the man is angry or getting angry: whereas when he has given himself away we say that we know.[33]

The word "physical" also, as used by Mr. Wisdom in contrast to "mental," seems to me abused, though I am not confident as to whether this abuse is misleading in the current case. He evidently does not wish to call a man's feelings, which he cites as a typical example of a "mental" event, *physical*. Yet this is what we ordinarily often do. There are many physical feelings, such as giddiness, hunger, or fatigue: and these are included by some doctors among the physical signs of various complaints. Most feelings we do not speak of as either mental or physical, especially emotions, such as jealousy or anger itself: we do not assign them to the *mind* but to the *heart*. Where we do describe a feeling as mental, it is because we are using a word normally used to describe a physical feeling in a special transferred sense, as when we talk about "mental" discomfort or fatigue.

It is then, clear, that more is involved in being, for example, angry than simply showing the symptoms and feeling the feeling. For there is also the display or manifestation. And it is to be noted that the feeling is related in a unique sort of way to the display. When we are angry, we have an impulse felt and/or acted on, to do actions of particular kinds, and, unless we suppress the anger, we do actually proceed to do them. There is a peculiar and intimate relationship between the emotion and the natural manner of venting it, with which, having been angry ourselves, we are acquainted. The ways in which anger is normally manifested are *natural* to anger just as there are tones *naturally* expressive of various emotions (indignation, etc.). There is not normally taken to be [34] such a thing as "being angry" apart from any impulse, however vague, to vent the anger in the natural way.

Moreover, besides the natural expressions of anger, there are also the natural *occasions* of anger, of which we have also had experience, which are similarly connected in an intimate way with the "being angry." It would be as nonsensical to class these as "causes" in some supposedly obvious and "external" sense, as it would be to class the venting of anger as the "effect" of the emotion in a supposedly obvious and "external" sense. Equally it would be nonsensical to say that there are three wholly distinct phenomena, (1) cause or occasion, (2) feeling or emotion, and (3) effect or manifestation, which are related together "by definition" as all necessary to anger, though this would perhaps be less misleading than the other.

It seems fair to say that "being angry" is in many respects like "having mumps." It is a description of a whole pattern of events, including occasion, symptoms, feeling and manifestation, and possibly other factors besides. It is as silly to ask "What, really, *is* the anger *itself*?" as to attempt to fine down "the disease" to some one chosen item ("the functional disorder"). That the man feels angry (and we don't) is, in the absence of Mr. Wisdom's variety of telepathy [35] evident enough, and incidentally nothing to complain about as a "predicament": but there is no call to say that "that" ("the feeling") [36] is the *anger*. The pattern of events whatever its precise form, is, fairly clearly, peculiar to the case of "feelings" (emotions)— it *is* not by any means exactly like the case of diseases: and it seems to be this peculiarity which makes us prone to say that, unless we have had experience of a feeling ourselves, we cannot know when someone else is experiencing it. Moreover, it is our confidence in the general pattern that makes us apt to say we "know" another man is angry when we have only observed parts of the pattern: for the parts of the pattern are related to each other very much more intimately than, for example, newspapermen scurrying in Brighton are related to a fire in Fleet Street.[37]

The man himself, such is the overriding power of the pattern, will sometimes accept corrections from outsiders about his own emotions, i.e. about the correct description of them. He may be got to agree that he was not really angry so much as, rather, indignant or jealous, and even that he was not in pain, but only fancied he was. And this is not surprising, especially in view of the fact that he, like all of us, has primarily learnt to use the expression "I am angry" of himself by (a) noting the occasion, symptoms, manifestation, etc., in cases where other persons say "I am angry" of *themselves*; (b) being told by others, who have noted all that can be observed about *him* on certain occasions, that "You are angry," i.e. that he should say "I am angry." On the whole, "mere" feelings or emotions, if there are such things genuinely detectable, are certainly very hard to be sure about, even harder than, say, tastes, which we already choose to describe, normally, only by their occasions (the taste "of tar," "of pineapple," etc.).

All words for emotions are, besides, on the vague side, in two ways, leading to further hesitations about whether we "know" when he's angry. They tend to cover a rather wide and ill-defined variety of situations: and the patterns they cover tend to be, each of them, rather complex (though common and so not difficult to recognize, very often), so that it is easy for one of the more or less necessary features to be omitted, and thus to give rise to hesitation about what exactly we should say in such an unorthodox case. We realize, well enough, that the challenge to which we are exposed if we say we *know* is to *prove* it, and in this respect vagueness of terminology is a crippling handicap.

So far, enough has perhaps been said to show that most of the difficulties which stand in the way of our saying we know a thing is a goldfinch arise in rather greater strength in the case where we want to say we know another man is angry. But there is still a feeling, and I think a justified feeling, that there is a further and quite *special* difficulty in the latter case.

This difficulty seems to be of the sort that Mr. Wisdom raises at the very outset of his series of articles on "Other Minds." It is asked, might the man not exhibit all the symptoms (and display and everything else) of anger, even *ad infinitum,* and yet still *not (really) be* angry? It will be remembered that he there treats it, no doubt provisionally, as a difficulty similar to that which can arise concerning the reality of any "material object." But in fact, it has special features of its own.

There seem to be three distinguishable doubts which may arise:

(1) When to all appearances angry, might he not really be labouring under some other emotion, in that, though he normally feels the same emotion as we should on occasions when we, in his position, should feel anger and in making displays such as we make when angry, in this particular case he is acting abnormally?

(2) When to all appearances angry, might he not really be labouring under some other emotion, in that he normally feels, on occasions when we in his position should feel anger and when acting as we should act if we felt anger, some feeling which we, if we experienced it, should distinguish from anger?

(3) When to all appearances angry, might he not really be feeling no emotion at all?

In everyday life, all these problems arise in special cases, and occasion genuine worry. We may worry (1) as to whether someone is *deceiving* us, by suppressing his emotions, or by feigning emotions which he does not feel: we may worry (2) as to whether we are *misunderstanding* someone (or he us), in wrongly supposing that he does "feel like us," that he does share emotions like ours: or we may worry (3) as to whether some action of another person is really deliberate, or perhaps only involuntary or inadvertent in some manner or other. All three varieties of worry may rise, and often do, in connexion with the actions of persons whom we know very well.[38] Any or all of them may be at the bottom of the passage from Mrs. Woolf:[39] all work together in the feeling of loneliness which affects everybody at times.

None of these three special difficulties about "reality" arises in connexion with goldfinches or bread, any more than the special difficulties about, for example, the oasis arise in connexion with the reality of another person's emotions. The goldfinch cannot be assumed, nor the bread suppressed: we may be deceived by the appearance of an oasis, or misinterpret the signs of the weather, but the oasis cannot lie to us and we cannot misunderstand the storm in the way we misunderstand the man.

Though the difficulties are very special, the ways of dealing with them are, initially, similar to those employed in the case of the goldfinch. There are (more or less roughly) established procedures for dealing with suspected cases of deception or of misunderstanding or of inadvertence. By these means we do very often establish (though we do not expect *always* to establish) that someone is acting, or that we were misunderstanding him, or that he is simply impervious to a certain emotion, or that he was not acting voluntarily. These special cases where doubts arise and require resolving, are contrasted with the normal cases which hold the field [40] *unless* there is some special suggestion that deceit, etc., is involved, and deceit, moreover, of an intelligible kind in the circumstances, that is, or a kind that can be looked into because motive, etc., is specially suggested. There is no suggestion that I *never* know what other people's emotions are, nor yet that in particular cases I might be wrong for no special reason or in no special way.

Extraordinary cases of deceit, misunderstanding, etc. (which are themselves not the normal) do not, *ex vi termini* [by the very force of the term], ordinarily occur: we have a working knowledge of the occasions for, the temptations to, the practical limits of, and the normal types of deceit and misunderstanding. Nevertheless, they *may* occur, and there may be varieties which are common without our yet having become aware of the fact. If this happens, we are in a certain sense wrong, because our terminology is inadequate to the facts, and we shall have thenceforward to be more wary about saying we know, or shall have to revise our ideas and terminology. This we are constantly ready to do in a field so complex and baffling as that of the emotions.

There remains, however, one further special feature of the case, which also differentiates it radically from the goldfinch case. The goldfinch, the material object, is, as we insisted above, uninscribed and *mute:* but the man *speaks.* In the complex of occurrences which induces us to say we know another man is angry, the complex of symptoms, occasion, display, and the rest, a peculiar place is occupied by the man's own statement as to what his feelings are. In the usual case, we accept this statement without question, and we then say that we know (as it were "at second-hand") what his feelings are: though of course "at second-hand" here could not be used to imply that anybody but he could know "at first-hand," and hence perhaps it is not in fact used. In unusual cases, where his statement conflicts with the description we should otherwise have been inclined to give of the case, we do not feel bound to accept it, though we always feel some uneasiness in rejecting it. If the man is an habitual liar or self-deceiver, or if there are patent reasons why he should be lying or deceiving himself on this occasion, then we feel reasonably happy: but if such a case occurred as the imagined one where a man, having given throughout life every appearance of holding a certain pointless belief, leaves behind a remark in his private diary to the effect that he never did believe it, then we probably should not know what to say.

I should like to make in conclusion some further remarks about this crucial matter of our believing what the man says about his own feelings. Although I know very well that I do not see my way clearly in this, I cannot help feeling sure that it is fundamental to the whole Predicament, and that it has not been given the attention it deserves, possibly just because it is so obvious.

The man's own statement is not (is not treated primarily as) a sign or symptom, although it can, secondarily and artificially, be treated as such. A unique place is reserved for it in the summary of the facts of the case. The question then is: "Why believe him ever?" not simply as "Why believe him this time?" We may say that the man's statements on matters other than his own feelings have constantly been before us in the past, and have been regularly verified by our own observations of the facts he reported: so that we have in fact some basis for an induction about his general reliability. Or we may say that his behaviour is most simply "explained" on the view that he does feel emotions like ours, just as psycho-analysts "explain" erratic behaviour by analogy with normal behaviour when they use the terminology of "unconscious desires."

These answers are, however, dangerous and unhelpful. They are so obvious that they please nobody: while on the other hand they encourage the questioner to push his question to "profounder" depths, encouraging us, in turn, to exaggerate these answers until they become distortions.

The question, pushed further, becomes a challenge to the very possibility of "believing another man," in its ordinarily accepted sense, at all. What "justification" is there for supposing that there is another mind communicating with you at all? How can you know what it would be like for another mind to feel anything, and so how can you understand it? It is then that we are tempted to say that we only mean by "believing him" that we take certain vocal noises as signs of certain impending behaviour, and that "other minds" are no more really real than unconscious desires.

This, however, is distortion. It seems, rather, that believing in other persons, in authority and testimony, is an essential part of the act of communicating, an act which we all constantly perform. It is as much an irreducible part of our experience as, say, giving promises, or playing competitive games, or even sensing coloured patches. We can state certain advantages of such performances, and we can elaborate rules of a kind for their "rational" conduct (as the Law Courts and historians and psychologists work out the rules for accepting testimony). But there is no "justification" for our doing them as such.

FINAL NOTE

One speaker at Manchester said roundly that the real crux of the matter remains still that "I ought not to say that I know Tom is angry, because I don't introspect his feelings": and this no doubt is just what many people do boggle at. The gist of what I have been trying to bring out is simply:

(1) *Of course* I *don't* introspect Tom's feelings (we should be in a pretty predicament if I did).

(2) Of *course* I *do* sometimes know Tom is angry. Hence

(3) to suppose that the question "How do I know that Tom is angry?" is meant to mean "How do I introspect Tom's feelings?" (because, as we know, that's the sort of thing that knowing is or ought to be), is simply barking our way up the wrong gum tree.

GUIDE TO FURTHER READINGS IN CONTEMPORARY PHILOSOPHICAL ANALYSIS

ANALYSIS AND ETHICS

Alfred J. Ayer (1910–   ) first gained prominence as an exponent of logical positivism in England. Although recently his approach to philosophy has been changing, he is still associated with the view, emphasized by the Vienna Circle, that the proper sphere of philosophical inquiry is limited. He showed that the positivist dictum—only analytic and empirically verifiable statements have cognitive meaning—forces one to the position that ethical utterances such as "Killing is evil" or "One ought to love his parents" merely express feelings or emotions. Ayer concludes that ethics is not, as tradition would have it, a science. The function of an ethical theorist is simply to explore the logical relations obtaining among ethical terms. See especially *Language, Truth and Logic* (New York: Dover, 1946).

Charles L. Stevenson (1908–), like Ayer, adopts the perspective of logical positivism but, unlike Ayer, refuses to regard emotive meaning as either unimportant or unrelated to cognitive meaning. He stresses the persuasive role of ethical utterances in influencing human decisions. See especially *Ethics and Language* (New Haven: Yale University Press, 1944).

Stephen Toulmin's (1922–) thinking in ethics is rooted in the philosophy of the later Wittgenstein. Toulmin argues that the traditional theorists have been asking unanswerable questions. Instead of the older preoccupation with such things as the "ultimate referent" of the term "good," he recommends that we concern ourselves with what count as "good reasons" in the course of making ethical decisions. See especially *The Place of Reason in Ethics* (Cambridge: Cambridge University Press, 1950).

Additional Readings

Ayer, A. J., "On the Analysis of Moral Judgments," *Horizon*, 20 (Sept. 1949):171–184.

Hare, R., *The Language of Morals*. Oxford: Clarendon Press, 1952.

Ross, W. D., *Foundations of Ethics*. New York: Oxford University Press, 1939.

Schlick, M., *Problems of Ethics*. New York: Prentice-Hall, 1939.

ANALYSIS AND KNOWLEDGE

Otto Neurath's (1882–1945) work embodied, as much as anyone's, the dedication of the logical positivists to purge cognitive discourse of all metaphysical statements on the grounds that since they are neither mathematical nor physical statements they have no cognitive content. He proposed that all empirical statements must be impersonal in the manner of scientific laws or in the sense that they refer to behavioristic or public perceptual acts. Neurath held that a thoroughgoing program along these lines is a necessary condition for the unification of the sciences. See "Unified Science as Encyclopedic Integration," *International Encyclopedia of Unified Science* (Chicago: University of Chicago Press, 1938), Vol. I, No. 1.

A. J. Wisdom (1904–   ) led the first effective attack on logical positivism. Singling out the positivists' verification meaning criterion, he questioned the language employed therein, showing that it was not representative of the actual language of either mathematics or physics. He concluded cautiously that the positivist is himself on the horns of a dilemma; he cannot justify the verification principle itself if he applies his own meaning criterion; and if he accepts the criterion, he opens up the possibility of cognitive significance in statements other than those that satisfy the criterion. See his "Metaphysics and Verification," *Mind*, 47 (1938): 452–498.

Additional Readings

Ayer, A. J., *The Problem of Knowledge*. London: Macmillan, 1959.

Carnap, R., "Psychology in Physical Language," in *Logical Positivism*, ed. A. J. Ayer. Glencoe: Free Press, 1959.

Goodman, N., *Fact, Fiction and Forecast*. London: Athlone, 1954.

Urmson, J. O., "Are Necessary Truths True by Convention?," *Aristotelian Society Supplement* 21 (1947):104–117.

ANALYSIS AND LOGIC AND MATHEMATICS

Rudolf Carnap (1891–   ), one of the original members of the Vienna Circle, views the development of modern mathematical logic, from Leibniz through Boole, Frege, and Russell, as having brought about the possibility of genuine investigation of the foundations of knowledge. He sees a theory of knowledge, for example, as applied logic in much the same sense that modern physics is viewed as applied mathematics. Carnap has attempted to perfect logic itself and to employ it in the analysis of the statements and concepts of science. His treatment of logic is notable because of the sharp distinctions he draws and because of his confidence in logic as the ultimate tool of philosophy. See his "Foundations of Logic and Mathematics," *International Encyclopedia of Unified Science* (Chicago: University of Chicago Press, 1939), Vol. I, No. 3.

Peter F. Strawson (1919–   ) provided the first well-developed attack on mathematical logic from the viewpoint of ordinary-language philosophy. The crux of his objection is that whereas the standard logic is useful for the analysis of the statements of such disciplines as mathematics and physics, in which the importance of context is minimal, mathematical logic is systematically misleading when applied to ordinary discourse. The logician traditionally has failed to recognize or acknowledge that language in its ordinary use is rich in meaning and varied in its roles, and that therefore its proper analysis is extremely dependent on context. It was clear to Strawson that earlier analysts mistakenly equate the scrutiny of language with respect to the dictums of formal logic with the analysis of language. See *Introduction of Logical Theory* (London: Methuen, 1952).

Additional Readings

Carnap, R., *Logical Syntax of Language.* New York: Harcourt, Brace, 1937.

Quine, W. V. O., *From a Logical Point of View.* Cambridge: Harvard University Press, 1953.

Toulmin, S., *The Uses of Argument.* London: Cambridge University Press, 1958.

Waismann, J., *Introduction to Mathematical Thinking.* London: Hafner, 1951.

ANALYSIS AND THEORY OF MIND

Carl G. Hempel (1905–), like many logical positivists, is concerned to provide an analysis of psychological propositions that show them to be of a kind with physical propositions, that is, to have their meaning established by the procedures of their verification. He concludes that although minds, feelings, thoughts, and the like may exist in some sense, psychological propositions must be translated into behavioristic, publicly verifiable propositions to be meaningful. See "The Logical Analysis of Psychology," in H. Feigl and W. Sellars (eds.), *Readings in Philosophical Analysis* (New York: Appleton-Century-Crofts, 1949).

Gilbert Ryle (1900–) exerted a notable influence on ordinary-language philosophy through his extensive investigation of psychological concepts. He began by attacking what he holds to be a myth—the Cartesian myth—which forestalled proper investigation of the notion of "mind" for centuries. Our preoccupation with finding the "Ghost in the Machine," with finding an entity called "mind" somehow analogous to an entity called "body," is properly abandoned. Ryle insists that we remain systematically attentive to the actual use of psychological terminology and resolutely refuse to misuse it; in this way we eliminate the mind-body puzzle that has plagued philosophy. See *The Concept of Mind* (New York: Barnes and Noble, 1949).

Additional Readings
   Bergmann, G., "Psychoanalysis and Experimental Psychology," *Mind* 53 (1953):122–140.
   Brunswick, E., "The Conceptual Framework of Psychology," *International Encyclopedia of Unified Science*. Chicago: University of Chicago Press, 1952: Vol. I, No. 10.
   Malcolm, N., "Wittgenstein's Philosophical Investigations," in V. C. Chappell, ed., *The Philosophy of Mind*. Englewood Cliffs: Prentice-Hall, 1962.
   Wisdom, A. J., *Philosophy and Psycho-analysis*. Oxford: Blackwell, 1953.

ANALYSIS AND PHILOSOPHY OF SCIENCE

Philipp Frank (1884–   ), a philosopher and physicist, has been part of the movement to bring philosophy into the closest possible contact with the natural sciences. He envisions the role of the philosopher of science as one of making clear which statements in physics are descriptive of fact and which statements describe the interrelations among the symbols employed by the physicist. Great stress is placed on the notion of operational definition of terms and on the relationship between physical theories and logicomathematical systems. See especially "Foundations of Physics," *International Encyclopedia of Unified Science* (Chicago: University of Chicago Press, 1946), Vol. I, No. 7.

W. H. Watson (1899–   ), one of Wittgenstein's students, was influenced both by his teacher's *Tractatus* and by his teacher's later views. Watson's thesis is that scientific theories are neither, as the classical physicist thought, descriptions of an underlying reality nor, as the positivist contends, true or false descriptions of the observable world. To put Watson's position negatively, a scientific theory should be viewed as nondescriptive and, accordingly, as neither true nor false; to put his view positively, a theory is a set of rules to guide us in representing the phenomena of the natural world. As a set of rules for representation—that is, as a highly structured, systematized, and specialized language—a theory in itself says nothing about the world even though the theory may be a necessary instrument for a satisfactory understanding of the world; it is no better or worse in this regard than another theory. See *Understanding Physics* (New York: Harper, 1959).

Additional Readings

Braithwaite, R., *Scientific Explanation*. London: Cambridge University Press, 1953.

Nagel, E., *The Structure of Science*. New York: Harcourt, Brace, 1961.

Popper, K., *The Logic of Discovery*. London: Hutchinson, 1958.

Toulmin, S., *The Philosophy of Science*. London: Hutchinson, 1953.

NOTES FOR CHAPTER V

1. B. Jowett (trans.), *The Dialogues of Plato* (New York: Random House, 1937), I, 386, 387–8, 389.
2. *Ibid.*, II, 165–66.
3. *Ibid.*, II, 91–92.
4. Leibniz, in a famous exchange with Locke on this point, indicated that the latter's argument in favor of empiricism is inconclusive, if not fallacious: In his second and more forceful argument, Locke eliminated the possibility of innate ideas on the ground that the proponents of innate ideas have not demonstrated that certain ideas *could not* come from experience, whereas, according to Leibniz, *Locke* would be required to show that these ideas could not have any origin *other than* experience. Or, to put it another way, Locke's argument is weakened if the advocate of innate ideas simply can show, not that certain ideas *could not* come from experience, but that they *were not* derived from experience. That is, Leibniz contended that the burden of proof is on Locke. Furthermore, if Locke were to offer such a demonstration, he would be required to show that the principles of the demonstration themselves originate solely in experience.
5. John Locke, *An Essay Concerning Human Understanding* (New York: Dutton, 1947), pp. 26–27.
6. *Ibid.*, p. 97.
7. George Berkeley, *A Treatise Concerning the Principles of Human Knowledge* (New York: Liberal Arts Press, 1957), pp. 24–25.
8. B. Russell, "Logical Atomism" in *Contemporary British Philosophy* (1st Series) (New York: Macmillan, 1924), p. 368.
9. Russell and Whitehead, *Principia Mathematica*, Vol. 1 (Cambridge, 1935), p. 66.
10. *Ibid.*
11. B. Russell, *A History of Western Philosophy* (New York: Simon and Schuster, 1944), p. 835.
12. But in special senses and cases, there is—e.g., if someone has announced some top secret information, we can ask, "How do *you* know?," nastily. [Austin's note.]
13. An interesting variant in the case of knowing would be "You oughtn't *to say* (you've no business to say) you know it at all." But of course this is only superficially similar to "You oughtn't to believe it": you ought to

say you believe it, if you do believe it, however poor the evidence. [Austin's note.]

14 "I know, *I know*, I've seen it a hundred times, don't keep on telling me" complains of a superabundance of opportunity: "knowing a hawk from a handsaw" lays down a minimum of acumen in recognition or classification. "As well as I know my own name" is said to typify something I must have experienced and must have learned to discriminate. [Austin's note.]

15 The adverbs that can be inserted in "How . . . do you know?" are few in number and fall into still fewer classes. There is practically no overlap with those that can be inserted in "How . . . do you believe?" (firmly, sincerely, genuinely, &c.). [Austin's note.]

16 Knowing at second hand, or on authority, is not the same as "knowing indirectly," whatever precisely that difficult and perhaps artificial expression may mean. If a murderer "confesses," then whatever our opinion of the worth of the "confession," we cannot say that "we (only) know indirectly that he did it," nor can we so speak when a witness, reliable or unreliable, has stated that he saw the man do it. Consequently, it is not correct, either, to say that the murderer himself knows "directly" that he did it, whatever precisely "knowing directly" may mean. [Austin's note.]

17 Reliance on the authority of others is fundamental, too, in various special matters, for example, for corroboration and for the correctness of our own use of words, which we learn from others. [Austin's note.]

18 Misnaming is not a trivial or laughing matter. If I misname I shall mislead others, and I shall also misunderstand information given by others to me. "Of course I knew all about his condition perfectly, but I never realized that was diabetes: I thought it was cancer, and all the books agree that's incurable: if I'd only known it was *diabetes*, I should have thought of insulin at once." Knowing *what a thing is* is, to an important extent, knowing what the name for it, and the right name for it, is. [Austin's note.]

19 Conjurers, too, trade on this. "Will some gentleman kindly satisfy himself that this is a perfectly ordinary hat?" This leaves us baffled and uneasy: sheepishly we agree that it seems all right, while conscious that we have not the least idea what to guard against. [Austin's note.]

20 The awkwardness about some snarks being boojums. [Austin's note.]

21 Sometimes, on the basis of the new special feature, we distinguish, not between "Cs" and "real Cs," but rather between Cs and Ds. There is a reason for choosing the one procedure rather than the other: all cases where we use the "real" formula exhibit (complicated and serpentine) likeness, as do all cases where we use "proper," a word which behaves in many ways like "real," and is no less more profound. [Austin's note.]

22 And yet she always *thought* his shirt was white until she saw it against Tommy's Persil-washed one. [Austin's note.]

23 Or, of course, related to it in some other way than by "similarity" (in any ordinary sense of "similarity"), which is yet sufficient reason for describing it by the same word. [Austin's note.]

24 This appears to cover cases of dull or careless or uninstructed perception, as opposed to cases of diseased or drugged perception. [Austin's note.]
25 There are, of course, legitimate uses of the direct object after *know*, and of the possessive pronoun before words for feelings. "He knows the town well," "He has known much suffering," "My old vanity, how well I know it!"—even the pleonastic "Where does he feel his (=the) pain?" and the educative tautology "He feels *his* pain." But none of these really lends support to the metaphysical "He *knows* his pain (in a way we can't)." [Austin's note.]
26 It is the use of the expressions "I know" and "I promise" (first person singular, present indicative tense) alone that is being considered. "If I knew, I can't have been wrong" or "If she can't be wrong" are not worrying in the way that "If I ('you') know I ('you') can't be wrong" is worrying. Or again, "I promise" is quite different from "he promises": if I say "I promise," I don't say I *say* I promise, I *promise*, just as if he says he promises, he doesn't say he says he promises, he promises: whereas if I say "he promises," I do (only) say he *says* he promises—in the other "sense" of "promise," the "sense" in which I say I promise, only *he* can say he promises. I *describe* his promising, but I *do* my own promising and he must do *his* own. [Austin's note.]
27 If "Figs never grow on thistles" is taken to mean "None ever have and none ever will," then it is implied that I *know* that none ever have, but only that I *believe* that none ever will. [Austin's note.]
28 "Swear," "guarantee," "give my word," "promise," all these and similar words cover cases both of "knowing" and of "promising" thus suggesting the two are analogous. Of course they differ subtly from each other; for example, *know* and *promise* are in a certain sense "unlimited" expressions, while when I swear I swear *upon* something, and when I guarantee I guarantee that, upon some adverse and more or less to be expected circumstance arising, I will take *some more or less definite action* to nullify it. [Austin's note.]
29 "You can't warn someone of something that isn't going to happen" parallels "You can't know what isn't true." [Austin's note.]
30 We say we don't know what it must feel like to be a king, whereas we do know what one of our friends must have felt when mortified. In this ordinary (imprecise and evidently not whole-hog) sense of "knowing what it would be like" we do often know what it would be like to be our neighbour drawing his sword, whereas we don't know (can't even guess or imagine), really, what it would feel like to be a cat or a cockroach. But of course we don't ever "know" what in our neighbour accompanies the drawing of his sword in Mr. Wisdom's peculiar sense of "know what" as equivalent to "directly experience that which." [Austin's note.]
31 Doctors nowadays draw a distinction of their own between "symptoms" and "(physical) signs": but the distinction is not here relevant, and perhaps not very clear. [Austin's note.]
32 There are some, more complicated, cases like that of inflation, where the signs of incipient inflation are of the same nature as inflation itself, but

of a less intensity or at a slower tempo. Here, especially, it is a matter for decision where the signs or "tendencies" end and where the state itself sets in: moreover, with inflation, as with some diseases, we can in some contexts go on talking of signs or symptoms even when the item itself is quite fairly decidedly present, because it is such as not to be patent to simple observation. [Austin's note.]

33 Sometimes, it is said, we use "I know" where we should be prepared to substitute "I believe," as when we say "I know he's in, because his hat is in the hall": thus "know" is used loosely for "believe," so why should we suppose there is a fundamental difference between them? But the question is, what exactly do we man by "prepared to substitute" and "loosely"? We are "prepared to substitute" *believe* for *know* not as an *equivalent* expression but as a weaker and therefore preferable expression, in view of the seriousness with which, as has become apparent, the matter is to be treated: the presence of the hat, which would serve as a proof of its owner's presence in many circumstances, could only through laxity be adduced as a proof in a court of law. [Austin's note.]

34 A new language is naturally necessary if we are to admit unconscious feelings, and feelings which express themselves in paradoxical manners, such as the psycho-analysts describe. [Austin's note.]

35 There is, it seems to me, something which does actually happen, rather different from Mr. Wisdom's telepathy, which does sometimes contribute towards our knowledge of the other people's feelings. We do talk, for example, of "feeling another person's displeasure," and say, for example, "his anger could be felt," and there seems to be something genuine about this. But the feeling we feel, though a genuine "feeling," is *not* in these cases, displeasure or anger but a special *counterpart* feeling. [Austin's note.]

36 The "feelings," i.e. sensations, we can observe in ourselves when angry are such things as a pounding of the heart or tensing of the muscles, which cannot in themselves be justifiably called "the feeling of anger." [Austin's note.]

37 It is therefore misleading to ask "How do I get from the scowl to the anger?" [Austin's note.]

38 There is, too, a special way in which we can doubt the "reality" of our own emotions, can doubt whether we are not "acting to ourselves." Professional actors may reach a state where they never really know what their genuine feelings are. [Austin's note.]

39 Quoted by Wisdom in his contribution to this Symposium. [Ed.]

40 "You cannot fool all of the people all of the time" is "analytic." [Austin's note.]

Index to Text

Abelard, Peter, 243; and concepts, 242
Absolute Idea, 82–3
Absurd, the, 230
Aeschylus, 235
Alexander, Samuel: and emergent evolution, 60 and reality, 60
Analysis, 239, 242, 253
"Analytic," the (Kant), 249
Antithesis (Hegel), 82
Apodictic judgments, 78, 249
Apology, 184
A posteriori truth, 249
A priori; the: judgment, 125; and Kant, 82, 132–3; 249–50; method, 139; Mill's rejection of, 135; Nietzsche's attack on, 136
Aquinas, 127, 128, 231
Aristotle, 61, 72, 73, 119, 123, 124, 186, 189, 193, 231; and change, 239, 240; form, 240; and God, 71; and immanent teleology, 71; and language, 240–41; and nondemonstrable knowledge, 185; and substance, 240; and universals, 69, 70, 73; criticism of Plato, 69, 70; importance of idealism, 71
Atomism, 2–4, 80–81, 122, 124
Augustine, 71, 83, 128, 185, 231; and divine ideas, 73; and faith, 127, 142; and God, 72, 73, 187; and happiness, 186; and knowledge of God, 187; and Platonic ideas, 73, 74
Austin, John, 253, 255, 317, 318, 319, 320
"Authentic living," 193, 197
Ayer, A. J., 312, 314; and emotive theory of ethics, 313

Bacon, Francis, 128; and inductive method, 129; and hypothesis, 130
Barth, Karl, 228, 229
Beauvoir, Simone, 230
Becoming (Hegel), 82
Behaviorism, 315
Being: in Hegel, 82; in Parmenides, 65
Benjamin, A. C., 179
Bergmann, G., 316
Bergson, Henri, 229, 231; and intuition, 194; and metaphysics, 194; and symbolic communication, 194–5

Berkeley, George, 62, 84, 116, 119, 246, 253, 317; and abstract ideas, 74–5, 245; and God, 9, 76; and ideas, 8, 9, 75, 245; and particular ideas, 245; and presentative theory, 9; and solipsism, 9; and subjective idealism, 74, 80, 81; and the real, 8, 76; *esse est percipi*, 8; philosophical convictions, 74
Blake, R., 181
Blanshard, Brand, 84
Boole, George, 250, 314
Bosanquet, Bernard, 83
Bowne, B. P., 117
Bradley, F. H., 15, 62, 84, 119; and thought as relational, 83
Braithwaite, R. B., 317
Brentano, F., 61; and intentionality, 12
Bridgman, Percy, 178; and operationalism, 179
Brightman, E. S., 117
Brunner, E., 229
Brunswick, E., 316
Buber, Martin, 228; and love, 229
Buchler, J., 181
Burtt, E. A., 62

Calkins, M. W., 119
Camus, Albert, 230
Carlyle, T., 83
Carnap, Rudolph, 314, 315
Cassirer, Ernst: and symbolism, 118
Categorical imperative, 133
Categories of the understanding, the, 11, 79, 82, 133
Causality: as empirical generalization, 135; final, 70; and the idea of "necessary connection," 248; Kant's theory of, 11, 135
Champeaux, William of, 241, 242
Change, the problem of, 240
Chappell, V. C., 316
Chrysippus, 235
Churchman, C. W., 180
Cohen, M., 61
Coleridge, S. T., 83
Collingwood, R. G., 116, 119
Common sense, 9, 252
Comte, Auguste, 132, 135, 136; and metaphysics, 134; and theory of evolution, 134

Concept formation, 242
Conceptualism, 243
Confessions, The, 186
Consciousness, 5–6, 188–9
Conventionalism, 136
Copernicus, 128, 130, 131
Cowan, M., 181
Creighton, J. E., 84
Critical Realists, 18, 58
Croce, Benedetto, 115, 116

Daimon, 184
Dasein, 196–7
Democracy: demands of, 178; pragmatic appraisal of, 177
Democritus, 125; and atoms, 2, 80, 81; and necessity, 2; and sense knowledge, 2; and void, 2; theory of perception, 2–3
Dennes, William R., 180
Descartes, René, 195, 196, 231, 234; and doubt, 6; and God, 6; and mathematics, 6; and matter, 6; and mind, 5–6; and mind-body relationship, 6; *cogito ergo sum,* 6; metaphysical dualism, 5–6, 7
Descriptions, Russell's theory of, 251
Determinism: in Democritus, 2; in Hobbes, 4; in Spinoza, 77
Dewey, John, 120, 142, 177, 178, 179, 180; and instrumentalism, 143
Dialectic: Hegel's, 81–2, 188–9; Kierkegaard's criticism of, 190
Ding an sich, 79
Dostoyevsky, Fyodor, 192, 230
Drake, D., 18, 59
Dualism: Berkeley's resolution of, 8; Cartesian, 5–6, 195–6; Marcel's criticism of, 229–30
Ducasse, C. J., 181

Ego: in Hegel, 191; in Husserl, natural, 195–6; transcendental, 196
Egocentric predicament, the, 59
Empiricism, 125, 135, 246–8
Epicurus, 2, 186; and atoms, 3; and hypothetical nature of truth, 126; and pleasure-pain, 124–5; and qualities, 3; and task of metaphysics, 3
Epiphenomenalism, 3–4
Esse est percipi, 8, 13, 15, 116
Essences, 61, 58
Eternal truths, 73, 186
Eubulides, 234, 235
Euripides, 235
Euthyphro, 232–4
Evolution, emergent, 60; *see also* Comte
Ewing, A. C., 59

Faith: and the absurd, 192; as knowledge, 58; as necessary for knowledge, 127, 142; and reason, 186–7, 190–91
Farber, Marvin, 61
Feigl, H., 315
Final causality, 70
Flewelling, Ralph Tyler, 117
Forms: Aristotle's criticism of, 72; Augustinian theory of, 72; Platonic theory of, 237–8; Plato's criticism of, 238–9
Frank, Philipp, 316
Freedom: as defining man, 190–91; as dynamic, 193–4; as presupposition of the categorical imperative, 133
Frege, G., 250, 314

Galileo Galilei, 62, 128, 130; and qualities, 5; and hypothesis, 131
Gibson, W. R. B., 61
Gilbert, 129
Gilson, Etienne, 60, 230, 231
God: our belief in, 187; as an encounter with truth, 192; our knowledge of, 9, 18, 72–3, 76–7, 131, 142, 187; our love for, 229; in Plato, 239; in revelation, 127; as unmoved mover, 71–2
"God is dead," 194
Good, the, 69, 72, 184
Goodman, N., 314
Green, T. H., 83

Happiness: and conformity, 122; and immortality, 186; and pleasure, 124–5
Harari, M., 230
Hare, R., 313
Hartmann, N., values as essences, 59
Hartshorne, Charles, 181
Harvey, 129
Hegel, G. W. F., 74, 76, 77, 78, 190, 191, 196, 231; and absolute idea, 82, 83; and alienation, 188; and Berkeley, 81; and categories, 82; and consciousness, 188–9; and Democritus, 80–81; and dialectic, 81–2, 188–9; and Heraclitus, 82; and Kant, 80; and knower-known relation, 79, 80, 81; and nature, 83; and Parmenides, 80; and Spinoza, 80; and Spirit, 83; and truth, 189; and universals, 80, 81, 82
Heidegger, Martin, 195; and authenticity, 197; and *Dasein,* 196–7
Hempel, C., 315
Heraclitus, 68, 121, 239; and objects of knowledge, 64
Herbart, Johann, 11
Hobbes, Thomas, 62; and atoms, 4; and knowledge, 4; and matter, 4

Hocking, W., 117
Hölderlin, 193
Holt, E. B., 16, 59, 60, 62
Hook, Sidney, 177
Hope, R., 119
Hoskyns, E., 228
Hulme, T. E., 231
Hume, David, 245, 249, 253; and criticism of necessary connections, 248; and general terms, 246; and ideas, 247–8; and impressions, 247, 248; and skepticism, 78
Husserl, Edmund: and intentionality, 61, 196; and the ego, 195–6
Hypotheses: as "convenient fictions," 130–31; their predictive function, 141; reduction of knowledge to, 125, 135

Idealism, 8–9, 11, 13–14, 58, 63–119, 136, 141; objective (Hegelian), 15, 74, 76, 83–4; reductive, 61; subjective, 74, 80–81
Ideas, 61
Ideas, 10, 14, 67–9, 73–5; complex and simple, 244, 247; innate, 243–4; true and false, 141; *see also* Forms, Meaning, Universals
Immanent teleology, 70
Impressions, 247–8
Induction, 129
Innate Ideas, 243–4
Instrumentalism, 143, 178
Intentionality, 12, 61, 84, 195–6
I-Thou relationship, 230

James, William, 143, 178, 181; and God, 142; pragmatic method, 139–140; theory of truth, 140, 141, 142
Jaspers, K., 183, 190, 229, 230, 231
Jessop, B., 62
Jesus, 193
Joachim, H. H., 84
Johnson, Samuel, 253
Jowett, Benjamin, 118, 180, 231, 317

Kant, Immanuel, 76, 80, 82, 119, 132, 134, 135, 136, 137, 229; and categorical imperative, 133; and categories, 11, 79, 133; and *Ding an sich*, 11, 79; and experience, 11, 79; and Hume, 78; and kinds of judgments, 249; and mathematical statements, 249, 250; on space, 78–9; relation to idealism, 78, 79
Kierkegaard, Sören, 193, 194, 231; and faith, 192; and freedom, 190–1; and God, 192; and the individual, 189, 190, 191

"Know thyself," 183, 187, 195
Knower-known relation, 6, 79–81, 188
Knowledge: and faith, 58, 127, 142; of God, 9, 18, 72–3, 76–7, 131, 142, 187; as intuition, 194; as nondemonstrable, 185; as predictive, 123, 126, 129, 138–9, 140–3, 314; as restricted to ideas, 243; scientific, 132–5, 240; self-evident, 125–6, 139; sense, 2, 4, 6–7, 9–11, 247
Krikorian, Y. H., 177, 180

Langer, S., 118
Leibniz, G., 250, 314, 317
Lepley, R., 178, 179
Leucippus, 2
Lewis, C. I., 143, 178
Lindemann, E. C., 178
Locke, John, 245, 246, 247, 317; and analysis, 242; and conceptualism, 243; and experience, 243; and ideas, 243, 244; innate ideas, 243, 244; and language, 243; and representative theory of perception, 7; and substance, 244; and universals, 242, 243
Logic: formal, 240–41; the pragmatic sanction applied to, 179; and mathematics, 250, 314
Logical atomism, 252
Logical positivism, 252–3, 312; criticism of, 314
Lotze, R., 1, 62
Lovejoy, A., 18
Lowenberg, J., 231
Luce, A. A., 62

Madden, E., 181
Malcolm, Norman, 316
"Man is the measure of all things," 66, 122, 123, 142
Manheim, R., 118
Marcel, Gabriel, 229, 230
Maritain, J., 231
Marvin, W. T., 16
Materialism, 2, 4, 61, 80–1
Mathematical statements, 13, 135–6, 248–50
Mathematics and logic, 250, 314
Matter, 4, 6, 8–9, 75–6
McClure, M., 181
McKeon, R., 231
McTaggart, J. M. E., 84
Mead, H., 178
Meaning: internal and external, 84; nonliteral, 118; pragmatic theory of, 133–4, 138, 140, 142; problem of, 254–5; and use of language, 253–4; *see also*, Intentionality

Mechanism, 4, 131, 134, 136, 194
Meinong, Alexius, 61; and act-object distinction, 13; general theory of objects, 12
Metaphysics, definition of, 195; process, 60; as speculative, 133-4; *see also* Idealism, Logical Atomism, Materialism, Realism
Mill, John Stuart, 83, 132, 142, 181; and empirical generalization, 135-6
Mind-body relation, 6
Molesworth, William, 62
Monism, 234
Montague, W. P., 16
Moore, George Edward, 60; and act-object distinction, 14; and analysis, 252-3; and common sense, 253; and good, 59; and ordinary language, 252, 253; and relations, 15
Moral good, the, 178
Morris, C. W., 180

Nagel, E., 179-180, 317
Nahm, M., 118
Neo-Kantianism, 118
Neo-Realism, 178
Neurath, O., 313, 314
New Realists, 16, 17, 18
Niebuhr, Reinhold, 229
Nietzsche, Friedrich, 136, 192; and human freedom, 193-4; and the will to power, 136, 193; "God is dead," 194
Nominalism, 74, 241, 243, 250; *see also* Realism

Oates, W., 180
Objective Idealism, *see* Idealism
Objectivism, 195
Ockham, William of, 74, 250
Ockham's razor, 74, 250
Operationalism, 179
Ordinary language, 252; philosophy of, 253, 314
Organon, 240
Osiander, 130, 131
Otto, M., 179

Parmenides, 80, 82, 118, 121, 234, 238, 239; and being, 65; and real as unchanging, 64
Participation, the Platonic theory of, 239
Pascal, Blaise, 133, 142, 185, 188, 231; and belief in God, 187; and knowledge of God, 131; Pascal's wager, 131-2
Paul, E., 229

Peirce, Charles S., 137, 140, 179, 180, 181; and meaning, 138, 142; and scientific method, 139
Perception, 10
Perry, Ralph Barton, 16, 58, 60, 62, 178
Personalism, 117
Phantasm, 4
Phenomenalism, 139
Phenomenology, *see* Husserl
Philosophical analysis, 239, 242, 253
Philosophical Investigations, 253
Philosophy of Mind, 188
Pitkin, W. B., 16
Plato, 63, 66, 70, 71, 72, 73, 82, 117, 118, 119, 138, 180, 184, 186, 231; and God, 239; and relation of forms to sense objects, 238, 239; and the Good, 69, 184; and theory of forms (Ideas), 67, 68, 69, 237-8; criticism of knowledge as perception, 236-7; criticism of relativism, 123-4; criticism of theory of forms, 238-9
Platonism, 184
Pluralism, 234
Poincaré, Henri, 137; and conventionalism, 136
Popper, K., 317
Positivism, *see* Comte; Logical Positivism
Pragmatism, 120-179; method of, 139-140
Pratt, J. B., 18
Presentative theory of perception, 9, 66
Principia Ethica, 252
Protagoras, 66, 122, 123; "man is the measure of all things," 142
Pythagoras, 234
Pythagoreanism, 122

Qualities, primary and secondary, 7
Quine, W. V. O., 315

Rationalism, 6, 125, 129
Realism: metaphysical, 1-63; extreme, 241-2; moderate, 243; presentative, 58; representative, 11, 58; *see also* Nominalism
Reality: as distorted by reason, 189; propositions reflect, 240; *see also* Metaphysics
Reason: limits of, 66, 131, 137, 142, 183-7, 189-91, 192-5; man of, 182-3
Refutation of idealism, 50; *see also* Moore
Reid, Thomas, 9, 62; and act-object distinction, 10; and common sense realism, 9-10
Relations: external, 15; internal, 15, 83

Relativism, 66, 122, 142; criticism of, 123-4, 236-7
Representational theory of perception, 4-5, 7, 11
Republic, The, 238
Revolt against institutions, 189-90, 193
Rilke, 193
Rogers, A. K., 18
Roscellinus, 242, 243; and nominalism, 241
Ross, W. D., 313
Rousseau, Jean-Jacques, 132
Royce, Josiah: and objective idealism, 84; and the absolute, 84
Runes, Dagobert, 181
Ruskin, 83
Russell, Bertrand, 59, 60, 62; and ideal language, 252; and incomplete symbols, 251; and logical atomism, 252; and metaphysics, 250, 251, 252; and relation of mathematics to logic, 250; and theory of descriptions, 251; criticism of Berkeley, 14-5
Ryle, Gilbert, 253, 315

Santayana, George, 18, 62; and essences, 58; and knowledge, 58
Sartre, Jean Paul, 198, 230
Schiller, F., 181
Schilpp, P., 62, 116
Schneider, H. W., 180
Schopenhauer, Arthur, 132, 136
Schlick, Moritz, 252, 255, 313
Scientific reductionism, 231
Scotus, John Duns, 128; and universals, 127; criticism of Augustine and Aquinas, 127
Self-knowledge, 182, 190, 192
Sellars, R. W., 18
Sellars, W., 315
Sensation: Hobbes' definition of, 4; Reid's definition of, 9-10
Sense experience, 121-2, 125, 132, 135
Skepticism, 78, 248
Skepticism and Animal Faith, 58
Smith, N. K., 119
Smith, T. V., 178
Socrates, 67, 123, 124, 183, 233, 236, 237, 239, 253; and his *Daimon,* 184; and the Sophists, 66; general philosophic position, 66; *see also* Plato
Solipsism, 9
Sophocles, 235
Sophists, 66, 121-3
Space: and God, 77; infinity of, 245; Kant on, 78

Spaulding, E. G., 16
Spinoza, Benedict, 78, 80, 119, 231; and God, 77; and knowledge of God, 77; and substance, 77; philosophic position of, 76-7; relation to objective idealism, 76, 77-8
Sprigge, S., 116
Stace, W. T., and external world, 116
Stevenson, C. L., 313
Strawson, P. F., 314, 315
Strong, C. A., 18
Subjective idealism, *see* Idealism
Subjectivism, 15, 122, 195-6
Substance, 77, 240, 244
Swenson, D. F., 231
Symbolism, 118, 194-5, 229, 243
Synthesis, 82-3
"Synthetic," the (Kant), 249

Tertullian, 127
Theaetetus, 236
Theology, and Buber, 228; and Copernicus, 128, 130-1
Thesis (Hegel), 82-3
Things-in-themselves, 11; *see also* Kant
Thomism, 230-31
Thought: as identical with Being, 65; as relational, 83; *see also* Idealism
Thrasymachus, 122
Tillich, Paul, 198
Timaeus, 239
Toulmin, S., 313, 315, 317
Tractatus Logico-Philosophicus, 253; *see also* Wittgenstein
Trotter, W. F., 231
Truth, *see* Knowledge

Universals, 69, 70, 73, 80, 81, 82, 127, 242, 243
Urban, Wilbur M., 117, 118
Urmson, J. O., 314

Vaihinger, Hans, 137
Verification criterion of truth, 123, 126, 129, 138-9, 140-3, 314
Vienna Circle, the, 252, 313, 314
Voluntarism, 128, 142

Waismann, F., 315
Wallace, W., 231
Watson, W. H., 316
Weiss, Paul, 181
Werkmeister, W. H., 117
Whitehead, Alfred North, 61, 250, 317; and process metaphysics, 60

Wild, John, 119
Will to power, the, 136, 193
Wisdom, J. O., 253, 316, 319, 320; and positivism, 314
Wittgenstein, Ludwig, 313; and logical grammar, 254; and logical positivism, 252, 253; and meaning, 253, 254,

Wittgenstein, Ludwig (*Cont.*): 255; ordinary language school, 253; and use, 253, 254
Wood, L., 117
Woodbridge, F. J. E., 61, 180

Zeno, 118, 234